History of the American Continent

Editor

Silvia Herbert

Scribbles

Year of Publication 2018

ISBN : 9789352979684

Book Published by
Scribbles

(An Imprint of Alpha Editions)

email - alphaedis@gmail.com

Produced by: PediaPress GmbH
Limburg an der Lahn
Germany
http://pediapress.com/

The content within this book was generated collaboratively by volunteers. Please be advised that nothing found here has necessarily been reviewed by people with the expertise required to provide you with complete, accurate or reliable information. Some information in this book may be misleading or simply wrong. Alpha Editions and PediaPress does not guarantee the validity of the information found here. If you need specific advice (for example, medical, legal, financial, or risk management) please seek a professional who is licensed or knowledgeable in that area.

Sources, licenses and contributors of the articles and images are listed in the section entitled "References". Parts of the books may be licensed under the GNU Free Documentation License. A copy of this license is included in the section entitled "GNU Free Documentation License"

The views and characters expressed in the book are those of the contributors and his/her imagination and do not represent the views of the Publisher.

Contents

Articles 1

Introduction 1
    History of Asia 1

Prehistory 27
    Prehistoric Asia 27

Ancient 39
    Ancient Near East 39

Medieval Middle East 55
    History of the Middle East 55

Central Asia 89
    History of Central Asia 89

Medieval India 119
    Medieval India 119

Medieval China 125
    History of China 125

Medieval Japan 195
    History of Japan 195

Medieval Southeast Asia   **243**
    History of Southeast Asia 243

Appendix   277
    References 277
    Article Sources and Contributors 292
    Image Sources, Licenses and Contributors 294

Article Licenses   299

Index   301

Introduction

History of Asia

The **history of Asia** can be seen as the collective history of several distinct peripheral coastal regions such as, East Asia, South Asia, and the Middle East linked by the interior mass of the Eurasian steppe.

The coastal periphery was the home to some of the world's earliest known civilizations, with each of the three regions developing early civilizations around fertile river valleys. These valleys were fertile because the soil there was rich and could bear many root crops. The civilizations in Mesopotamia, India, and China shared many similarities and likely exchanged technologies and ideas such as mathematics and the wheel. Other notions such as that of writing likely developed individually in each area. Cities, states and then empires developed in these lowlands.

The steppe region had long been inhabited by mounted nomads, and from the central steppes they could reach all areas of the Asian continent. The northern part of the continent, covering much of Siberia was also inaccessible to the steppe nomads due to the dense forests and the tundra. These areas in Siberia were very sparsely populated.

The centre and periphery were kept separate by mountains and deserts. The Caucasus, Himalaya, Karakum Desert, and Gobi Desert formed barriers that the steppe horsemen could only cross with difficulty. While technologically and culturally the city dwellers were more advanced, they could do little militarily to defend against the mounted hordes of the steppe. However, the lowlands did not have enough open grasslands to support a large horsebound force. Thus the nomads who conquered states in the Middle East were soon forced to adapt to the local societies.

Asia's history would feature major developments seen in other parts of the world, as well as events that would affect those other regions. These include

Figure 1: *Detail of Chinese silk from the 4th century BCE. The characteristic trade of silk through the Silk Road connected various regions from China, India, Central Asia, and the Middle East to Europe and Africa.*

the trade of the Silk Road, which spread cultures, languages, religion, and disease throughout Afro-Eurasian trade. Another major advancement was the innovation of gunpowder in medieval China, which led to advanced warfare through the use of guns.

Prehistory

A report by archaeologist Rakesh Tewari on Lahuradewa, India shows new C14 datings that range between 9000 and 8000 BCE associated with rice, making Lahuradewa the earliest Neolithic site in entire South Asia.

The prehistoric Beifudi site near Yixian in Hebei Province, China, contains relics of a culture contemporaneous with the Cishan and Xinglongwa cultures of about 8000–7000 BCE, neolithic cultures east of the Taihang Mountains, filling in an archaeological gap between the two Northern Chinese cultures. The total excavated area is more than 1,200 square meters and the collection of neolithic findings at the site consists of two phases.

Around 5500 BCE the Halafian culture appeared in Lebanon, Israel, Syria, Anatolia, and northern Mesopotamia, based upon dryland agriculture.

In southern Mesopotamia were the alluvial plains of Sumer and Elam. Since there was little rainfall, irrigation systems were necessary. The Ubaid culture flourished from 5500 BCE.

Ancient

Bronze Age

The Chalcolithic period (or Copper Age) began about 4500 BCE, then the Bronze Age began about 3500 BCE, replacing the Neolithic cultures.

The Indus Valley Civilization (IVC) was a Bronze Age civilization (3300–1300 BCE; mature period 2600–1900 BCE) which was centered mostly in the western part of the Indian Subcontinent; it is considered that an early form of Hinduism was performed during this civilization. Some of the great cities of this civilization include Harappa and Mohenjo-daro, which had a high level of town planning and arts. The cause of the destruction of these regions around 1700 BCE is debatable, although evidence suggests it was caused by natural disasters (especially flooding). This era marks Vedic period in India, which lasted from roughly 1500 to 500 BCE. During this period, the Sanskrit language developed and the Vedas were written, epic hymns that told tales of gods and wars. This was the basis for the Vedic religion, which would eventually sophisticate and develop into Hinduism.[1]

China and Vietnam were also centres of metalworking. Dating back to the Neolithic Age, the first bronze drums, called the Dong Son drums have been uncovered in and around the Red River Delta regions of Vietnam and Southern China. These relate to the prehistoric Dong Son Culture of Vietnam. Song Da bronze drum's surface, Dong Son culture, Vietnam

In Ban Chiang, Thailand (Southeast Asia), bronze artifacts have been discovered dating to 2100 BCE.

In Nyaunggan, Burma bronze tools have been excavated along with ceramics and stone artifacts. Dating is still currently broad (3500–500 BCE).

Iron Age

The Iron Age saw the widespread use of iron tools, weaponry, and armor throughout the major civilizations of Asia.

Middle East

The Achaemenid dynasty of the Persian Empire, founded by Cyrus the Great, ruled an area from Greece and Turkey to the Indus River and Central Asia during the 6th to 4th centuries BCE. Persian politics included a tolerance for other cultures, a highly centralized government, and significant infrastructure developments. Later, in Darius the Great's rule, the territories were integrated, a bureaucracy was developed, nobility were assigned military positions, tax collection was carefully organized, and spies were used to ensure the loyalty of regional officials. The primary religion of Persia at this time was Zoroastrianism, developed by the philosopher Zoroaster. It introduced an early form of monotheism to the area. The religion banned animal sacrifice and the use of intoxicants in rituals; and introduced the concept of spiritual salvation through personal moral action, an end time, and both general and Particular judgment with a heaven or hell. These concepts would heavily influence later emperors and the masses. More importantly, Zoroastrianism would be an important precursor for the Abrahamic religions such as Christianity, Islam, or Judaism. The Persian Empire was successful in establishing peace and stability throughout the Middle East and were a major influence in art, politics (affecting Hellenistic leaders), and religion.

Alexander the Great conquered this dynasty in the 4th century BCE, creating the brief Hellenistic period. He was unable to establish stability and after his death, Persia broke into small, weak dynasties including the Seleucid Empire, followed by the Parthian Empire. By the end of the Classical age, Persia had been reconsolidated into the Sassanid Empire, also known as the second Persian Empire.

The Roman Empire would later control parts of Western Asia. The Seleucid, Parthian and Sassanid dynasties of Persia dominated Western Asia for centuries.

India

The Maurya and Gupta empires are called the Golden Age of India and were marked by extensive inventions and discoveries in science, technology, art, religion, and philosophy that crystallized the elements of what is generally known as Indian culture. The religions of Hinduism and Buddhism, which began in Indian sub-continent, were an important influence on South, East and Southeast Asia.

By 600 BCE, India had been divided into 17 regional states that would occasionally feud amongst themselves. In 327 BCE, Alexander the Great came to India with a vision of conquering the whole world. He crossed northwestern India and created the province Bactria but could not move further because his army wanted to go back to their family. Shortly prior, the soldier Chandragupta Maurya began to take control of the Ganges river and soon established the Maurya Empire. The Maurya Empire (Sanskrit: मौर्य राजवंश, Maurya Rājavanśha) was the geographically extensive and powerful empire in ancient India, ruled by the Mauryan dynasty from 321 to 185 BCE. It was one of the world's largest empires in its time, stretching to the Himalayas in the north, what is now Assam in the east, probably beyond modern Pakistan in the west, and annexing Balochistan and much of what is now Afghanistan, at its greatest extent. South of Mauryan empire was the Tamilakam an independent country dominated by three dynasties, the Pandyans, Cholas and Cheras. The government established by Chandragupta was led by an autocratic king, who primarily relied on the military to assert his power.[2] It also applied the use of a bureaucracy and even sponsored a postal service.[2] Chandragupta's grandson, Ashoka, greatly extended the empire by conquering most of modern-day India (save for the southern tip). He eventually converted to Buddhism, though, and began a peaceful life where he promoted the religion as well as humane methods throughout India. The Maurya Empire would disintegrate soon after Ashoka's death and was conquered by the Kushan invaders from the northwest, establishing the Kushan Empire. Their conversion to Buddhism caused the religion to be associated with foreigners and therefore a decline in its popularity occurred.[2]

The Kushan Empire would fall apart by 220 CE, creating more political turmoil in India. Then in 320, the Gupta Empire (Sanskrit: गुप्त राजवंश, Gupta Rājavanśha) was established and covered much of the Indian Subcontinent. Founded by Maharaja Sri-Gupta, the dynasty was the model of a classical civilization. Gupta kings united the area primarily through negotiation of local leaders and families as well as strategical intermarriage.[3] Their rule covered less land than the Maurya Empire, but established the greatest stability.[3] In 535, the empire ended when India was overrun by the Huns.

Classical China

Zhou Dynasty

Since 1029 BCE, the Zhou Dynasty (Chinese: 周朝 ; pinyin: *Zhōu Cháo*; Wade–Giles: *Chou Ch'ao* [tʂóʊ tʂʰɑ̌ʊ]), had existed in China and it would continue to until 258 BCE.[4] The Zhou dynasty had been using a feudal system by giving power to local nobility and relying on their loyalty in order to control its large territory.[4] As a result, the Chinese government at this time tended to be very decentralized and weak, and there was often little the emperor could do to resolve national issues. Nonetheless, the government was able to retain its position with the creation of the Mandate of Heaven, which could establish an emperor as divinely chosen to rule. The Zhou additionally discouraged the human sacrifice of the preceding eras and unified the Chinese language. Finally, the Zhou government encouraged settlers to move into the Yangtze River valley, thus creating the Chinese Middle Kingdom.

But by 500 BCE, its political stability began to decline due to repeated nomadic incursions[4] and internal conflict derived from the fighting princes and families. This was lessened by the many philosophical movements, starting with the life of Confucius. His philosophical writings (called Confucianism) concerning the respect of elders and of the state would later be popularly used in the Han Dynasty. Additionally, Laozi's concepts of Taoism, including yin and yang and the innate duality and balance of nature and the universe, became popular throughout this period. Nevertheless, the Zhou Dynasty eventually disintegrated as the local nobles began to gain more power and their conflict devolved into the Warring States period, from 402 to 201 BCE.[5]

Qin Dynasty

One leader eventually came on top, Qin Shi Huang (Chinese: 始皇帝 , Shǐ Huángdì), who overthrew the last Zhou emperor and established the Qin dynasty.[4] The Qin Dynasty (Chinese: 秦朝 ; pinyin: Qín Cháo) was the first ruling dynasty of Imperial China, lasting from 221 to 207 BCE.[6] The new Emperor abolished the feudal system and directly appointed a bureaucracy that would rely on him for power. Huang's imperial forces crushed any regional resistance, and they furthered the Chinese empire by expanding down to the South China Sea and northern Vietnam. Greater organization brought a uniform tax system, a national census, regulated road building (and cart width), standard measurements, standard coinage, and an official written and spoken language.[7] Further reforms included new irrigation projects, the encouragement of silk manufacturing,[7] and (most famously) the beginning of the construction of the Great Wall of China—designed to keep out the nomadic raiders who'd constantly badger the Chinese people. However, Shi Huang was infamous for his tyranny, forcing laborers to build the Wall, ordering heavy taxes, and severely punishing all who opposed him. He oppressed Confucians and promoted Legalism, the idea that people were inherently evil, and that a strong, forceful government was needed to control them. Legalism was infused with realistic, logical views and rejected the pleasures of educated conversation as frivolous. All of this made Shi Huang extremely unpopular with the people. As the Qin began to weaken, various factions began to fight for control of China.

History of Asia

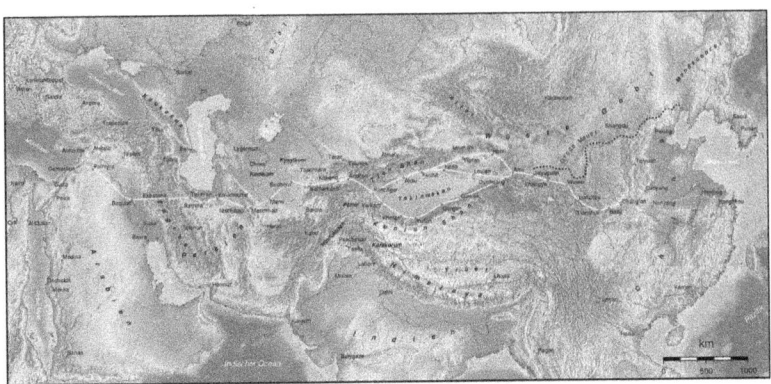

Figure 2: *The Silk Road in Asia*

Han Dynasty

The Han Dynasty (simplified Chinese: 汉朝 ; traditional Chinese: 漢朝 ; pinyin: Hàn Cháo ;206 BCE – 220 CE) was the second imperial dynasty of China, preceded by the Qin Dynasty and succeeded by the Three Kingdoms (220–265 CE). Spanning over four centuries, the period of the Han Dynasty is considered a golden age in Chinese history. One of the Han Dynasty's greatest emperors, Emperor Wu of Han, established a peace throughout China comparable to the Pax Romana seen in the Mediterranean a hundred years later.[7] To this day, China's majority ethnic group refers to itself as the "Han people". The Han Dynasty was established when two peasants succeeded in rising up against Shi Huang's significantly weaker successor-son. The new Han government retained the centralization and bureaucracy of the Qin, but greatly reduced the repression seen before. They expanded their territory into Korea, Vietnam, and Central Asia, creating an even larger empire than the Qin.

The Han developed contacts with the Persian Empire in the Middle East and the Romans, through the Silk Road, with which they were able to trade many commodities—primarily silk. Many ancient civilizations were influenced by the Silk Road, which connected China, India, the Middle East and Europe. Han emperors like Wu also promoted Confucianism as the national "religion" (although it is debated by theologians as to whether it is defined as such or as a philosophy). Shrines devoted to Confucius were built and Confucian philosophy was taught to all scholars who entered the Chinese bureaucracy. The bureaucracy was further improved with the introduction of an examination system that selected scholars of high merit. These bureaucrats were often upper-class people educated in special schools, but whose power was often checked by the lower-class brought into the bureaucracy through their skill. The Chinese imperial bureaucracy was very effective and highly respected by all in the realm and would last over 2,000 years. The Han government was highly organized and it commanded the military, judicial law (which used a system of courts and strict laws), agricultural production, the economy, and the general lives of its people. The government also promoted intellectual philosophy, scientific research, and detailed historical records.

However, despite all of this impressive stability, central power began to lose control by the turn of the Common Era. As the Han Dynasty declined, many factors continued to pummel it into submission until China was left in a state of chaos. By 100 CE, philosophical activity slowed, and corruption ran rampant in the bureaucracy. Local landlords began to take control as the scholars neglected their duties, and this resulted in heavy taxation of the peasantry. Taoists began to gain significant ground and protested the decline. They started to proclaim magical powers and promised to save China with them; the Taoist Yellow Turban Rebellion in 184 (led by rebels in yellow scarves) failed but was able to weaken the government. The aforementioned Huns combined with diseases killed up to half of the population and officially ended the Han Dynasty by 220. The ensuing period of chaos was so terrible it lasted for three centuries, where many weak regional rulers and dynasties failed to establish order in China. This period of chaos and attempts at order is commonly known as that of the Six Dynasties. The first part of this included the Three Kingdoms which started in 220 and describes the brief and weak successor "dynasties" that followed the Han. In 265, the Jin dynasty of China was started and this soon split into two different empires in control of northwestern and southeastern China. In 420, the conquest and abdication of those two dynasties resulted in the first of the Southern and Northern Dynasties. The Northern and Southern Dynasties passed through until finally, by 557, the Northern Zhou Dynasty ruled the north and the Chen Dynasty ruled the south.

Medieval

During this period, the Eastern world empires continued to expand through trade, migration and conquests of neighboring areas. Gunpowder was widely used as early as the 11th century and they were using moveable type printing five hundred years before Gutenberg created his press. Buddhism, Taoism, Confucianism were the dominant philosophies of the Far East during the Middle Ages. Marco Polo was not the first Westerner to travel to the Orient and return with amazing stories of this different culture, but his accounts published in the late 13th and early 14th centuries were the first to be widely read throughout Europe.

Western Asia (Middle East)

The Arabian peninsula and the surrounding Middle East and Near East regions saw dramatic change during the Medieval era caused primarily by the spread of Islam and the establishment of the Arabian Empires.

In the 5th century, the Middle East was separated into small, weak states; the two most prominent were the Sasanian Empire of the Persians in what is now Iran and Iraq, and the Byzantine Empire in Anatolia (modern-day Turkey). The Byzantines and Sasanians fought with each other continually, a reflection of the rivalry between the Roman Empire and the Persian Empire seen during the previous five hundred years. The fighting weakened both states, leaving the stage open to a new power. Meanwhile, the nomadic Bedouin tribes who dominated the Arabian desert saw a period of tribal stability, greater trade networking and a familiarity with Abrahamic religions or monotheism.

While the Byzantine Roman and Sassanid Persian empires were both weakened by the Byzantine–Sasanian War of 602–628, a new power in the form of Islam grew in the Middle East under Muhammad in Medina. In a series of rapid Muslim conquests, the Rashidun army, led by the Caliphs and skilled military commanders such as Khalid ibn al-Walid, swept through most of the Middle East, taking more than half of Byzantine territory in the Arab–Byzantine wars and completely engulfing Persia in the Muslim conquest of Persia. It would be the Arab Caliphates of the Middle Ages that would first unify the entire Middle East as a distinct region and create the dominant ethnic identity that persists today. These Caliphates included the Rashidun Caliphate, Umayyad Caliphate, Abbasid Caliphate, and later the Seljuq Empire.

After Muhammad introduced Islam, it jump-started Middle Eastern culture into an Islamic Golden Age, inspiring achievements in architecture, the revival of old advances in science and technology, and the formation of a distinct way of life. Muslims saved and spread Greek advances in medicine, algebra, geometry, astronomy, anatomy, and ethics that would later finds it way back to Western Europe.

The dominance of the Arabs came to a sudden end in the mid-11th century with the arrival of the Seljuq Turks, migrating south from the Turkic homelands in Central Asia. They conquered Persia, Iraq (capturing Baghdad in 1055), Syria, Palestine, and the Hejaz. This was followed by a series of Christian Western Europe invasions. The fragmentation of the Middle East allowed joined forces, mainly from England, France, and the emerging Holy Roman Empire, to enter the region. In 1099 the knights of the First Crusade captured Jerusalem and founded the Kingdom of Jerusalem, which survived until 1187, when Saladin retook the city. Smaller crusader fiefdoms survived until 1291. In the early 13th century, a new wave of invaders, the armies of the

Mongol Empire, swept through the region, sacking Baghdad in the Siege of Baghdad (1258) and advancing as far south as the border of Egypt in what became known as the Mongol conquests. The Mongols eventually retreated in 1335, but the chaos that ensued throughout the empire deposed the Seljuq Turks. In 1401, the region was further plagued by the Turko-Mongol, Timur, and his ferocious raids. By then, another group of Turks had arisen as well, the Ottomans.

Central Asia

Mongol Empire

The Mongol Empire conquered a large part of Asia in the 13th century, an area extending from China to Europe. Medieval Asia was the kingdom of the Khans. Never before had any person controlled as much land as Genghis Khan. He built his power unifying separate Mongol tribes before expanding his kingdom south and west. He and his grandson, Kublai Khan, controlled lands in China, Burma, Central Asia, Russia, Iran, the Middle East, and Eastern Europe. Estimates are that the Mongol armies reduced the population of China by nearly a third. Genghis Khan was a pagan who tolerated nearly every religion, and their culture often suffered the harshest treatment from Mongol armies. The Khan armies pushed as far west as Jerusalem before being defeated in 1260.

South Asia

India

The Indian early medieval age, 600 to 1200, is defined by regional kingdoms and cultural diversity. When Harsha of Kannauj, who ruled much of the Indo-Gangetic Plain from 606 to 647, attempted to expand southwards, he was defeated by the Chalukya ruler of the Deccan. When his successor attempted to expand eastwards, he was defeated by the Pala king of Bengal. When the Chalukyas attempted to expand southwards, they were defeated by the Pallavas from farther south, who in turn were opposed by the Pandyas and the Cholas from still farther south. The Cholas could under the rule of Raja Raja Chola defeat their rivals and rise to a regional power. Cholas expanded northward and defeated Eastern Chalukya, Kalinga and the Pala. Under Rajendra Chola the Cholas created the first notable navy of Indian subcontinent. The Chola navy extended the influence of Chola empire to southeast asia. During this time, pastoral peoples whose land had been cleared to make way for the growing agricultural economy were accommodated within caste society, as were new non-traditional ruling classes.

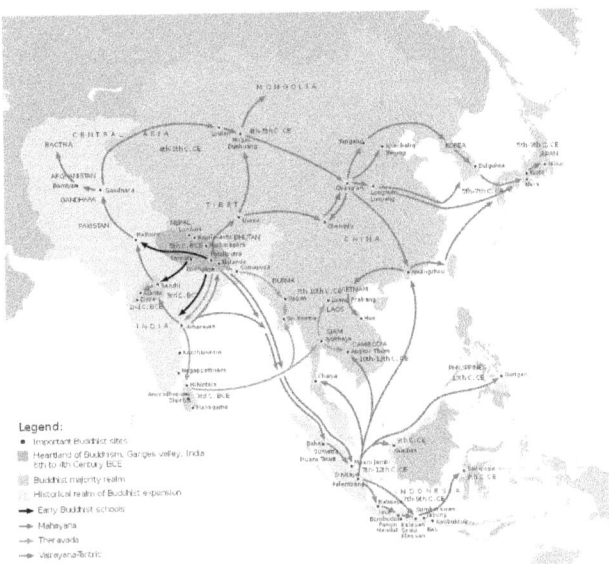

Figure 3: *Buddhist adoption in Asia, Mahayana Buddhism first entered China through Silk Road.*

The Muslim conquest in the Indian subcontinent mainly took place from the 12th century onwards, though earlier Muslim conquests made limited inroads into the region, beginning during the period of the ascendancy of the Rajput Kingdoms in North India, although Sindh and Multan were captured in 8th century.

East Asia

China

China saw the rise and fall of the Sui, Tang, Song, and Yuan dynasties and therefore improvements in its bureaucracy, the spread of Buddhism, and the advent of Neo-Confucianism. It was an unsurpassed era for Chinese ceramics and painting. Medieval architectural masterpieces the Great South Gate in Todaiji, Japan, and the Tien-ning Temple in Peking, China are some of the surviving constructs from this era.

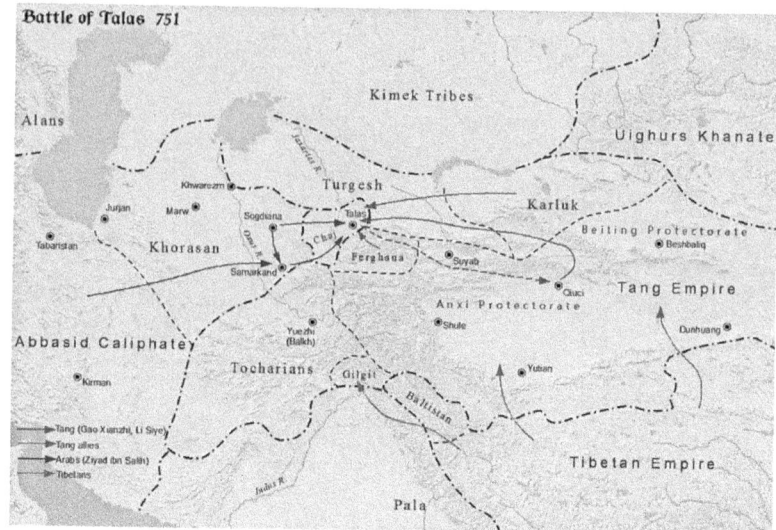

Figure 4: *Battle of Talas between Tang dynasty and Abbasid Caliphate c. 751*

Sui Dynasty

A new powerful dynasty began to rise in the 580s, amongst the divided factions of China. This was started when an aristocrat named Yang Jian married his daughter into the Northern Zhou Dynasty. He proclaimed himself Emperor Wen of Sui and appeased the nomadic military by abandoning the Confucian scholar-gentry. Emperor Wen soon led the conquest of the southern Chen Dynasty and united China once more under the Sui Dynasty. The emperor lowered taxes and constructed granaries that he used to prevent famine and control the market. Later Wen's son would murder him for the throne and declare himself Emperor Yang of Sui. Emperor Yang revived the Confucian scholars and the bureaucracy, much to anger of the aristocrats and nomadic military leaders. Yang became an excessive leader who overused China's resources for personal luxury and perpetuated exhaustive attempts to reconquer Korea. His military failures and neglect of the empire forced his own ministers to assassinate him in 618, ending the Sui Dynasty.

Tang dynasty

Fortunately, one of Yang's most respectable advisors, Li Yuan, was able to claim the throne quickly, preventing a chaotic collapse. He proclaimed himself Emperor Gaozu, and established the Tang dynasty in 623. The Tang saw expansion of China through conquest to Tibet in the west, Vietnam in the south, and Manchuria in the north. Tang emperors also improved the education of scholars in the Chinese bureaucracy. A Ministry of Rites was established and the examination system was improved to better qualify scholars for their jobs.[8] In addition, Buddhism became popular in China with two different strains between the peasantry and the elite, the Pure Land and Zen strains, respectively.[9] Greatly supporting the spread of Buddhism was Empress Wu, who additionally claimed an unofficial "Zhou Dynasty" and displayed China's tolerance of a woman ruler, which was rare at the time. However, Buddhism would also experience some backlash, especially from Confucianists and Taoists. This would usually involve criticism about how it was costing the state money, since the government was unable to tax Buddhist monasteries, and additionally sent many grants and gifts to them.[10]

The Tang dynasty began to decline under the rule of Emperor Xuanzong, who began to neglect the economy and military and caused unrest amongst the court officials due to the excessive influence of his concubine, Yang Guifei, and her family.[11] This eventually sparked a revolt in 755.[11] Although the revolt failed, subduing it required involvement with the unruly nomadic tribes outside of China and distributing more power to local leaders—leaving the government and economy in a degraded state. The Tang dynasty officially ended in 907 and various factions led by the aforementioned nomadic tribes and local leaders would fight for control of China in the Five Dynasties and Ten Kingdoms period.

Liao, Song and Jin dynasties

By 960, most of China proper had been reunited under the Song dynasty, although it lost territories in the north and could not defeat one of the nomadic tribes there—the Liao dynasty of the highly sinicized Khitan people. From then on, the Song would have to pay tribute to avoid invasion and thus set the precedent for other nomadic kingdoms to oppress them. The Song also saw the revival of Confucianism in the form of Neo-Confucianism. This had the effect of putting the Confucian scholars at a higher status than aristocrats or Buddhists and also intensified the reduction of power in women. The infamous practice of foot binding developed in this period as a result. Eventually the Liao dynasty in the north was overthrown by the Jin dynasty of the Manchu-related Jurchen people. The new Jin kingdom invaded northern China, leaving the Song to flee farther south and creating the Southern Song dynasty in 1126. There, cultural life flourished.

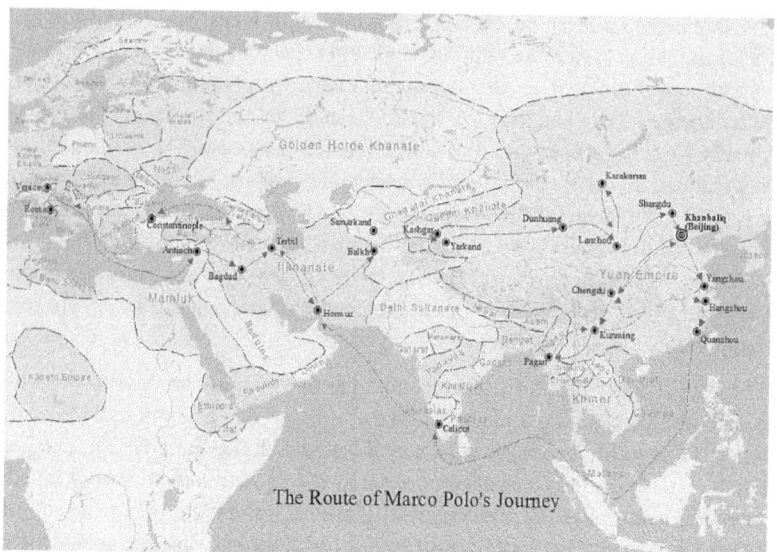

Figure 5: *Map of Marco Polo's travels*

Yuan Dynasty

By 1227, the Mongols had conquered the Western Xia kingdom northwest of China. Soon the Mongols incurred upon the Jin empire of the Jurchens. Chinese cities were soon besieged by the Mongol hordes that showed little mercy for those who resisted and the Southern Song Chinese were quickly losing territory. In 1271 the current great khan, Kublai Khan, claimed himself Emperor of China and officially established the Yuan Dynasty. By 1290, all of China was under control of the Mongols, marking the first time they were ever completely conquered by a foreign invader; the new capital was established at Khanbaliq (modern-day Beijing). Kublai Khan segregated Mongol culture from Chinese culture by discouraging interactions between the two peoples, separating living spaces and places of worship, and reserving top administrative positions to Mongols, thus preventing Confucian scholars to continue the bureaucratic system. Nevertheless, Kublai remained fascinated with Chinese thinking, surrounding himself with Chinese Buddhist, Taoist, or Confucian advisors.

Mongol women displayed a contrasting independent nature compared to the Chinese women who continued to be suppressed. Mongol women often rode out on hunts or even to war. Kublai's wife, Chabi, was a perfect example of this; Chabi advised her husband on several political and diplomatic matters; she convinced him that the Chinese were to be respected and well-treated in

Figure 6: *Sculpture of Prince Shōtoku*

order to make them easier to rule.[12] However this was not enough to affect Chinese women's position, and the increasingly Neo-Confucian successors of Kublai further repressed Chinese and even Mongol women.

The Black Death, which would later ravage Western Europe, had its beginnings in Asia, where it wiped out large populations in China in 1331.

Japan

Asuka period

Japan's medieval history began with the Asuka period, from around 600 to 710. The time was characterized by the Taika Reform and imperial centralization, both of which were a direct result of growing Chinese contact and influences. In 603, Prince Shōtoku of the Yamato dynasty began significant political and cultural changes. He issued the Seventeen-article constitution in 604, centralizing power towards the emperor (under the title *tenno*, or heavenly sovereign) and removing the power to levy taxes from provincial lords. Shōtoku was also a patron of Buddhism and he encouraged building temples competitively.[13]

Nara period

Shōtoku's reforms transitioned Japan to the Nara period (c. 710 to c. 794), with the moving of the Japanese capital to Nara in Honshu. This period saw the culmination of Chinese-style writing, etiquette, and architecture in Japan along with Confucian ideals[14] to supplement the already present Buddhism. Peasants revered both Confucian scholars and Buddhist monks. However, Buddhism gained the status of state religion, and the government ordered the construction of Buddhist temples, monasteries, and statues.[13] The lavish spending combined with the fact that many aristocrats did not pay taxes, put a heavy burden on peasantry that caused poverty and famine.[13] Eventually the Buddhist position got out of control, threatening to seize imperial power and causing Emperor Kanmu to move the capital to Heian-kyō to avoid a Buddhist takeover.[14] This marked the beginning of the Heian period and the end of Taika reform.

Heian period

With the Heian period (from 794 to 1185) came a decline of imperial power. Chinese influence also declined, as a result of its correlation with imperial centralization and the heavenly mandate, which came to be regarded as ineffective. By 838, the Japanese court discontinued its embassies in China; only traders and Buddhist monks continued to travel to China. Buddhism itself came to be considered more Japanese than Chinese, and persisted to be popular in Japan. Buddhists monks and monasteries continued their attempts to gather personal power in courts, along with aristocrats. One particular noble family that dominated influence in the imperial bureaucracy was the Fujiwara clan. During this time cultural life in the imperial court flourished. There was a focus on beauty and social interaction and writing and literature was considered refined. Noblewomen were cultured the same as noblemen, dabbling in creative works and politics. A prime example of both Japanese literature and women's role in high-class culture at this time was *The Tale of Genji*, written by the lady-in-waiting Murasaki Shikibu. Popularization of wooden palaces and shōji sliding doors amongst the nobility also occurred.

Loss of imperial power also led to the rise of provincial warrior elites. Small lords began to function independently. They administered laws, supervised public works projects, and collected revenue for themselves instead of the imperial court. Regional lords also began to build their own armies. These warriors were loyal only their local lords and not the emperor, although the imperial government increasingly called them in to protect the capital. The regional warrior class developed into the samurai, which created its own culture: including specialized weapons such as the katana and a form of chivalry, bushido. The imperial government's loss of control in the second half of the

Heian period allowed banditry to grow, requiring both feudal lords and Buddhist monasteries to procure warriors for protection. As imperial control over Japan declined, feudal lords also became more independent and seceded from the empire. These feudal states squandered the peasants living in them, reducing the farmers to an almost serfdom status. Peasants were also rigidly restricted from rising to the samurai class, being physically set off by dress and weapon restrictions. As a result of their oppression, many peasants turned to Buddhism as a hope for reward in the afterlife for upright behavior.[15]

With the increase of feudalism, families in the imperial court began to depend on alliances with regional lords. The Fujiwara clan declined from power, replaced by a rivalry between the Taira clan and the Minamoto clan. This rivalry grew into the Genpei War in the early 1180s. This war saw the use of both samurai and peasant soldiers. For the samurai, battle was ritual and they often easily cut down the poorly trained peasantry. The Minamoto clan proved successful due to their rural alliances. Once the Taira was destroyed, the Minamoto established a military government called the shogunate (or bakufu), centered in Kamakura.

Kamakura period

The end of the Genpei War and the establishment of the Kamakura shogunate marked the end of the Heian period and the beginning of the Kamakura period in 1185, solidifying feudal Japan.

Korea

Korea was fought between the three local kingdoms: Silla, Baekje, and Goguryeo. This continued until the Silla allied with Tang China to conquer all of Korea. Attempts at sinicization occurred.

Early modern

The Russian Empire began to expand into Asia from the 17th century, and would eventually take control of all of Siberia and most of Central Asia by the end of the 19th century. The Ottoman Empire controlled Anatolia, the Middle East, North Africa and the Balkans from the 16th century onwards. In the 17th century, the Manchu conquered China and established the Qing Dynasty. In the 16th century, the Mughal Empire controlled much of India and initiated the second golden age for India. China was the largest economy in the world for much of the time, followed by India until the 18th century.

Figure 7: *A 1796 map of Asia (or the "Eastern world"), which also included the continent of Australia (then known as New Holland) within its realm.*

Ming China

By 1368, Zhu Yuanzhang had claimed himself Hongwu Emperor and established the Ming Dynasty of China. Immediately, the new emperor and his followers drove the Mongols and their culture out of China and beyond the Great Wall.[16] The new emperor was somewhat suspicious of the scholars that dominated China's bureaucracy, for he had been born a peasant and was uneducated.[16] Nevertheless, Confucian scholars were necessary to China's bureaucracy and were reestablished as well as reforms that would improve the exam systems and make them more important in entering the bureaucracy than ever before. The exams became more rigorous, cut down harshly on cheating, and those who excelled were more highly appraised. Finally, Hongwu also directed more power towards the role of emperor so as to end the corrupt influences of the bureaucrats.

Society and economy

The Hongwu emperor, perhaps for his sympathy of the common-folk, had built many irrigation systems and other public projects that provided help for the peasant farmers.[17] They were also allowed to cultivate and claim unoccupied land without having to pay any taxes and labor demands were lowered.[17]

However, none of this was able to stop the rising landlord class that gained many privileges from the government and slowly gained control of the peasantry. Moneylenders foreclosed on peasant debt in exchange for mortgages and bought up farmer land, forcing them to become the landlords' tenants or to wander elsewhere for work.[18] Also during this time, Neo-Confucianism intensified even more than the previous two dynasties (the Song and Yuan). Focus on the superiority of elders over youth, men over women, and teachers over students resulted in minor discrimination of the "inferior" classes. The fine arts grew in the Ming era, with improved techniques in brush painting that depicted scenes of court, city or country life; people such as scholars or travelers; or the beauty of mountains, lakes, or marshes. The Chinese novel fully developed in this era, with such classics written such as *Water Margin*, *Journey to the West*, and *Jin Ping Mei*.

Economics grew rapidly in the Ming Dynasty as well. The introduction of American crops such as maize, sweet potatoes, and peanuts allowed for cultivation of crops in infertile land and helped prevent famine. The population boom that began in the Song dynasty accelerated until China's population went from 80 or 90 million to 150 million in three centuries, culminating in 1600.[19] This paralleled the market economy that was growing both internally and externally. Silk, tea, ceramics, and lacquer-ware were produced by artisans that traded them in Asia and to Europeans. Westerners began to trade (with some Chinese-assigned limits), primarily in the port-towns of Macau and Canton. Although merchants benefited greatly from this, land remained the primary symbol of wealth in China and traders' riches were often put into acquiring more land.[19] Therefore, little of these riches were used in private enterprises that could've allowed for China to develop the market economy that often accompanied the highly-successful Western countries.

Foreign interests

In the interest of national glory, the Chinese began sending impressive junk ships across the South China Sea and the Indian Ocean. From 1403 to 1433, the Yongle Emperor commissioned expeditions led by the admiral Zheng He, a Muslim eunuch from China. Chinese junks carrying hundreds of soldiers, goods, and animals for zoos, traveled to Southeast Asia, Persia, southern Arabia, and east Africa to show off Chinese power. Their prowess exceeded that of current Europeans at the time, and had these expeditions not ended, the world economy may be different from today.[20] In 1433, the Chinese government decided that the cost of a navy was an unnecessary expense. The Chinese navy was slowly dismantled and focus on interior reform and military defense began. It was China's longstanding priority that they protect themselves from nomads and they have accordingly returned to it. The growing limits on the Chinese navy would leave them vulnerable to foreign invasion by sea later on.

Figure 8: *A view of the Fort St George in 18th-century Madras.*

Figure 9: *Here a Jesuit, Adam Schall von Bell (1592–1666), is dressed as an official of the Chinese Department of Astronomy.*

History of Asia

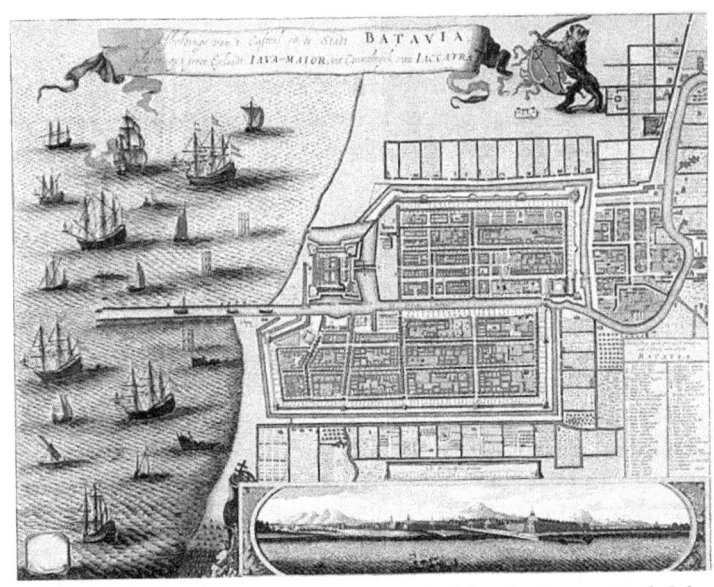

Figure 10: *Dutch Batavia in the 17th century, built in what is now North Jakarta*

As was inevitable, Westerners arrived on the Chinese east coast, primarily Jesuit missionaries which reached the mainland in 1582. They attempted to convert the Chinese people to Christianity by first converting the top of the social hierarchy and allowing the lower classes to subsequently convert. To further gain support, many Jesuits adopted Chinese dress, customs, and language.[21] Some Chinese scholars were interested in certain Western teachings and especially in Western technology. By the 1580s, Jesuit scholars like Matteo Ricci and Adam Schall amazed the Chinese elite with technological advances such as European clocks, improved calendars and cannons, and the accurate prediction of eclipses.[21] Although some the scholar-gentry converted, many were suspicious of the Westerners whom they called "barbarians" and even resented them for the embarrassment they received at the hand of Western correction. Nevertheless, a small group of Jesuit scholars remained at the court to impress the emperor and his advisors.

Decline

Near the end of the 1500s, the extremely centralized government that gave so much power to the emperor had begun to fail as more incompetent rulers took the mantle. Along with these weak rulers came increasingly corrupt officials who took advantage of the decline. Once more the public projects fell into disrepair due to neglect by the bureaucracy and resulted in floods, drought, and famine that rocked the peasantry. The famine soon became so terrible that some peasants resorted to selling their children to slavery to save them from starvation, or to eating bark, the feces of geese, or other people.[22] Many landlords abused the situation by building large estates where desperate farmers would work and be exploited. In turn, many of these farmers resorted to flight, banditry, and open rebellion.

All of this corresponded with the usual dynastic decline of China seen before, as well as the growing foreign threats. In the mid-16th century, Japanese and ethnic Chinese pirates began to raid the southern coast, and neither the bureaucracy nor the military were able to stop them.[23] The threat of the northern Manchu people also grew. The Manchu were an already large state north of China, when in the early 17th century a local leader named Nurhaci suddenly united them under the Eight Banners—armies that the opposing families were organized into. The Manchus adopted many Chinese customs, specifically taking after their bureaucracy. Nevertheless, the Manchus still remained a Chinese vassal. In 1644 Chinese administration became so weak, the 16th and last emperor, the Chongzhen Emperor, did not respond to the severity of an ensuing rebellion by local dissenters until the enemy had invaded the Forbidden City (his personal estate). He soon hanged himself in the imperial gardens.[23] For a brief amount of time, the Shun Dynasty was claimed, until a loyalist Ming official called support from the Manchus to put down the new dynasty. The Shun Dynasty ended within a year and the Manchu were now within the Great Wall. Taking advantage of the situation, the Manchus marched on the Chinese capital of Beijing. Within two decades all of China belonged to the Manchu and the Qing Dynasty was established.

Late modern

Qing China

By 1644, the northern Manchu people had conquered China and established a foreign dynasty—the Qing Dynasty—once more. The Manchu Qing emperors, especially Confucian scholar Kangxi, remained largely conservative—retaining the bureaucracy and the scholars within it, as well as the Confucian ideals present in Chinese society. However, changes in the economy and new attempts at resolving certain issues occurred too. These included increased trade with Western countries that brought large amounts of silver into the Chinese economy in exchange for tea, porcelain, and silk textiles. This allowed for a new merchant-class, the compradors, to develop. In addition, repairs were done on existing dikes, canals, roadways, and irrigation works. This, combined with the lowering of taxes and government-assigned labor, was supposed to calm peasant unrest. However, the Qing failed to control the growing landlord class which had begun to exploit the peasantry and abuse their position.

By the late 18th century, both internal and external issues began to arise in Qing China's politics, society, and economy. The exam system with which scholars were assigned into the bureaucracy became increasingly corrupt; bribes and other forms of cheating allowed for inexperienced and inept scholars to enter the bureaucracy and this eventually caused rampant neglect of the peasantry, military, and the previously mentioned infrastructure projects. Poverty and banditry steadily rose, especially in rural areas, and mass migrations looking for work throughout China occurred. The perpetually conservative government refused to make reforms that could resolve these issues.

Opium War

China saw its status reduced by what it perceived as parasitic trade with Westerners. Originally, European traders were at a disadvantage because the Chinese cared little for their goods, while European demand for Chinese commodities such as tea and porcelain only grew. In order to tip the trade imbalance in their favor, British merchants began to sell Indian opium to the Chinese. Not only did this sap Chinese bullion reserves, it also led to widespread drug addiction amongst the bureaucracy and society in general. A ban was placed on opium as early as 1729 by the Yongzheng Emperor, but little was done to enforce it. By the early 19th century, under the new Daoguang Emperor, the government began serious efforts to eradicate opium from Chinese society. Leading this endeavour were respected scholar-officials including Imperial Commissioner Lin Zexu.

After Lin destroyed more than 20,000 chests of opium in the summer of 1839, Europeans demanded compensation for what they saw as unwarranted Chinese interference in their affairs. When it was not paid, the British declared war later the same year, starting what became known as the First Opium War. The outdated Chinese junks were no match for the advanced British gunboats, and soon the Yangzi River region came under threat of British bombardment and invasion. The emperor had no choice but to sue for peace, resulting in the exile of Lin and the making of the Treaty of Nanking, which ceded the British control of Hong Kong and opened up trade and diplomacy with other European countries, including Germany, France, and the USA.

Contemporary

The European powers had control of other parts of Asia by the early 20th century, such as British India, French Indochina, Spanish East Indies, and Portuguese Macau and Goa. The Great Game between Russia and Britain was the

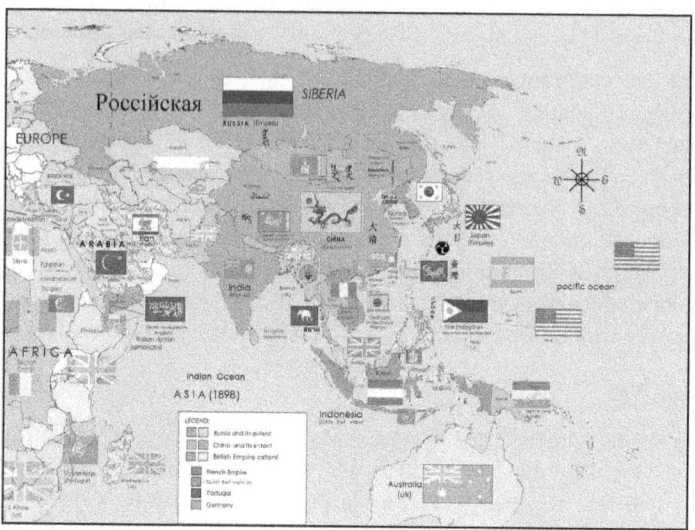

Figure 11: *Map of Asia for early 20th century*

struggle for power in the Central Asian region in the nineteenth century. The Trans-Siberian Railway, crossing Asia by train, was complete by 1916. Parts of Asia remained free from European control, although not influence, such as Persia, Thailand and most of China. In the twentieth century, Imperial Japan expanded into China and Southeast Asia during the Second World War. After the war, many Asian countries became independent from European powers. During the Cold War, the northern parts of Asia were communist controlled with the Soviet Union and People's Republic of China, while western allies formed pacts such as CENTO and SEATO. Conflicts such as the Korean War, Vietnam War and Soviet invasion of Afghanistan were fought between communists and anti-communists. In the decades after the Second World War, a massive restructuring plan drove Japan to become the world's second-largest economy, a phenomenon known as the Japanese post-war economic miracle. The Arab–Israeli conflict has dominated much of the recent history of the Middle East. After the Soviet Union's collapse in 1991, there were many new independent nations in Central Asia.

China

Prior to World War II, China faced a civil war between Mao Zedong's Communist party and Chiang Kai-shek's nationalist party; the nationalists appeared to be in the lead. However, once the Japanese invaded in 1937, the two parties were forced to form a temporary cease-fire in order to defend China. The nationalists faced many military failures that caused them to lose territory and subsequently, respect from the Chinese masses. In contrast, the communists' use of guerilla warfare (led by Lin Biao) proved effective against the Japanese's conventional methods and put the Communist Party on top by 1945. They also gained popularity for the reforms they were already applying in controlled areas, including land redistribution, education reforms, and widespread health care. For the next four years, the nationalists would be forced to retreat to the small island east of China, known as Taiwan (formerly known as Formosa), where they remain today. In mainland China, the People's Republic of China was established by the Communist Party, with Mao Zedong as its state chairman.

The communist government in China was defined by the party cadres. These hard-line officers controlled the People's Liberation Army, which itself controlled large amounts of the bureaucracy. This system was further controlled by the Central Committee, which additionally supported the state chairman who was considered the head of the government. The People's Republic's foreign policies included the repressing of secession attempts in Mongolia and Tibet and supporting of North Korea and North Vietnam in the Korean War and Vietnam War, respectively. Additionally, by 1960 China began to cut off its connections with the Soviet Union due to border disputes and an increasing Chinese sense of superiority, especially the personal feeling of Mao over the Russian premier, Nikita Khrushchev.

Today China, India, South Korea, Japan and Russia play important roles in world economics and politics. China today is the world's second largest economy and the second fastest growing economy. Indian economy is the seventh-largest in the world by nominal GDP and the third-largest by purchasing power parity and is the fastest growing economy.

Bibliography

<templatestyles src="Template:Refbegin/styles.css" />

- "Asia Reborn: A Continent Rises from the Ravages of Colonialism and War to a New Dynamism" by Prasenjit K. Basu,Publisher: Aleph Book Company

- Bowman, John S. (2000), *Columbia Chronologies of Asian History and Culture*[24], New York City: Columbia University Press, ISBN 0-231-50004-1<templatestyles src="Module:Citation/CS1/styles.css"></templatestyles>
- Holcombe, Charles. *A History of East Asia: From the Origins of Civilization to the Twenty-First Century* (2010).
- Ludden, David. *India and South Asia: A Short History* (2013).
- Mansfield, Peter, and Nicolas Pelham, *A History of the Middle East* (4th ed, 2013).
- Moffett, Samuel Hugh. *A History of Christianity in Asia, Vol. II: 1500-1900* (2003) excerpt[25]
- Murphey, Rhoads. *A History of Asia* (7th ed, 2016) excerpt[26]
- Stearns, Peter N.; Michael Adas; Stuart B. Schwartz; Marc Jason Gilbert (2011), *World Civilizations: The Global Experience* (Textbook) (6th ed.), One Lake St., Upper Saddle River, NJ 07458: Longman, ISBN 978-0-13-136020-4<templatestyles src="Module:Citation/CS1/styles.css"></templatestyles>

Prehistory

Prehistoric Asia

Prehistoric Asia refers to events in Asia during the period of human existence prior to the invention of writing systems or the documentation of recorded history. This includes portions of the Eurasian land mass currently or traditionally considered as the continent of Asia. The continent is commonly described as the region east of the Ural Mountains, the Caucasus Mountains, the Caspian Sea and Black Sea, bounded by the Pacific, Indian, and Arctic Oceans. This article gives an overview of the many regions of Asia during prehistoric times.

Origin of Asian hominids

Early hominids

About 1.8 million years ago, some hominids left the African continent.[27] *Homo erectus* ("upright man") is believed to have lived in East and Southeast Asia from 1.8 million to 40,000 years ago. Their regional distinction is classified as *Homo erectus sensu stricto*.[28] The females weighed an average of 52 kilograms (115 lb) and were on average 1.5 metres (4.9 ft) tall. The males weighed an average of 58 kilograms (128 lb) and were on average 1.7 metres (5.6 ft) tall. They are believed to have had a vegetarian diet with some meat. They had small brains, when compared to the later *Homo sapiens* and used simple tools.

The earliest human fossils found outside of Africa are skulls and mandibles of the Asian *Homo erectus* from Dmanisi (modern Republic of Georgia) in Caucasus, which is a land corridor that led to North Asia from Africa and Near East or Middle East. They are approximately 1.8 Ma (Megaannum, or million years) old. Archaeologists have named these fossils *Homo erectus georgicus*.[29,30] There were also some remains that looked similar to the *Homo ergaster*, which may mean that there were several species living about that time

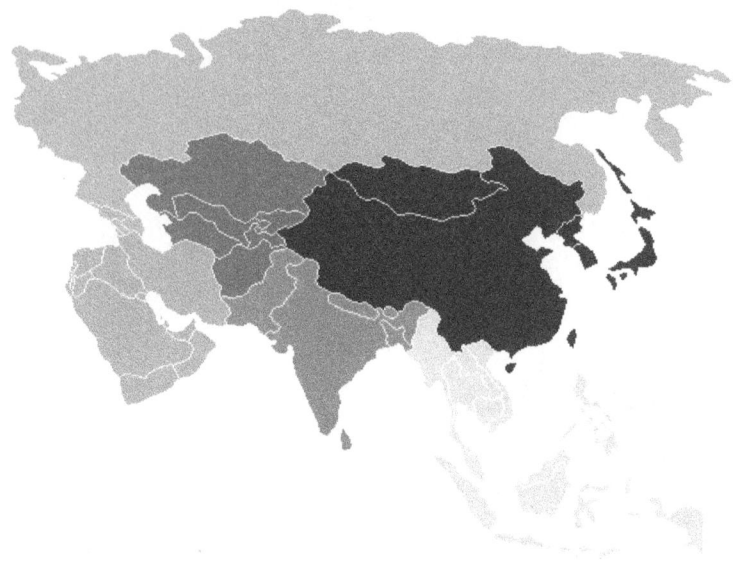

Figure 12:
Map of AsiaWikipedia:Citation needed
North Asia/Eurasia
Central Asia
East Asia
Near East/Middle East
South Asia
Southeast Asia

in Caucasus. Bones of animals found near the human remains included short-necked giraffes, ostriches, ancient rhinoceroses from Africa and saber-toothed tigers and wolves from Eurasia. Tools found with the human fossils include simple stone tools like those used in Africa: a cutting flake, core and a chopper.

The oldest Southeast Asian *Homo* fossils, known as the *Homo erectus* Java Man, were found between layers of volcanic debris in Java, Indonesia. Fossils representing 40 *Homo erectus* individuals, known as Peking Man, were found near Beijing at Zhoukoudian that date to about 400,000 years ago. The species was believed to have lived for at least several hundred thousand years in China,[31] and possibly until 200,000 years ago in Indonesia. They may have been the first to use fire and cook food.[32]

Skulls were found in Java of *Homo erectus* that dated to about 300,000 years ago.[33] A skull was found in Central China that was similar to the *Homo heidelbergensis* remains that were found in Europe and Africa and are dated between

Figure 13: *This skull of Homo erectus georgicus from Dmanisi in modern Georgia (Caucasus) is the earliest evidence for the presence of early humans outside the African continent.*

Figure 14: *Illustration of what Peking Man may have looked like.*

200,000 and 50,000 years ago.[34]

Homo sapiens

Between 60,000 and 100,000 years ago, *Homo sapiens* came to Southeast Asia by migrating from Africa, known as the "Out of Africa" model.[35] *Homo sapiens* are believed to have migrated through the Middle East on their way out of Africa about 100,000 years ago.[36] Near Nazareth, remains of skeletons, including a double grave of a mother and child, dating to about 93,000 years ago were found in a Jebel Qafzeh cave. Included among the remains was a skeleton of another species which was not *Homo sapiens*; it had a "distinct and undivided browridge that is continuous across the eye sockets" and other discrepancies.[37]

Researchers believe that the modern human, or *Homo sapiens*, migrated about 60,000 years ago to South Asia along the Indian Ocean, because people living in the most isolated areas of the Indian Ocean have the oldest non-African DNA markers. Humans migrated into inland Asia, likely by following herds of bison and mammoth and arrived in southern Siberia by about 43,000 years ago and some people move south or east from there.[38,39] By about 40,000 years ago *Homo sapiens* made it to Indonesia, where a skull was found on Borneo in Niah Cave.

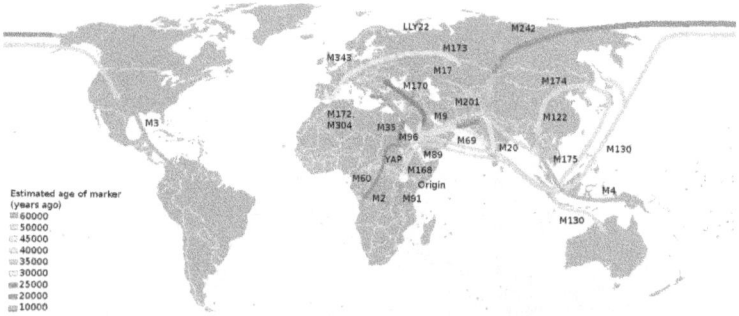

Figure 15: *Homo sapiens migration map, based upon DNA markers*

Homo sapiens females weighed an average of 54 kilograms (119 lb) and were on average 1.6 metres (5.2 ft) tall. The males weighed an average of 65 kilograms (143 lb) and were on average 1.7 metres (5.6 ft) tall. They were omnivorous. As compared to earlier hominids, *Homo sapiens* had larger brains and used more complex tools, including, blades, awls, and microliths out of antlers, bones and ivory. They were the only hominids to develop language, make clothes, create shelters, and store food underground for preservation. In addition, language was formed, rituals were created and art was made.[40]

Prehistoric Asia

Written language

Date	Writing system	Attestation	Location	Region
c. 2600–2500 BC	Sumerian	Cuneiform texts from Shuruppak and Abu Salabikh (Fara period)[41]	Mesopotamia	Near East
c. 2400 BC	Akkadian	A few dozen pre-Sargonic texts from Mari and other sites in northern Babylonia	Syria	Near East
c. 2400 BC	Eblaite	Ebla tablets	Syria	Near East
c. 2300 BC	Elamite	Awan dynasty peace treaty with Naram-Sin	Iran / Iraq	Near East
21st century BC	Hurrian	Temple inscription of Tish-atal in Urkesh	Mesopotamia	Near East
c. 1650 BC	Hittite	Various cuneiform texts and Palace Chronicles written during the reign of Hattusili I, from the archives at Hattusa	Turkey	Near East
c. 1300 BC	Ugaritic	Tablets from Ugarit	Syria	Near East
c. 1200 BC	Old Chinese	Oracle bone and bronze inscriptions from the reign of Wu Ding[42,43]	China	East Asia
c. 1000 BC	Phoenician	Ahiram epitaph	Canaan	Near East
10th century BC	Aramaic			Near East
10th century BC	Hebrew	Gezer calendar	Canaan	Near East
c. 850 BC	Ammonite	Amman Citadel Inscription	Jordan	Near East
c. 840 BC	Moabite	Mesha Stele	Jordan	Near East
c. 800 BC	Phrygian		Asia Minor	Near East
c. 800 BC	Old North Arabian		Northern Arabian Peninsula	Near East
c. 800 BC	Old South Arabian		Southern Arabian Peninsula	Near East
c. 600 BC	Lydian		Anatolia	Near East
c. 600 BC	Carian		Anatolia	Near East
c. 500 BC	Old Persian	Behistun inscription	Iran	Near East

c. 500-300 BC	Tamil Brahmi	cave inscriptions and potsherds in Tamil Nadu[44]	Sri Lanka / India	South Asia
c. 260 BC	Middle Indo-Aryan (Prakrit)	Edicts of Ashoka[45,46] (Pottery inscriptions from Anuradhapura have been dated c. 400 BC.[47])	India	South Asia
c. 170–130 BC	Pahlavi		Iran	Near East

Prehistory by region

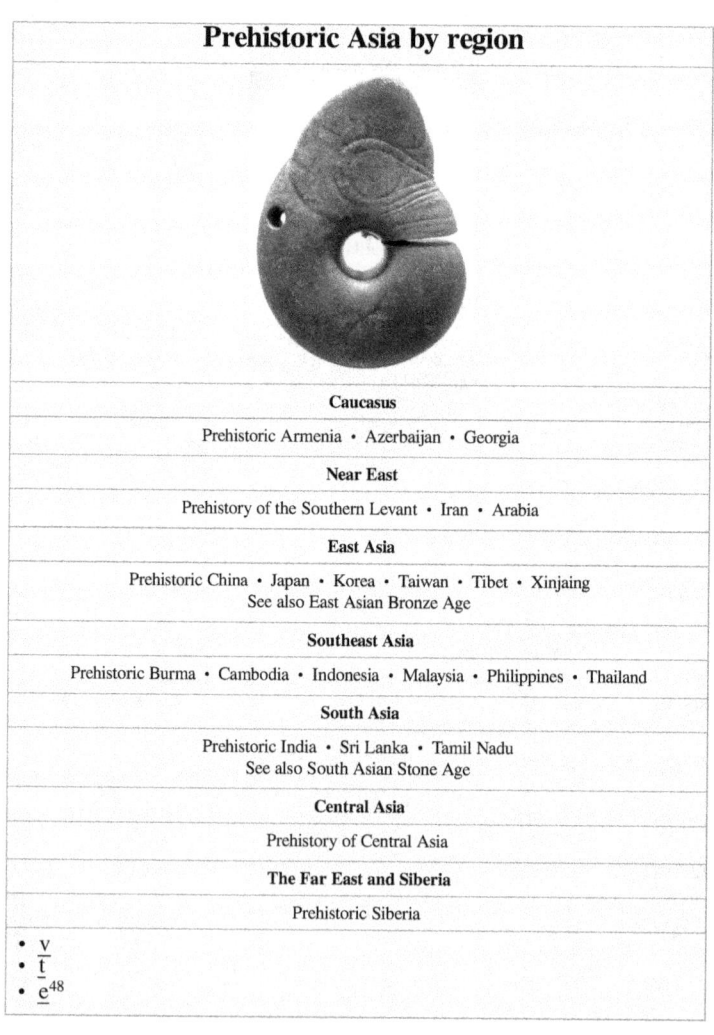

Prehistoric Asia by region
Caucasus
Prehistoric Armenia • Azerbaijan • Georgia
Near East
Prehistory of the Southern Levant • Iran • Arabia
East Asia
Prehistoric China • Japan • Korea • Taiwan • Tibet • Xinjaing See also East Asian Bronze Age
Southeast Asia
Prehistoric Burma • Cambodia • Indonesia • Malaysia • Philippines • Thailand
South Asia
Prehistoric India • Sri Lanka • Tamil Nadu See also South Asian Stone Age
Central Asia
Prehistory of Central Asia
The Far East and Siberia
Prehistoric Siberia
• v • t • e[48]

North Asia

Above China is North Asia or Eurasia, in which Siberia, and Russian Far East are extensive geographical regions which has been part of Russia since the seventeenth century.

At the southwestern edge of North Asia is Caucasus. It is a region at the border of Europe and Asia, situated between the Black and the Caspian seas. Caucasus is home to the Caucasus Mountains, which contain Europe's highest mountain, Mount Elbrus. The southern part of the Caucasus consists of independent sovereign states, whereas the northern parts are under the jurisdiction of the Russian Federation.

The Armenian Highland, in Prehistoric Armenia, shows traces of settlement from the Neolithic era. The Shulaveri-Shomu culture of the central Transcaucasus region is one of the earliest known prehistoric culture in the area, carbon-dated to roughly 6000–4000 BC. Another early culture in the area is the Kura-Araxes culture, assigned to the period of ca. 3300–2000 BC, succeeded by the Georgian Trialeti culture (ca. 3000–1500 BC).

The prehistory of Georgia is the period between the first human habitation of the territory of modern-day nation of Georgia and the time when Assyrian and Urartian, and more firmly, the Classical accounts, brought the proto-Georgian tribes into the scope of recorded history.

Central Asia

Central Asia is the core region of the Asian continent and stretches from the Caspian Sea in the west to China in the east and from Afghanistan in the south to Russia in the north. It is also sometimes referred to as Middle Asia, and, colloquially, "the 'stans" (as the six countries generally considered to be within the region all have names ending with the Persian suffix "-stan", meaning "land of") and is within the scope of the wider Eurasian continent. The countries are Kazakhstan, Kyrgyzstan, Tajikistan, Turkmenistan, Uzbekistan, and Afghanistan.

East Asia

East Asia, for the purpose of this discussion, includes the prehistoric regions of China, Taiwan, Tibet, Xinjiang and Korea. Study of Prehistoric China includes its paleolithic sites, neolithic cultures, Chalcolithic cultures, the Chinese Bronze Age, and the Bronze Age sites.

China

The earliest traces of early humans, *Homo erectus*, in East Asia have been found in China. Fossilized remains of Yuanmou Man were found in Yunnan province in southwest China and have been dated to 1.7 Ma. Stone tools from the Nihewan Basin of the Hebei province in northern China are 1.66 million years old.[49]

Early humans were attracted to what was the warm, fertile climate of Central China more than 500,000 years ago.[50] Skeletal remains of about 45 individuals, known collectively as Peking Man were found in a limestone cave in Yunnan province at Zhoukoudian. They date from 400,000 to 600,000 years ago and some researchers believe that evidence of hearths and artifacts means that they controlled fire, although this is challenged by other archaeologists. About 800 miles west of this site, near Xi'an in the Shaanxi province are remains of a hominid who lived earlier than Peking Man.

Between 100,000 and 200,000 years ago, Neanderthals lived in various places in China. After 100,000 BCE, *Homo sapiens* lived in China and by 25,000 BCE the modern humans lived in isolated locations on the North China Plain, where they fished and hunted for food. They made artifacts of bone and shell.

Starting about 5000 BCE humans lived in Yellow River valley settlements were they farmed, fished, raised pigs and dogs for food, and grew millet and rice. Begun during the late Neolithic period, they were the earliest communities in China. Its artifacts include ceramic pots, fishhooks, knives, arrows and needles. In the northwest Shaanxi, Gansu and Henan provinces two cultures were established by about the sixth millennium BCE. They produced red pottery. Other cultures that emerged, that also made pottery, include the Bao-chi and Banpo people of Shaanxi and the Chishan people of Hebei.

The Yangshao people, who existed between 5000 and 2500 BCE, were farmers who lived in distinctive dwelling which were partly below the surface. Their pottery included designs which may have been symbols that later evolved into written language. Their villages were in western Henan, southwestern Shanxi and central Shaanxi. Between 2500 to 1000 BCE the Longshan culture existed in southern, eastern and northeastern China and into Manchuria. They had superior farming and ceramic making techniques to that of the Yangshao people and had ritualistic burial practices and worshiped their ancestors.[51] Subsequent dynasties include the Xia, Shang, and Zhou dynasties, when the Old Chinese language developed.[52]

Bronze Age China Dynasties

Dates are approximate, consult particular article for details

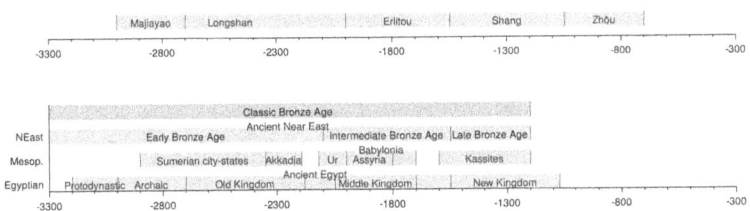

Taiwan

The Prehistory of Taiwan ended with the arrival of the Dutch East India Company in 1624, and is known from archaeological finds throughout the island. The earliest evidence of human habitation dates back 50,000 years or more, when the Taiwan Strait was exposed by lower sea levels as a land bridge. Around 5000 years ago farmers from mainland China settled on the island. These people are believed to have been speakers of Austronesian languages, which dispersed from Taiwan across the islands of the Pacific and Indian Oceans. The current Taiwanese aborigines are believed to be their descendants.

Korea

Prehistoric Korea is the era of human existence in the Korean Peninsula for which written records did not exist. It, however, constitutes the greatest segment of the Korean past and is the major object of study in the disciplines of archaeology, geology, and palaeontology.

Japan

The study of Prehistoric Japan includes Japanese Paleolithic and Jōmon.

Near East

The Near East is a geographical term that roughly encompasses Western Asia. Despite having varying definitions within different academic circles, the term was originally applied to the maximum extent of the Ottoman Empire, but has since been gradually replaced by the term Middle East. The region is sometimes called the Levant.

At 1.4 million years, Ubeidiya in the northern Jordan River Valley is the earliest *Homo erectus* site in the Levant.[53]

Near East Bronze Age timeline

Dates are approximate, consult particular article for details

Figure 16: *Dolmen from Godavari district, Andhra Pradesh, India. Woodcut from the article "Indiska fornsaker" by Hans Hildebrand.*

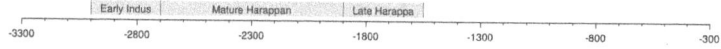

South Asia

South Asia is the southern region of the Asian continent, which comprises the sub-Himalayan countries and, for some authorities, also includes the adjoining countries to the west and the east. Topographically, it is dominated by the Indian Plate, which rises above sea level as the Indian subcontinent south of the Himalayas and the Hindu Kush. South Asia is bounded on the south by the Indian Ocean and on land (clockwise, from west) by West Asia, Central Asia, East Asia, and Southeast Asia.

The Riwat site in modern-day Pakistan contains a few artifacts – a core and two flakes – that might date human activity there to 1.9 million years ago, but these dates are still controversial.[54]

The South Asian prehistory is explored in the articles about Prehistoric Sri Lanka, India and Tamil Nadu

Bronze Age India timeline

Dates are approximate, consult particular article for details

Southeast Asia

Southeast Asia is a subregion of Asia, consisting of the countries that are geographically south of China, east of India, west of New Guinea and north of Australia. The region lies on the intersection of geological plates, with heavy seismic and volcanic activity. Southeast Asia consists of two geographic regions: (1) Mainland Southeast Asia, also known as Indochina, comprising Cambodia, Laos, Myanmar (Burma), Thailand, and Vietnam; and (2) Maritime Southeast Asia, comprising Brunei, Malaysia, East Timor, Indonesia, Philippines, and Singapore.

The rich Sangiran Formation in Central Java (Indonesia) has yielded the earliest evidence of hominin presence in Southeast Asia. These *Homo erectus* fossils date to more than 1.6 Ma.[55] Remains found in Mojokerto have been dated to 1.49 Ma.[56]

Its history is told by region, including the Early history of Burma and Cambodia, as well as the articles about Prehistoric Philippines, Thailand, Malaysia and Indonesia.

Skeleton remains were found of a hominid that was only 3 feet (0.91 m) tall as an adult in Indonesia on the island of Flores. It had a small brain and, nicknamed "the Hobbit" for its diminutive structure, was classified distinctly as *Homo floresiensis*. The small hominid lived about 18,000 years ago.[57]

Works cited

- Dennell, Robin (2007), "'Resource-rich, stone-poor': Early hominin land use in large river systems of Northern India and Pakistan", in Michael D. Petraglia and Bridget Allchin (eds), *The Evolution and History of Human Populations in South Asia: Inter-disciplinary Studies in Archaeology, Biological Anthropology, Linguistics and Genetics*, Vertebrate Paleobiology and Paleoanthropology Series, Dordrecht: Springer, pp. 41–68, ISBN 978-1-4020-5561-4<templatestyles src="Module:Citation/CS1/styles.css"></templatestyles>.
- Dennell, Robin (2010), "'Out of Africa I': Current Problems and Future Prospects", in John G. Fleagle et al. (eds), *Out of Africa I: The First Hominin Colonization of Eurasia*, Vertebrate Paleobiology and Paleoanthropology Series, Dordrecht: Springer, pp. 247–74, ISBN 978-90-481-9036-2<templatestyles src="Module:Citation/CS1/styles.css"></templatestyles>.

- Morwood, M. J.; O'Sullivan, P.; Susanto, E. E.; Aziz, F. (2003), "Revised age for Mojokerto 1, an early *Homo erectus* cranium from East Java, Indonesia"[58], *Australian Archaeology*, **57**: 1–4, archived from the original[59] on 2014-03-10<templatestyles src="Module:Citation/CS1/styles.css"></templatestyles>.
- Rightmire, G. Philip; Lordkipanidze, David (2010), "Fossil Skulls from Dmanisi: A Paleodeme Representing Early *Homo* in Asia", in John G. Fleagle et al. (eds), *Out of Africa I: The First Hominin Colonization of Eurasia*, Vertebrate Paleobiology and Paleoanthropology Series, Dordrecht: Springer, pp. 225–44, ISBN 978-90-481-9036-2<templatestyles src="Module:Citation/CS1/styles.css"></templatestyles>.
- Swisher, C. C.; Curtis, G. H.; Jacob, T.; Getty, A. G.; Suprijo, A.; Widiasmoro (1994), "Age of the earliest known hominin in Java, Indonesia", *Science*, **263**: 1118–21, doi: 10.1126/science.8108729[60], PMID 8108729[61]<templatestyles src="Module:Citation/CS1/styles.css"></templatestyles>.
- Tchernov, E. (1987), "The age of the 'Ubeidiya Formation, and Early Pleistocene hominid site in the Jordan River Valley, Israel", *Israel J. Earth Sci.*, **36**: 3–30<templatestyles src="Module:Citation/CS1/styles.css"></templatestyles>.

Ancient

Ancient Near East

The ancient Near East
Regions and states

	Fertile Crescent
	Mesopotamia
• Akkadian Empire	
• Assyria	
• Babylonia	
• Neo-Assyrian Empire	
• Neo-Babylonian Empire	
• Sumer	
	Egypt
• Ancient Egypt	
	Persia
• Achaemenid Empire	
• Elam	
• Medes	
	Anatolia
• Hittites	
• Hurrians	
• Neo-Hittite states	
• Urartu	
	The Levant
• Ancient Israel	
• Phoenicia	

Archaeological periods
• Chronology
• Bronze Age
• Bronze Age collapse
• Iron Age

Languages
• Akkadian
• Aramaic
• Assyriology
• Cuneiform script
• Elamite
• Hebrew
• Hittite
• Hurrian
• Phoenician
• Sumerian
• Urartian

Literature
• Babylonian
• Hittite texts
• Sumerian

Mythology
• Babylonian
• Hittite
• Mesopotamian
• Egyptian

Other topics
• Cradle of civilization
• Assyrian law
• Babylonian astronomy
• Babylonian law
• Babylonian mathematics
• Cuneiform law
• History of the Middle East
• $\underline{v}$
• $\underline{t}$
• $\underline{e}$[62]

The **ancient Near East** was the home of early civilizations within a region roughly corresponding to the modern Middle East: Mesopotamia (modern Iraq, southeast Turkey, southwest Iran, northeastern Syria and Kuwait), ancient Egypt, ancient Iran (Elam, Media, Parthia and Persia), Anatolia/Asia Minor and Armenian Highlands (Turkey's Eastern Anatolia Region, Armenia, northwestern Iran, southern Georgia, and western Azerbaijan), the Levant (modern Syria, Lebanon, Palestine, Israel, and Jordan), Cyprus and the Arabian Peninsula. The ancient Near East is studied in the fields of Near Eastern archaeology and ancient history.

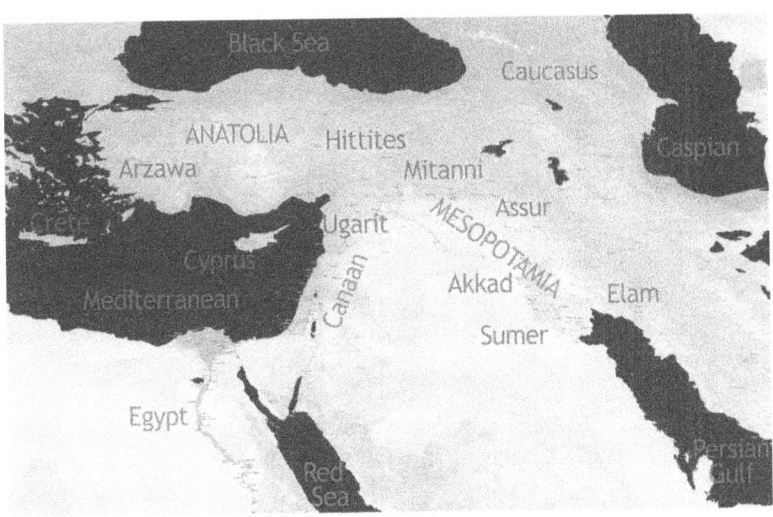

Figure 17: *Overview map of the ancient Near East*

The history of the ancient Near East begins with the rise of Sumer in the 4th millennium BC, though the date it ends varies. The term covers the Bronze Age and the Iron Age in the region, until either the conquest by the Achaemenid Empire in the 6th century BC, that by Macedonian Empire in the 4th century BC, or the Muslim conquests in the 7th century AD.

The ancient Near East is considered[63] one of the cradles of civilization. It was here that intensive year-round agriculture was first practiced, leading to the rise of the first dense urban settlements and the development of many familiar institutions of civilization, such as social stratification, centralized government and empires, organized religion and organized warfare. It also saw the creation of the first writing system and law codes, early advances that laid the foundations of astronomy and mathematics, and the invention of the wheel.

During the period, states became increasingly large, until the region became controlled by militaristic empires that had conquered a number of different cultures.

Concept of Near East

The phrase "ancient Near East" utilizes the 19th-century distinction between Near East and Far East as global regions of interest to the British Empire. The distinction began during the Crimean War. The last major exclusive partition of the east between these two terms was current in diplomacy in the late 19th century, with the Hamidian Massacres of the Armenians and Assyrians by the Ottoman Empire in 1894-1896 and the Sino-Japanese War of 1894-1895. The two theatres were described by the statesmen and advisors of the British Empire as "the Near East" and "the Far East". Shortly after, they were to share the stage with Middle East, which came to prevail in the 20th century and continues in modern times.

As *Near East* had meant the lands of the Ottoman Empire at roughly its maximum extent, on the fall of that empire, the use of Near East in diplomacy was reduced significantly in favor of the Middle East. Meanwhile, the ancient Near East had become distinct. The Ottoman rule over the Near East ranged from Vienna (to the north) to the tip of the Arabian Peninsula (to the south), from Egypt (in the west) to the borders of Iraq (in the east). The 19th-century archaeologists added Iran to their definition, which was never under the Ottomans, but they excluded all of Europe and, generally, Egypt, which had parts in the empire.

Periodization

Ancient Near East periodization is the attempt to categorize or divide time into discrete named blocks, or eras, of the Near East. The result is a descriptive abstraction that provides a useful handle on Near East periods of time with relatively stable characteristics.

Copper Age	Chalcolithic (4500 - 3300 BC)	Early Chalcolithic	4500 - 4000 BC	Ubaid period in Mesopotamia
		Late Chalcolithic	4000 - 3300 BC	Ghassulian, Sumerian Uruk period in Mesopotamia, Gerzeh, Predynastic Egypt, Proto-Elamite
Bronze Age (3300 - 1200 BC)	Early Bronze Age (3300 - 2000 BC)	Early Bronze Age I	3300 - 3000 BC	Protodynastic to Early Dynastic Period of Egypt, settlement of Phoenicians
		Early Bronze Age II	3000 - 2700 BC	Early Dynastic Period of Sumer
		Early Bronze Age III	2700 - 2200 BC	Old Kingdom of Egypt, Akkadian Empire, early Assyria, Old Elamite period, Sumero-Akkadian states
		Early Bronze Age IV	2200 - 2100 BC	First Intermediate Period of Egypt
	Middle Bronze Age (2000 - 1550 BC)	Middle Bronze Age I	2100 - 2000 BC	Third Dynasty of Ur

Ancient Near East

		Middle Bronze Age II A	2000 - 1750 BC	Minoan civilization, early Babylonia, Egyptian Middle Kingdom
		Middle Bronze Age II B	1750 - 1650 BC	Second Intermediate Period of Egypt
		Middle Bronze Age II C	1650 - 1550 BC	Hittite Old Kingdom, Minoan eruption
	Late Bronze Age (1550 - 1200 BC)	Late Bronze Age I	1550 - 1400 BC	Hittite Middle Kingdom, Hayasa-Azzi, Middle Elamite period, New Kingdom of Egypt
		Late Bronze Age II A	1400 - 1300 BC	Hittite New Kingdom, Mitanni, Hayasa-Azzi, Ugarit, Mycenaean Greece
		Late Bronze Age II B	1300 - 1200 BC	Middle Assyrian Empire, beginning of the high point of Phoenicians
Iron Age (1200 - 539 BC)	Iron Age I (1200 - 1000 BC)	Iron Age I A	1200 - 1150 BC	Troy VII, Hekla 3 eruption, Bronze Age collapse, Sea Peoples
		Iron Age I B	1150 - 1000 BC	Neo-Hittite states, Neo Elamite period, Aramean states
	Iron Age II (1000 - 539 BC)	Iron Age II A	1000 - 900 BC	Greek Dark Ages, traditional date of the United Monarchy of Israel
		Iron Age II B	900 - 700 BC	Kingdom of Israel, Urartu, Phrygia, Neo-Assyrian Empire, Kingdom of Judah, first settlement of Carthage
		Iron Age II C	700 - 539 BC	Neo-Babylonian Empire, Median Empire, fall of the Neo-Assyrian Empire, Phoenicia, Archaic Greece, rise of Achaemenid Persia
Classical Antiquity (post-ANE) (539 BC - 634 AD)		Achaemenid	539 – 330 BC	Persian Achaemenid Empire
		Hellenistic & Parthian	330 - 31 BC	Macedonian Empire, Seleucid Empire, Kingdom of Pergamon, Ptolemaic Kingdom, Parthian Empire
		Roman & Persian	31 BC - 634 AD	Roman-Persian Wars, Roman Empire, Parthian Empire, Sassanid Empire, Byzantine Empire, Muslim conquests

History

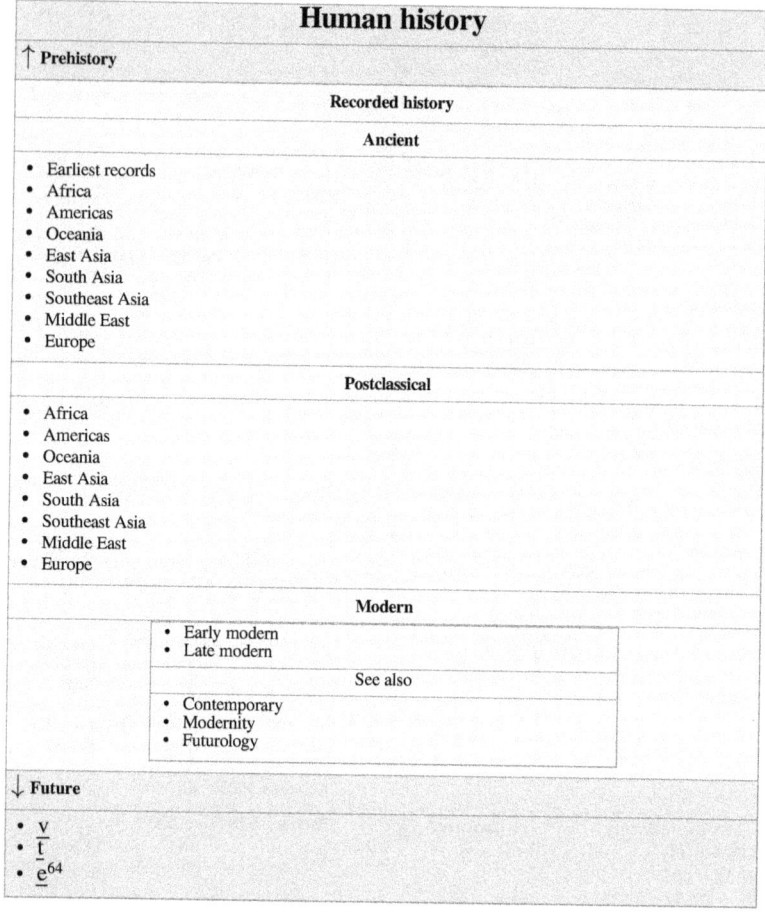

Prehistory

- Paleolithic
- Epipaleolithic and mesolithic
  - Kebaran culture
  - Natufian culture (founding of Göbekli Tepe ceremonial site)
- Pre-pottery Neolithic A
- Pre-pottery Neolithic B
- Pre-pottery Neolithic C
- Pottery Neolithic

Chalcolithic

Early Mesopotamia

The Uruk period (c. 4000 to 3100 BC) existed from the protohistoric Chalcolithic to the Early Bronze Age period in the history of Mesopotamia, following the Ubaid period.[65] Named after the Sumerian city of Uruk, this period saw the emergence of urban life in Mesopotamia. It was followed by the Sumerian civilization.[66] The late Uruk period (34–32 centuries) saw the gradual emergence of the cuneiform script and corresponds to the Early Bronze Age.

Bronze Age

Bronze Age
- v
- t
- e[67]

↑ Chalcolithic

Near East (c. 3300–1200 BC)
Anatolia, Caucasus, Elam, Egypt, Levant, Mesopotamia, Sistan, Canaan
Late Bronze Age collapse

South Asia (c. 3300–1200 BC)
Indus Valley Civilization
Bronze Age South Asia
Ochre Coloured Pottery
Cemetery H

Europe (c. 3200–600 BC)
Aegean (Cycladic, Minoan, Mycenaean), Caucasus, Catacomb culture, Srubna culture, Beaker culture, Unetice culture, Tumulus culture, Urnfield culture, Hallstatt culture, Apennine culture, Canegrate culture, Golasecca culture, Atlantic Bronze Age, Bronze Age Britain, Nordic Bronze Age

East Asia (c. 2000–300 BC)
Erlitou, Erligang, Gojoseon, Jomon, Majiayao, Mumun, Qijia, Siwa, Wucheng, Xindian, Yueshi

- arsenical bronze
- writing
- literature
- sword
- chariot

↓ Iron Age

- ○ Category
- ⊙ Commons
- Portal

Early Bronze Age

Sumer and Akkad

Sumer, located in southern Mesopotamia, is the earliest known civilization in the world. It lasted from the first settlement of Eridu in the Ubaid period (late 6th millennium BC) through the Uruk period (4th millennium BC) and the Dynastic periods (3rd millennium BC) until the rise of Assyria and Babylon in the late 3rd millennium BC and early 2nd millennium BC respectively. The Akkadian Empire, founded by Sargon the Great, lasted from the 24th to the 21st century BC, and was regarded by many as the world's first empire. The Akkadians eventually fragmented into Assyria and Babylonia.

Elam

Ancient Elam lay to the east of Sumer and Akkad, in the far west and southwest of modern-day Iran, stretching from the lowlands of Khuzestan and Ilam Province. In the Old Elamite period, c. 3200 BC, it consisted of kingdoms on the Iranian plateau, centered on Anshan, and from the mid-2nd millennium BC, it was centered on Susa in the Khuzestan lowlands. Elam was absorbed into the Assyrian Empire in the 9th to 7th centuries BC; however, the civilization endured up until 539 BC when it was finally overrun by the Iranian Persians. The Proto-Elamite civilization existed from c. 3200 BC to 2700 BC, when Susa, the later capital of the Elamites, began to receive influence from the cultures of the Iranian plateau. In archaeological terms, this corresponds to the late Banesh period. This civilization is recognized as the oldest in Iran and was largely contemporary with its neighbour, the Sumerian civilization. The Proto-Elamite script is an Early Bronze Age writing system briefly in use for the ancient Elamite language (which was a Language isolate) before the introduction of Elamite Cuneiform.

The Amorites

The Amorites were a nomadic Semitic people who occupied the country west of the Euphrates from the second half of the 3rd millennium BC. In the earliest Sumerian sources, beginning about 2400 BC, the land of the Amorites ("the *Mar.tu* land") is associated with the West, including Syria and Canaan, although their ultimate origin may have been Arabia.[68] They ultimately settled in Mesopotamia, ruling Isin, Larsa, and later Babylon.

Middle Bronze Age

- Assyria, after enduring a short period of Mitanni domination, emerged as a great power from the accession of Ashur-uballit I in 1365 BC to the death of Tiglath-Pileser I in 1076 BC. Assyria rivalled Egypt during this period, and dominated much of the near east.
- Babylonia, founded as a state by Amorite tribes, found itself under the rule of Kassites for 435 years. The nation stagnated during the Kassite period, and Babylonia often found itself under Assyrian or Elamite domination.
- Canaan: Ugarit, Kadesh, Megiddo, Kingdom of IsraelWikipedia:Accuracy dispute#Disputed statement
- The Hittite Empire was founded some time after 2000 BC, and existed as a major power, dominating Asia Minor and the Levant until 1200 BC, when it was first overrun by the Phrygians, and then appropriated by Assyria.

Late Bronze Age

The Hurrians lived in northern Mesopotamia and areas to the immediate east and west, beginning approximately 2500 BC. They probably originated in the Caucasus and entered from the north, but this is not certain. Their known homeland was centred on Subartu, the Khabur River valley, and later they established themselves as rulers of small kingdoms throughout northern Mesopotamia and Syria. The largest and most influential Hurrian nation was the kingdom of Mitanni. The Hurrians played a substantial part in the History of the Hittites.

Ishuwa was an ancient kingdom in Anatolia. The name is first attested in the second millennium BC, and is also spelled Išuwa. In the classical period, the land was a part of Armenia. Ishuwa was one of the places where agriculture developed very early on in the Neolithic. Urban centres emerged in the upper Euphrates river valley around 3500 BC. The first states followed in the third millennium BC. The name Ishuwa is not known until the literate period of the second millennium BC. Few literate sources from within Ishuwa have been discovered and the primary source material comes from Hittite texts. To the west of Ishuwa lay the kingdom of the Hittites, and this nation was an untrustworthy neighbour. The Hittite king Hattusili I (c. 1600 BC) is reported to have marched his army across the Euphrates river and destroyed the cities there. This corresponds well with burnt destruction layers discovered by archaeologists at town sites in Ishuwa of roughly the same date. After the end of the Hittite empire in the early 12th century BC a new state emerged in Ishuwa. The city of Malatya became the centre of one of the so-called Neo-Hittite kingdom. The movement of nomadic people may have weakened the kingdom of

Malatya before the final Assyrian invasion. The decline of the settlements and culture in Ishuwa from the 7th century BC until the Roman period was probably caused by this movement of people. The Armenians later settled in the area since they were natives of the Armenian Plateau and related to the earlier inhabitants of Ishuwa.

Kizzuwatna is the name of an ancient kingdom of the second millennium BC. It was situated in the highlands of southeastern Anatolia, near the Gulf of İskenderun in modern-day Turkey. It encircled the Taurus Mountains and the Ceyhan river. The centre of the kingdom was the city of Kummanni, situated in the highlands. In a later era, the same region was known as Cilicia.

Luwian is an extinct language of the Anatolian branch of the Indo-European language family. Luwian speakers gradually spread through Anatolia and became a contributing factor to the downfall, after c. 1180 BC, of the Hittite Empire, where it was already widely spoken. Luwian was also the language spoken in the Neo-Hittite states of Syria, such as Melid and Carchemish, as well as in the central Anatolian kingdom of Tabal that flourished around 900 BC. Luwian has been preserved in two forms, named after the writing systems used to represent them: Cuneiform Luwian, and Hieroglyphic Luwian.

Mari was an ancient Sumerian and Amorite city, located 11 kilometres northwest of the modern town of Abu Kamal on the western bank of Euphrates river, some 120 km southeast of Deir ez-Zor, Syria. It is thought to have been inhabited since the 5th millennium BC, although it flourished from 2900 BC until 1759 BC, when it was sacked by Hammurabi.

Mitanni was a Hurrian kingdom in northern Mesopotamia from c. 1500 BC, at the height of its power, during the 14th century BC, encompassing what is today southeastern Turkey, northern Syria and northern Iraq (roughly corresponding to Kurdistan), centred on the capital Washukanni whose precise location has not yet been determined by archaeologists. The Mitanni kingdom is thought to have been a feudal state led by a warrior nobility of Indo-Aryan descent, who invaded the Levant region at some point during the 17th century BC, their influence apparent in a linguistic superstratum in Mitanni records. The spread to Syria of a distinct pottery type associated with the Kura-Araxes culture has been connected with this movement, although its date is somewhat too early.[69] Yamhad was an ancient Amorite kingdom. A substantial Hurrian population also settled in the kingdom, and the Hurrian culture influenced the area. The kingdom was powerful during the Middle Bronze Age, c. 1800-1600 BC. Its biggest rival was Qatna further south. Yamhad was finally destroyed by the Hittites in the 16th century BC.

The Aramaeans were a Semitic (West Semitic language group), semi-nomadic and pastoralist people who had lived in upper Mesopotamia and Syria. Aramaeans have never had a unified empire; they were divided into independent kingdoms all across the Near East. Yet to these Aramaeans befell the privilege of imposing their language and culture upon the entire Near East and beyond, fostered in part by the mass relocations enacted by successive empires, including the Assyrians and Babylonians. Scholars even have used the term 'Aramaization' for the Assyro-Babylonian peoples' languages and cultures, that have become Aramaic-speaking.[70]

The Sea peoples is the term used for a confederacy of seafaring raiders of the second millennium BC who sailed into the eastern shores of the Mediterranean, caused political unrest, and attempted to enter or control Egyptian territory during the late 19th dynasty, and especially during Year 8 of Ramesses III of the 20th Dynasty.[71] The Egyptian Pharaoh Merneptah explicitly refers to them by the term "the foreign-countries (or 'peoples'[72]) of the sea"[73,74] in his Great Karnak Inscription.[75] Although some scholars believe that they "invaded" Cyprus, Hatti and the Levant, this hypothesis is disputed.[76]

Bronze Age collapse

The *Bronze Age collapse* is the name given by those historians who see the transition from the Late Bronze Age to the Early Iron Age as violent, sudden and culturally disruptive, expressed by the collapse of palace economies of the Aegean and Anatolia, which were replaced after a hiatus by the isolated village cultures of the Dark Age period in history of the ancient Middle East. Some have gone so far as to call the catalyst that ended the Bronze Age a "catastrophe". The Bronze Age collapse may be seen in the context of a technological history that saw the slow, comparatively continuous spread of iron-working technology in the region, beginning with precocious iron-working in what is now Romania in the 13th and 12th centuries.[77] The cultural collapse of the Mycenaean kingdoms, the Hittite Empire in Anatolia and Syria, and the Egyptian Empire in Syria and Israel, the scission of long-distance trade contacts and sudden eclipse of literacy occurred between 1206 and 1150 BC. In the first phase of this period, almost every city between Troy and Gaza was violently destroyed, and often left unoccupied thereafter (for example, Hattusas, Mycenae, Ugarit). The gradual end of the Dark Age that ensued saw the rise of settled Neo-Hittite and Aramaean kingdoms of the mid-10th century BC, and the rise of the Neo-Assyrian Empire.

Iron Age

Iron Age This box: • view • talk • edit[78]
↑ Bronze Age
Ancient Near East (1200 – 550 BC) Bronze Age collapse (1200 – 1150 BC) Anatolia, Caucasus, Levant **Europe** Aegean (1190 – 700 BC) Italy (1100 – 700 BC) Balkans (1100 BC – AD 150) Eastern Europe (900 – 650 BC) Central Europe (800 – 50 BC) Great Britain (800 BC – AD 100) Northern Europe (500 BC – AD 800) **South Asia (1200 – 200 BC)** **East Asia (500 BC – AD 300)** **Iron metallurgy in Africa**
Iron Age metallurgy Ancient iron production
↓ Ancient history Mediterranean, Greater Persia, South Asia, China
Historiography Greek, Roman, Chinese, Medieval

During the Early Iron Age, from 911 BC, the Neo-Assyrian Empire arose, vying with Babylonia and other lesser powers for dominance of the region, though not until the reforms of Tiglath-Pileser III in the 8th century BC,[79,80] did it become a powerful and vast empire. In the Middle Assyrian period of the Late Bronze Age, Assyria had been a kingdom of northern Mesopotamia (modern-day northern Iraq), competing for dominance with its southern Mesopotamian rival Babylonia. From 1365-1076 it had been a major imperial power, rivaling Egypt and the Hittite Empire. Beginning with the campaign of Adad-nirari II, it became a vast empire, overthrowing 25th dynasty Egypt and conquering Egypt, the Middle East, and large swaths of Asia Minor, ancient Iran, the Caucasus and east Mediterranean. The Neo-Assyrian Empire succeeded the Middle Assyrian period (14th to 10th century BC). Some scholars, such as Richard Nelson Frye, regard the Neo-Assyrian Empire to be the first real empire in human history. During this period, Aramaic was also made an official language of the empire, alongside the Akkadian language.

The states of the Neo-Hittite kingdoms were Luwian, Aramaic and Phoenician-speaking political entities of Iron Age northern Syria and southern Anatolia that arose following the collapse of the Hittite Empire around 1180 BC and lasted until roughly 700 BC. The term "Neo-Hittite" is sometimes reserved specifically for the Luwian-speaking principalities like Melid (Malatya) and Karkamish (Carchemish), although in a wider sense the broader cultural term "Syro-Hittite" is now applied to all the entities that arose in south-central Anatolia following the Hittite collapse – such as Tabal and Quwê – as well as those of northern and coastal Syria.[81]

Urartu was an ancient kingdom of Armenia and North Mesopotamia[82] which existed from c. 860 BC, emerging from the Late Bronze Age until 585 BC. The Kingdom of Urartu was located in the mountainous plateau between Asia Minor, the Iranian Plateau, Mesopotamia, and the Caucasus mountains, later known as the Armenian Highland, and it centered on Lake Van (present-day eastern Turkey). The name corresponds to the Biblical *Ararat*.

The term Neo-Babylonian Empire refers to Babylonia under the rule of the 11th ("Chaldean") dynasty, from the revolt of Nabopolassar in 623 BC until the invasion of Cyrus the Great in 539 BC (Although the last ruler of Babylonia (Nabonidus) was in fact from the Assyrian city of Harran and not Chaldean), notably including the reign of Nebuchadrezzar II. Through the centuries of Assyrian domination, Babylonia enjoyed a prominent status, and revolted at the slightest indication that it did not. However, the Assyrians always managed to restore Babylonian loyalty, whether through the granting of increased privileges, or militarily. That finally changed in 627 BC with the death of the last strong Assyrian ruler, Ashurbanipal, and Babylonia rebelled under Nabopolassar the Chaldean a few years later. In alliance with the Medes and Scythians, Nineveh was sacked in 612 and Harran in 608 BC, and the seat of empire was again transferred to Babylonia. Subsequently, the Medes controlled much of the ancient Near East from their base in Ecbatana (modern-day Hamadan, Iran), most notably most of what is now Turkey, Iran, Iraq, and the South Caucasus.

Following the fall of the Medes, the Achaemenid Empire was the first of the Persian Empires to rule over most of the Near East and far beyond, and the second great Iranian empire (after the Median Empire). At the height of its power, encompassing approximately 7.5 million square kilometers, the Achaemenid Empire was territorially the largest empire of classical antiquity, and the first world empire. It spanned three continents (Europe, Asia, and Africa), including apart from its core in modern-day Iran, the territories of modern Iraq, the Caucasus (Armenia, Georgia, Azerbaijan, Dagestan, Abkhazia), Asia Minor (Turkey), Thrace, Bulgaria, Greece, many of the Black Sea coastal regions, northern Saudi Arabia, Jordan, Israel, Lebanon, Syria, Afghanistan, Central Asia, parts of Pakistan, and all significant population centers of ancient Egypt as far west as Libya.[83] It is noted in western history as the foe of the Greek city states in the Greco-Persian Wars, for freeing the Israelites from their Babylonian captivity, and for instituting Aramaic as the empire's official language.

Religions

Ancient civilizations in the Near East were deeply influenced by their spiritual beliefs, which generally did not distinguish between heaven and Earth. They believed that divine action influenced all mundane matters, and also believed in divination (ability to predict the future). Omens were often inscribed in ancient Egypt and Mesopotamia, as were records of major events.

Further reading

- Fletcher, Banister; Cruickshank, Dan, *Sir Banister Fletcher's a History of Architecture*[84], Architectural Press, 20th edition, 1996 (first published 1896). <templatestyles src="Module:Citation/CS1/styles.css" />ISBN 0-7506-2267-9. Cf. Part One, Chapter 4.
- William W. Hallo & William Kelly Simpson, *The Ancient Near East: A History*, Holt Rinehart and Winston Publishers, 2nd edition, 1997. <templatestyles src="Module:Citation/CS1/styles.css" />ISBN 0-15-503819-2.
- Jack Sasson, *The Civilizations of the Ancient Near East*, New York, 1995
- Marc Van de Mieroop, *History of the Ancient Near East: Ca. 3000-323 B.C.*, Blackwell Publishers, 2nd edition, 2006 (first published 2003). <templatestyles src="Module:Citation/CS1/styles.css" />ISBN 1-4051-4911-6.
- Pittman, Holly (1984). *Art of the Bronze Age: southeastern Iran, western Central Asia, and the Indus Valley*[85]. New York: The Metropolitan Museum of Art. ISBN 9780870993657.<templatestyles src="Module:Citation/CS1/styles.css"></templatestyles>

External links

- The History of the Ancient Near East[86] – A database of the prehistoric Near East as well as its ancient history up to approximately the destruction of Jerusalem by the Romans ...
- Vicino Oriente[87] Wikipedia:Link rot – Vicino Oriente is the journal of the Section Near East of the Department of Historical, Archaeological and Anthropological Sciences of Antiquity of Rome 'La Sapienza' University. The Journal, which is published yearly, deals with Near Eastern History, Archaeology, Epigraphy, extending its view also on the whole Mediterranean with the study of Phoenician and Punic documents. It is accompanied by 'Quaderni di Vicino Oriente', a monograph series.

- Ancient Near East.net[88] – an information and content portal for the archaeology, ancient history, and culture of the ancient Near East and Egypt
- Freer Gallery of Art, Smithsonian Institution[89] The Freer Gallery houses a famous collection of ancient Near Eastern artefacts and records, notebooks and photographs of excavations in Samarra (Iraq), Persepolis and Pasargadae (Iran)
- The Freer Gallery of Art and Arthur M. Sackler Gallery Archives[90] The archives for The Freer Gallery of Art and Arthur M. Sackler Gallery houses the papers of Ernst Herzfeld regarding his many excavations, along with records of other archeological excavations in the ancient Near East.
- Archaeowiki.org[91]—a wiki for the research and documentation of the ancient Near East and Egypt
- ETANA[92] – website hosted by a consortium of universities in the interests of providing digitized resources and relevant web links
- Ancient Near East Photographs[93] This collection, created by Professor Scott Noegel, documents artifacts and archaeological sites of the ancient Near East; from the University of Washington Libraries Digital Image Collection
- Near East Images[94] A directory of archaeological images of the ancient Near East
- Bioarchaeology of the Near East[95] An Open Access journal

Medieval Middle East

History of the Middle East

Home to the Cradle of Civilization, the Middle East (usually interchangeable with the Near East) has seen many of the world's oldest cultures and civilizations. This history started from the earliest human settlements, continuing through several major pre- and post-Islamic Empires through to the nation-states of the Middle East today.

Human history
↑ **Prehistory**
Recorded history
Ancient
<ul><li>Earliest records</li><li>Africa</li><li>Americas</li><li>Oceania</li><li>East Asia</li><li>South Asia</li><li>Southeast Asia</li><li>Middle East</li><li>Europe</li></ul>
Postclassical
<ul><li>Africa</li><li>Americas</li><li>Oceania</li><li>East Asia</li><li>South Asia</li><li>Southeast Asia</li><li>Middle East</li><li>Europe</li></ul>
Modern

	• Early modern • Late modern	
	See also	
	• Contemporary • Modernity • Futurology	

↓ **Future**

- $\underline{v}$
- $\underline{t}$
- $\underline{e}$[96]

Egyptian civilization coalesced around 3150 BC with the political unification of Upper and Lower Egypt under the first pharaoh. Mesopotamia was home to several powerful empires that came to rule almost the entire Middle East—particularly the Assyrian Empires of 1365–1076 BC and the Neo-Assyrian Empire of 911–609 BC. From the early 7th century BC and onwards, the Iranian Medes followed by Achaemenid Persia and other subsequent Iranian states empires dominated the region. In the 1st century BC, the expanding Roman Republic absorbed the whole Eastern Mediterranean, which included much of the Near East. The Eastern Roman Empire, today commonly known as the Byzantine Empire, ruling from the Balkans to the Euphrates, became increasingly defined by and dogmatic about Christianity, gradually creating religious rifts between the doctrines dictated by the establishment in Constantinople and believers in many parts of the Middle East. From the 3rd up to the course of the 7th century AD, the entire Middle East was dominated by the Byzantines and Sassanid Persia. From the 7th century, a new power was rising in the Middle East, that of Islam. The dominance of the Arabs came to a sudden end in the mid-11th century with the arrival of the Seljuq Turks. In the early 13th century, a new wave of invaders, the armies of the Mongol Empire, mainly Turkic, swept through the region. By the early 15th century, a new power had arisen in western Anatolia, the Ottoman emirs, linguistically Turkic and religiously Islamic, who in 1453 captured the Christian Byzantine capital of Constantinople and made themselves sultans.

Large parts of the Middle East became a warground between the Ottomans and Iranian Safavids for centuries starting in the early 16th century. By 1700, the Ottomans had been driven out of Hungary and the balance of power along the frontier had shifted decisively in favor of the West. The British also established effective control of the Persian Gulf, and the French extended their influence into Lebanon and Syria. In 1912, the Italians seized Libya and the Dodecanese islands, just off the coast of the Ottoman heartland of Anatolia. In the late 19th and early 20th centuries, Middle Eastern rulers tried to modernize their states to compete more effectively with the European powers. A turning point in the **history of the Middle East** came when oil was discovered, first in Persia in

History of the Middle East 57

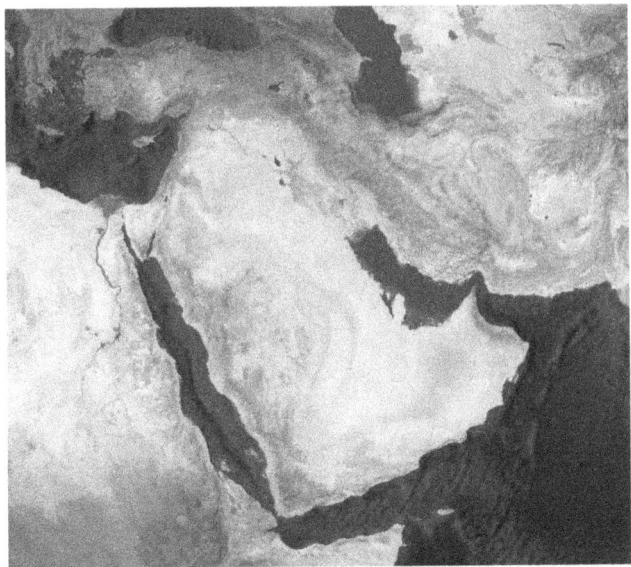

Figure 18: *A map showing territories commonly considered part of the Near East*

1908 and later in Saudi Arabia (in 1938) and the other Persian Gulf states, and also in Libya and Algeria. A Western dependence on Middle Eastern oil and the decline of British influence led to a growing American interest in the region.

During the 1920s, 1930s, and 1940s, Syria and Egypt made moves towards independence. The British, the French, and the Soviets departed from many parts of the Middle East during and after World War II (1939–1945). The struggle between the Arabs and the Jews in Palestine culminated in the 1947 United Nations plan to partition Palestine. Later in the midst of Cold War tensions, the Arabic-speaking countries of Western Asia and Northern Africa saw the rise of pan-Arabism. The departure of the European powers from direct control of the region, the establishment of Israel, and the increasing importance of the oil industry, marked the creation of the modern Middle East. In most Middle Eastern countries, the growth of market economies was inhibited by political restrictions, corruption and cronyism, overspending on arms and prestige projects, and over-dependence on oil revenues. The wealthiest economies in the region per capita are the small oil-rich countries of Persian Gulf: Qatar, Kuwait, Bahrain, and the United Arab Emirates.

A combination of factors—among them the 1967 Six-Day War,[97] the 1970s energy crisis beginning with the 1973 OPEC oil embargo in response to

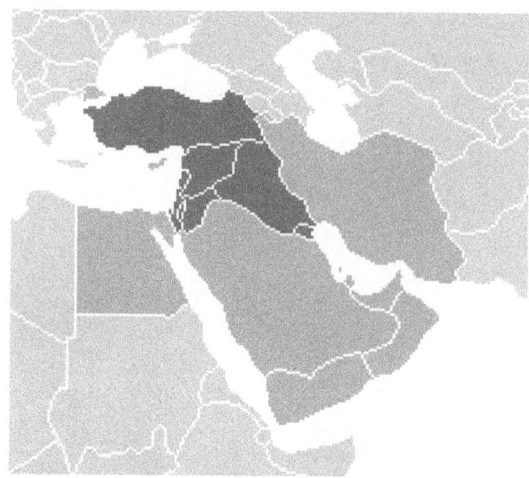

Figure 19:
*The limited modern archaeological and historical context of the Near East
Middle East and Near East*

U.S. support of Israel in the Yom Kippur War,[98] the concurrent Saudi-led popularization of Salafism/Wahhabism, and the 1978-79 Iranian Revolution—promoted the increasing rise of Islamism and the ongoing Islamic revival (*Tajdid*). The Fall of the Soviet Union in 1991 brought a global security refocus from the Cold War to a War on Terror. Starting in the early 2010s, a revolutionary wave popularly known as the Arab Spring brought major protests, uprisings, and revolutions to several Middle Eastern and Maghreb countries. Clashes in western Iraq on 30 December 2013 were preliminary to the Sunni pan-Islamist ISIL uprising.

The term *Near East* can be used interchangeably with *Middle East*, but in a different context, especially when discussing ancient times, it may have a limited meaning, namely the northern, historically Aramaic-speaking Semitic area and adjacent Anatolian territories, marked in the two maps below.

General

Geographically, the Middle East can be thought of as Western Asia with the addition of Egypt (which is the non-Maghreb region of Northern Africa) and with the exclusion of the Caucasus. The Middle East was the first to experience a Neolithic Revolution (c. the 10th millennium BC), as well as the first to enter the Bronze Age (c. 3300–1200 BC) and Iron Age (c. 1200–500 BC).

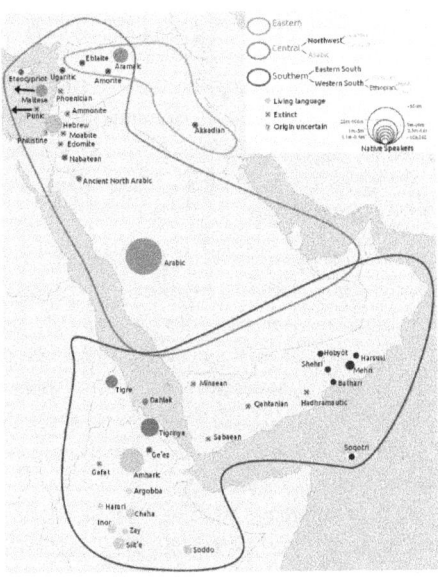

Figure 20: *The historical Semitic region, defined by the pre-Islamic distribution of Semitic languages and coinciding very roughly with the Arabian plate. Not so much lingually but rather culturally, politically and historically, the most significant division here has been between the north and the south, to some degree isolated from each other by the sparsely populated Arabian Desert. The north comprises Mesopotamia and the Levant, which, together with the lower Nile (i.e., Egypt), constitute the Fertile Crescent.*

Historically human populations have tended to settle around bodies of water, which is reflected in modern population density patterns. Irrigation systems were extremely important for the agricultural Middle East: for Egypt that of the lower Nile River, and for Mesopotamia that of the Tigris and Euphrates rivers. Levantine agriculture depended on precipitation rather than on the river-based irrigation of Egypt and Mesopotamia, resulting in preference for different crops. Since travel was faster and easier by sea, civilizations along the Mediterranean, such as Phoenicia and later Greece, participated in intense trade. Similarly, Ancient Yemen, much more conducive to agriculture than the rest of the Arabian Peninsula, sea traded heavily with the Horn of Africa, some of which it lingually Semitized. The Adnanite Arabs, inhabiting the drier desert areas of the Middle East, were all nomadic pastoralists before some began settling in city states, with the geo-linguistic distribution today being divided between Persian Gulf, the Najd and the Hejaz in the Peninsula, as well as the Bedouin areas beyond the Peninsula.

Since ancient times the Middle East has had several lingue franche: Akkadian (c. 14th – 8th century BC), Aramaic (c. 8th century BC – 8th century AD), Greek (c. 4th century BC – 8th century AD), and Arabic (c. 8th century AD – present). Familiarity with English is not uncommon among the middle and upper classes. Arabic is not commonly spoken in Turkey, Iran, and Israel, and some varieties of Arabic lack mutual intelligibility, thus qualifying as distinct languages by this linguistic criterion.

The Middle East was the birthplace of the Abrahamic, Gnostic, and most Iranian religions. Initially the ancient inhabitants of the region followed various ethnic religions, but most of those began to be gradually replaced at first by Christianity (even before the 313 AD Edict of Milan) and finally by Islam (after the spread of the Muslim conquests beyond the Arabian Peninsula in 634 AD). To this day, however, the Middle East has, in particular, some sizable, ethnically distinct Christian minority groups, as well as Jews, concentrated in Israel, and followers of Iranian religions, such as Yazdânism and Zoroastrianism. Some of the smaller ethnoreligious minorities include the Shabak people, the Mandaeans and the Samaritans. It is somewhat controversial whether the Druze religion is a distinct religion in its own right or merely a part of the Ismailist branch of Shia Islam.

Prehistory

The Arabian Tectonic Plate was part of the African Plate during much of the Phanerozoic Eon (Paleozoic–Cenozoic), until the Oligocene Epoch of the Cenozoic Era. Red Sea rifting began in the Eocene, but the separation of Africa and Arabia occurred in the Oligocene, and since then the Arabian Plate has been slowly moving toward the Eurasian Plate.

The collision between the Arabian Plate and Eurasia is pushing up the Zagros Mountains of Iran. Because the Arabian Plate and Eurasia plate collide, many cities are in danger such as those in south eastern Turkey (which is on the Arabian Plate). These dangers include earthquakes, tsunamis, and volcanoes.

The earliest human migrations out of Africa occurred through the Middle East, namely over the Levantine corridor, with the pre-modern *Homo erectus* about 1.8 million years BP. One of the potential routes for early human migrations toward southern and eastern Asia is Iran.

Haplogroup J-P209, the most common human Y-chromosome DNA haplogroup in the Middle East today, is believed to have arisen in the region 31,700±12,800 years ago. The two main current subgroups, J-M267 and J-M172, which now comprise between them almost all of the population of the haplogroup, are both believed to have arisen very early, at least 10,000 years

History of the Middle East 61

ago. Nonetheless, Y-chromosomes F-M89* and IJ-M429* were reported to have been observed in the Iranian plateau.

There is evidence of rock carvings along the Nile terraces and in desert oases. In the 10th millennium BC, a culture of hunter-gatherers and fishermen was replaced by a grain-grinding culture. Climate changes and/or overgrazing around 6000 BC began to desiccate the pastoral lands of Egypt, forming the Sahara. Early tribal peoples migrated to the Nile River, where they developed a settled agricultural economy and more centralized society.[99]

Ancient Near East

The symbol of the winged sun was found throughout the Middle East.

It was associated with divinity, royalty, and power. The above is an Egyptian version. The modern-day Assyrian flag and Aramean flag feature different versions of the symbol. The Israelite royal Seals of Hezekiah also featured one, sometimes flanked on either side with the Egyptian ankh symbol. The Iranian religion of Zoroastrianism has a related symbol called Faravahar.

The ancient Near East
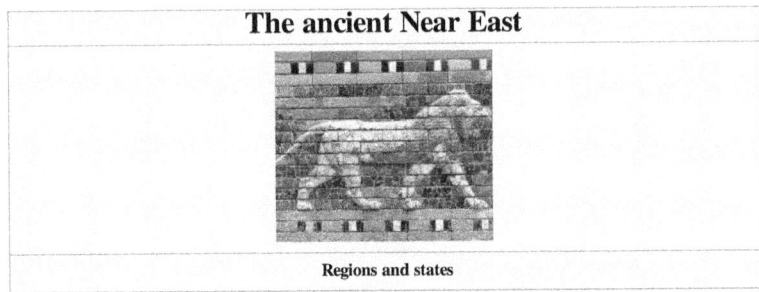
Regions and states

Fertile Crescent
Mesopotamia

- Akkadian Empire
- Assyria
- Babylonia
- Neo-Assyrian Empire
- Neo-Babylonian Empire
- Sumer

Egypt

- Ancient Egypt

Persia

- Achaemenid Empire
- Elam
- Medes

Anatolia

- Hittites
- Hurrians
- Neo-Hittite states
- Urartu

The Levant

- Ancient Israel
- Phoenicia

Archaeological periods

- Chronology
- Bronze Age
- Bronze Age collapse
- Iron Age

Languages

- Akkadian
- Aramaic
- Assyriology
- Cuneiform script
- Elamite
- Hebrew
- Hittite
- Hurrian
- Phoenician
- Sumerian
- Urartian

Literature

- Babylonian
- Hittite texts
- Sumerian

Mythology

- Babylonian
- Hittite
- Mesopotamian
- Egyptian

Other topics

- Cradle of civilization

- Assyrian law
- Babylonian astronomy
- Babylonian law
- Babylonian mathematics
- Cuneiform law
- History of the Middle East
- $\underline{v}$
- $\underline{t}$
- $\underline{e}^{100}$

The ancient Near East was the first to practice intensive year-round agriculture and currency-mediated trade (as opposed to barter), gave the rest of the world the first writing system, invented the potter's wheel and then the vehicular and mill wheel, created the first centralized governments and law codes, served as birthplace to the first city-states with their high degree of division of labor, as well as laying the foundation for the fields of astronomy and mathematics. However, its empires also introduced rigid social stratification, slavery, and organized warfare.

Cradle of civilization, Sumer and Akkad

The earliest civilizations in history were established in the region now known as the Middle East around 3500 BC by the Sumerians, in Mesopotamia (Iraq), widely regarded as the cradle of civilization. The Sumerians and the Akkadians (later known as Babylonians and Assyrians) all flourished in this region.

"In the course of the fourth millennium BC, city-states developed in southern Mesopotamia that were dominated by temples whose priests represented the cities' patron deities. The most prominent of the city-states was Sumer, which gave its language to the area, [presumably the first written language,] and became the first great civilization of mankind. About 2340 BC, Sargon the Great (c. 2360–2305 BC) united the city-states in the south and founded the Akkadian dynasty, the world's first empire."

During this same time period, Sargon the Great appointed his daughter, Enheduanna, as High Priestess of Inanna at Ur.[101] Her writings, which established her as the first known author in world history, also helped cement Sargon's position in the region.

Egypt

Soon after the Sumerian civilization began, the Nile valley of Lower and Upper Egypt was unified under the Pharaohs approximately around 3150 BC. Since then, Ancient Egypt experienced 3 high points of civilization, the so-called "Kingdom" periods:

- The Old Kingdom (2686–2181),
- The Middle Kingdom (2055–1650) and, most notably,
- The New Kingdom (1550–1069).

The history of Ancient Egypt is concluded by the Late Period (664–332 BC), immediately followed by the history of Egypt in Classical Antiquity, beginning with Ptolemaic Egypt.

The Levant and Anatolia

Thereafter, civilization quickly spread through the Fertile Crescent to the east coast of the Mediterranean Sea and throughout the Levant, as well as to ancient Anatolia. Ancient Levantine kingdoms and city states included Ebla City, Ugarit City, Kingdom of Aram-Damascus, Kingdom of Israel, Kingdom of Judah, Kingdom of Ammon, Kingdom of Moab, Kingdom of Edom, and the Nabatean kingdom. The Phoenician civilization, encompassing several city states, was a maritime trading culture that established colonial cities in the Mediterranean Basin, most notably Carthage, in 814 BC.

Assyrian empires

Mesopotamia was home to several powerful empires that came to rule almost the entire Middle East—particularly the Assyrian Empires of 1365–1076 BC and the Neo-Assyrian Empire of 911–605 BC. The Assyrian Empire, at its peak, was the largest the world had seen. It ruled all of what is now Iraq, Syria, Lebanon, Israel, Palestine, Kuwait, Jordan, Egypt, Cyprus, and Bahrain—with large swathes of Iran, Turkey, Armenia, Georgia, Sudan, and Arabia. "The Assyrian empires, particularly the third, had a profound and lasting impact on the Near East. Before Assyrian hegemony ended, the Assyrians brought the highest civilization to the then known world. From the Caspian to Cyprus, from Anatolia to Egypt, Assyrian imperial expansion would bring into the Assyrian sphere nomadic and barbaric communities, and would bestow the gift of civilization upon them."

Neo-Babylonian and Persian empires

From the early 6th century BC onwards, several Persian states dominated the region, beginning with the Medes and non-Persian Neo-Babylonian Empire, then their successor the Achaemenid Empire known as the first Persian Empire, conquered in the late 4th century BC. by the very short-lived Macedonian Empire of Alexander the Great, and then successor kingdoms such as Ptolemaic Egypt and the Seleucid state in Western Asia.

After a century of hiatus, the idea of the Persian Empire was revived by the Parthians in the 3rd century BC—and continued by their successors, the Sassanids from the 3rd century AD. This empire dominated sizable parts of what is now the Asian part of the Middle East and continued to influence the rest of the Asiatic and African Middle East region, until the Arab Muslim conquest of Persia in the mid-7th century AD. Between the 1st century BC and the early 7th century AD, the region was completely dominated by the Romans and the Parthians and Sassanids on the other hand, which often culminated in various Roman-Persian Wars over the seven centuries. Eastern Rite, Church of the East Christianity took hold in Persian-ruled Mesopotamia, particularly in Assyria from the 1st century AD onwards, and the region became a center of a flourishing Syriac–Assyrian literary tradition.

Greek and Roman Empire

In the 1st century BC, the expanding Roman Republic absorbed the whole Eastern Mediterranean, which included much of the Near East. The Roman Empire united the region with most of Europe and North Africa in a single political and economic unit. Even areas not directly annexed were strongly influenced by the Empire, which was the most powerful political and cultural entity for centuries. Though Roman culture spread across the region, the Greek culture and language first established in the region by the Macedonian Empire continued to dominate throughout the Roman period. Cities in the Middle East, especially Alexandria, became major urban centers for the Empire and the region became the Empire's "bread basket" as the key agricultural producer. Ægyptus was by far the most wealthy Roman province.[102,103]

As the Christian religion spread throughout the Roman and Persian Empires, it took root in the Middle East, and cities such as Alexandria and Edessa became important centers of Christian scholarship. By the 5th century, Christianity was the dominant religion in the Middle East, with other faiths (gradually including *heretical* Christian sects) being actively repressed. The Middle East's ties to the city of Rome were gradually severed as the Empire split into East and West, with the Middle East tied to the new Roman capital of Constantinople. The subsequent Fall of the Western Roman Empire therefore, had minimal direct impact on the region.

Byzantine empire (Eastern Roman Empire)

The Eastern Roman Empire, today commonly known as the Byzantine Empire, ruling from the Balkans to the Euphrates, became increasingly defined by and dogmatic about Christianity, gradually creating religious rifts between the doctrines dictated by the establishment in Constantinople and believers in many parts of the Middle East. By this time, Greek had become the 'lingua franca' of the region, although ethnicities such as the Syriacs and the Hebrew continued to exist. Under Byzantine/Greek rule the area of the Levant met an era of stability and prosperity.

Medieval Middle East

Pre-Islam

In the 5th century, the Middle East was separated into small, weak states; the two most prominent were the Sasanian Empire of the Persians in what is now Iran and Iraq, and the Byzantine Empire in Anatolia (modern-day Turkey). The Byzantines and Sasanians fought with each other a reflection of the rivalry between the Roman Empire and the Persian Empire seen during the previous five hundred years. The Byzantine-Sasanian rivalry was also seen through their respective cultures and religions. The Byzantines considered themselves champions of Hellenism and Christianity. Meanwhile, the Sasanians thought themselves heroes of ancient Iranian and Semitic traditions and of the traditional Persian religion, Zoroastrianism.[104]

The Arabian peninsula already played a role in the power struggles of the Byzantines and Sasanians. While Byzantium allied itself with the Kingdom of Aksum in the horn of Africa, the Sasanian Empire assisted the Himyarite Kingdom in what is now Yemen (southwest Arabia). Thus the clash between the kingdoms of Aksum and Himyar in 525 displayed a higher power struggle between Byzantium and Persia for control of the Red Sea trade. Territorial wars soon became common, with the Byzantines and Sasanians fighting over upper Mesopotamia and Armenia and key cities that facilitated trade from Arabia, India, and China.[105] Byzantium, as the continuation of the Eastern Roman Empire, continued control of the latter's territories in the Middle East. Since 527, this included Anatolia, Syria, Lebanon, Palestine, and Egypt. But in 603 the Sasanians invaded, conquering Damascus and Egypt. It was Emperor Heraclius who was able to repel these invasions, and in 628 he replaced the Sasanian Great King with a more docile one. But the fighting weakened both states, leaving the stage open to a new power.[106,107]

The nomadic Bedouin tribes dominated the Arabian desert, where they worshiped idols and remained in small clans tied together by kinship. Urbanization

History of the Middle East

Figure 21: *Late-12th-century plaque of Byzantine Emperor Heraclius submitting the Sasanian King Khosrau II.*

and agriculture was limited in Arabia, save for a few regions near the coast. Mecca and Medina (then called Yathrib) were two such cities that were important hubs for trade between Africa and Eurasia. This commerce was central to city-life, where most inhabitants were merchants.[108] Nevertheless, some Arabs saw it fit to migrate to the northern regions of the Fertile Crescent, a Persian region so named for its place between the Tigris and Euphrates rivers that offered it fertile land. This included entire tribal chiefdoms such as the Lakhmids in a less controlled area of the Sasanian Empire, and the Ghassanids in a similar area inside of Byzantine territory; these political units of Arab origin offered a surprising stability that was rare in the region and offered Arabia further connections to the outside world. The Lakhmid capital, Hira was a center for Christianity and Jewish craftsmen, merchants, and farmers were common in western Arabia as were Christian monks in central Arabia. Thus pre-Islamic Arabia was no stranger to Abrahamic religions or monotheism, for that matter.[109]

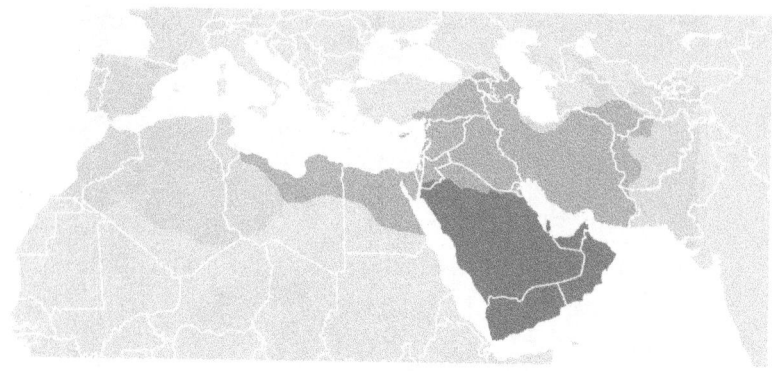

Figure 22:
Age of the Caliphs
Expansion under Muhammad, 622–632
Expansion during the Rashidun Caliphate, 632–661
Expansion during the Umayyad Caliphate, 661–750

Islamic caliphate

While the Byzantine Roman and Sassanid Persian empires were both weakened by warfare (602–628), a new power in the form of Islam grew in the Middle East. In a series of rapid Muslim conquests, Arab armies, led by the Caliphs and skilled military commanders such as Khalid ibn al-Walid, swept through most of the Middle East, taking more than half of Byzantine territory and completely engulfing the Persian lands. In Anatolia, they were stopped in the Siege of Constantinople (717–18) by the Byzantines, who were helped by the Bulgarians.

The Byzantine provinces of Roman Syria, North Africa, and Sicily, however, could not mount such a resistance, and the Muslim conquerors swept through those regions. At the far west, they crossed the sea taking Visigothic Hispania before being halted in southern France in the Battle of Tours by the Franks. At its greatest extent, the Arab Empire was the first empire to control the entire Middle East, as well three-quarters of the Mediterranean region, the only other empire besides the Roman Empire to control most of the Mediterranean Sea.[110] It would be the Arab Caliphates of the Middle Ages that would first unify the entire Middle East as a distinct region and create the dominant ethnic identity that persists today. The Seljuq Empire would also later dominate the region.

Much of North Africa became a peripheral area to the main Muslim centres in the Middle East, but Iberia (Al-Andalus) and Morocco soon broke away from this distant control and founded one of the world's most advanced societies at the time, along with Baghdad in the eastern Mediterranean. Between 831 and

History of the Middle East

Figure 23: *The interior of the former mosque of Córdoba, showing its distinctive arches.*

1071, the Emirate of Sicily was one of the major centres of Islamic culture in the Mediterranean. After its conquest by the Normans the island developed its own distinct culture with the fusion of Arab, Western, and Byzantine influences. Palermo remained a leading artistic and commercial centre of the Mediterranean well into the Middle Ages.

Africa was reviving, however, as more organized and centralized states began to form in the later Middle Ages after the Renaissance of the 12th century. Motivated by religion and conquest, the kings of Europe launched a number of Crusades to try to roll back Muslim power and retake the Holy Land. The Crusades were unsuccessful but were far more effective in weakening the already tottering Byzantine Empire. They also rearranged the balance of power in the Muslim world as Egypt once again emerged as a major power.

Islamic culture and science

Religion always played a prevalent role in Middle Eastern culture, affecting learning, architecture, and the ebb and flow of cultures. When Muhammad introduced Islam, it jump-started Middle Eastern culture, inspiring achievements in architecture, the revival of old advances in science and technology, and the formation of a distinct way of life. Islam primarily consisted of the five pillars of belief, including confession of faith, the five prayers a day, to fast during the holy month of Ramadan, to pay the tax for charity (the zakāt), and the hajj, or the pilgrimage that a Muslim needed to take at least once in their lifetime, according to the five (or six) pillars of Islam. Islam also created the need for spectacularly built mosques which created a distinct form of architecture. Some of the more magnificent mosques include the Al-Aqsa Mosque and the former Mosque of Cordoba. Islam unified the Middle East and helped the empires there to remain stable. Missionaries and warriors spread the religion from Arabia to North and Sudanic Africa, South and Southeast Asia, and the Mesopotamia area. This created a mix of cultures, especially in Africa, and the mawali demographic. Although the mawali would experience discrimination from the Umayyad, they would gain widespread acceptance from the Abbasids and it was because of this that allowed for mass conversions in foreign areas. "People of the book" or dhimmi were always treated well; these people included Christians, Jews, Hindus, and Zoroastrians. However, the crusades started a new thinking in the Islamic empires, that non-Islamic ideas were immoral or inferior; this was primarily perpetrated by the ulama (علماء) scholars.[111]

Arabian culture took off during the early Abbasid age, despite the prevalent political issues. Muslims saved and spread Greek advances in medicine, algebra, geometry, astronomy, anatomy, and ethics that would later finds it way back to Western Europe. The works of Aristotle, Galen, Hippocrates, Ptolemy, and Euclid were saved and distributed throughout the empire (and eventually into Europe) in this manner. Muslim scholars also discovered the Hindu-Arabic numeral system in their conquests of south Asia. The use of this system in Muslim trade and political institutions allowed for the eventual popularization of it around the world; this number system would be critical to the Scientific revolution in Europe. Muslim intellectuals would become experts in chemistry, optics, and mapmaking during the Abbasid Caliphate. In the arts, Abbasid architecture expanded upon Umayyad architecture, with larger and more extravagant mosques. Persian literature grew based on ethical values. Astronomy was stressed in art. Much of this learning would find its way to the West. This was especially true during the crusades, as warriors would bring back Muslim treasures, weapons, and medicinal methods.[112]

Turks, Crusaders, and Mongols

The dominance of the Arabs came to a sudden end in the mid-11th century with the arrival of the Seljuq Turks, migrating south from the Turkic homelands in Central Asia. They conquered Persia, Iraq (capturing Baghdad in 1055), Syria, Palestine, and the Hejaz. Egypt held out under the Fatimid caliphs until 1169, when it too fell to the Turks.

Despite massive territorial losses in the 7th century, the Christian Byzantine Empire continued to be a potent military and economic force in the Mediterranean, preventing Arab expansion into much of Europe. The Seljuqs' defeat of the Byzantine military in the Battle of Manzikert in the 11th century and settling in Anatolia effectively marked the end of Byzantine power. The Seljuks ruled most of the Middle East region for the next 200 years, but their empire soon broke up into a number of smaller sultanates.

Christian Western Europe staged a remarkable economic and demographic recovery in the 11th century since its nadir in the 7th century. The fragmentation of the Middle East allowed joined forces, mainly from England, France, and the emerging Holy Roman Empire, to enter the region. In 1095, Pope Urban II responded to pleas from the flagging Byzantine Empire and summoned the European aristocracy to recapture the Holy Land for Christianity. In 1099 the knights of the First Crusade captured Jerusalem and founded the Kingdom of Jerusalem, which survived until 1187, when Saladin retook the city. Smaller crusader fiefdoms survived until 1291.

Mongol rule

The conquest of Baghdad and the death of the caliph in 1258 officiated the end of the Abbasid Caliphate and annexed its territories to the Mongol Empire, excluding Mamluk Egypt and the majority of Arabia.[113] When the Khagan (or Great Khan) of the Mongol Empire, Möngke Khan, died in 1259, any further expansion by Hulegu was halted, as he had to return to the Mongol capital Karakorum for the election of a new khagan. His absence resulted in the first defeat of the Mongols (by the Mamluk Egyptians) during the Battle of Ain Jalut in 1260.[114] Issues began to arise when the Mongols grew increasingly unable to reach a consensus as to who to elect khagan. Additionally, societal clashing occurred between traditionalists who wished to retain their nomadic culture and Mongols moving towards sedentary agriculture. All of this led to the fragmentation of the empire in 1260. Hulegu carved out his Middle Eastern territory into the independent Ilkhanate, which included most of Armenia, Anatolia, Azerbaijan, Mesopotamia, and Iran.

The Mongols eventually retreated in 1335, but the chaos that ensued throughout the empire deposed the Seljuq Turks. In 1401, the region was further plagued by the Turko-Mongol, Timur, and his ferocious raids. By then, another group of Turks had arisen as well, the Ottomans. Based in Anatolia, by 1566 they would conquer the Iraq-Iran region, the Balkans, Greece, Byzantium, most of Egypt, most of north Africa, and parts of Arabia, unifying them under the Ottoman Empire. The rule of the Ottoman sultans marked the end of the Medieval (Postclassical) Era in the Middle East.

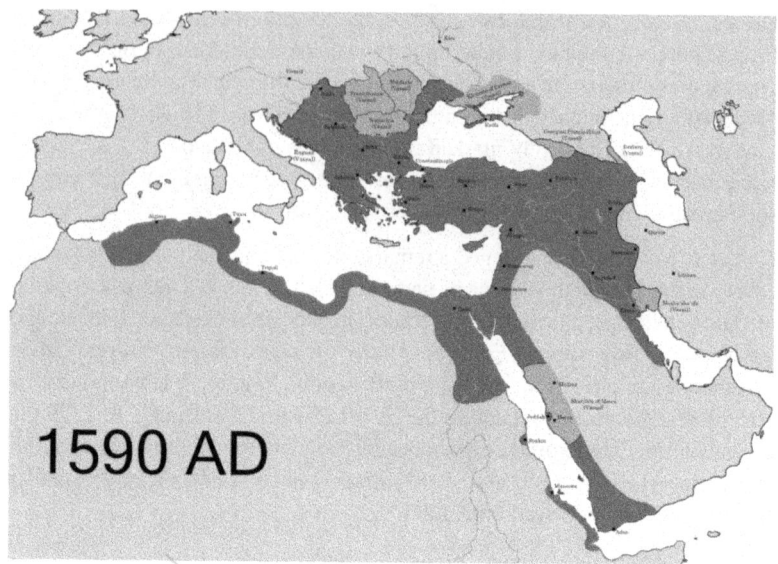

Figure 24: *The Ottoman Empire at its greatest extent in the Middle East.*

Early Modern Near East

The Ottoman Empire (1299–1918)

By the early 15th century, a new power had arisen in western Anatolia, the Ottoman Empire. Ottoman khans, who in 1453 captured the Christian Byzantine capitol of Constantinople and made themselves sultans. The Mamluks held the Ottomans out of the Middle East for a century, but in 1514 Selim the Grim began the systematic Ottoman conquest of the region. Syria was occupied in 1516 and Egypt in 1517, extinguishing the Mameluk line. Iraq was conquered almost in 40 years from the Iranian Safavids, who were successors of the Aq Qoyunlu.

The Ottomans united the whole region under one ruler for the first time since the reign of the Abbasid caliphs of the 10th century, and they kept control of it for 400 years, despite brief intermissions created by the Iranian Safavids and Afsharids.[115] By this time the Ottomans also held Greece, the Balkans, and most of Hungary, setting the new frontier between east and west far to the north of the Danube.

In the west, Europe was rapidly expanding, demographically, economically, and culturally. By 1700, the Ottomans had been driven out of Hungary. Although some areas of Ottoman Europe, such as Albania and Bosnia, saw many

Figure 25: *Selim the Grim, Ottoman conqueror of the Middle East*

Figure 26: *Inhabitants of the Middle East by the end of the Ottoman era*

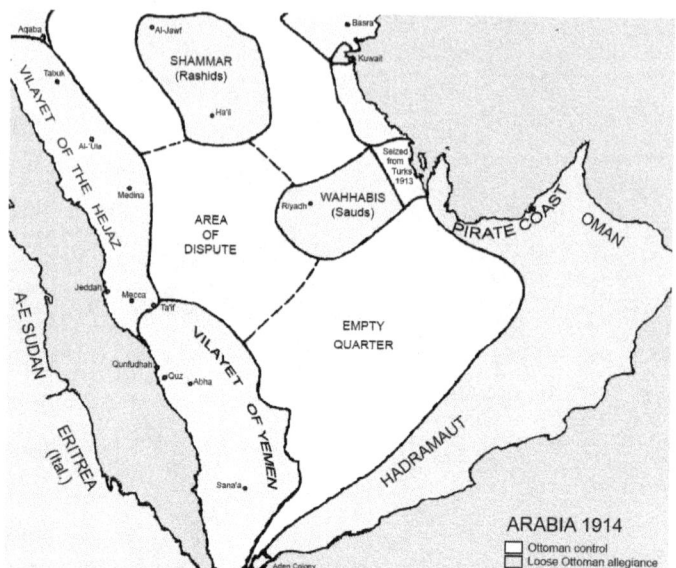

Figure 27: *Middle East Map 1890–1914. Ottoman Empire (Hejaz Vilayet and Yemen Vilayet), Jabal Shammar, Aden Protectorate, Emirate of Nejd and Hasa, and Hadhramaut.*

conversions to Islam, the area was never culturally absorbed into the Muslim world. From 1768 to 1918, the Ottomans gradually lost territory. By the 19th century, Europe had overtaken the Muslim world in wealth, population, and—most importantly—technology. The industrial revolution fueled a boom that laid the foundations for the growth of capitalism. During the 19th century, Greece, Serbia, Romania, and Bulgaria claimed independence, and the Ottoman Empire became known as the "sick man of Europe", increasingly under the financial control of European powers. Domination soon turned to outright conquest: the French annexed Algeria in 1830 and Tunisia in 1878 and the British occupied Egypt in 1882, though it remained under nominal Ottoman sovereignty. In the Balkan Wars of 1912–13 the Ottomans were driven out of Europe altogether, except for the city of Constantinople and its hinterland.

The British also established effective control of the Persian Gulf, and the French extended their influence into Lebanon and Syria. In 1912, the Italians seized Libya and the Dodecanese islands, just off the coast of the Ottoman heartland of Anatolia. The Ottomans turned to Germany to protect them from the western powers, but the result was increasing financial and military dependence on Germany.

Ottoman reform efforts

In the late 19th and early 20th centuries, Middle Eastern rulers tried to modernize their states to compete more effectively with Europe. In the Ottoman Empire, the Tanzimat reforms re-invigorated Ottoman rule and were furthered by the Young Ottomans in the late 19th century, leading to the First Constitutional Era in the Empire that included the writing of the 1876 constitution and the establishment of the Ottoman Parliament. The authors of the 1906 revolution in Persia all sought to import versions of the western model of constitutional government, civil law, secular education, and industrial development into their countries. Throughout the region, railways and telegraph lines were constructed, schools and universities were opened, and a new class of army officers, lawyers, teachers, and administrators emerged, challenging the traditional leadership of Islamic scholars.

This first Ottoman constitutional experiment ended soon after it began, however, when the autocratic Sultan Abdul Hamid II abolished the parliament and the constitution in favor of personal rule. Abdul Hamid ruled by decree for the next 30 years, stirring democratic resentment. The reform movement known as the Young Turks emerged in the 1890s against his rule, which included massacres against minorities. The Young Turks seized power in the 1908 Young Turk Revolution and established the Second Constitutional Era, leading to a pluralist and multiparty elections in the Empire for the first time in 1908. The Young Turks split into two parties, the pro-German and pro-centralization Committee of Union and Progress and the pro-British and pro-decentralization Freedom and Accord Party. The former was led by an ambitious pair of army officers, Ismail Enver Bey (later Pasha) and Ahmed Cemal Pasha, and a radical lawyer, Mehmed Talaat Bey (later Pasha). After a power struggle between the two parties of Young Turks, the Committee emerged victorious and became a ruling junta, with Talaat as Grand Vizier and Enver as War Minister, and established a German-funded modernisation program across the Empire.[116]

Enver Bey's alliance with Germany, which he considered the most advanced military power in Europe, was enabled by British demands that the Ottoman Empire cede their formal capital Edirne (Adrianople) to the Bulgarians after losing the First Balkan War, which the Turks saw as a betrayal by Britain. These demands cost Britain the support of the Turks, as the pro-British Freedom and Accord Party was now repressed under the pro-German Committee for, in Enver's words, "shamefully delivering the country to the enemy" (Britain) after agreeing to the demands to give up Edirne.

Figure 28: *Mustafa Kemal Atatürk, founder of modern Turkey*

Modern Middle East

Final years of the Ottoman Empire

In 1878, as the result of the Cyprus Convention, the United Kingdom took over the government of Cyprus as a protectorate from the Ottoman Empire. While the Cypriots at first welcomed British rule, hoping that they would gradually achieve prosperity, democracy and national liberation, they soon became disillusioned. The British imposed heavy taxes to cover the compensation they paid to the Sultan for conceding Cyprus to them. Moreover, the people were not given the right to participate in the administration of the island, since all powers were reserved to the High Commissioner and to London. In 1819, the Government of Lord Liverpool created the *Six Acts*, which established press censorship, the banning of political parties (mainly the communist party), the dissolution of municipal elections, as well as the out-ruling of trade unions, meetings of more than five individuals, and the tolling of church bells outside services.[117]

Meanwhile, the fall of the Ottomans and the partitioning of Anatolia by the Allies led to resistance by the Turkish population, under the Turkish National Movement led by Mustafa Kemal Atatürk, the Turkish victory against the invading powers during the Turkish War of Independence, and the founding of the modern Republic of Turkey in 1923. As the first President of Turkey, Atatürk embarked on a program of modernisation and secularisation. He abolished the caliphate, emancipated women, enforced western dress and the use of a new Turkish alphabet based on Latin script in place of the Arabic alphabet, and abolished the jurisdiction of the Islamic courts. In effect, Turkey, having given up rule over the Arab world, was now determined to secede from the Middle East and become culturally part of Europe.

Another turning point came when oil was discovered, first in Persia (1908) and later in Saudi Arabia (1938) as well as the other Persian Gulf states, Libya, and Algeria. The Middle East, it turned out, possessed the world's largest easily accessible reserves of crude oil, the most important commodity in the 20th century. While western oil companies pumped and exported nearly all of it to fuel the rapidly expanding automobile industry among other developments, the kings and emirs of these oil states became immensely rich, allowing them to consolidate their hold on power and giving them a stake in preserving western hegemony over the region.

A Western dependence on Middle Eastern oil and the decline of British influence led to a growing American interest in the region. Initially, the Western oil companies established a dominance over oil production and extraction. However, indigenous movements towards nationalizing oil assets, oil sharing, and the advent of OPEC ensured a shift in the balance of power towards the Arab oil states. Oil wealth also had the effect of suffocating whatever economic, political, or social reform might have emerged in the Arab world under the influence of the Kemalist revolution in Turkey.

World War I

In 1914, Enver Pasha's alliance with Germany led the Ottoman Empire into the fatal step of joining Germany and Austria-Hungary in World War I, against Britain and France. The British saw the Ottomans as the weak link in the enemy alliance, and concentrated on knocking them out of the war. When a direct assault failed at Gallipoli in 1915, they turned to fomenting revolution in the Ottoman domains, exploiting the awakening force of Arab, Armenian, and Assyrian nationalism against the Ottomans.

The British found an ally in Sharif Hussein, the hereditary ruler of Mecca (and believed by Muslims to be a descendant of Muhammad), who led an Arab Revolt against Ottoman rule, after being promised independence.

The Allies, led by Britain, won the war and seized most of the Ottoman territories; Turkey just managed to survive. The war transformed the region in terms of increased British and French involvement; the creation of the Middle Eastern state system as seen in Turkey and Saudi Arabia; the emergence of explicitly more nationalist politics, as seen in Turkey and Egypt; and the rapid growth of the Middle Eastern oil industry.[118]

Ottoman defeat and partition (1918–22)

When the Ottoman Empire was defeated by an Arab uprising and the British forces after the Sinai and Palestine Campaign in 1918, the Arab population did not get what it wanted. Islamic activists of more recent times have described as an Anglo-French betrayal. British and French governments concluded a secret treaty (the Sykes–Picot Agreement) to partition the Middle East between them. The British in 1917 announced the Balfour Declaration promised the international Zionist movement their support in re-creating the historic Jewish homeland in Palestine.

When the Ottomans departed, the Arabs proclaimed an independent state in Damascus, but were too weak, militarily and economically, to resist the European powers for long, and Britain and France soon established control and re-arranged the Middle East to suit themselves.

Syria became a French protectorate as a League of Nations mandate. The Christian coastal areas were split off to become Lebanon, another French protectorate. Iraq and Palestine became British mandated territories. Iraq became the "Kingdom of Iraq" and one of Sharif Hussein's sons, Faisal, was installed as the King of Iraq. Iraq incorporated large populations of Kurds, Assyrians and Turkmens, many of whom had been promised independent states of their own.

Palestine became the "British Mandate of Palestine" and was split in half. The eastern half of Palestine became the "Emirate of Transjordan" to provide a throne for another of Husayn's sons, Abdullah. The western half of Palestine was placed under direct British administration. The Jewish population of Palestine which numbered less than 8 percent in 1918 was given free rein to immigrate, buy land from absentee landlords, set up a shadow government in waiting and establish the nucleus of a state under the protection of the British Army which suppressed a Palestinian revolt in 1936.[119] Most of the Arabian peninsula fell to another British ally, Ibn Saud. Saud created the Kingdom of Saudi Arabia in 1932.

1920–1945

During the 1920s, 1930s, and 1940s, Syria and Egypt made moves towards independence. In 1919, Egypt's Saad Zaghloul orchestrated mass demonstrations in Egypt known as the First Revolution. While Zaghloul would later become Prime Minister, the British repression of the anticolonial riots led to around 800 deaths. In 1920, Syrian forces were defeated by the French in the

Battle of Maysalun and Iraqi forces were defeated by the British when they revolted. In 1922, the (nominally) independent Kingdom of Egypt was created following the British government's issuance of the Unilateral Declaration of Egyptian Independence.

Although the Kingdom of Egypt was technically "neutral" during World War II, Cairo soon became a major military base for the British and the country was occupied. The British cited the 1936 treaty that allowed it to station troops on Egyptian soil to protect the Suez Canal. In 1941, the Rashīd 'Alī al-Gaylānī coup in Iraq led to the British to invade, leading to the Anglo-Iraqi War. This was followed by the Allied invasion of Syria–Lebanon and the Anglo-Soviet invasion of Iran.

In Palestine, conflicting forces of Arab nationalism and Zionism created a situation the British could neither resolve nor extricate themselves from. The rise of German dictator Adolf Hitler had created a new urgency in the Zionist quest to immigrate to Palestine and create a Jewish state. A Palestinian state was also an attractive alternative to the Arab and Persian leaders, instead of the de facto British, French, and perceived Jewish colonialism or imperialism, under the logic of "the enemy of my enemy is my friend".[120]

New states after World War II

The British,[121] French, and Soviets departed from many parts of the Middle East during and after World War II. Iran, Turkey, Saudi Arabia, and the states in the Arabian Peninsula generally kept their boundaries. After the war, however, seven Middle East states gained (or regained) their independence:

- 22 November 1943 – Lebanon
- 1 January 1944 – Syria
- 22 May 1946 – Jordan (British mandate ended)
- 1947 – Iraq (forces of the United Kingdom withdrawn)
- 1947 – Egypt (forces of the United Kingdom withdrawn to the Suez Canal area)
- 1948 – Israel (forces of the United Kingdom withdrawn)
- August 16, 1960 – Cyprus

The struggle between the Arabs and the Jews in Palestine culminated in the 1947 United Nations plan to partition Palestine. This plan sought to create an Arab state and a separate Jewish state in the narrow space between the Jordan River and the Mediterranean. The Jewish leaders accepted it, but the Arab leaders rejected this plan.

On 14 May 1948, when the British Mandate expired, the Zionist leadership declared the State of Israel. In the 1948 Arab–Israeli War which immediately followed, the armies of Egypt, Syria, Transjordan, Lebanon, Iraq, and Saudi

Figure 29: *1963 film about contemporary events in the Middle East*

Arabia intervened and were defeated by Israel. About 800,000 Palestinians fled from areas annexed by Israel and became refugees in neighbouring countries, thus creating the "Palestinian problem", which has troubled the region ever since. Approximately two-thirds of 758,000–866,000 of the Jews expelled or who fled from Arab lands after 1948 were absorbed and naturalized by the State of Israel.

On August 16, 1960, Cyprus gained its independence from the United Kingdom. Archbishop Makarios III, a charismatic religious and political leader, was elected its first independent president, and in 1961 it became the 99th member of the United Nations.

Modern states

The modern Middle East was shaped by three things: departure of European powers, the founding of Israel, and the growing importance of the oil industry. These developments led increased U.S. involvement in Middle East. The United States was the ultimate guarantor of the region's stability as well as the dominant force in the oil industry after the 1950s. When revolutions brought radical anti-Western regimes to power in Egypt (1954), Syria (1963), Iraq (1968), and Libya (1969), the Soviet Union, seeking to open a new arena of

Figure 30: *Menachem Begin, Jimmy Carter and Anwar Sadat concluded a peace treaty in 1978.*

the Cold War, allied itself with Arab socialist rulers like Gamal Abdel Nasser in Egypt and Saddam Hussein in Iraq.

These regimes gained popular support with promises to destroy the state of Israel, defeat the United States and other "western imperialists", and to bring prosperity to the Arab masses. When the Six-Day War of 1967 with Israel ended in a decisive loss for the Muslim side, many viewed defeat as the failure of Arab socialism. This represents a turning point when "fundamental and militant Islam began to fill the political vacuum created".[122]

The United States, in response, felt obliged to defend its remaining allies, the conservative monarchies of Saudi Arabia, Jordan, Iran, and the Persian Gulf emirates, whose methods of rule were almost as unattractive in western eyes as those of the anti-western regimes. Iran in particular became a key U.S. ally, until a revolution led by the Shi'a clergy overthrew the monarchy in 1979 and established a theocratic regime that was even more anti-western than the secular regimes in Iraq or Syria. This forced the United States into a close alliance with Saudi Arabia. The list of Arab-Israeli wars includes a great number of major wars such as 1948 Arab–Israeli War, 1956 Suez War, 1967 Six-Day War, 1970 War of Attrition, 1973 Yom Kippur War, 1982 Lebanon War, as well as a number of lesser conflicts.

Between 1963 and 1974, conflict arising between Greek Cypriots and Turkish Cypriots in British colonial Cyprus led to Cypriot intercommunal violence and the Turkish invasion of Cyprus. The Cyprus dispute remains unresolved.

In the mid-to-late 1960s, the Arab Socialist Ba'ath Party led by Michel Aflaq and Salah al-Din al-Bitar took power in both Iraq and Syria. Iraq was first ruled by Ahmed Hassan al-Bakr, but was succeeded by Saddam Hussein in 1979, and Syria was ruled first by a Military Committee led by Salah Jadid, and later Hafez al-Assad until 2000, when he was succeeded by his son, Bashar al-Assad.

In 1979, Egypt under Nasser's successor, Anwar Sadat, concluded a peace treaty with Israel, ending the prospects of a united Arab military front. From the 1970s the Palestinians, led by Yasser Arafat's Palestine Liberation Organization, resorted to a prolonged campaign of violence against Israel and against American, Jewish, and western targets generally, as a means of weakening Israeli resolve and undermining western support for Israel. The Palestinians were supported in this, to varying degrees, by the regimes in Syria, Libya, Iran, and Iraq. The high point of this campaign came in the 1975 United Nations General Assembly Resolution 3379 condemning Zionism as a form of racism and the reception given to Arafat by the United Nations General Assembly. Resolution 3379 was revoked in 1991 by the United Nations General Assembly Resolution 4686.

Due to many of the frantic events of the late 1970s in the Middle East it culimated in the Iran–Iraq War between neighbouring Iran and Iraq. The war, started by Iraq, who invaded Iranian Khuzestan in 1980 at the behest of the latter's chaotic state of country due to the 1979 Islamic Revolution, eventually turned into a stalemate with hundreds of thousands of dead on both sides.

The fall of the Soviet Union and the collapse of communism in the early 1990s had several consequences for the Middle East. It allowed large numbers of Soviet Jews to emigrate from Russia and Ukraine to Israel, further strengthening the Jewish state. It cut off the easiest source of credit, armaments, and diplomatic support to the anti-western Arab regimes, weakening their position. It opened up the prospect of cheap oil from Russia, driving down the price of oil and reducing the west's dependence on oil from the Arab states. It discredited the model of development through authoritarian state socialism, which Egypt (under Nasser), Algeria, Syria, and Iraq had followed since the 1960s, leaving these regimes politically and economically stranded. Rulers such as Iraq's Saddam Hussein increasingly relied on Arab nationalism as a substitute for socialism.

Saddam Hussein led Iraq into a prolonged and costly war with Iran from 1980 to 1988, and then into its fateful invasion of Kuwait in 1990. Kuwait

History of the Middle East

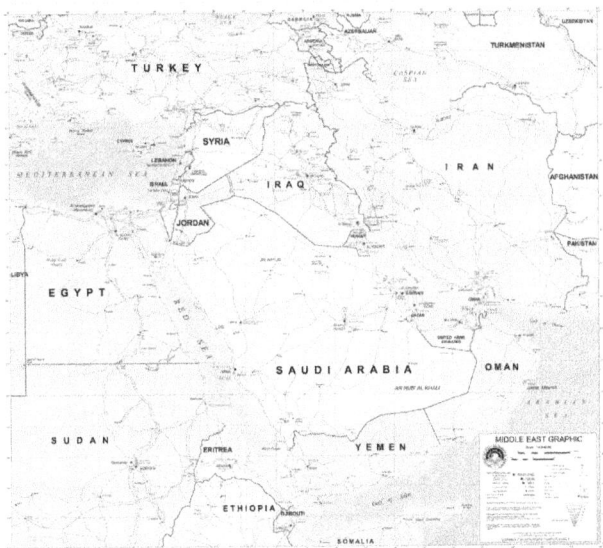

Figure 31: *A map of the Middle East (2003)*

had been part of the Ottoman province of Basra before 1918, and thus in a sense part of Iraq, even though Iraq had recognized its independence in 1961. In response, the United States formed a coalition of allies with Saudi Arabia, Egypt, and Syria, gained UN approval, and evicted Iraq from Kuwait by force in the Gulf War. President George H. W. Bush did not, however, attempt to overthrow Saddam Hussein, which the United States later came to regret.Wikipedia:Citation needed The Gulf War led to a permanent U.S. military presence in the Persian Gulf, particularly in Saudi Arabia, which offended many Muslims, and was a reason often cited by Osama bin Laden as justification for the September 11 attacks.

1990s–present

The worldwide change of governance in Eastern Europe, Latin America, East Asia, and parts of Africa following the dissolution of the Soviet Union did not occur in the Middle East. In the whole region, only Israel, Turkey and to some extent Lebanon and the Palestinian territories were considered to be democracies. Some countries had legislative bodies, but these were said to have little power. In the Persian Gulf states the majority of the population could not vote because they were guest workers rather than citizens.

In most Middle Eastern countries, the growth of market economies was said to be limited by political restrictions, corruption, and cronyism, overspending on arms and prestige projects and over-dependence on oil revenues. The successful economies were countries that had oil wealth and low populations, such as Qatar, Bahrain, Kuwait and the United Arab Emirates, where the ruling emirs allowed some political and social liberalization, but without giving up any of their own power. Lebanon also rebuilt a fairly successful economy after a prolonged civil war in the 1980s.

At the beginning of the 21st century, all these factors intensified conflict in the Middle East, which affected the entire world. Bill Clinton's failed attempt to broker a peace deal between Israel and Palestine at the Camp David Summit in 2000 led directly to the election of Ariel Sharon as Prime Minister of Israel and to the Second Intifada, which conducted suicide bombings on Israeli civilians. This was the first major outbreak of violence since the Oslo Peace Accords of 1993.

At the same time, the failures of most of the Arab governments and the bankruptcy of secular Arab radicalism led a section of educated Arabs (and other Muslims) to embrace Islamism, promoted both by Iran's Shi'a clerics as well as by Saudi Arabia's powerful Wahhabist sect. Many of the militant Islamists gained their military training while fighting Soviet forces in Afghanistan.Wikipedia:Accuracy dispute#Disputed statement Many of the Afghan jihadists, though supposedly none of the Arab volunteers, were funded by the United States under Operation Cyclone as part of the Reagan Doctrine, one of the longest and most expensive CIA covert operations ever.[123]

One of these Arab militants was a wealthy Saudi Arabian named Osama bin Laden. After fighting against the Soviets in Afghanistan in the 1980s, he formed the al-Qaida organization, which was responsible for the 1998 U.S. embassy bombings, the USS *Cole* bombing and the September 11, 2001 attacks on the United States.Wikipedia:Citation needed The September 11 attacks led the George W. Bush administration to invade Afghanistan in 2001 to overthrow the Taliban regime, which had been harbouring Bin Laden and al-Qaida. The United States and its allies described this operation as part of a global "War on Terror".

In 2002, U.S. Defense Secretary Donald Rumsfeld developed a plan to invade Iraq, remove Saddam from power, and turn Iraq into a democratic state with a free-market economy, which they hoped would serve as a model for the rest of the Middle East. The United States and its principal allies—Britain, Italy, Spain, and Australia—could not secure United Nations approval for the execution of the numerous UN resolutions, so they launched an invasion of Iraq and deposed Saddam without much difficulty in April 2003.

The advent of a new western army of occupation in a Middle Eastern capital marked a turning point in the history of the region. Despite successful elections (although boycotted by large portions of Iraq's Sunni population) held in January 2005, much of Iraq had all but disintegrated, due to a post-war insurgency which morphed into persistent ethnic violence that the American army was initially unable to quell. Many of Iraq's intellectual and business elite fled the country, and many Iraqi refugees left as a result of the insurgency, further destabilizing the region. A responsive surge in U.S. forces in Iraq was largely successful in controlling the insurgency and stabilizing the country. U.S. forces withdrew from Iraq by December 2011.

By 2005, President George W. Bush's Road map for peace between Israel and the Palestinians was stalled, although this situation had begun to change with Yasser Arafat's death in 2004. In response, Israel moved towards a unilateral solution, pushing ahead with the Israeli West Bank barrier to protect Israel from Palestinian suicide bombers and proposed unilateral withdrawal from Gaza. The barrier if completed would amount to a *de facto* annexation of areas of the West Bank by Israel. In 2006 a new conflict erupted between Israel and Hezbollah Shi'a militia in southern Lebanon, further setting back any "prospects for peace".

In the early 2010s, a revolutionary wave popularly known as the Arab Spring brought major protests, uprisings, and revolutions to several Middle Eastern countries, followed by prolonged civil wars in Syria, Iraq, Yemen, and Libya. In 2014, a terrorist group and self-proclaimed caliphate calling itself the Islamic State made rapid territorial gains in western Iraq and eastern Syria, prompting international military intervention. At its peak, the group controlled an area containing an estimated 2.8 to 8 million people, 98% of which was lost by December 2017.

References

Works cited

- Esposito, John L. (1999), *The Oxford History of Islam*[124] (Illustrated ed.), New York City: Oxford University Press, ISBN 978-0-19-510799-9<templatestyles src="Module:Citation/CS1/styles.css"></templatestyles>
- Guzman, Gregory (1985), "Christian Europe and Mongol Asia: First Medieval Intercultural Contact Between East and West"[125] (PDF), *Essays in Medieval Studies*, West Virginia University Press, 2<templatestyles src="Module:Citation/CS1/styles.css"></templatestyles>
- Hourani, Albert (2013), *A History of the Arab Peoples*[126] (Updated ed.), Faber and Faber, ISBN 978-0-571-30249-9<templatestyles src="Module:Citation/CS1/styles.css"></templatestyles>

- Stearns, Peter N. (2007), *A Brief History of the World*, The Teaching Company<templatestyles src="Module:Citation/CS1/styles.css"></templatestyles>
- Wawro, Geoffrey (2008), *Historical Atlas: A Comprehensive History of the World*, Elanora Heights, NSW, Australia: Millennium House, ISBN 978-1-921209-23-9<templatestyles src="Module:Citation/CS1/styles.css"></templatestyles>

Further reading

- Cheta, Omar Youssef. "The economy by other means: The historiography of capitalism in the modern Middle East." *History Compass* (April 2018) 16#4 DOI: 10.1111/hic3.12444
- Cleveland, William L. and Martin Bunton. (2016) *A History of the Modern Middle East*. 6th ed. Westview Press.
- Fawaz, Leila Tarazi. *A Land of Aching Hearts: The Middle East in the Great War* (2014)
- Fawcett, Louise, ed. *International relations of the Middle East* (Oxford University Press, 2013)
- Lewis, Bernard (1995), *The Middle East: A Brief History of the Last 2,000 Years*, New York: Scribner<templatestyles src="Module:Citation/CS1/styles.css"></templatestyles>
- Goldschmidt, Arthur, and Lawrence Davidson. *A concise history of the Middle East* (Westview Press, 1991)
- Issawi, Charles. *An economic history of the Middle East and North Africa* (Routledge, 2013) Excerpt and text search[127]
- Kirk, George Eden. *A short history of the Middle East: from the rise of Islam to modern times*(Methuen, 1964)
- Monroe, Elizabeth. *Britain's Moment in the Middle East, 1914-1956* (1963) online[128]
- Mansfield, Peter; Pelham, Nicolas (2013), *A History of the Middle East* (4 ed.), Penguin Books, ISBN 978-0-7181-9967-8<templatestyles src="Module:Citation/CS1/styles.css"></templatestyles>
- Rogan, Eugene (2009), *The Arabs: A History*<templatestyles src="Module:Citation/CS1/styles.css"></templatestyles>
- Quataert, Donald (2000), *The Ottoman Empire, 1700-1922*[129], Cambridge University Press, ISBN 978-1-139-44591-7<templatestyles src="Module:Citation/CS1/styles.css"></templatestyles>

External links

- Articles From Our Experts[130] – Qatar Digital Library - an online portal providing access to previously undigitised British Library archive materials relating to Persian Gulf history and Arabic science
- The Middle East : peace and the changing order[131] from the Dean Peter Krogh Foreign Affairs Digital Archives
- Ancient Civilizations Medicine[132]
- Assyrians[133]
- Middle East: Primary Cultural and Historical Zones[134]

 Wikimedia Commons has media related to *History of the Middle East*.

Central Asia

History of Central Asia

Human history		
↑ **Prehistory**		
Recorded history		
Ancient		
<ul><li>Earliest records</li><li>Africa</li><li>Americas</li><li>Oceania</li><li>East Asia</li><li>South Asia</li><li>Southeast Asia</li><li>Middle East</li><li>Europe</li></ul>		
Postclassical		
<ul><li>Africa</li><li>Americas</li><li>Oceania</li><li>East Asia</li><li>South Asia</li><li>Southeast Asia</li><li>Middle East</li><li>Europe</li></ul>		
Modern		
	<ul><li>Early modern</li><li>Late modern</li></ul>	
	See also	
	<ul><li>Contemporary</li><li>Modernity</li><li>Futurology</li></ul>	
↓ **Future**		
<ul><li>v</li><li>t</li><li>e[135]</li></ul>		

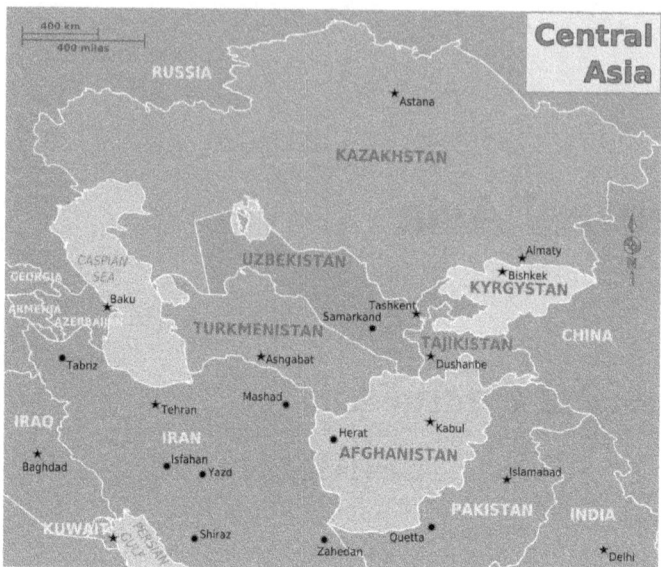

Figure 32: *Central Asian Countries*

The **history of Central Asia** concerns the history of the various peoples that have inhabited Central Asia. The lifestyle of such people has been determined primarily by the area's climate and geography. The aridity of the region makes agriculture difficult and distance from the sea cut it off from much trade. Thus, few major cities developed in the region. Nomadic horse peoples of the steppe dominated the area for millennia.

Relations between the steppe nomads and the settled people in and around Central Asia were marked by conflict. The nomadic lifestyle was well suited to warfare, and the steppe horse riders became some of the most militarily potent people in the world, due to the devastating techniques and ability of their horse archers.[136] Periodically, tribal leaders or changing conditions would organise several tribes into a single military force, which would then often launch campaigns of conquest, especially into more 'civilised' areas. A few of these types of tribal coalitions included the Huns' invasion of Europe, various Turkic migrations into Transoxiana, the Wu Hu attacks on China and most notably the Mongol conquest of much of Eurasia.

The dominance of the nomads ended in the 16th century as firearms allowed settled people to gain control of the region. The Russian Empire, the Qing Dynasty of China, and other powers expanded into the area and seized the bulk of Central Asia by the end of the 19th century. After the Russian Revolution of 1917, the Soviet Union incorporated most of Central Asia; only Mongolia and Afghanistan remained nominally independent, although Mongolia existed as a Soviet satellite state and Soviet troops invaded Afghanistan in the late 20th century. The Soviet areas of Central Asia saw much industrialisation and construction of infrastructure, but also the suppression of local cultures and a lasting legacy of ethnic tensions and environmental problems.

With the collapse of the Soviet Union in 1991, five Central Asian countries gained independence — Kazakhstan, Uzbekistan, Turkmenistan, Kyrgyzstan, and Tajikistan. In all of the new states, former Communist Party officials retained power as local strongmen.

Prehistory

<templatestyles src="Multiple_image/styles.css" />

Left image: The Sampul tapestry, a woolen wall hanging from Lop County, Xinjiang, China, showing a possibly Greek soldier from the Greco-Bactrian kingdom (250–125 BC), with blue eyes, wielding a spear, and wearing what appears to be a *diadem* headband; depicted above him is a centaur, from Greek mythology, a common motif in Hellenistic art

Right image: painted clay and alabaster head of a Zoroastrian priest wearing a distinctive Bactrian-style headdress, Takhti-Sangin, Tajikistan, 3rd–2nd century BC

<templatestyles src="Multiple_image/styles.css" />

A Sogdian silk brocade textile fragment, dated c. 700 AD (left image), and a Sogdian silver wine cup with mercury gilding, 7th century (right image)

Anatomically modern humans (*Homo sapiens*) reached Central Asia by 50,000 to 40,000 years ago. The Tibetan Plateau is thought to have been reached by 38,000 years ago.[137] Populations who lived in Siberia during the Last Glacial Maximum have also contributed significantly to the populations of both Europe and the Americas.[138]

The term Ceramic Mesolithic is used of late Mesolithic cultures of Central Asia, during the 6th to 5th millennia BC (in Russian archaeology, these cultures are described as Neolithic even though farming is absent). It is characterized by its distinctive type of pottery, with point or knob base and flared rims, manufactured by methods not used by the Neolithic farmers. The earliest manifestation of this type of pottery may be in the region around Lake Baikal in Siberia. It appears in the Elshan or Yelshanka or Samara culture on the Volga in Russia by about 7000 BC. and from there spread via the Dnieper-Donets culture to the Narva culture of the Eastern Baltic.

In the Pontic-Caspian steppe, Chalcolithic cultures develop in the second half of the 5th millennium BC, small communities in permanent settlements which began to engage in agricultural practices as well as herding. Around this time, some of these communities began the domestication of the horse. According to the Kurgan hypothesis, the north-west of the region is also considered to be the source of the root of the Indo-European languages. The horse-drawn chariot appears in the 3rd millennium BC, by 2000 BC, in the form of war chariots with spoked wheels, thus being made more manoeuvrable, and dominated the battlefields. The growing use of the horse, combined with the failure, roughly around 2000 BC, of the always precarious irrigation systems that had allowed for extensive agriculture in the region, gave rise and dominance of pastoral nomadism by 1000 BC, a way of life that would dominate the region for the next several millennia, giving rise to the Scythian expansion of the Iron Age.

Scattered nomadic groups maintained herds of sheep, goats, horses, and camels, and conducted annual migrations to find new pastures (a practice known as transhumance). The people lived in yurts (or gers) – tents made of hides and wood that could be disassembled and transported. Each group had several yurts, each accommodating about five people.

While the semi-arid plains were dominated by the nomads, small city-states and sedentary agrarian societies arose in the more humid areas of Central Asia. The Bactria-Margiana Archaeological Complex of the early 2nd millennium BC was the first sedentary civilisation of the region, practicing irrigation farming of wheat and barley and possibly a form of writing. Bactria-Margiana probably interacted with the contemporary Bronze Age nomads of the Andronovo culture, the originators of the spoke-wheeled chariot, who lived to their north in western Siberia, Russia, and parts of Kazakhstan, and survived as a culture until the 1st millennium BC. These cultures, particularly Bactria-Margiana, have been posited as possible representatives of the hypothetical Aryan culture ancestral to the speakers of the Indo-Iranian languages (see Indo-Iranians).

Later the strongest of Sogdian city states of the Fergana Valley rose to prominence. After the 1st century BC, these cities became home to the traders of the Silk Road and grew wealthy from this trade. The steppe nomads were dependent on these settled people for a wide array of goods that were impossible for transient populations to produce. The nomads traded for these when they could, but because they generally did not produce goods of interest to sedentary people, the popular alternative was to carry out raids.

A wide variety of people came to populate the steppes. Nomadic groups in Central Asia included the Huns and other Turks, as well as Indo-Europeans such as the Tocharians, Persians, Scythians, Saka, Yuezhi, Wusun, and others, and a number of Mongol groups. Despite these ethnic and linguistic differences, the steppe lifestyle led to the adoption of very similar culture across the region.

Ancient era

In the 2nd and 1st millennia BC, a series of large and powerful states developed on the southern periphery of Central Asia (the Ancient Near East). These empires launched several attempts to conquer the steppe people, but met with

Figure 33: *Tetradrachm of the Greco-Bactrian King Eucratides (171–145 BC).*

Figure 34: *A monumental Sogdian wall mural of Samarkand, dated c. 650 AD, known as the Ambassordors' Painting, found in the hall of the ruin of an aristocratic house in Afrasiab, commissioned by the Sogdian king of Samarkand, Varkhuman*

Figure 35: *Two Buddhist monks on a mural of the Bezeklik Thousand Buddha Caves near Turpan, Xinjiang, China, 9th century AD; although Albert von Le Coq (1913) assumed the blue-eyed, red-haired monk was a Tocharian,*[139] *modern scholarship has identified similar Caucasian figures of the same cave temple (No. 9) as ethnic Sogdians,*[140] *an Eastern Iranian people who inhabited Turfan as an ethnic minority community during the phases of Tang Chinese (7th–8th century) and Uyghur rule (9th–13th century).*[141]

only mixed success. The Median Empire and Achaemenid Empire both ruled parts of Central Asia. The Xiongnu Empire (209 BC-93 (156) AD) may be seen as the first central Asian empire which set an example for later Göktürk and Mongol empires.[142] Xiongnu's ancestor Xianyu tribe founded Zhongshan state (c. 6th century BC – c. 296 BC) in Hebei province, China. The title chanyu was used by the Xiongnu rulers before Modun Chanyu so it is possible that statehood history of the Xiongnu began long before Modun's rule.

Following the success of the Han–Xiongnu War, Chinese states would also regularly strive to extend their power westwards. Despite their military might, these states found it difficult to conquer the whole region.

When faced by a stronger force, the nomads could simply retreat deep into the steppe and wait for the invaders to leave. With no cities and little wealth other than the herds they took with them the nomads had nothing they could be forced to defend. An example of this is given by Herodotus's detailed account of the futile Persian campaigns against the Scythians. The Scythians, like most nomad empires, had permanent settlements of various sizes, representing various degrees of civilisation.[143] The vast fortified settlement of Kamenka on the Dnieper River, settled since the end of the 5th century BC, became the centre of the Scythian kingdom ruled by Ateas, who lost his life in a battle against Philip II of Macedon in 339 BC.

Some empires, such as the Persian and Macedonian empires, did make deep inroads into Central Asia by founding cities and gaining control of the trading centres. Alexander the Great's conquests spread Hellenistic civilisation all the way to Alexandria Eschate (Lit. "Alexandria the Furthest"), established in 329 BC in modern Tajikistan. After Alexander's death in 323 BC, his Central Asian territory fell to the Seleucid Empire during the Wars of the Diadochi.

In 250 BC, the Central Asian portion of the empire (Bactria) seceded as the Greco-Bactrian Kingdom, which had extensive contacts with India and China until its end in 125 BC. The Indo-Greek Kingdom, mostly based in the Punjab region but controlling a fair part of Afghanistan, pioneered the development of Greco-Buddhism. The Kushan Kingdom thrived across a wide swath of the region from the 2nd century BC to the 4th century AD, and continued Hellenistic and Buddhist traditions. These states prospered from their position on the Silk Road linking China and Europe.

Likewise, in eastern Central Asia, the Chinese Han Dynasty expanded into the region at the height of its imperial power. From roughly 115 to 60 BC, Han forces fought the Xiongnu over control of the oasis city-states in the Tarim Basin. The Han was eventually victorious and established the Protectorate of the Western Regions in 60 BC, which dealt with the region's defence and foreign affairs. Chinese rule in Tarim Basin was replaced successively with Kushans and Hephthalites.

Later, external powers such as the Sassanid Empire would come to dominate this trade. One of those powers, the Parthian Empire, was of Central Asian origin, but adopted Persian-Greek cultural traditions. This is an early example of a recurring theme of Central Asian history: occasionally nomads of Central Asian origin would conquer the kingdoms and empires surrounding the region, but quickly merge into the culture of the conquered peoples.

At this time Central Asia was a heterogeneous region with a mixture of cultures and religions. Buddhism remained the largest religion, but was concentrated in the east. Around Persia, Zoroastrianism became important. Nestorian Christianity entered the area, but was never more than a minority faith. More successful was Manichaeism, which became the third largest faith. Many Central Asians practised more than one faith, and almost all of the local religions were infused with local shamanistic traditions. Wikipedia:Citation needed

History of Central Asia

Figure 36: *A Tang period gilt-silver jar, shaped in the style of northern nomad's leather bag decorated with a horse dancing with a cup of wine in its mouth, as the horses of Emperor Xuanzong were trained to do.*

Turkic expansion began in the 6th century, and following the Göktürk empire, Turkic tribes quickly spread westward across all of Central Asia. The Turkic speaking Uyghurs were one of many distinct cultural groups brought together by the trade of the Silk Route at Turfan, which was then ruled by China's Tang Dynasty. The Uyghurs, primarily pastoral nomads, observed a number of religions including Manichaeism, Buddhism, and Nestorian Christianity. Many of the artefacts from this period were found in the 19th century in this remote desert region.

Medieval

Sui and early Tang Dynasty

It was during the Sui and Tang dynasties that China expanded into eastern Central Asia. Chinese foreign policy to the north and west now had to deal with Turkic nomads, who were becoming the most dominant ethnic group in Central Asia. To handle and avoid any threats posed by the Turks, the Sui government repaired fortifications and received their trade and tribute missions. They sent royal princesses off to marry Turkic clan leaders, a total of four of

Figure 37: *The monumental Sogdian wall murals of Panjakent (modern Tajikistan), showing cavalry and horse riders, dated c. 740 AD*

them in 597, 599, 614, and 617. The Sui stirred trouble and conflict amongst ethnic groups against the Turks.

As early as the Sui Dynasty, the Turks had become a major militarised force employed by the Chinese. When the Khitans began raiding north-east China in 605, a Chinese general led 20,000 Turks against them, distributing Khitan livestock and women to the Turks as a reward. On two occasions between 635 and 636, Tang royal princesses were married to Turk mercenaries or generals in Chinese service.

Throughout the Tang Dynasty until the end of 755, there were approximately ten Turkic generals serving under the Tang. While most of the Tang army was made of *fubing(府兵)* Chinese conscripts, the majority of the troops led by Turkic generals were of non-Chinese origin, campaigning largely in the western frontier where the presence of *fubing(府兵)* troops was low. Some "Turkic" troops were nomadisized Han Chinese, a desinicized people.

Civil war in China was almost totally diminished by 626, along with the defeat in 628 of the Ordos Chinese warlord Liang Shidu; after these internal conflicts, the Tang began an offensive against the Turks. In the year 630, Tang armies captured areas of the Ordos Desert, modern-day Inner Mongolia province, and southern Mongolia from the Turks.

After this military victory, Emperor Taizong won the title of Great Khan amongst the various Turks in the region who pledged their allegiance to him and the Chinese empire (with several thousand Turks traveling into China to live at Chang'an). On June 11, 631, Emperor Taizong also sent envoys to the Xueyantuo bearing gold and silk in order to persuade the release of enslaved Chinese prisoners who were captured during the transition from Sui to Tang from the northern frontier; this embassy succeeded in freeing 80,000 Chinese men and women who were then returned to China.

While the Turks were settled in the Ordos region (former territory of the Xiongnu), the Tang government took on the military policy of dominating the central steppe. Like the earlier Han Dynasty, the Tang Dynasty, along with Turkic allies like the Uyghurs, conquered and subdued Central Asia during the 640s and 650s. During Emperor Taizong's reign alone, large campaigns were launched against not only the Göktürks, but also separate campaigns against the Tuyuhun, and the Xueyantuo. Taizong also launched campaigns against the oasis states of the Tarim Basin, beginning with the annexation of Gaochang in 640. The nearby kingdom of Karasahr was captured by the Tang in 644 and the kingdom of Kucha was conquered in 649.

The expansion into Central Asia continued under Taizong's successor, Emperor Gaozong, who invaded the Western Turks ruled by the qaghan Ashina Helu in 657 with an army led by Su Dingfang. Ashina was defeated and the khaganate was absorbed into the Tang empire. The territory was administered through the Anxi Protectorate and the Four Garrisons of Anxi. Tang hegemony beyond the Pamir Mountains in modern Tajikistan and Afghanistan ended with revolts by the Turks, but the Tang retained a military presence in Xinjiang. These holdings were later invaded by the Tibetan Empire to the south in 670. For the remainder of the Tang Dynasty, the Tarim Basin alternated between Tang and Tibetan rule as they competed for control of Central Asia.

Tang rivalry with the Tibetan Empire

The Tang Empire competed with the Tibetan Empire for control of areas in Inner and Central Asia, which was at times settled with marriage alliances such as the marrying of Princess Wencheng (d. 680) to Songtsän Gampo (d. 649). A Tibetan tradition mentions that after Songtsän Gampo's death in 649 AD, Chinese troops captured Lhasa. The Tibetan scholar Tsepon W. D. Shakabpa believes that the tradition is in error and that "those histories reporting the arrival of Chinese troops are not correct" and claims that the event is mentioned neither in the Chinese annals nor in the manuscripts of Dunhuang.

There was a long string of conflicts with Tibet over territories in the Tarim Basin between 670–692 and in 763 the Tibetans even captured the capital of

Figure 38: *A lion motif on Sogdian polychrome silk, 8th century AD, most likely from Bukhara*

China, Chang'an, for fifteen days during the An Shi Rebellion. In fact, it was during this rebellion that the Tang withdrew its western garrisons stationed in what is now Gansu and Qinghai, which the Tibetans then occupied along with the territory of what is now Xinjiang. Hostilities between the Tang and Tibet continued until they signed a formal peace treaty in 821. The terms of this treaty, including the fixed borders between the two countries, are recorded in a bilingual inscription on a stone pillar outside the Jokhang temple in Lhasa.

Islamic empires

In the 8th century, Islam began to penetrate the region, the desert nomads of Arabia could militarily match the nomads of the steppe, and the early Arab Empire gained control over parts of Central Asia. The early conquests under Qutayba ibn Muslim (705–715) were soon reversed by a combination of native uprisings and invasion by the Turgesh, but the collapse of the Turgesh khaganate after 738 opened the way for the re-imposition of Muslim authority under Nasr ibn Sayyar.

The Arab invasion also saw Chinese influence expelled from western Central Asia. At the Battle of Talas in 751 an Arab army decisively defeated a Tang Dynasty force, and for the next several centuries Middle Eastern influences

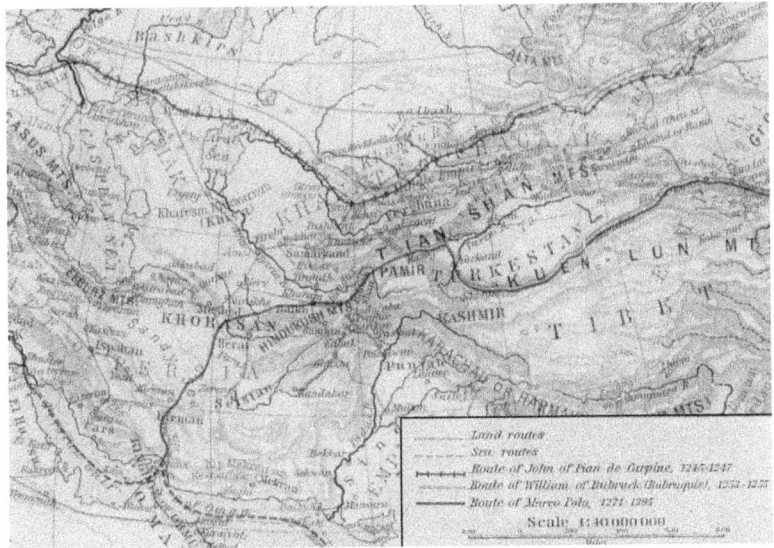

Figure 39: *A map showing the major trade routes of Central Asia in the 13th century.*

would dominate the region. Large-scale Islamization however did not begin until the 9th century, running parallel with the fragmentation of Abbasid political authority and the emergence of local Iranian and Turkic dynasties like the Samanids.

Steppe empires

Over time, as new technologies were introduced, the nomadic horsemen grew in power. The Scythians developed the saddle, and by the time of the Alans the use of the stirrup had begun. Horses continued to grow larger and sturdier so that chariots were no longer needed as the horses could carry men with ease. This greatly increased the mobility of the nomads; it also freed their hands, allowing them to use the bow from horseback.

Using small but powerful composite bows, the steppe people gradually became the most powerful military force in the world. From a young age, almost the entire male population was trained in riding and archery, both of which were necessary skills for survival on the steppe. By adulthood, these activities were second nature. These mounted archers were more mobile than any other force at the time, being able to travel forty miles per day with ease. Wikipedia:Citation needed

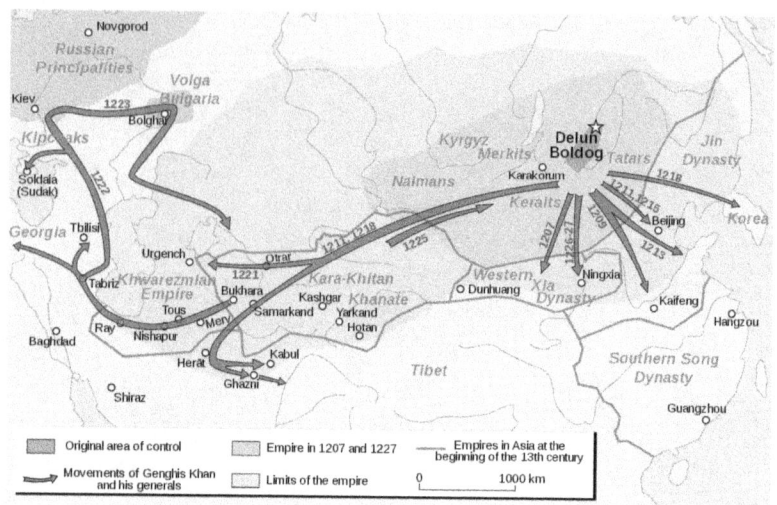

Figure 40: *Mongol invasions and conquests seriously depopulated large areas of Muslim Central Asia*

The steppe peoples quickly came to dominate Central Asia, forcing the scattered city states and kingdoms to pay them tribute or face annihilation. The martial ability of the steppe peoples was limited, however, by the lack of political structure within the tribes. Confederations of various groups would sometimes form under a ruler known as a khan. When large numbers of nomads acted in unison they could be devastating, as when the Huns arrived in Western Europe. However, tradition dictated that any dominion conquered in such wars should be divided among all of the khan's sons, so these empires often declined as quickly as they formed.

Once the foreign powers were expelled, several indigenous empires formed in Central Asia. The Hephthalites were the most powerful of these nomad groups in the 6th and 7th century and controlled much of the region. In the 10th and 11th centuries the region was divided between several powerful states including the Samanid dynasty, that of the Seljuk Turks, and the Khwarezmid Empire.

The most spectacular power to rise out of Central Asia developed when Genghis Khan united the tribes of Mongolia. Using superior military techniques, the Mongol Empire spread to comprise all of Central Asia and China as well as large parts of Russia, and the Middle East. After Genghis Khan died in 1227, most of Central Asia continued to be dominated by the successor Chagatai Khanate. This state proved to be short lived, as in 1369 Timur, a Turkic leader in the Mongol military tradition, conquered most of the region.

Even harder than keeping a steppe empire together was governing conquered lands outside the region. While the steppe peoples of Central Asia found conquest of these areas easy, they found governing almost impossible. The diffuse political structure of the steppe confederacies was maladapted to the complex states of the settled peoples. Moreover, the armies of the nomads were based upon large numbers of horses, generally three or four for each warrior. Maintaining these forces required large stretches of grazing land, not present outside the steppe. Any extended time away from the homeland would thus cause the steppe armies to gradually disintegrate. To govern settled peoples the steppe peoples were forced to rely on the local bureaucracy, a factor that would lead to the rapid assimilation of the nomads into the culture of those they had conquered. Another important limit was that the armies, for the most part, were unable to penetrate the forested regions to the north; thus, such states as Novgorod and Muscovy began to grow in power.

In the 14th century much of Central Asia, and many areas beyond it, were conquered by Timur (1336–1405) who is known in the west as Tamerlane. It was during Timur's reign that the nomadic steppe culture of Central Asia fused with the settled culture of Iran. One of its consequences was an entirely new visual language that glorified Timur and subsequent Timurid rulers. This visual language was also used to articulate their commitment to Islam.[144] Timur's large empire collapsed soon after his death, however. The region then became divided among a series of smaller Khanates, including the Khanate of Khiva, the Khanate of Bukhara, the Khanate of Kokand, and the Khanate of Kashgar.

Early modern period (16th to 19th centuries)

The lifestyle that had existed largely unchanged since 500 BCE began to disappear after 1500. Important change to the world economy in the 14th and 15th century reflected the impact of the development of nautical technology. Ocean trade routes were pioneered by the Europeans, who had been cut off from the Silk Road by the Muslim states that controlled its western termini. The long-distance trade linking East Asia and India to Western Europe increasingly began to move over the seas and not through Central Asia. However, the emergence of Russia as a world power enabled Central Asia to continue its role as a conduit for overland trade of other sorts, now linking India with Russia on a north-south axis.

An even more important development was the introduction of gunpowder-based weapons. The gunpowder revolution allowed settled peoples to defeat the steppe horsemen in open battle for the first time. Construction of these weapons required the infrastructure and economies of large societies and were thus impractical for nomadic peoples to produce. The domain of the nomads

Figure 41: *A native Turkmen man in traditional dress with his dromedary camel in Turkmenistan, c. 1915.*

began to shrink as, beginning in the 15th century, the settled powers gradually began to conquer Central Asia.

The last steppe empire to emerge was that of the Dzungars who conquered much of East Turkestan and Mongolia. However, in a sign of the changed times they proved unable to match the Chinese and were decisively defeated by the forces of the Qing Dynasty. In the 18th century the Qing emperors, themselves originally from the far eastern edge of the steppe, campaigned in the west and in Mongolia, with the Qianlong Emperor taking control of Xinjiang in 1758. The Mongol threat was overcome and much of Inner Mongolia was annexed to China.

The Chinese dominions stretched into the heart of Central Asia and included the Khanate of Kokand, which paid tribute to Beijing. Outer Mongolia and Xinjiang did not become provinces of the Chinese empire, but rather were directly administered by the Qing dynasty. The fact that there was no provincial governor meant that the local rulers retained most of their powers and this special status also prevented emigration from the rest of China into the region. Persia also began to expand north, especially under the rule of Nadir Shah, who extended Persian dominion well past the Oxus. After his death, however, the Persian empire rapidly crumbled.

Figure 42: *Russian wars of conquest in Turkestan*

Russian expansion into Central Asia (19th century)

The Russians also expanded south, first with the transformation of the Ukrainian steppe into an agricultural heartland, and subsequently onto the fringe of the Kazakh steppes, beginning with the foundation of the fortress of Orenburg. The slow Russian conquest of the heart of Central Asia began in the early 19th century, although Peter the Great had sent a failed expedition under Prince Bekovitch-Cherkassky against Khiva as early as the 1720s.

By the 1800s, the locals could do little to resist the Russian advance, although the Kazakhs of the Great Horde under Kenesary Kasimov rose in rebellion from 1837–46. Until the 1870s, for the most part, Russian interference was minimal, leaving native ways of life intact and local government structures in place. With the conquest of Turkestan after 1865 and the consequent securing of the frontier, the Russians gradually expropriated large parts of the steppe and gave these lands to Russian farmers, who began to arrive in large numbers. This process was initially limited to the northern fringes of the steppe and it was only in the 1890s that significant numbers of Russians began to settle farther south, especially in Zhetysu (Semirechye).

The Great Game

Russian campaigns

The forces of the khanates were poorly equipped and could do little to resist Russia's advances, although the Kokandian commander Alimqul led a quixotic campaign before being killed outside Chimkent. The main opposition to Russian expansion into Turkestan came from the British, who felt that Russia was growing too powerful and threatening the northwest frontiers of British India. This rivalry came to be known as The Great Game, where both powers

Figure 43: *Prisoners in a zindan, a traditional Central Asian prison, in the Bukharan Protectorate under Imperial Russia, ca. 1910*

competed to advance their own interests in the region. It did little to slow the pace of conquest north of the Oxus, but did ensure that Afghanistan remained independent as a buffer state between the two Empires.

After the fall of Tashkent to General Cherniaev in 1865, Khodjend, Djizak, and Samarkand fell to the Russians in quick succession over the next three years as the Khanate of Kokand and the Emirate of Bukhara were repeatedly defeated. In 1867 the Governor-Generalship of Russian Turkestan was established under General Konstantin Petrovich Von Kaufman, with its headquarters at Tashkent. In 1881–85 the Transcaspian region was annexed in the course of a campaign led by Generals Mikhail Annenkov and Mikhail Skobelev, and Ashkhabad (from Persia), Merv and Pendjeh (from Afghanistan) all came under Russian control.

Russian expansion was halted in 1887 when Russia and Great Britain delineated the northern border of Afghanistan. Bukhara and the Khanate of Khiva remained quasi-independent, but were essentially protectorates along the lines of the Princely States of British India. Although the conquest was prompted by almost purely military concerns, in the 1870s and 1880s Turkestan came to play a reasonably important economic role within the Russian Empire.

Because of the American Civil War, cotton shot up in price in the 1860s, becoming an increasingly important commodity in the region, although its cultivation was on a much lesser scale than during the Soviet period. The cotton trade led to improvements: the Transcaspian Railway from Krasnovodsk to Samarkand and Tashkent, and the Trans-Aral Railway from Orenburg to Tashkent were constructed. In the long term the development of a cotton monoculture would render Turkestan dependent on food imports from Western Siberia, and the Turkestan-Siberia Railway was already planned when the First World War broke out.

Russian rule still remained distant from the local populace, mostly concerning itself with the small minority of Russian inhabitants of the region. The local Muslims were not considered full Russian citizens. They did not have the full privileges of Russians, but nor did they have the same obligations, such as military service. The Tsarist regime left substantial elements of the previous regimes (such as Muslim religious courts) intact, and local self-government at the village level was quite extensive.

Qing Dynasty

During the 17th and 18th centuries the Qing Dynasty made several campaigns to conquer the Dzungar Mongols. In the meantime, they incorporated parts of Central Asia into the Chinese Empire. Internal turmoil largely halted Chinese expansion in the 19th century. In 1867 Yakub Beg led a rebellion that saw Kashgar declaring its independence as the Taiping and Nian Rebellions in the heartland of the Empire prevented the Chinese from reasserting their control.

Instead, the Russians expanded, annexing the Chu and Ili Valleys and the city of Kuldja from the Chinese Empire. After Yakub Beg's death at Korla in 1877 his state collapsed as the area was reconquered by China. After lengthy negotiations Kuldja was returned to Beijing by Russia in 1884.

Revolution and revolt

During the First World War the Muslim exemption from conscription was removed by the Russians, sparking the Central Asian Revolt of 1916. When the Russian Revolution of 1917 occurred, a provisional Government of Jadid Reformers, also known as the Turkestan Muslim Council met in Kokand and declared Turkestan's autonomy. This new government was quickly crushed by the forces of the Tashkent Soviet, and the semi-autonomous states of Bukhara and Khiva were also invaded. The main independence forces were rapidly crushed, but guerrillas known as basmachi continued to fight the Communists until 1924. Mongolia was also swept up by the Russian Revolution and, though it never became a Soviet republic, it became a communist People's Republic in 1924.

The creation of the Republic of China in 1911 and the general turmoil in China affected the Qing Dynasty's holdings in Central Asia. Republic of China's control of the region was relegated to southern Xinjiang and there was a dual threat from Islamic separatists and communists. Eventually the region became largely independent under the control of the provincial governor. Rather than invade, the Soviet Union established a network of consulates in the region and sent aid and technical advisors.

By the 1930s, the governor of Xinjiang's relationship with Moscow was far more important than that with Nanking. The Chinese Civil War further destabilised the region and saw Turkic nationalists make attempts at independence. In 1933, the First East Turkestan Republic was declared, but it was destroyed soon after with the aid of the Soviet troops.

After the German invasion of the Soviet Union in 1941, Governor Sheng Shicai of Xinjiang gambled and broke his links to Moscow, moving to ally himself with the Kuomintang. This led to a civil war within the region. Sheng was eventually forced to flee and the Soviet-backed Second East Turkestan Republic was formed in northern Dzungaria, while the Republic of China retained control of southern Xinjiang. Both states were annexed by the People's Republic of China in 1949.

Soviet era (1918–1991)

After being conquered by Bolshevik forces, Soviet Central Asia experienced a flurry of administrative reorganisation. In 1918 the Bolsheviks set up the Turkestan Autonomous Soviet Socialist Republic, and Bukhara and Khiva also became SSRs. In 1919 the Conciliatory Commission for Turkestan Affairs was established, to try to improve relations between the locals and the Communists. New policies were introduced, respecting local customs and religion. In 1920, the Kirghiz Autonomous Soviet Socialist Republic, covering modern Kazakhstan, was set up. It was renamed the Kazakh Autonomous Soviet Socialist Republic in 1925. In 1924, the Soviets created the Uzbek SSR and the Turkmen SSR. In 1929 the Tajik SSR was split from the Uzbek SSR. The Kyrgyz Autonomous Oblast became an SSR in 1936.

These borders had little to do with ethnic make-up, but the Soviets felt it important to divide the region. They saw both Pan-Turkism and Pan-Islamism as threats, which dividing Turkestan would limit. Under the Soviets, the local languages and cultures were systematised and codified, and their differences clearly demarcated and encouraged. New Cyrillic writing systems were introduced, to break links with Turkey and Iran. Under the Soviets the southern border was almost completely closed and all travel and trade was directed north through Russia.

During the period of forced collectivisation under Joseph Stalin at least a million persons died, mostly in the Kazakh SSR. Islam, as well as other religions, were also attacked. In the Second World War several million refugees and hundreds of factories were moved to the relative security of Central Asia; and the region permanently became an important part of the Soviet industrial complex. Several important military facilities were also located in the region, including nuclear testing facilities and the Baikonur Cosmodrome. The Virgin Lands Campaign, starting in 1954, was a massive Soviet agricultural resettlement program that brought more than 300,000 individuals, mostly from the Ukraine, to the northern Kazakh SSR and the Altai region of the Russian SFSR. This was a major change in the ethnicity of the region.

Similar processes occurred in Xinjiang and the rest of Western China where the PRC quickly established control from the Second East Turkestan Republic that controlled northern Xinjiang and the Republic of China forces that controlled southern Xinjiang after the Qing Dynasty. The area was subject to a number of development schemes and, like Soviet Central Asia, one focus was on the growing of the cotton cash crop. These efforts were overseen by the Xinjiang Production and Construction Corps. The XPCC also encouraged Han Chinese to return to Xinjiang after many had migrated out during the Muslim revolts against the Qing Dynasty.

Political turmoil has led to major demographic shifts in the region: During the Qing Dynasty there were 60% Turkic and 30% Han Chinese in the region, after the Muslim revolts the percentage of Han Chinese dropped to as low as 7%,[145] and by the year 2000 some 40% of the population of Xinjiang were Han.[146] As with the Soviet Union local languages and cultures were mostly encouraged and Xinjiang was granted autonomous status. However, Islam was much persecuted, especially during the Cultural Revolution. Many people from other parts of China fled to Xinjiang due to the failed agricultural policies of the Great Leap Forward in other provinces. However, the Great Leap Forward did not affect much of Xinjiang due to its geographical isolation from other parts of China.

Soviet Evacuation and Population Deportations During World War II

The Second World War sparked the widespread migration of Soviet citizens to the rear of the USSR. Much of this movement was directed to Soviet Central Asia. These migrations included official, state-organised evacuations and deportations as well as the non-sanctioned, panicked flight from the front by both general citizenry and important officials. The evacuation of Soviet citizens and industry during World War II was an essential element of their overall success in the war, and Central Asia served as a main destination for evacuees.

The German invasion of the Soviet Union began on June 22, 1941. A decree from the Presidium of the Executive Committee on the same day forbade the entry or exit from the USSR's border regions, which were under a state of martial law. Such mandates demonstrated the Soviets' fear of spreading panic and their commitment to asserting direct state control over wartime relocations to maintain order. Soviet wartime population policy consisted of two distinct operations: deportation and evacuation. Deportation aimed to clear regions near the front of potentially insidious anti-Soviet elements that could hamper the war effort, while evacuation policy aimed to move Soviet industry and intelligentsia to the rear, where they would be safe.

Deportations along ethnic lines

Soviet officials organised their wartime deportation policy largely along ethnic lines. As a response to the German invasion, Soviet citizens of German descent in border regions were targeted for deportation to the rear where Soviet authorities had no need to worry of their conspiring with the enemy. Such dubious ethnically-derived logic was not reserved for Germans. Many Finns were also forcibly relocated in the first year of the war simply for their heritage, though they were mainly sent to remote areas in the northern rear, such as Siberia, rather than Central Asia. A large portion of the German deportees, however, were sent to Kazakhstan. The remobilisation of relocated human resources into the labour force was pivotal to Soviet wartime production policy, and to that end many able-bodied deportees were conscripted into a "labour army" with military style discipline.

By early 1942 as many as 20,800 ethnic Germans had been organised into battalions in this labour army, though this number would grow to as much as 222,000 by early 1944 as conscription criteria were broadened. The NKVD employed about 101,000 members of the labour army at construction sites to develop infrastructure for the war effort. Those who were not assigned to the labour army were used for timber harvesting, the construction of railways and other infrastructure, or sent to collective farms.

As the tide turned in the war, and the Soviets began to reclaim the territories they lost to the initial German advance, they began a new wave of deportations of unfavoured ethnic groups. Karachais, Kalmyks, Chechens, Ingushetians, Kabardians, and Crimean Tatars were all deported to Central Asia for their supposed fraternisation with occupying German forces. These groups were sent mostly to Kazakhstan, Kyrgyzstan, and Uzbekistan for their infidelity. These punitive deportations were also conducted to keep "anti-Soviet elements" far from the border – where the Soviet offensive against Germany was progressing – for fear of spying or sabotage.

Evacuation of Soviet citizens to Central Asia

Many Soviet citizens ended up in Central Asia during World War II, not as a result of deportation, but evacuation. The evacuation focused on the movement of critical wartime industry and the factory workers responsible for overseeing such production. Whole factories and their employees were moved together via railway eastward to cities like Tashkent, which received a lion's share of the evacuees.

The initial attempts at evacuation while the war was still in its early stages through early 1942 were a far cry from the organised affair that the Soviet central bureaucracy envisaged. Throughout the summer and fall of 1941, numerous Soviet frontier cities evacuated in a haphazard and panicked fashion before the German onslaught. A number of factors led to this lack of organisation. For one, the Soviet evacuation plans were thrown together fairly hurriedly, and a lot of the logistical planning was done on the fly as the German advance was already sweeping through the Soviet border zone. The German invasion also hampered the effectiveness of the Soviet response by shattering their communications in the war's early stages; many Soviet leaders were unable to gather reliable information about the positions of German forces until it was too late to effect an orderly evacuation.

There was also a desire on the part of Soviet officials to forestall any evacuations until it was absolutely necessary, the marching orders were often to continue factory production until the eve of occupation before hurriedly dismantling and transporting factory equipment, and destroying what couldn't be moved in time. As a result of the delay in evacuations, they were often carried out under German aerial bombardment, which led to additional confusion among the frightened citizenry. Historian Rebecca Manley describes these early evacuations as being charactered by "three phenomena: the 'flight' of officials, the flight of the population, and 'panic'".

The early flight of Soviet officials who were supposed to manage the evacuation was roundly condemned by Soviet leaders, but often their retreat resulted from a realisation that evacuation procedures had started too late, and that there was no way to effectively execute it. Additionally, Soviet officials who remained in a city captured by German forces feared execution by Nazis on the hunt for communists. Avoiding that, the officials knew that they would be subject to intense interrogation as to what happened by suspicious Soviets upon returning to the fold.

Despite these setbacks in the implementation of evacuation policy early in the war, around 12 million Soviet citizens successfully evacuated in 1941, even if a number of these were the result of disorganised, "spontaneous self-evacuation," and another 4.5 million evacuated the following year. In addition, the factories that were successfully evacuated to the Central Asian rear would help provide the productive capacity the Soviets needed to eventually win the war, as well as preventing the Germans from acquiring additional industrial resources. By providing a safe haven from the German advance for Soviet citizens, Central Asia played a critical role in securing Allied victory. The evacuation itself was only part of the difficulty, however, as evacuees arriving in Central Asia faced many trials and tribulations.

Due to the haphazard nature of evacuation, many labourers did not arrive with their factory, and had to find labour on their own, though jobs were hard to come by. Additionally, cities like Tashkent became overwhelmed at the sheer volume of people arriving at its gates and had great difficulty supplying the food and shelter necessary for evacuees. Upon arrival, many evacuees died of illness or starvation in extreme poverty in Central Asia. Uzbek officials set up aid stations at Tashkent, which were mirrored at other railway stations to help combat the poverty, but they could only do so much as little could be spared economically for the war effort. Despite these troubles, the ability of Central Asia to absorb Soviet industry and population to the extent that it did and in the harried manner that it did was impressive. The Germans certainly didn't foresee the preparedness of Soviet Central Asia, and in the end they paid dearly for it.

Since 1991

From 1988 to 1992, a free press and multi-party system developed in the Central Asian republics as perestroika pressured the local Communist parties to open up. What Svat Soucek calls the "Central Asian Spring" was very short-lived, as soon after independence former Communist Party officials recast themselves as local strongmen. Political stability in the region has mostly been maintained, with the major exception of the Tajik Civil War that lasted from 1992 to 1997. 2005 also saw the largely peaceful ousting of Kyrgyz president Askar Akayev in the Tulip Revolution and an outbreak of violence in Andijan, Uzbekistan.

Much of the population of Soviet Central Asia was indifferent to the collapse of the Soviet Union, even the large Russian populations in Kazakhstan (roughly 40% of the total) and Tashkent, Uzbekistan. Aid from the Kremlin had also been central to the economies of Central Asia, each of the republics receiving massive transfers of funds from Moscow.

Independence largely resulted from the efforts of the small groups of nationalistic, mostly local intellectuals, and from little interest in Moscow for retaining

Figure 44: *The independent states of Central Asia with their Soviet-drawn borders.*

the expensive region. While never a part of the Soviet Union, Mongolia followed a somewhat similar path. Often acting as the unofficial sixteenth Soviet republic, it shed the communist system only in 1996, but quickly ran into economic problems. See: History of independent Mongolia.

The economic performance of the region since independence has been mixed. It contains some of the largest reserves of natural resources in the world, but there are important difficulties in transporting them. Since it lies farther from the ocean than anywhere else in the world, and its southern borders lay closed for decades, the main trade routes and pipelines run through Russia. As a result, Russia still exerts more influence over the region than in any other former Soviet republics. Nevertheless, the rising energy importance of the Caspian Sea entails a great involvement in the region by the US. The former Soviet republics of the Caucasus now have their own US Special Envoy and interagency working groups. Former US Secretary of Energy Bill Richardson had claimed that "the Caspian region will hopefully save us [the US] from total dependence on Middle East oil".

Some analysts, such as Myers Jaffe and Robert A. Manning, estimate however that US' entry into the region (with initiatives such as the US-favored Baku-Tbilisi-Ceyhan pipeline) as a major actor may complicate Moscow's chances of making a decisive break with its past economic mistakes and geopolitical excesses in Central Asia. They also regard as a myth the assertion that Caspian oil and gas will be a cheaper and more secure alternative to supplies from the Persian Gulf.

Despite these reservations and fears, since the late 1980s, Azerbaijan, Kazakhstan, and Turkmenistan have gradually moved to centre stage in the global energy markets and are now regarded as key factors of the international energy security. Azerbaijan and Kazakhstan in particular have succeeded in attracting massive foreign investment to their oil and gas sectors. According to Gawdat Bahgat, the investment flow suggests that the geological potential of the Caspian region as a major source of oil and gas is not in doubt.

Russia and Kazakhstan started a closer energy co-operation in 1998, which was further consolidated in May 2002, when Presidents Vladimir Putin and Nursultan Nazarbayev signed a protocol dividing three gas fields – Kurmangazy, Tsentralnoye, and Khvalynskoye – on an equal basis. Following the ratification of bilateral treaties, Russia, Kazakhstan and Azerbaijan declared that the northern Caspian was open for business and investment as they had reached a consensus on the legal status of the basin. Iran and Turkmenistan refused however to recognise the validity of these bilateral agreements; Iran is rejecting any bilateral agreement to divide the Caspian. On the other hand, US' choices in the region (within the framework of the so-called "pipeline diplomacy"), such as the strong support of the Baku pipeline (the project was eventually approved and was completed in 2005), reflect a political desire to avoid both Russia and Iran.

Increasingly, other powers have begun to involve themselves in Central Asia. Soon after the Central Asian states won their independence, Turkey began to look east, and a number of organizations are attempting to build links between the western and eastern Turks. Iran, which for millennia had close links with the region, has also been working to build ties and the Central Asian states now have good relations with the Islamic Republic. One important player in the new Central Asia has been Saudi Arabia, which has been funding the Islamic revival in the region. Olcott notes that soon after independence Saudi money paid for massive shipments of Qur'ans to the region and for the construction and repair of a large number of mosques. In Tajikistan alone an estimated 500 mosques per year have been erected with Saudi money.[147]

The formerly atheistic Communist Party leaders have mostly converted to Islam. Small Islamist groups have formed in several of the countries, but radical Islam has little history in the region; the Central Asian societies have remained largely secular and all five states enjoy good relations with Israel. Central Asia is still home to a large Jewish population, the largest group being the Bukharan Jews, and important trade and business links have developed between those that left for Israel after independence and those remaining.

The People's Republic of China sees the region as an essential future source of raw materials; most Central Asian countries are members of the Shanghai Cooperation Organization. This has affected Xinjiang and other parts of western China that have seen infrastructure programs building new links and also new military facilities. Chinese Central Asia has been far from the centre of that country's economic boom and the area has remained considerably poorer than the coast. China also sees a threat in the potential of the new states to support separatist movements among its own Turkic minorities.

One important Soviet legacy that has only gradually been appreciated is the vast ecological destruction. Most notable is the gradual drying of the Aral Sea. During the Soviet era, it was decided that the traditional crops of melons and vegetables would be replaced by water-intensive growing of cotton for Soviet textile mills. Massive irrigation efforts were launched that diverted a considerable percentage of the annual inflow to the sea, causing it to shrink steadily. Furthermore, vast tracts of Kazakhstan were used for nuclear testing, and there exists a plethora of decrepit factories and mines.

In the first part of 2008 Central Asia experienced a severe energy crisis, a shortage of both electricity and fuel, aggravated by abnormally cold temperatures, failing infrastructure, and a shortage of food in which aid from the west began to assist the region.

Further reading

- S. Frederick Starr, *Rediscovering Central Asia*[148]
- V.V. Barthold, *Turkestan Down to the Mongol Invasion* (London) 1968 (Third Edition)
- Brower, Daniel *Turkestan and the Fate of the Russian Empire* (London) 2003. <templatestyles src="Module:Citation/CS1/styles.css" />ISBN 0-415-29744-3
- Dani, A.H. and V.M. Masson eds. *UNESCO History of Civilizations of Central Asia*[149] (Paris: UNESCO) 1992–
- Hildinger, Erik. *Warriors of the Steppe: A Military History of Central Asia, 500 BC. to 1700 AD.* (Cambridge: Da Capo) 2001. <templatestyles src="Module:Citation/CS1/styles.css" />ISBN 0-306-81065-4
- Maitdinova, Guzel. The Dialogue of Civilizations in the Central Asian area of the Great Silk Route: Historical experience of integration and reference points of XXI century. Dushanbe: 2015.
- Maitdinova, Guzel. The Kirpand State – an Empire in Middle Asia. Dushanbe: 2011.
- O'Brien, Patrick K. (General Editor). *Oxford Atlas of World History*. New York: Oxford University Press, 2005.

- Olcott, Martha Brill. *Central Asia's New States: Independence, Foreign policy, and Regional security*. (Washington, D.C.: United States Institute of Peace Press) 1996. <templatestyles src="Module:Citation/CS1/styles.css" />ISBN 1-878379-51-8
- Sinor, Denis *The Cambridge History of Early Inner Asia* (Cambridge) 1990 (2nd Edition). <templatestyles src="Module:Citation/CS1/styles.css" />ISBN 0-521-24304-1
- В.В. Бартольд *История Культурной Жизни Туркестана*

(*"Istoriya Kul'turnoy zhizni Turkestana"*) (Москва) 1927

- Н.А. Халфин; *Россия и Ханства Средней Азии* (*"Rossiya i Hanstva Sredney Azii"*) (Москва) 1974
- Encyclopædia Iranica: Central Asia in pre-Islamic Times (R. Fryer)[150]
- Encyclopædia Iranica: Central Asia from the Islamic Period to the Mongol Conquest (C. Bosworth)[151]
- Encyclopædia Iranica: Central Asia in the Mongol and Timurid Periods (B. Spuler)[152]
- Encyclopædia Iranica: Central Asia from the 16th to the 18th centuries (R.D. McChesney)[153] Wikipedia:Link rot
- Encyclopædia Iranica: Central Asia in the 18th–19th centuries ([[Yuri Bregel[154]])]
- Center for the Study of Eurasian Nomads[155]

Notes

References

<templatestyles src="Template:Refbegin/styles.css" />

- Altschuler, Mordechai (1993), "Escape and Evacuation of Soviet Jews at the Time of the Nazi Invasion", in Lucjan Dobroszycki & Jeffrey S. Gurock, *The Holocaust in the Soviet Union*, New York, NY: M. E. Sharpe<templatestyles src="Module:Citation/CS1/styles.css"></templatestyles>
- Bahgat, Gawdat (March 2006), "Central Asia and Energy Security", *Asian Affairs*, Routledge – Taylor and Francis Group, **37** (1): 1–16, doi:10.1080/03068370500456819[156]<templatestyles src="Module:Citation/CS1/styles.css"></templatestyles>
- Beckwith, Christopher I. (1987), *The Tibetan Empire in Central Asia*, Princeton: Princeton University Press, ISBN 0-691-02469-3<templatestyles src="Module:Citation/CS1/styles.css"></templatestyles>

- Chang, Chun-shu (2007), *The Rise of the Chinese Empire: Volume II; Frontier, Immigration, & Empire in Han China, 130 B.C. – A.D. 157*, Ann Arbor, MI: University of Michigan Press, ISBN 0-472-11534-0<templatestyles src="Module:Citation/CS1/styles.css"></templatestyles>
- Cui, Mingde (2005), *The History of Chinese Heqin*, Beijing: Renmin Chubanshe, ISBN 7-01-004828-2<templatestyles src="Module:Citation/CS1/styles.css"></templatestyles>
- Di Cosmo, Nicola (2002), *Ancient China and Its Enemies: the Rise of Nomadic Power in East Asian History*, Cambridge: Cambridge University Press, ISBN 0-521-77064-5<templatestyles src="Module:Citation/CS1/styles.css"></templatestyles>
- Ebrey, Patricia Buckley; Walthall, Anne; Palais, James B. (2006), *East Asia: A Cultural, Social, and Political History*, Boston: Houghton Mifflin, ISBN 0-618-13384-4<templatestyles src="Module:Citation/CS1/styles.css"></templatestyles>
- Ebrey, Patricia Buckley (1999), *The Cambridge Illustrated History of China*, Cambridge: Cambridge University Press, ISBN 0-521-66991-X<templatestyles src="Module:Citation/CS1/styles.css"></templatestyles>
- Herodotus, *Histories*, IV. See original text in perseus project[157].
- Gernet, Jacques (1996), *A History of Chinese Civilization* (2nd ed.), New York: Cambridge University Press, doi: 10.2277/0521497817[158], ISBN 978-0-521-49781-7<templatestyles src="Module:Citation/CS1/styles.css"></templatestyles>
- Loewe, Michael (1986), "The Former Han Dynasty", in Denis Twitchett & Michael Loewe, *The Cambridge History of China: Volume I: the Ch'in and Han Empires, 221 B.C. – A.D. 220*, Cambridge: Cambridge University Press, pp. 103–222, ISBN 0-521-24327-0<templatestyles src="Module:Citation/CS1/styles.css"></templatestyles>
- Liu, Zhaoxiang (2000), *History of Military Legal System, et al.*, Beijing: Encyclopedia of China Publishing House, ISBN 7-5000-6303-2<templatestyles src="Module:Citation/CS1/styles.css"></templatestyles>
- Manley, Rebecca (2009), *To the Tashkent Station*, Ithaca, NY: Cornell University Press<templatestyles src="Module:Citation/CS1/styles.css"></templatestyles>
- Manning, R.; Jaffe, A. (1998), "The myth of the Caspian "Great Game": the real geopolitics of energy", *Survival: Global Politics and Strategy*, International Institute for Strategic Studies, **40** (4): 112–129, doi: 10.1080/713660015[159]<templatestyles src="Module:Citation/CS1/styles.css"></templatestyles>
- Polian, Pavel (2004), "Forced migrations during and after the Second World War (1939–1953)", *Against Their Will: the History and Geog-*

raphy of Forced Migrations in the USSR, Budapest: Central European University Press<templatestyles src="Module:Citation/CS1/styles.css"></templatestyles>
- Sen, Tansen (2003), *Buddhism, Diplomacy, and Trade: The Realignment of Sino-Indian Relations, 600–1400*, Manoa: Asian Interactions and Comparisons, a joint publication of the University of Hawaii Press and the Association for Asian Studies, ISBN 0-8248-2593-4<templatestyles src="Module:Citation/CS1/styles.css"></templatestyles>
- Soucek, Svat (2000), *A History of Inner Asia*, Cambridge: Cambridge University Press, ISBN 0-521-65169-7<templatestyles src="Module:Citation/CS1/styles.css"></templatestyles>
- Stein, R. A. (1972) [1962], *Tibetan Civilization* (1st English ed.), Stanford: Stanford University Press, ISBN 0-8047-0806-1<templatestyles src="Module:Citation/CS1/styles.css"></templatestyles>
- Twitchett, Denis (2000), "Tibet in Tang's Grand Strategy", in van de Ven, Hans, *Warfare in Chinese History*, Leiden: Koninklijke Brill, pp. 106–179, ISBN 90-04-11774-1<templatestyles src="Module:Citation/CS1/styles.css"></templatestyles>
- Whitfield, Susan (2004), *The Silk Road: Trade, Travel, War and Faith*, Chicago: Serindia, ISBN 1-932476-12-1<templatestyles src="Module:Citation/CS1/styles.css"></templatestyles>
- Xue, Zongzheng (薛宗正) (1992), *Turkic peoples (*突厥史 *)*, Beijing: 中国社会科学出版社 , ISBN 7-5004-0432-8<templatestyles src="Module:Citation/CS1/styles.css"></templatestyles>
- Yü, Ying-shih (1986), "Han Foreign Relations", in Denis Twitchett & Michael Loewe, *The Cambridge History of China: Volume I: the Ch'in and Han Empires, 221 B.C. – A.D. 220*, Cambridge: Cambridge University Press, pp. 377–462, ISBN 0-521-24327-0<templatestyles src="Module:Citation/CS1/styles.css"></templatestyles>

External links

- New Directions Post-Independence[160] from the Dean Peter Krogh Foreign Affairs Digital Archives[161]

Medieval India

Medieval India

Medieval India refers to a long period of the history of the Indian subcontinent between the "ancient period" and "modern period". Definitions of the period itself vary widely, and partly for this reason, many historians now prefer to avoid the term completely.[162]

One definition, used in the rest of this article, includes the period from the 8th century to the 16th century, essentially the same period as the Middle Ages of Europe. It may be divided into two periods: The 'early medieval period' which lasted from the 6th to the 13th century and the 'late medieval period' which lasted from the 13th to the 16th century, ending with the start of the Mughal Empire in 1526. The Mughal era, from the 16th century to the 18th century, is often referred to as the early modern period, but is sometimes also included in the 'late medieval' period.

An alternative definition, often seen in those more recent authors who still use the term at all, brings the start of the medieval period forward, either to about 1000 CE, or to the 12th century. The end may be pushed back to the 18th century, making the period in effect that between the start of Muslim domination (at least in northern India) and British India. Or the "early medieval" period is begun in the 8th century, ending with the 11th.[163]

The use of "medieval" at all as a term for periods in Indian history has often been objected to, and is probably becoming more rare (there is a similar discussion in terms of the history of China).[164] It is argued that neither the start nor the end of the period really mark fundamental changes in Indian history, comparable to the European equivalents.[165] Burton Stein still used the concept in his *A History of India* (1998, referring to the period from the Guptas to the Mughals), but most recent authors using it are Indian. Understandably, they often specify the period they cover within their titles.[166] The critic Peter Hardy argues that Muslim historiography on medieval India is often motivated by Islamic apologetics, which tries to justify "the life of medieval Muslims to the modern world".[167]

Early medieval period

The start of the period is typically taken to be the slow collapse of the Gupta Empire from about 480 to 550,[168] ending the "classical" period, as well as "ancient India",[169] although both these terms may be used for periods with widely different dates, especially in specialized fields such as the history of art or religion.[170] At least in northern India, there was no comparably large state until perhaps the Delhi Sultanate, or certainly the Mughal Empire,[171] but there were several different dynasties ruling large areas for long periods, as well as many other dynasties ruling smaller areas, often paying some form of tribute to larger states. John Keay puts the typical number of dynasties within the subcontinent at any one time at between 20 and 40,[172] not including local rajas.

- Rashtrakuta dynasty, was a Kannada Dynasty ruling large parts of the Indian subcontinent between the 6th and the 10th centuries and one who built World Heritage center Ellora, Maharashtra.
- Eastern Chalukyas, 7th to 12th centuries, a South Indian Kannada dynasty whose kingdom was located in the present-day Andhra Pradesh they were the descendants of Western Chalukyas.
- Pallava dynasty, rulers of Telugu and some Tamil areas from the 6th to 9th centuries.
- Pala Empire, the last major Buddhist rulers, from the 8th to 12th centuries in Bengal. Briefly controlled most of north India in the 9th century.
- Chola Empire, a South Indian empire which ruled from Tamil Nadu and extended to include South-east Asian territories at its height. From 9th century to 13th century.
- Empire of Harsha, a brief period of control of most of north India, from 601 to 647, under Harsha of the Vardhana dynasty.
- Western Chalukya Empire, ruled most of the western Deccan and some of South India, between the 10th and 12th centuries. Kannada-speaking, with capital at Badami.
- Kalachuri dynasty, ruled areas in Central India during 10th-12th centuries.
- Western Ganga dynasty, was an important ruling dynasty of ancient Karnataka, often under the overlordship of larger states, from about 350 to 1000 AD. The large monolithic Bahubali of Shravanabelagola was built during their rule.

- Eastern Ganga dynasty, was a royal dynasty ruling Odisha region who are descendants of Kannada Western Ganga Dynasty and Tamil Chola Empire. They have built famous Konark Sun Temple and Jagannath Temple, Puri.
- Hoysala Empire, a prominent South Indian Kannadiga empire that ruled most of the modern day state of Karnataka between the 10th and the 14th centuries. The capital of the Hoysalas was initially located at Belur but was later moved to Halebidu.
- Kakatiya Kingdom, a Telugu dynasty that ruled most of current day Andhra Pradesh, India from 1083 to 1323 CE.
- The Sena dynasty, was a Hindu dynasty that ruled from Bengal through the 11th and 12th centuries. The empire at its peak covered much of the north-eastern region of the Indian subcontinent. The rulers of the Sena Dynasty traced their origin to the south Indian region of Karnataka.

Late medieval era

- Delhi Sultanate, five short-lived dynasties, based in Delhi, from 1206 to 1526, when it fell to the Mughal Empire.
- Bengal Sultanate, 1352 to 1576, ruled over Bengal and much of Burma.
- Ahom Kingdom, 1228–1826, Brahmaputra valley in Assam, resisted the Mughals, eventually taken by the British.
- Reddy Kingdom, 1325 to 1448, in Andhra Pradesh.
- Seuna (Yadava) dynasty, 1190-1315, an old Kannada-Maratha dynasty, which at its peak ruled a kingdom stretching from the Tungabhadra to the Narmada rivers, including present-day Maharashtra, north Karnataka and parts of Madhya Pradesh, from its capital at Devagiri.
- Rajput States, were a group of Rajput Hindu states that ruled present-day Rajasthan, and at times much of Madhya Pradesh, Gujarat, Uttaranchal, Himachal Pradesh, Western Uttar Pradesh and Central Uttar Pradesh. Many Rajput kingdoms continued under the Mughals and as Princely States in British India until Indian independence.
- Vijayanagara Empire, 1336–1646, a Hindu-Kannadiga empire based in Karnataka, in the Deccan Plateau region. UNESCO World Heritage site Hampi in Karnataka district of Bellary was their capital city.
- Gajapati Kingdom, was a medieval Hindu dynasty that ruled over Kalinga (the present day Orissa).

Early modern era

The start of the Mughal Empire in 1526 marked the beginning of the early modern period of Indian history, often referred to as the Mughal era. Sometimes, the Mughal era is also referred to as the 'late medieval' period.

- Mughal Empire, was an imperial state founded by Babar, who had Turco-Mongol origin from Central Asia. The empire ruled most of the Indian subcontinent from 16th to 18th century, though it lingered for another century, formally ending in 1857.
- Maratha Empire, was an imperial power based in modern-day Maharashtra in western India. Marathas replaced the Mughal rule over large parts of India in the 18th century, but lost the Anglo-Maratha Wars in the early 19th century, and became rulers of Princely States.
- Kingdom of Mysore, was a Kannada kingdom have been founded in 1399 in the vicinity of the modern city of Mysore. Fully independent after the fall of the Vijayanagara Empire in 1646, reduced in size by the British, but ruled until 1947.
- Nayak dynasty of Kannada, Telugu, Tamil kings ruled parts of south India after the fall of the Vijayanagara Empire in 1646. Their contribution can be seen in Ikkeri, Sri Ranga, Madurai, and Chitradurga.
- Sikh Empire, was a major power in the Northwestern part of the Indian subcontinent, which arose under the leadership of Maharaja Ranjit Singh in the Punjab region. They were usurped by the British East India Company between early and mid 19th century, following the British victory in the Anglo-Sikh wars.

References

- Avari, Burjor, *India: The Ancient Past: A History of the Indian Subcontinent from C. 7000 BCE to CE 1200*, 2016 (2nd edn), Routledge, <templatestyles src="Module:Citation/CS1/styles.css" />ISBN 1317236734, 9781317236733, google books[173]
- Farooqui, Salma Ahmed, *A Comprehensive History of Medieval India: From Twelfth to the Mid-Eighteenth Century*, 2011, Pearson Education India, <templatestyles src="Module:Citation/CS1/styles.css" />ISBN 8131732029, 9788131732021, google books[174]
- Harle, J.C., *The Art and Architecture of the Indian Subcontinent*, 2nd edn. 1994, Yale University Press Pelican History of Art, <templatestyles src="Module:Citation/CS1/styles.css" />ISBN 0300062176
- Keay, John, *India, a History*, 2000, HarperCollins, <templatestyles src="Module:Citation/CS1/styles.css" />ISBN 0002557177

- Michell, George, (1977) *The Hindu Temple: An Introduction to its Meaning and Forms*, 1977, University of Chicago Press, <templatestyles src="Module:Citation/CS1/styles.css" />ISBN 978-0-226-53230-1
- Rowland, Benjamin, *The Art and Architecture of India: Buddhist, Hindu, Jain*, 1967 (3rd edn.), Pelican History of Art, Penguin, <templatestyles src="Module:Citation/CS1/styles.css" />ISBN 0140561021

Further reading

<templatestyles src="Template:Refbegin/styles.css" />

- Satish Chandra; Historiography, Religion and State in Medieval India, Har-Anand Publications, 2010.
- Elliot and Dowson: The History of India as told by its own Historians, New Delhi reprint, 1990.
- Elliot, Sir H. M., Edited by Dowson, John. The History of India, as Told by Its Own Historians. The Muhammadan Period; published by London Trubner Company 1867–1877. (Online Copy: The History of India, as Told by Its Own Historians. The Muhammadan Period; by Sir H. M. Elliot; Edited by John Dowson; London Trubner Company 1867–1877[175] – This online Copy has been posted by: The Packard Humanities Institute; Persian Texts in Translation; Also find other historical books: Author List and Title List[176])
- Gommans, Jos J. L. (2002), Mughal Warfare: Indian Frontiers and Highroads to Empire, 1500-1700, Routledge, <templatestyles src="Module:Citation/CS1/styles.css" />ISBN 0-415-23989-3.
- Lal, K. S. (1999). Theory and practice of Muslim state in India. New Delhi: Aditya Prakashan.
- Majumdar, Ramesh Chandra; Pusalker, A. D.; Majumdar, A. K., eds. (1960). *The History and Culture of the Indian People*. VI: The Delhi Sultanate. Bombay: Bharatiya Vidya Bhavan.<templatestyles src="Module:Citation/CS1/styles.css"></templatestyles>
- Majumdar, Ramesh Chandra; Pusalker, A. D.; Majumdar, A. K., eds. (1973). *The History and Culture of the Indian People*. VII: The Mughal Empire. Bombay: Bharatiya Vidya Bhavan.<templatestyles src="Module:Citation/CS1/styles.css"></templatestyles>
- Misra, R. G. (1993). Indian resistance to early Muslim invaders up to 1206 AD. Meerut City: Anu Books.
- Sarkar, Jadunath. (1997). Fall of the Mughal Empire: Vol. 1-4. Hyderabad: Orient Longman.
- Sarkar, Jadunath. (1975). Studies in economic life in Mughal India. Delhi: Oriental Publishers & Distributors.; (1987). Mughal economy: Organization and working. Calcutta, India: Naya Prokash.

- Srivastava, A. L. (1970). The Mughal Empire, 1526-1803 A.D. ... Seventh revised edition. Agra: Shiva Lal Agarwala & Co.
- Srivastava, A. L. (1975). Medieval Indian culture. Agra: Agarwala.
- Wink, André (2004). *Indo-Islamic society: 14th - 15th centuries*[177]. Volume 3 of Al-Hind Series. BRILL. ISBN 9004135618. Retrieved 24 April 2014.<templatestyles src="Module:Citation/CS1/styles.css"></templatestyles>
- Wink, André (1996). Al-Hind: The Making of the Indo-Islamic Worlds Vol 1. E. J. Brill. <templatestyles src="Module:Citation/CS1/styles.css" />ISBN 0-391-04173-8.

Primary Sources

- Babur, ., & Thackston, W. M. (2002). The Baburnama: Memoirs of Babur, prince and emperor. New York: Modern Library.
- Muḥammad, A. K., & Pandit, K. N. (2009). A Muslim missionary in mediaeval Kashmir: Being the English translation of Tohfatu'l-ahbab.
- V. S. Bhatnagar (1991). *Kānhaḍade Prabandha, India's Greatest Patriotic Saga of Medieval Times: Padmanābha's Epic Account of Kānhaḍade*. Aditya Prakashan. ISBN 978-81-85179-54-4.<templatestyles src="Module:Citation/CS1/styles.css"></templatestyles>
- Jain, M. The India They Saw : Foreign Accounts (4 Volumes) Delhi: Ocean Books, 2011.

External links.com

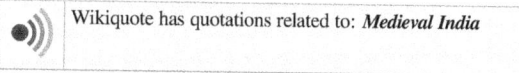

Wikiquote has quotations related to: *Medieval India*

- Online Copy: The History of India, as Told by Its Own Historians. The Muhammadan Period; by Sir H. M. Elliot; Edited by John Dowson; London Trubner Company 1867–1877[175] – This online Copy has been postesd by: The Packard Humanities Institute; Persian Texts in Translation; Also find other historical books: Author List and Title List[176]

Medieval China

History of China

<indicator name="pp-default"> 🔒 </indicator>

History of China
ANCIENT
Neolithic c. 8500 – c. 2070 BC
Xia dynasty c. 2070 – c. 1600 BC
Shang dynasty c. 1600 – c. 1046 BC
Zhou dynasty c. 1046 – 256 BC
Western Zhou
Eastern Zhou
Spring and Autumn
Warring States
IMPERIAL
Qin dynasty 221–206 BC
Han dynasty 206 BC – 220 AD
Western Han
Xin dynasty
Eastern Han
Three Kingdoms 220–280
Wei, Shu and Wu
Jin dynasty 265–420

Western Jin		
Eastern Jin	Sixteen Kingdoms	
Northern and Southern dynasties 420–589		
Sui dynasty 581–618		
Tang dynasty 618–907		
(Second Zhou dynasty 690–705)		
Five Dynasties and Ten Kingdoms 907–960	Liao dynasty 907–1125	
Song dynasty 960–1279		
Northern Song		Western Xia
Southern Song	Jin	
Yuan dynasty 1271–1368		
Ming dynasty 1368–1644		
Qing dynasty 1644–1912		
MODERN		
Republic of China 1912–1949		
People's Republic of China 1949–present		
Related articles • Chinese historiography • Timeline of Chinese history • Dynasties in Chinese history • Linguistic history • Art history • Economic history • Education history • Science and technology history • Legal history • Media history • Military history • Naval history		
• view • talk • edit[178]		

The earliest known written records of the **history of China** date from as early as 1250 BC,[179,180] from the Shang dynasty (c. 1600–1046 BC). Ancient historical texts such as the *Records of the Grand Historian* (c. 100 BC) and the *Bamboo Annals* (296 BC) describe a Xia dynasty (c. 2070–1600 BC) before the Shang, but no writing is known from the period, and Shang writings do not indicate the existence of the Xia. The Shang ruled in the Yellow River valley, which is commonly held to be the cradle of Chinese civilization. However, Neolithic civilizations originated at various cultural centers along both the Yellow

History of China

Figure 45: *Along the River During the Qingming Festival (Qing Court Version). The original version dated to the Song dynasty (960–1279 CE). It captures the daily life of people and the landscape of the capital, Bianjing (present-day Kaifeng) during the Northern Song.*

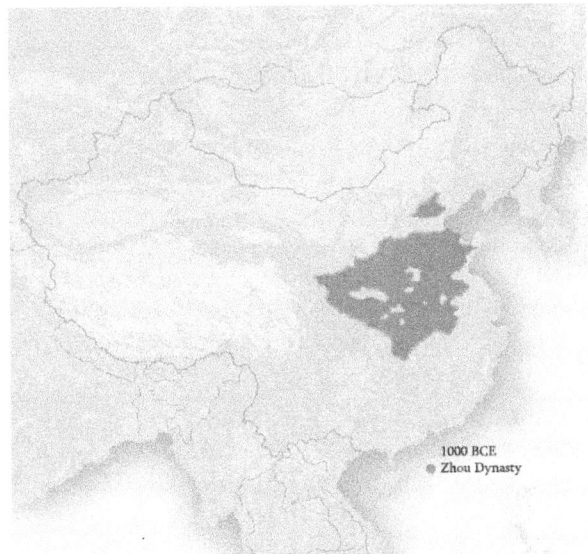

Figure 46: *Approximate territories occupied by the various dynasties and states throughout the history of China*

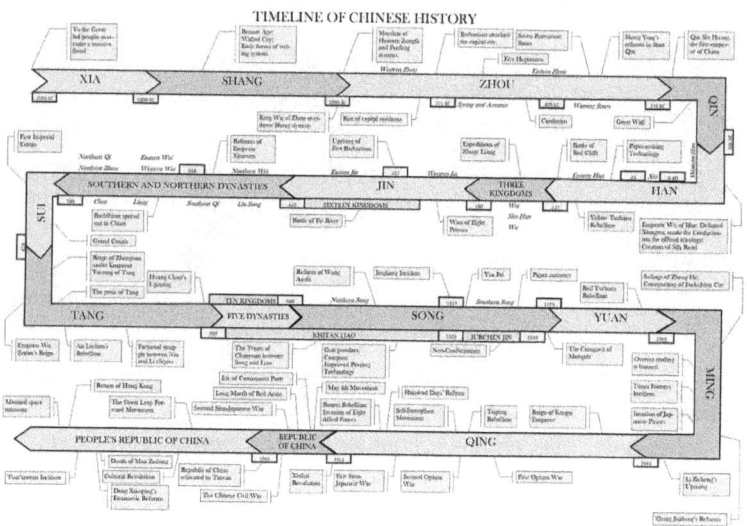

Figure 47: *Timeline of Chinese history*

River and Yangtze River. These Yellow River and Yangtze civilizations arose millennia before the Shang. With thousands of years of continuous history, China is one of the world's oldest civilizations, and is regarded as one of the cradles of civilization.[181]

The Zhou dynasty (1046–256 BC) supplanted the Shang, and introduced the concept of the Mandate of Heaven to justify their rule. The central Zhou government began to weaken due to external and internal pressures in the 8th century BC, and the country eventually splintered into smaller states during the Spring and Autumn period. These states became independent and warred with one another in the following Warring States period. Much of traditional Chinese culture, literature and philosophy first developed during those troubled times.

In 221 BC Qin Shi Huang conquered the various warring states and created for himself the title of *Huangdi* or "emperor" of the Qin, marking the beginning of imperial China. However, the oppressive government fell soon after his death, and was supplanted by the longer lived Han dynasty (206 BC–220 AD). Successive dynasties developed bureaucratic systems that enabled the emperor to control vast territories directly. In the 21 centuries from 206 BC until AD 1912, routine administrative tasks were handled by a special elite of *scholar-officials*. Young men, well-versed in calligraphy, history, literature,

History of China

and philosophy, were carefully selected through difficult government examinations. China's last dynasty was the Qing (1644–1912), which was replaced by the Republic of China in 1912, and in the mainland by the People's Republic of China in 1949, resulting in two *de facto* states claiming to be the legitimate government of all China.

Chinese history has alternated between periods of political unity and peace, and periods of war and failed statehood – the most recent being the Chinese Civil War (1927–1949). China was occasionally dominated by steppe peoples, most of whom were eventually assimilated into the Han Chinese culture and population. Between eras of multiple kingdoms and warlordism, Chinese dynasties have ruled parts or all of China; in some eras control stretched as far as Xinjiang and Tibet, as at present. Traditional culture, and influences from other parts of Asia and the Western world (carried by waves of immigration, cultural assimilation, expansion, and foreign contact), form the basis of the modern culture of China.

Prehistory

Paleolithic (3.3 Ma ∼ 12 ka)

<templatestyles src="Multiple_image/styles.css" />

Linheraptor, a genus of dromaeosaurid dinosaur which lived in what is now China in the Late Cretaceous.

Tarbosaurus, a genus of tyrannosaurid theropod dinosaur that lived at the end of the Late Cretaceous Period. Fossils have been recovered in the Gobi Desert.

What is now China was inhabited by *Homo erectus* more than a million years ago. Recent study shows that the stone tools found at Xiaochangliang site are magnetostratigraphically dated to 1.36 million years ago. The archaeological site of Xihoudu in Shanxi Province is the earliest recorded use of fire by *Homo erectus*, which is dated 1.27 million years ago. The excavations at Yuanmou and later Lantian show early habitation. Perhaps the most famous specimen of *Homo erectus* found in China is the so-called Peking Man discovered in 1923–27. Fossilised teeth of *Homo sapiens* dating to 125,000–80,000 BC have been discovered in Fuyan Cave in Dao County in Hunan.

Neolithic

<templatestyles src="Multiple_image/styles.css" />

Neolithic

10,000 years old pottery, Xianren Cave culture (18000–7000BC)

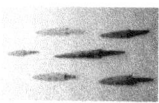

Bone Arrowheads, Peiligang culture (7000-5000 BC)

Butterfly-shaped ivory vessel with the pattern of two birds facing the sun, Hemudu culture (5500-3300 BC)

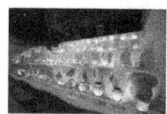

Pottery artifacts from the Hemudu culture.

The Neolithic age in China can be traced back to about 18,000 BC.

Early evidence for proto-Chinese millet agriculture is radiocarbon-dated to about 7000 BC. The earliest evidence of cultivated rice, found by the Yangtze River, is carbon-dated to 8,000 years ago. Farming gave rise to the Jiahu culture (7000 to 5800 BC). At Damaidi in Ningxia, 3,172 cliff carvings dating to 6000–5000 BC have been discovered, "featuring 8,453 individual characters such as the sun, moon, stars, gods and scenes of hunting or grazing". These pictographs are reputed to be similar to the earliest characters confirmed to be written Chinese. Chinese proto-writing existed in Jiahu around 7000 BC, Dadiwan from 5800 BC to 5400 BC, Damaidi around 6000 BC[182] and Banpo dating from the 5th millennium BC. Some scholars have suggested that Jiahu symbols (7th millennium BC) were the earliest Chinese writing system. Excavation of a Peiligang culture site in Xinzheng county, Henan, found a community that flourished in 5,500 to 4,900 BC, with evidence of agriculture, constructed buildings, pottery, and burial of the dead. With agriculture came increased population, the ability to store and redistribute crops, and the potential to support specialist craftsmen and administrators. In late Neolithic times, the Yellow River valley began to establish itself as a center of Yangshao culture (5000 BC to 3000 BC), and the first villages were founded; the most archaeologically significant of these was found at Banpo, Xi'an. Later, Yangshao culture was superseded by the Longshan culture, which was also centered on the Yellow River from about 3000 BC to 2000 BC.

Bronze Age

<templatestyles src="Multiple_image/styles.css" />

Bronze Age

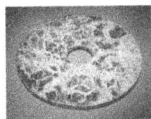

Jade bi from the Liangzhu culture (3400–2250 BC).

Bronze *jue* (wine vessel) from Erlitou culture (1900–1500 BC).

Bronze artifacts have been found at the Majiayao culture site (between 3100 and 2700 BC), The Bronze Age is also represented at the Lower Xiajiadian culture (2200–1600 BC[183]) site in northeast China. Sanxingdui located in what is now Sichuan province is believed to be the site of a major ancient city, of a previously unknown Bronze Age culture (between 2000 and 1200 BC). The site was first discovered in 1929 and then re-discovered in 1986. Chinese archaeologists have identified the Sanxingdui culture to be part of the ancient kingdom of Shu, linking the artifacts found at the site to its early legendary kings.

Ferrous metallurgy begins to appear in the late 6th century in the Yangzi Valley.[184] An bronze tomahawk with a blade of meteoric iron excavated near the city of Gaocheng in Shijiazhuang (now Hebei province) has been dated to the 14th century BC. For this reason, authors such as Liana Chua and Mark Elliott have used the term "Iron Age" by convention for the transitional period of c. 500 BC to 100 BC, roughly corresponding to the Warring States period of Chinese historiography.[185] An Iron Age culture of the Tibetan Plateau has tentatively been associated with the Zhang Zhung culture described in early Tibetan writings.

Ancient China

Xia dynasty (2070–1600 BC)

The Xia dynasty of China (from c. 2070 to c. 1600 BC) is the first dynasty to be described in ancient historical records such as Sima Qian's *Records of the Grand Historian* and *Bamboo Annals*.

The dynasty was considered mythical by historians until scientific excavations found early Bronze Age sites at Erlitou, Henan in 1959.[186] With few clear records matching the Shang oracle bones, it remains unclear whether these sites are the remains of the Xia dynasty or of another culture from the same period. Excavations that overlap the alleged time period of the Xia indicate a type of culturally similar groupings of chiefdoms. Early markings from this period found on pottery and shells are thought to be ancestral to modern Chinese characters.[187]

According to ancient records, the dynasty ended around 1600 BC as a consequence of the Battle of Mingtiao.

Shang dynasty (1600–1046 BC)

<templatestyles src="Multiple_image/styles.css" />

Shang dynasty (1600–1046 BC)

Map of the Shang Dynasty

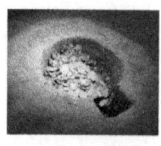

Oracle bones pit at Yin

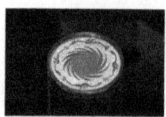

The Golden Sun Bird, a ring-shaped piece of foil, made of nearly pure gold. Late Sanxingdui culture (Shang Period).

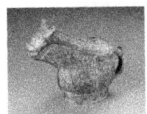

Guang, a Shang Period ritual Wine Vessel.

<templatestyles src="Multiple_image/styles.css" />

Bronze square ding (cauldron) with human faces

Ding, a Shang dynasty bronze

Bronze Battle Axe, Shang Dynasty (1600 - 1046 B.C.). Excavated at Yidu, Shangdong Province.

Archaeological findings providing evidence for the existence of the Shang dynasty, c. 1600–1046 BC, are divided into two sets. The first set, from the earlier Shang period, comes from sources at Erligang, Zhengzhou, and Shangcheng. The second set, from the later Shang or Yin (殷) period, is at Anyang, in modern-day Henan, which has been confirmed as the last of the Shang's nine capitals (c. 1300–1046 BC).Wikipedia:Citation needed The findings at Anyang include the earliest written record of Chinese past so far discovered: inscriptions of divination records in ancient Chinese writing on the bones or shells of animals — the "oracle bones", dating from around 1250 BC.

A series of thirty-one kings reigned over the Shang dynasty. During their reign, according to the *Records of the Grand Historian*, the capital city was moved six times.[188] The final (and most important) move was to Yin in 1350 BC which led to the dynasty's golden age. The term Yin dynasty has been synonymous with the Shang dynasty in history, although it has lately been used to refer specifically to the latter half of the Shang dynasty.

Chinese historians living in later periods were accustomed to the notion of one dynasty succeeding another, but the actual political situation in early China is known to have been much more complicated. Hence, as some scholars of China suggest, the Xia and the Shang can possibly refer to political entities that existed concurrently, just as the early Zhou is known to have existed at the same time as the Shang.Wikipedia:Citation needed

Although written records found at Anyang confirm the existence of the Shang dynasty, Western scholars are often hesitant to associate settlements that are contemporaneous with the Anyang settlement with the Shang dynasty. For example, archaeological findings at Sanxingdui suggest a technologically advanced civilization culturally unlike Anyang. The evidence is inconclusive in proving how far the Shang realm extended from Anyang. The leading hypothesis is that Anyang, ruled by the same Shang in the official history, coexisted and traded with numerous other culturally diverse settlements in the area that is now referred to as China proper.Wikipedia:Citation needed

Zhou dynasty (1046–256 BC)

<templatestyles src="Multiple_image/styles.css" />

Zhou dynasty (1046–256 BC)

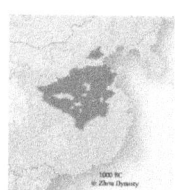

The approximate territory of the Zhou dynasty in China.

Spear of Fuchai

Bronze ritual vessel (You), Western Zhou dynasty

Ji, a Chinese polearm combining a spear and dagger-axe, Zhou dynasty (1046–256 BC)

The Zhou dynasty (1046 BC to approximately 256 BC) was the longest-lasting dynasty in Chinese history. By the end of the 2nd millennium BC, the Zhou dynasty began to emerge in the Yellow River valley, overrunning the territory of the Shang. The Zhou appeared to have begun their rule under a semi-feudal system. The Zhou lived west of the Shang, and the Zhou leader had been appointed Western Protector by the Shang. The ruler of the Zhou, King Wu, with the assistance of his brother, the Duke of Zhou, as regent, managed to defeat the Shang at the Battle of Muye.

The king of Zhou at this time invoked the concept of the Mandate of Heaven to legitimize his rule, a concept that would be influential for almost every succeeding dynasty.Wikipedia:Citation needed Like Shangdi, Heaven (*tian*) ruled over all the other gods, and it decided who would rule China.Wikipedia:Citation needed It was believed that a ruler had lost the Mandate of Heaven when natural disasters occurred in great number, and when, more realistically, the sovereign had apparently lost his concern for the people. In response, the royal house would be overthrown, and a new house would rule, having been granted the Mandate of Heaven.

The Zhou initially moved their capital west to an area near modern Xi'an, on the Wei River, a tributary of the Yellow River, but they would preside over a series of expansions into the Yangtze River valley. This would be the first of many population migrations from north to south in Chinese history.

Spring and Autumn period (722–476 BC)

<templatestyles src="Multiple_image/styles.css" />

Spring and Autumn period (722–476 BC)

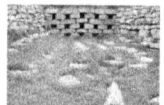

Map of the Five Hegemons during the
Spring and Autumn period of Zhou Dynasty

Remains of city sewer passing underneath the former
city wall in Ancient Linzi, Spring and Autumn period.

Sword of Goujian, Hubei Provincial Museum

The Sun Gao Bianzhong, Spring and Autumn period (770-476 B.C.), excavated in 1978 from a tomb in Yingchuan, Henan.

Capitals: several (multiple states)

In the 8th century BC, power became decentralized during the Spring and Autumn period, named after the influential *Spring and Autumn Annals*. In this period, local military leaders used by the Zhou began to assert their power and vie for hegemony. The situation was aggravated by the invasion of other peoples from the northwest, such as the Qin, forcing the Zhou to move their capital east to Luoyang. This marks the second major phase of the Zhou dynasty: the Eastern Zhou. The Spring and Autumn period is marked by a falling apart of the central Zhou power. In each of the hundreds of states that eventually arose, local strongmen held most of the political power and continued their subservience to the Zhou kings in name only. Some local leaders even started using royal titles for themselves. China now consisted of hundreds of states, some of them only as large as a village with a fort.

As the era continued, larger and more powerful states annexed or claimed suzerainty over smaller ones. By the 6th century BC most small states had disappeared from being annexed and just a few large and powerful principalities dominated China. Some southern states, such as Chu and Wu, claimed independence from the Zhou, who undertook wars against some of them (Wu and Yue). Many new cities were established in this period and Chinese culture was slowly shaped.

Once all these powerful rulers had firmly established themselves within their respective dominions, the bloodshed focused more fully on interstate conflict in the Warring States period, which began when the three remaining élite families in the Jin state – Zhao, Wei and Han – partitioned the state. Many famous individuals such as Lao Zi, Confucius and Sun Tzu lived during this chaotic period.

The Hundred Schools of Thought of Chinese philosophy blossomed during this period, and such influential intellectual movements as Confucianism, Taoism, Legalism and Mohism were founded, partly in response to the changing political world. The first two philosophical thoughts would have an enormous influence on Chinese culture.

Warring States period (476–221 BC)

<templatestyles src="Multiple_image/styles.css" />

Warring States period (476–221 BC)

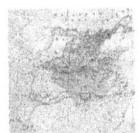

Map of the Warring States. Qin is shown in pink

Bronze halberd - Duo Ge Tong Ji, Warring States period (457-221 B.C.), excavated in 1994 in Henan.

Bi disc with a dual dragon motif, Warring States period

A cup carved from crystal, unearthed at Banshan, Hangzhou.

After further political consolidation, seven prominent states remained by the end of 5th century BC, and the years in which these few states battled each other are known as the Warring States period. Though there remained a nominal Zhou king until 256 BC, he was largely a figurehead and held little real power.

Numerous developments were made during this period in culture and mathematics, examples include an important literary achievement, the Zuo Commentary on the Spring and Autumn Annals, which summarizes the preceding Spring and Autumn period and the bundle of 21 bamboo slips from the Tsinghua collection, which was invented during this period dated to 305 BC, are the worlds' earliest example of a two digit decimal multiplication table, indicating that sophisticated commercial arithmetic was already established during this period.[189]

As neighboring territories of these warring states, including areas of modern Sichuan and Liaoning, were annexed, they were governed under the new local administrative system of commandery and prefecture. This system had been in use since the Spring and Autumn period, and parts can still be seen in the modern system of Sheng & Xian (province and county).

The final expansion in this period began during the reign of Ying Zheng, the king of Qin. His unification of the other six powers, and further annexations in the modern regions of Zhejiang, Fujian, Guangdong and Guangxi in 214 BC, enabled him to proclaim himself the First Emperor (Qin Shi Huang).

Imperial China

The Imperial China Period can be divided into three subperiods: Early, Middle, and Late.

Major events in the Early subperiod include the Qin unification of China and their replacement by the Han, the First Split followed by the Jin unification, and the loss of north China. The Middle subperiod was marked by the Sui unification and their supplementation by the Tang, the Second Split, and the Song unification. The Late subperiod included the Yuan, Ming, and Qing dynasties.

Qin dynasty (221–207 BC)

<templatestyles src="Multiple_image/styles.css" />

Qin dynasty (221–207 BC)

The territory of Qin dynasty, 210BCE.

The Terracotta Army of Qin Shi Huang

Dujiangyan, an irrigation project completed in 256 BC during the Warring States period of China by the State of Qin.

Ruins of the ancient Great Wall of Qi on Dafeng Mountain in the Changqing District of Jinan, Shandong province, dated back to the Warring States period

Historians often refer to the period from Qin dynasty to the end of Qing dynasty as Imperial China. Though the unified reign of the First Qin Emperor lasted only 12 years, he managed to subdue great parts of what constitutes the core of the Han Chinese homeland and to unite them under a tightly centralized Legalist government seated at Xianyang (close to modern Xi'an). The doctrine of Legalism that guided the Qin emphasized strict adherence to a legal code and the absolute power of the emperor. This philosophy, while effective for expanding the empire in a military fashion, proved unworkable for governing it in peacetime. The Qin Emperor presided over the brutal silencing of political opposition, including the event known as the burning of books and burying of scholars. This would be the impetus behind the later Han synthesis incorporating the more moderate schools of political governance.

Terracotta Army General (Left), Mid-rank officer of the Terracotta Army in Xi'an (Right)

Major contributions of the Qin include the concept of a centralized government, and the unification and development of the legal code, the written language, measurement, and currency of China after the tribulations of the Spring and Autumn and Warring States periods. Even something as basic as the length of axles for carts—which need to match ruts in the roads—had to be made uniform to ensure a viable trading system throughout the empire. Also as part of its centralization, the Qin connected the northern border walls of the states it defeated, making the first Great Wall of China.

A major Qin innovationWikipedia:Citation needed that lasted until 1912 was reliance upon a trained intellectual elite, the *Scholar-official* ("Scholar-gentlemen"). They were civil servants appointed by the Emperor to handle daily governance. Talented young men were selected through an elaborate process of imperial examination. They had to demonstrate skill at calligraphy, and had to know Confucian philosophy. Historian Wing-Tsit Chan concludes that:

> Generally speaking, the record of these scholar-gentlemen has been a worthy one. It was good enough to be praised and imitated in 18th century Europe. Nevertheless, it has given China a tremendous handicap in their transition from government by men to government by law, and personal considerations in Chinese government have been a curse.

After Emperor Qin Shi Huang's unnatural death due to the consumption of mercury pills, the Qin government drastically deteriorated and eventually capitulated in 207 BC after the Qin capital was captured and sacked by rebels, which would ultimately lead to the establishment of a new dynasty of a unified China.[190] Despite the short 15-year duration of the Qin dynasty, it was immensely influential on China and the structure of future Chinese dynasties.

Han dynasty (202 BC–AD 220)

<templatestyles src="Multiple_image/styles.css" />

Han dynasty (202 BC–AD 220)

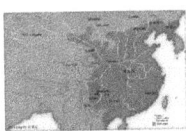

The territory of Han dynasty, 2nd century CE.

The ruins of a Han-dynasty watchtower made of rammed earth at Dunhuang, the eastern end of the Silk Road.

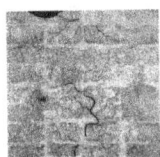

An early Western-Han silk map, depicting the Kingdom of Changsha and Kingdom of Nanyue in southern China.

A mural showing women dressed in traditional *Hanfu* silk robes, from the Dahuting Tomb of the late Eastern Han dynasty (25–220 AD), located in Zhengzhou, Henan province, China

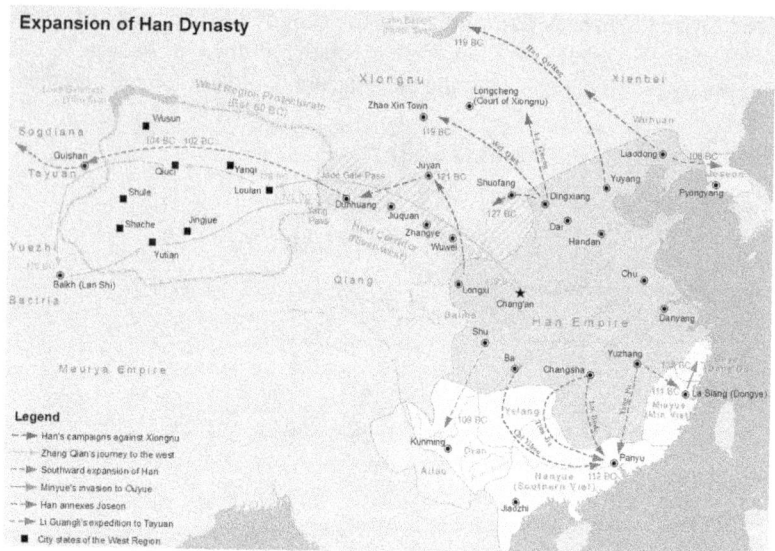

Figure 48: *Map showing the expansion of Han dynasty in 2nd century BC.*

Western Han

The Han dynasty was founded by Liu Bang, who emerged victorious in the Chu–Han Contention that followed the fall of the Qin dynasty. A golden age in Chinese history, the Han dynasty's long period of stability and prosperity consolidated the foundation of China as a unified state under a central imperial bureaucracy, which was to last intermittently for most of the next two millennia. During the Han dynasty, territory of China was extended to most of the China proper and to areas far west. Confucianism was officially elevated to orthodox status and was to shape the subsequent Chinese civilization. Art, culture and science all advanced to unprecedented heights. With the profound and lasting impacts of this period of Chinese history, the dynasty name "Han" had been taken as the name of the Chinese people, now the dominant ethnic group in modern China, and had been commonly used to refer to Chinese language and written characters. The Han dynasty also saw many mathematical innovations being invented such as the method of Gaussian elimination which appeared in the Chinese mathematical text Chapter Eight *Rectangular Arrays* of *The Nine Chapters on the Mathematical Art*. Its use is illustrated in eighteen problems, with two to five equations. The first reference to the book by this title is dated to 179 AD, but parts of it were written as early as approximately 150 BC, more than 1500 years before the Europeans came up with the method in the 18th century.[191]

After the initial Laissez-faire policies of Emperors Wen and Jing, the ambitious Emperor Wu brought the empire to its zenith. To consolidate his power, Confucianism, which emphasizes stability and order in a well-structured society, was given exclusive patronage to be the guiding philosophical thoughts and moral principles of the empire. Imperial Universities were established to support its study and further development, while other schools of thought were discouraged.

<templatestyles src="Multiple_image/styles.css" />

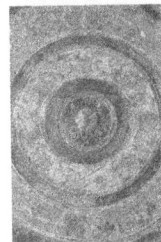

Left image: Western-Han painted ceramic jar decorated with raised reliefs of dragons, phoenixes, and *taotie*
Right image: Reverse side of a Western-Han bronze mirror with painted designs of a flower motif

Major military campaigns were launched to weaken the nomadic Xiongnu Empire, limiting their influence north of the Great Wall. Along with the diplomatic efforts led by Zhang Qian, the sphere of influence of the Han Empire extended to the states in the Tarim Basin, opened up the Silk Road that connected China to the west, stimulating bilateral trade and cultural exchange. To the south, various small kingdoms far beyond the Yangtze River Valley were formally incorporated into the empire.

<templatestyles src="Multiple_image/styles.css" />

A Chinese crossbow mechanism with a buttplate from either the late Warring States Period or the early Han dynasty; made of bronze and inlaid with silver

Emperor Wu also dispatched a series of military campaigns against the Baiyue tribes. The Han annexed Minyue in 135 BC and 111 BC, Nanyue in 111 BC, and Dian in 109 BC. Migration and military expeditions led to the cultural assimilation of the south. It also brought the Han into contact with kingdoms in Southeast Asia, introducing diplomacy and trade.

After Emperor Wu, the empire slipped into gradual stagnation and decline. Economically, the state treasury was strained by excessive campaigns and projects, while land acquisitions by elite families gradually drained the tax base. Various consort clans exerted increasing control over strings of incompetent emperors and eventually the dynasty was briefly interrupted by the usurpation of Wang Mang.

Xin dynasty

In AD 9, the usurper Wang Mang claimed that the Mandate of Heaven called for the end of the Han dynasty and the rise of his own, and he founded the short-lived Xin ("New") dynasty. Wang Mang started an extensive program of land and other economic reforms, including the outlawing of slavery and land nationalization and redistribution. These programs, however, were never supported by the landholding families, because they favored the peasants. The instability of power brought about chaos, uprisings, and loss of territories. This was compounded by mass flooding of the Yellow River; silt buildup caused it to split into two channels and displaced large numbers of farmers. Wang Mang was eventually killed in Weiyang Palace by an enraged peasant mob in AD 23.

Eastern Han

Emperor Guangwu reinstated the Han dynasty with the support of landholding and merchant families at Luoyang, *east* of the former capital Xi'an. Thus, this new era is termed the Eastern Han dynasty. With the capable administrations of Emperors Ming and Zhang, former glories of the dynasty was reclaimed, with brilliant military and cultural achievements. The Xiongnu Empire was decisively defeated. The diplomat and general Ban Chao further expanded the conquests across the Pamirs to the shores of the Caspian Sea,[192] thus reopening the Silk Road, and bringing trade, foreign cultures, along with the arrival of Buddhism. With extensive connections with the west, the first of several

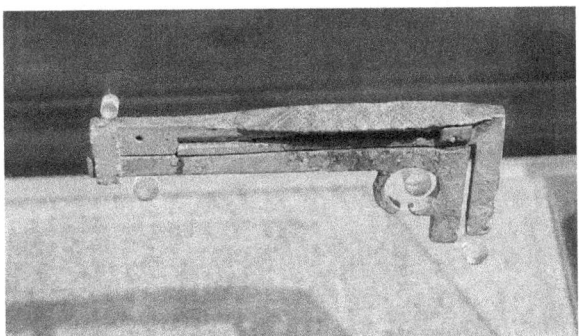

Figure 49: *A bronze caliper from the Eastern Han period.*

Roman embassies to China were recorded in Chinese sources, coming from the sea route in AD 166, and a second one in AD 284.

The Eastern Han dynasty was one of the most prolific era of science and technology in ancient China, notably the historic invention of papermaking by Cai Lun, and the numerous scientific and mathematical contributions by the famous polymath Zhang Heng.

Three Kingdoms (AD 220–280)

<templatestyles src="Multiple_image/styles.css" />

Three Kingdoms (AD 220–280)

Three Kingdoms in 262, on the eve of the conquest of Shu, Wei, and Wu.

Fresco of a tomb in Luoyang dated to the Cao Wei period (220–266 AD), showing seated men wearing *Hanfu* silk robes

By the 2nd century, the empire declined amidst land acquisitions, invasions, and feuding between consort clans and eunuchs. The Yellow Turban Rebellion broke out in AD 184, ushering in an era of warlords. In the ensuing turmoil, three states tried to gain predominance in the period of the Three Kingdoms. This time period has been greatly romanticized in works such as *Romance of the Three Kingdoms*.

After Cao Cao reunified the north in 208, his son proclaimed the Wei dynasty in 220. Soon, Wei's rivals Shu and Wu proclaimed their independence, leading China into the Three Kingdoms period. This period was characterized by a gradual decentralization of the state that had existed during the Qin and Han dynasties, and an increase in the power of great families.

In 266, the Jin dynasty overthrew the Wei and later unified the country in 280, but this union was short-lived.

Jin dynasty (AD 266–420)

<templatestyles src="Multiple_image/styles.css" />
Jin dynasty (AD 266–420)

Western Jin Dynasty, c. 280 CE

View of Maijishan hill caves, grottoes and stairways.

"The Painting of Goddess Luo Rhapsody"(in a part), Gu Kaizhi, Jin Dynasty

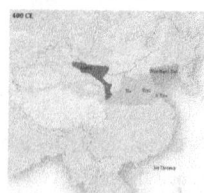

Eastern Jin Dynasty (Yellow), c. 400 CE

The Jin dynasty was severely weakened by internecine fighting among imperial princes and lost control of northern China after non-Han Chinese settlers rebelled and captured Luoyang and Chang'an. In 317, a Jin prince in modern-day Nanjing became emperor and continued the dynasty, now known as the Eastern Jin, which held southern China for another century. Prior to this move, historians refer to the Jin dynasty as the Western Jin.

Northern China fragmented into a series of independent kingdoms, most of which were founded by Xiongnu, Xianbei, Jie, Di and Qiang rulers. These non-Han peoples were ancestors of the Turks, Mongols, and Tibetans. Many had, to some extent, been "sinicized" long before their ascent to power. In fact, some of them, notably the Qiang and the Xiongnu, had already been allowed to live in the frontier regions within the Great Wall since late Han times. During the period of the Sixteen Kingdoms, warfare ravaged the north and prompted large-scale Han Chinese migration south to the Yangtze Basin and Delta.

Northern and Southern dynasties (AD 420–589)

<templatestyles src="Multiple_image/styles.css" />

Northern and Southern dynasties (AD 420–589)

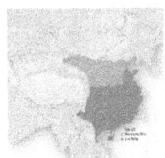

Southern and Northern Dynasties, 440 CE

Hanging Monastery, a temple with the combination of Taoism, Buddhism, and Confucianism.

Yungang Grottoes, an ancient Chinese Buddhist temple grottoes near the city of Datong in the province of Shanxi.

Mogao Caves, also known as the Thousand Buddha Grottoes, located at a religious and cultural crossroads on the Silk Road, in Gansu province.

In the early 5th century, China entered a period known as the Northern and Southern dynasties, in which parallel regimes ruled the northern and southern halves of the country. In the south, the Eastern Jin gave way to the Liu Song, Southern Qi, Liang and finally Chen. Each of these Southern dynasties were led by Han Chinese ruling families and used Jiankang (modern Nanjing) as the capital. They held off attacks from the north and preserved many aspects of Chinese civilization, while northern barbarian regimes began to sinify.

In the north, the last of the Sixteen Kingdoms was extinguished in 439 by the Northern Wei, a kingdom founded by the Xianbei, a nomadic people who unified northern China. The Northern Wei eventually split into the Eastern and Western Wei, which then became the Northern Qi and Northern Zhou. These regimes were dominated by Xianbei or Han Chinese who had married into Xianbei families. During this period most Xianbei people adopted Han surnames, eventually leading to complete assimilation into the Han.

Despite the division of the country, Buddhism spread throughout the land. In southern China, fierce debates about whether Buddhism should be allowed were held frequently by the royal court and nobles. By the end of the era, Buddhists and Taoists had become much more tolerant of each other.

Sui dynasty (581–618)

<templatestyles src="Multiple_image/styles.css" />

Sui dynasty (581–618)

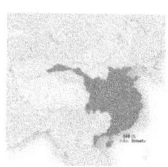

Sui dynasty c.609

The Anji Bridge, the world's oldest open-spandrel segmental arch bridge of stone construction.

Manshan Pavilion of the Tianlongshan Grottoes

Yang Guang depicted as Emperor of Sui

The short-lived Sui dynasty was a pivotal period in Chinese history. Founded by Emperor Wen in 581 in succession of the Northern Zhou, the Sui went on to conquer the Southern Chen in 589 to reunify China, ending three centuries of political division. The Sui pioneered many new institutions, including the government system of Three Departments and Six Ministries, imperial examinations for selecting officials from commoners, while improved on the systems of fubing system of the army conscription and the Equal-field system of land distributions. These policies, which were adopted by later dynasties, brought enormous population growth, and amassed excessive wealth to the state. Standardized coinage were enforced throughout the unified empire. Buddhism took root as a prominent religion and was supported officially. Sui China was known for its numerous mega-construction projects. Intended for grains shipment and transporting troops, the Grand Canal was constructed, linking the capitals Daxing (Chang'an) and Luoyang to the wealthy southeast region, and in another route, to the northeast border. The Great Wall was also expanded, while series of military conquests and diplomatic maneuvers further pacified its borders. However, the massive invasions of the Korean Peninsula during the Goguryeo–Sui War failed disastrously, triggering widespread revolts that led to the fall of the dynasty.

Tang dynasty (AD 618–907)

<templatestyles src="Multiple_image/styles.css" />

Tang dynasty (AD 618–907)

Tang Dynasty circa 700 CE

The Fengxian cave (c. 675 AD) of the Longmen Grottoes, commissioned by Wu Zetian.

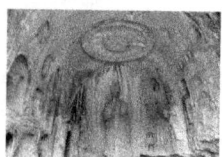

Inside a cave of Longmen Grottoes

The Dunhuang map is to date the world's oldest complete preserved star atlas.

The Tang dynasty was founded by Emperor Gaozu on 18 June 618. It was a golden age of Chinese civilization and considered to be the most prosperous period of China with significant developments in culture, art, literature, particularly poetry, and technology. Buddhism became the predominant religion for the common people. Chang'an (modern Xi'an), the national capital, was the largest city in the world during its time.[193]

The second emperor, Taizong, is widely regarded as one of the greatest emperors in Chinese history, who had laid the foundation for the dynasty to flourish for centuries beyond his reign. Combined military conquests and diplomatic

History of China

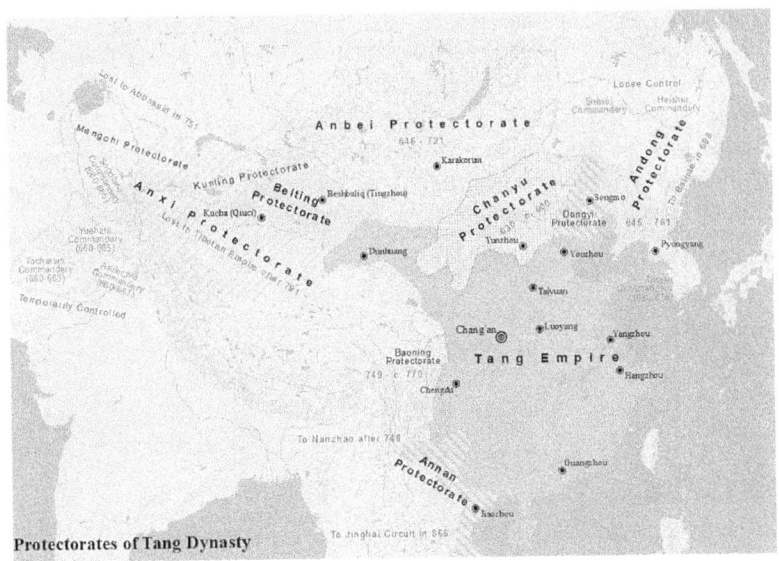

Figure 50: *Map of the six major protectorates during Tang dynasty.*

maneuvers were implemented to eliminate threats from nomadic tribes, extend the border, and submit neighboring states into a tributary system. Military victories in the Tarim Basin kept the Silk Road open, connecting Chang'an to Central Asia and areas far to the west. In the south, lucrative maritime trade routes began from port cities such as Guangzhou. There was extensive trade with distant foreign countries, and many foreign merchants settled in China, encouraging a cosmopolitan culture. The Tang culture and social systems were observed and imitated by neighboring countries, most notably, Japan. Internally the Grand Canal linked the political heartland in Chang'an to the agricultural and economic centers in the eastern and southern parts of the empire. Xuanzang, a Chinese Buddhist monk, scholar, traveller, and translator who travelled to India on his own, and returned with, "over six hundred Mahayana and Hinayana texts, seven statues of the Buddha and more than a hundred sarira relics."

Underlying the prosperity of the early Tang dynasty was a strong centralized bureaucracy with efficient policies. The government was organized as "Three Departments and Six Ministries" to separately draft, review, and implement policies. These departments were run by royal family members as well as scholar officials who were selected by imperial examinations. These practices, which matured in the Tang dynasty, were continued by the later dynasties, with some modifications.

Under the Tang "equal-field system" all land was owned by the Emperor and granted to people according to household size. Men granted land were conscripted for military service for a fixed period each year, a military policy known as the "Fubing system". These policies stimulated a rapid growth in productivity and a significant army without much burden on the state treasury. By the dynasty's midpoint, however, standing armies had replaced conscription, and land was continuously falling into the hands of private owners.

<templatestyles src="Multiple_image/styles.css" />

A gilt Buddhist reliquary with decorations of armored guards, from Silla, 7th-century

A Tang period gilt-silver jar, shaped in the style of northern nomad's leather bag[194] decorated with a horse dancing with a cup of wine in its mouth, as the horses of Emperor Xuanzong were trained to do.[194]

The dynasty continued to flourish under the rule of Empress Wu Zetian, the only empress regnant in Chinese history, and reached its zenith during the long reign of Emperor Xuanzong, who oversaw an empire that stretched from the Pacific to the Aral Sea with at least 50 million people. There were vibrant artistic and cultural creations, including works of the greatest Chinese poets, Li Bai, and Du Fu.

<templatestyles src="Multiple_image/styles.css" />

One of the Three Pagodas of Chong Shen Monastery in Dali.

The Giant Wild Goose Pagoda, Chang'an (modern-day Xi'an), built in 652, repaired by Empress Wu Zetian in 704.

The Small Wild Goose Pagoda, built by 709, was adjacent to the Dajianfu Temple in Chang'an, where Buddhist monks gathered to translate Sanskrit texts into Chinese[195]

At the zenith of prosperity of the empire, the An Lushan Rebellion from 755 to 763 was a watershed event that devastated the population and drastically weakened the central imperial government. Upon suppression of the rebellion, regional military governors, known as Jiedushi, gained increasingly autonomous status. With loss of revenue from land tax, the central imperial government relied heavily on salt monopoly. Externally, former submissive states raided the empire and the vast border territories were irreversibly lost for subsequent centuries. Nevertheless, civil society recovered and thrived amidst the weakened imperial bureaucracy.

In late Tang period, the empire was worn out by recurring revolts of regional warlords, while internally, as scholar-officials engaged in fierce factional strife, corrupted eunuchs amassed immense power. Catastrophically, the Huang Chao Rebellion, from 874 to 884, devastated the entire empire for a decade. The sack of the southern port Guangzhou in 879 was followed by the massacre of most of its inhabitants, along with the large foreign merchant enclaves. By 881, both capitals, Luoyang and Chang'an, fell successively. The reliance on ethnic Han and Turkic warlords in suppressing the rebellion increased their power and influence. Consequently, the fall of the dynasty following Zhu Wen's usurpation led to an era of division.

According to historian Mark Edward Lewis:

> Most Chinese regard the Tang dynasty (618–907) as the high point of Imperial China, both politically and culturally. The empire reached its greatest size prior to the Manchu Qing dynasty, becoming the center of an East Asian world linked by religion, script, and many economic and political institutions. Moreover, Tang writers produce the finest poetry in China's great lyric tradition.[196]

Five Dynasties and Ten Kingdoms (AD 907–960)

<templatestyles src="Multiple_image/styles.css" />

Zhenguo Pagoda of Kaiyuan Temple (Quanzhou)

Gongchen Bagoda, Lin'an, Hangzhou, China

<templatestyles src="Multiple_image/styles.css" />

Five Dynasties and Ten Kingdoms (AD 907–960)

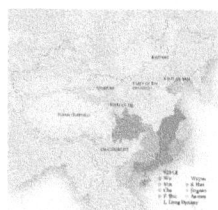

Five Dynasties Ten Kingdoms Period 923 CE

Yunyan Pagoda in Jiangsu Province of Eastern China.

Coins of the Five Dynasties and Ten Kingdoms

Section and detail of *Night Revels of Han Xizai*, by Gu Hongzhong

The period of political disunity between the Tang and the Song, known as the Five Dynasties and Ten Kingdoms period, lasted from 907 to 960. During this half-century, China was in all respects a multi-state system. Five regimes, namely, (Later) Liang, Tang, Jin, Han and Zhou, rapidly succeeded one another in control of the traditional Imperial heartland in northern China. Among the regimes, rulers of (Later) Tang, Jin and Han were sinicized Shatuo Turks, which ruled over the ethnic majority of Han Chinese. More stable and smaller regimes of mostly ethnic Han rulers coexisted in south and western China over the period, cumulatively constituted the "Ten Kingdoms".

Amidst political chaos in the north, the strategic Sixteen Prefectures (region along today's Great Wall) were ceded to the emerging Khitan Liao dynasty, which drastically weakened the defense of the China proper against northern nomadic empires. To the south, Vietnam gained lasting independence after being a Chinese prefecture for many centuries. With wars dominated in Northern China, there were mass southward migrations of population, which further enhanced the southward shift of cultural and economic centers in China. The era ended with the coup of Later Zhou general Zhao Kuangyin, and the establishment the Song dynasty in 960, which would eventually annihilated the remains of the "Ten Kingdoms" and reunified China.

Song, Liao, Jin, and Western Xia dynasties (AD 960–1234)

<templatestyles src="Multiple_image/styles.css" />

Song, Liao, Jin, and Western Xia dynasties (AD 960–1234)

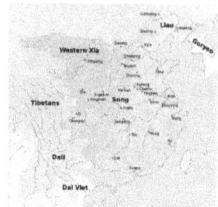

China during the Northern Song Dynasty

A wooden Bodhisattva from the Song dynasty (960–1279).

Earliest known written formula for gunpowder, from the *Wujing Zongyao* of 1044 AD.

A giant "squatting-tiger fire trebuchet" located at the Wolongtai Great Wall section, Xinyang, Henan, China.

In 960, the Song dynasty was founded by Emperor Taizu, with its capital established in Kaifeng (also known as Bianjing). In 979, the Song dynasty reunified most of the China proper, while large swaths of the outer territories were occupied by sinicized nomadic empires. The Khitan Liao dynasty, which lasted from 907 to 1125, ruled over Manchuria, Mongolia, and parts of Northern China. Meanwhile, in what are now the north-western Chinese provinces of

Gansu, Shaanxi, and Ningxia, the Tangut tribes founded the Western Xia dynasty from 1032 to 1227.

Aiming to recover the strategic Sixteen Prefectures lost in the previous dynasty, campaigns were launched against the Liao dynasty in the early Song period, which all ended in failure. Then in 1004, the Liao cavalry swept over the exposed North China Plain and reached the outskirts of Kaifeng, forcing the Song's submission and then agreement to the Chanyuan Treaty, which imposed heavy annual tributes from the Song treasury. The treaty was a significant reversal of Chinese dominance of the traditional tributary system. Yet the annual outflow of Song's silver to the Liao was paid back through the purchase of Chinese goods and products, which expanded the Song economy, and replenished its treasury. This dampened the incentive for the Song to further campaign against the Liao. Meanwhile, this cross-border trade and contact induced further sinicization within the Liao Empire, at the expense of its military might which was derived from its primitive nomadic lifestyle. Similar treaties and social-economical consequences occurred in Song's relations with the Jin dynasty.

<templatestyles src="Multiple_image/styles.css" />

Liaodi Pagoda, Song dynasty (960–1279)

The Pagoda of Tianing Temple, Liao Dynasty (1100-1120)

The Ten Thousand Copies of the Huayan Sutra Pagoda, commonly known as the White Pagoda, Liao dynasty (907-1125)

Poyang Yongfu Temple Pagoda, Song dynasty (960-1279)

Within the Liao Empire, the Jurchen tribes revolted against their overlords to establish the Jin dynasty in 1115. In 1125, the devastating Jin cataphract annihilated the Liao dynasty, while remnants of Liao court members fled to Central Asia to found the Qara Khitai Empire (Western Liao dynasty). Jin's invasion of the Song dynasty followed swiftly. In 1127, Kaifeng was sacked, a massive catastrophe known as the Jingkang Incident, ending the Northern Song dynasty. Later the entire north of China was conquered. The survived members of Song court regrouped in the new capital city of Hangzhou, and initiated the Southern Song dynasty, which ruled territories south of the Huai River. In the ensuing years, the territory and population of China were divided between the Song dynasty, the Jin dynasty and the Western Xia dynasty. The era ended with the Mongol conquest, as Western Xia fell in 1227, the Jin dynasty in 1234, and finally the Southern Song dynasty in 1279.

Despite its military weakness, the Song dynasty is widely considered to be the high point of classical Chinese civilization. The Song economy, facilitated by technology advancement, had reached a level of sophistication probably unseen in world history before its time. The population soared to over 100 million and the living standards of common people improved tremendously due to improvements in rice cultivation and the wide availability of coal for production. The capital cities of Kaifeng and subsequently Hangzhou were both the most populous cities in the world for their time, and encouraged vibrant civil societies unmatched by previous Chinese dynasties. Although land trading routes to the far west were blocked by nomadic empires, there were extensive maritime trade with neighbouring states, which facilitated the use of Song coinage as the de facto currency of exchange. Giant wooden vessels equipped with compasses travelled throughout the China Seas and northern Indian Ocean. The concept of insurance was practised by merchants to hedge the risks of such long-haul maritime shipments. With prosperous economic activities, the historically first use of paper currency emerged in the western city of Chengdu, as a supplement to the existing copper coins.

<templatestyles src="Multiple_image/styles.css" />

Beisi Pagoda, located at Bao'en Temple in Suzhou, Jiangsu Province.

Jingzhou Pagoda, Song dynasty (960–1279)

Northern Chaoyang Bagoda, located in Chaoyang, Liaoning Province. Liao Dynasty (1100-1120).

The Song dynasty was considered to be the golden age of great advancements in science and technology of China, thanks to innovative scholar-officials such as Su Song (1020–1101) and Shen Kuo (1031–1095). Inventions such as the hydro-mechanical astronomical clock, the first continuous and endless power-transmitting chain, woodblock printing and paper money were all invented during the Song dynasty.

<templatestyles src="Multiple_image/styles.css" />

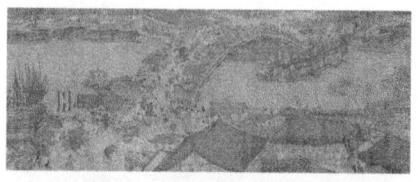
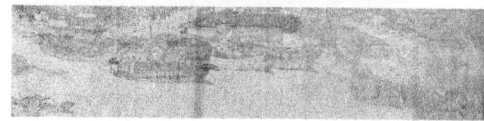

City views of Song dynasty from paintings. Clockwise from upper left: A Northern Song Dynasty (960-1127) era Chinese painting of a water-powered mill for grain, with surrounding river transport. The bridge scene from Zhang Zeduan's (1085–1145) painting *Along the River During Qingming Festival.* Chinese boats from *Along the River During Qingming Festival.* Leifeng Pagoda in the Southern Song Dynasty by Li Song.

There was court intrigue between the political reformers and conservatives, led by the chancellors Wang Anshi and Sima Guang, respectively. By the mid-to-late 13th century, the Chinese had adopted the dogma of Neo-Confucian philosophy formulated by Zhu Xi. Enormous literary works were compiled during the Song dynasty, such as the historical work, the *Zizhi Tongjian* ("Comprehensive Mirror to Aid in Government"). The invention of movable-type printing further facilitated the spread of knowledge. Culture and the arts flourished, with grandiose artworks such as *Along the River During the Qingming Festival* and *Eighteen Songs of a Nomad Flute*, along with great Buddhist painters such as the prolific Lin Tinggui.

The Song dynasty was also a period of major innovation in the history of warfare. Gunpowder, while invented in the Tang dynasty, was first put into use in battlefields by the Song army, inspiring a succession of new firearms and siege engines designs. During the Southern Song dynasty, as its survival hinged decisively on guarding the Yangtze and Huai River against the cavalry forces from the north, the first standing navy in China was assembled in 1132, with its admiral's headquarters established at Dinghai. Paddle-wheel warships equipped with trebuchets could launch incendiary bombs made of gunpowder and lime, as recorded in Song's victory over the invading Jin forces at the Battle of Tangdao in the East China Sea, and the Battle of Caishi on the Yangtze River in 1161.

History of China 161

The advances in civilization during the Song dynasty came to an abrupt end following the devastating Mongol conquest, during which the population sharply dwindled, with a marked contraction in economy. Despite viciously halting Mongol advance for more than three decades, the Southern Song capital Hangzhou fell in 1276, followed by the final annihilation of the Song standing navy at the Battle of Yamen in 1279.

Yuan dynasty (AD 1271–1368)

<templatestyles src="Multiple_image/styles.css" />

Yuan dynasty (AD 1271–1368)

The White Stupa of Miaoying Temple in Beijing.

Deva King of the East on the east wall of the Cloud Platform at Juyong Pass.

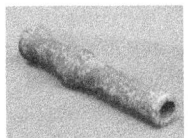

Yuan period bronze firearm on display at the Shaanxi History Museum in Xi'an.

Yuan dynasty banknote with its printing wood plate, 1287 CE.

The Yuan dynasty was formally proclaimed in 1271, when the Great Khan of Mongol, Kublai Khan, one of the grandsons of Genghis Khan, assumed the additional title of the Emperor of China, and considered his inherited part of

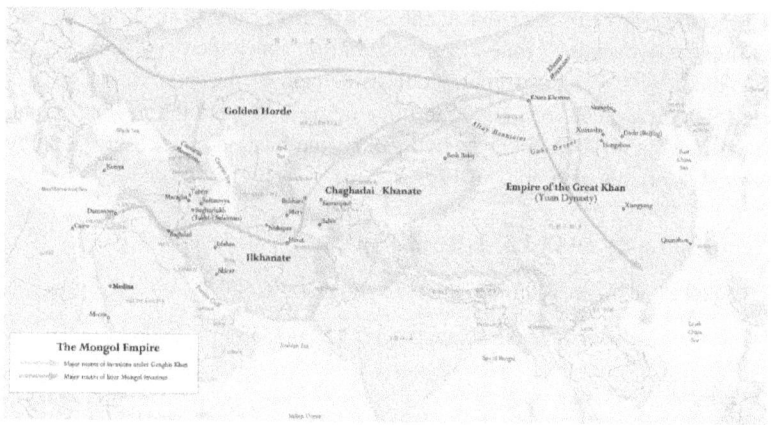

Figure 51: *Mongol successor khanates*

the Mongol Empire as a Chinese dynasty. In the preceding decades, the Mongols had conquered the Jin dynasty in Northern China, and the Southern Song dynasty fell in 1279 after a protracted and bloody war. The Mongol Yuan dynasty became the first conquest dynasty in Chinese history to rule the entire China proper and its population as an ethnic minority. The dynasty also directly controlled the Mongolian heartland and other regions, inheriting the largest share of territory of the divided Mongol Empire, which roughly coincided with the modern area of China and nearby regions in East Asia. Further expansion of the empire was halted after defeats in the invasions of Japan and Vietnam. Following the previous Jin dynasty, the capital of Yuan dynasty was established at Khanbaliq (also known as Dadu, modern-day Beijing). The Grand Canal was reconstructed to connect the remote capital city to economic hubs in southern part of China, setting the precedence and foundation where Beijing would largely remain as the capital of the successive regimes that unified China mainland.

After the peace treaty in 1304 that ended a series of Mongols civil wars, the emperors of the Yuan dynasty were upheld as the nominal Great Khan (Khagan) of the greater Mongol Empire over other Mongol Khanates, which nonetheless remained de facto autonomous. The era was known as *Pax Mongolica*, when much of the Asian continent was ruled by the Mongols. For the first and only time in history, the silk road was controlled entirely by a single state, facilitating the flow of people, trade, and cultural exchange. Network of roads and a postal system were established to connect the vast empire. Lucrative maritime trade, developed from the previous Song dynasty, continued to flourish, with Quanzhou and Hangzhou emerging as the largest ports in the world. Adventurous travelers from the far west, most notably the Venetian, Marco Polo, would have settled in China for decades. Upon his return, his detail travel record inspired generations of medieval Europeans with the splendors of the far East. The Yuan dynasty was the first ancient economy, where paper currency, known at the time as Chao, was used as the predominant medium of exchange. Its unrestricted issuance in the late Yuan dynasty inflicted hyperinflation, which eventually brought the downfall of the dynasty.

<templatestyles src="Multiple_image/styles.css" />

Dengfeng Observatory, the first in a series of 27 astronomical observatories built in the early Yuan dynasty.

The Pagoda of Bailin Temple, an octagonal-based brick pagoda built in 1330 during the reign of Emperor Wenzong, ruler of the Mongol-led Yuan Dynasty (1271–1368).

While the Mongol rulers of the Yuan dynasty adopted substantially to Chinese culture, their sinicization was of lesser extent compared to earlier conquest dynasties in Chinese history. For preserving racial superiority as the conqueror and ruling class, traditional nomadic customs and heritage from the Mongolian steppe were held in high regard. On the other hand, the Mongol rulers also adopted flexibly to a variety of cultures from many advanced civilizations within the vast empire. Traditional social structure and culture in China underwent immense transform during the Mongol dominance. Large group of foreign migrants settled in China, who enjoyed elevated social status over the majority Han Chinese, while enriching Chinese culture with foreign elements.

The class of scholar officials and intellectuals, traditional bearers of elite Chinese culture, lost substantial social status. This stimulated the development of culture of the common folks. There were prolific works in zaju variety shows and literary songs (sanqu), which were written in a distinctive poetry style known as qu. Novels of vernacular style gained unprecedented status and popularity.

<templatestyles src="Multiple_image/styles.css" />

The Ayuwang Stupa in northern Shanxi, China.

A stupa on top of an arch (*crossing street tower*), is a common form of architecture during Yuan period.

Before the Mongol invasion, Chinese dynasties reported approximately 120 million inhabitants; after the conquest had been completed in 1279, the 1300 census reported roughly 60 million people. This major decline is not necessarily due only to Mongol killings. Scholars such as Frederick W. Mote argue that the wide drop in numbers reflects an administrative failure to record rather than an actual decrease; others such as Timothy Brook argue that the Mongols created a system of enserfment among a huge portion of the Chinese populace, causing many to disappear from the census altogether; other historians including William McNeill and David Morgan consider that plague was the main factor behind the demographic decline during this period. In the 14th century China suffered additional depredations from epidemics of plague, estimated to have killed 25 million people, 30% of the population of China.

Throughout the Yuan dynasty, there was some general sentiment among the populace against the Mongol dominance. Yet rather than the nationalist cause, it was mainly strings of natural disasters and incompetent governance that triggered widespread peasant uprisings since the 1340s. After the massive naval engagement at Lake Poyang, Zhu Yuanzhang prevailed over other rebel forces in the south. He proclaimed himself emperor and founded the Ming dynasty in 1368. The same year his northern expedition army captured the capital Khanbaliq. The Yuan remnants fled back to Mongolia and sustained the regime. Other Mongol Khanates in Central Asia continued to exist after the fall of Yuan dynasty in China.

Ming dynasty (AD 1368–1644)

<templatestyles src="Multiple_image/styles.css" />

Residence of the Lu Family in Dongyang, built in the Ming period.

City wall of Xi'an, a UNESCO World Heritage Site built during the early Ming dynasty

Fenghuang County, an ancient town that harbors many architectural remains of Ming and Qing styles.

Hongcun, a village in Yi County in the historical Huizhou region of southern Anhui Province.

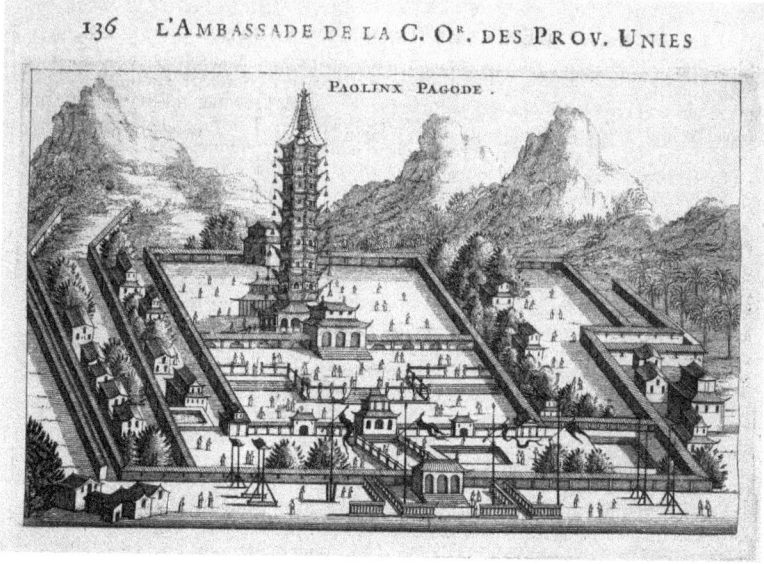

Figure 52: *Porcelain Tower, from An embassy from the East-India Company (1665) by Johan Nieuhof. It was first discovered by the Western world when travelers like Johan Nieuhof visited it, sometimes listing it as one of the Seven Wonders of the World.*

Xinye, a village noted for its well-preserved Ming and Qing era architecture and ancient residential buildings.

The Ming dynasty was founded by Zhu Yuanzhang in 1368, who proclaimed himself as the Hongwu Emperor. The capital was initially set at Nanjing, and was later moved to Beijing from Yongle Emperor's reign onward.

<templatestyles src="Multiple_image/styles.css" />

Haihui Temple Pagodas, built in the Ming period.

Pagoda of Chongjue Temple, dated to the Song dynasty. The onion-shaped Sōrin was a Ming dynasty addition.

Urbanization increased as the population grew and as the division of labor grew more complex. Large urban centers, such as Nanjing and Beijing, also contributed to the growth of private industry. In particular, small-scale industries grew up, often specializing in paper, silk, cotton, and porcelain goods. For the most part, however, relatively small urban centers with markets proliferated around the country. Town markets mainly traded food, with some necessary manufactures such as pins or oil.

Despite the xenophobia and intellectual introspection characteristic of the increasingly popular new school of neo-Confucianism, China under the early Ming dynasty was not isolated. Foreign trade and other contacts with the outside world, particularly Japan, increased considerably. Chinese merchants explored all of the Indian Ocean, reaching East Africa with the voyages of Zheng He.

The Hongwu Emperor, being the only founder of a Chinese dynasty who was also of peasant origin, had laid the foundation of a state that relied fundamentally in agriculture. Commerce and trade, which flourished in the previous Song and Yuan dynasties, were less emphasized. Neo-feudal landholdings of the Song and Mongol periods were expropriated by the Ming rulers. Land estates were confiscated by the government, fragmented, and rented out. Private slavery was forbidden. Consequently, after the death of the Yongle Emperor, independent peasant landholders predominated in Chinese agriculture. These laws might have paved the way to removing the worst of the poverty during the previous regimes. Towards later era of the Ming dynasty, with declining government control, commerce, trade and private industries revived.

The dynasty had a strong and complex central government that unified and controlled the empire. The emperor's role became more autocratic, although Hongwu Emperor necessarily continued to use what he called the "Grand Secretariat" to assist with the immense paperwork of the bureaucracy, including memorials (petitions and recommendations to the throne), imperial edicts in reply, reports of various kinds, and tax records. It was this same bureaucracy that later prevented the Ming government from being able to adapt to changes in society, and eventually led to its decline.

The Yongle Emperor strenuously tried to extend China's influence beyond its borders by demanding other rulers send ambassadors to China to present tribute. A large navy was built, including four-masted ships displacing 1,500 tons. A standing army of 1 million troops was created. The Chinese armies conquered and occupied Vietnam for around 20 years, while the Chinese fleet sailed the China seas and the Indian Ocean, cruising as far as the east coast of Africa. The Chinese gained influence in eastern Moghulistan. Several maritime Asian nations sent envoys with tribute for the Chinese emperor. Domestically, the Grand Canal was expanded and became a stimulus to domestic trade. Over 100,000 tons of iron per year were produced. Many books were printed using movable type. The imperial palace in Beijing's Forbidden City reached its current splendor. It was also during these centuries that the potential of south China came to be fully exploited. New crops were widely cultivated and industries such as those producing porcelain and textiles flourished.

In 1449 Esen Tayisi led an Oirat Mongol invasion of northern China which culminated in the capture of the Zhengtong Emperor at Tumu. Since then, the Ming became on the defensive on the northern frontier, which led to the Ming Great Wall being built. Most of what remains of the Great Wall of China today was either built or repaired by the Ming. The brick and granite work was enlarged, the watchtowers were redesigned, and cannons were placed along its length.

<templatestyles src="Multiple_image/styles.css" />

Eagles by Lin Liang. Located at the National Palace Museum.

Snow Plums and Twin Cranes by Bian Jingzhao. Located at the Guangdong Provincial Museum.

At sea, the Ming became increasingly isolationist after the death of the Yongle Emperor. The treasure voyages which sailed Indian Ocean were discontinued, and the maritime prohibition laws were set in place banning the Chinese from sailing abroad. European traders who reached China in the midst of the Age of Discovery were repeatedly rebuked in their requests for trade, with the Portuguese being repulsed by the Ming navy at Tuen Mun in 1521 and again in 1522. Domestic and foreign demands for overseas trade, deemed illegal by the state, led to widespread *wokou* piracy attacking the southeastern coastline during the rule of the Jiajing Emperor (1507–1567), which only subsided after the opening of ports in Guangdong and Fujian and much military suppression.[197] The Portuguese were allowed to settle in Macau in 1557 for trade, which remained in Portuguese hands until 1999. The Dutch entry into the Chinese seas was also met with fierce resistance, with the Dutch being chased off the Penghu islands in the Sino-Dutch conflicts of 1622–1624 and were forced to settle in Taiwan instead. The Dutch in Taiwan fought with the Ming in the Battle of Liaoluo Bay in 1633 and lost, and eventually surrendered to the Ming loyalist Koxinga in 1662, after the fall of the Ming dynasty.

In 1556, during the rule of the Jiajing Emperor, the Shaanxi earthquake killed about 830,000 people, the deadliest earthquake of all time.

The Ming dynasty intervened deeply in the Japanese invasions of Korea (1592–98), which ended with the withdrawal of all invading Japanese forces in Korea, and the restoration of the Joseon dynasty, its traditional ally and tributary state. The regional hegemony of the Ming dynasty was preserved at a toll on its resources. Coincidentally, with Ming's control in Manchuria in decline, the Manchu (Jurchen) tribes, under their chieftain Nurhaci, broke away from Ming's rule, and emerged as a powerful, unified state, which was later proclaimed as the Qing dynasty. It went on to subdue the much weakened Korea as its tributary, conquered Mongolia, and expanded its territory to the outskirt of the Great Wall. The most elite army of the Ming dynasty was to station at the Shanhai Pass to guard the last stronghold against the Manchus, which weakened its suppression of internal peasants uprisings.

Qing dynasty (AD 1644–1911)

<templatestyles src="Multiple_image/styles.css" />
Qing dynasty (AD 1644–1911)

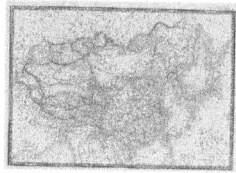

1836 map of China published by C. Picque.

Pilgrim flask, porcelain with underglaze blue and iron-red decoration.

A military attire of the Qianlong Emperor

A Qing period geomantic compass (c. 1760)

<templatestyles src="Multiple_image/styles.css" />

Summer Palace, an imperial garden in Qing Dynasty.

Putuo Zongcheng Temple, a Buddhist temple complex built between 1767 and 1771. The temple was modeled after the Potala Palace of Tibet.

The House of the Huangcheng Chancellor, a 10-hectare walled estate on Phoenix Hill in southeastern Shanxi, China.

Flower Theatre, a Qing period guildhall.

A residential building of Qiao Family Compound, built in the Qing period.

The Qing dynasty (1644–1911) was the last imperial dynasty in China. Founded by the Manchus, it was the second conquest dynasty to rule the entire territory of China and its people. The Manchus were formerly known as Jurchens, residing in the northeastern part of the Ming territory outside the Great Wall. They emerged as the major threat to the late Ming dynasty after Nurhaci united all Jurchen tribes and established an independent state. However, the Ming dynasty would be overthrown by Li Zicheng's peasants rebellion, with Beijing captured in 1644 and the Chongzhen Emperor, the last Ming emperor, committing suicide. The Manchus allied with the former Ming general Wu Sangui to seize Beijing, which was made the capital of the Qing dynasty, and then proceeded to subdue the Ming remnants in the south. The decades of Manchu conquest caused enormous loss of lives and the economic scale of China shrank drastically. In total, the Qing conquest of the Ming (1618–1683) cost as many as 25 million lives.[198] Nevertheless, the Manchus adopted the Confucian norms of traditional Chinese government in their rule and were considered a Chinese dynasty.

The Manchus enforced a 'queue order,' forcing the Han Chinese to adopt the Manchu queue hairstyle. Officials were required to wear Manchu-style clothing *Changshan* (bannermen dress and *Tangzhuang*), but ordinary Han civilians were allowed to wear traditional Han clothing, or *Hanfu*. Most Han then voluntarily shifted to wearing Qipao anyway. The Kangxi Emperor ordered the creation of the *Kangxi Dictionary*, the most complete dictionary of Chinese characters that had been compiled. The Qing dynasty set up the Eight Banners system that provided the basic framework for the Qing military organization. Bannermen could not undertake trade or manual labor; they had to petition to be removed from banner status. They were considered a form of nobility and were given preferential treatment in terms of annual pensions, land, and allotments of cloth.

Over the next half-century, all areas previously under the Ming dynasty were consolidated under the Qing. Xinjiang, Tibet, and Mongolia were also formally incorporated into Chinese territory. Between 1673 and 1681, the Kangxi Emperor suppressed the Revolt of the Three Feudatories, an uprising of three generals in Southern China who had been denied hereditary rule of large fiefdoms granted by the previous emperor. In 1683, the Qing staged an amphibious assault on southern Taiwan, bringing down the rebel Kingdom of Tungning, which was founded by the Ming loyalist Koxinga (Zheng Chenggong) in 1662 after the fall of the Southern Ming, and had served as a base for continued Ming resistance in Southern China. The Qing defeated the Russians at Albazin, resulting in the Treaty of Nerchinsk.

By the end of Qianlong Emperor's long reign, the Qing Empire was at its zenith. China ruled more than one-third of the world's population, and had the largest economy in the world. By area it was one of the largest empires ever.

In the 19th century the empire was internally stagnant and externally threatened by western powers. The defeat by the British Empire in the First Opium War (1840) led to the Treaty of Nanking (1842), under which Hong Kong was ceded to Britain and importation of opium (produced by British Empire territories) was allowed. Subsequent military defeats and unequal treaties with other western powers continued even after the fall of the Qing dynasty.

Internally the Taiping Rebellion (1851–1864), a quasi-Christian religious movement led by the "Heavenly King" Hong Xiuquan, raided roughly a third

Figure 53: *Qianlong Emperor*

Figure 54: *Li Hongzhang, a Chinese politician, general and diplomat of the late Qing dynasty.*

of Chinese territory for over a decade until they were finally crushed in the Third Battle of Nanking in 1864. This was one of the largest wars in the 19th century in terms of troop involvement; there was massive loss of life, with a death toll of about 20 million. A string of civil disturbances followed, including the Punti–Hakka Clan Wars, Nian Rebellion, Dungan Revolt, and Panthay Rebellion. All rebellions were ultimately put down, but at enormous cost and with millions dead, seriously weakening the central imperial authority. The Banner system that the Manchus had relied upon for so long failed: Banner forces were unable to suppress the rebels, and the government called upon local officials in the provinces, who raised "New Armies", which successfully crushed the challenges to Qing authority. China never rebuilt a strong central army, and many local officials became warlords who used military power to effectively rule independently in their provinces.[199]

In response to calamities within the empire and threats from imperialism, the Self-Strengthening Movement was an institutional reform in the second half of the 1800s. The aim was to modernize the empire, with prime emphasis on strengthening the military. However, the reform was undermined by corrupt officials, cynicism, and quarrels within the imperial family. As a result, the "Beiyang Fleet" were soundly defeated in the First Sino-Japanese War (1894–1895). The Guangxu Emperor and the reformists then launched a more comprehensive reform effort, the Hundred Days' Reform (1898), but it was soon overturned by the conservatives under Empress Dowager Cixi in a military coup.

At the turn of the 20th century, the violent Boxer Rebellion opposed foreign influence in Northern China, and attacked Chinese Christians and missionaries. When Boxers entered Beijing, the Qing government ordered all foreigners to leave. But instead the foreigners and many Chinese were besieged in the foreign legations quarter. The Eight-Nation Alliance sent the Seymour Expedition of Japanese, Russian, Italian, German, French, American, and Austrian troops to relieve the siege. The Expedition was stopped by the Boxers at the Battle of Langfang and forced to retreat. Due to the Alliance's attack on the Dagu Forts, the Qing government in response sided with the Boxers and declared war on the Alliance. There was fierce fighting at Tientsin. The Alliance formed the second, much larger Gaselee Expedition and finally reached Beijing; the Qing government evacuated to Xi'an. The Boxer Protocol ended the war.

Figure 55: *Nanjing Road during Xinhai Revolution, 1911.*

Modern China

Republic of China (since 1912)

Frustrated by the Qing court's resistance to reform and by China's weakness, young officials, military officers, and students began to advocate the overthrow of the Qing dynasty and the creation of a republic. They were inspired by the revolutionary ideas of Sun Yat-sen. A revolutionary military uprising, the Wuchang Uprising, began on 10 October 1911, in Wuhan. The provisional government of the Republic of China was formed in Nanjing on 12 March 1912. The Xinhai Revolution ended 2,000 years of dynastic rule in China.
<templatestyles src="Multiple_image/styles.css" />

Sun Yat-sen, the leader of the Xinhai Revolution and the first provisional president of the Republic of China.

Yuan Shikai, the first president of the Republic of China.

After the success of the overthrow of the Qing dynasty, Sun Yat-sen was declared President, but Sun was forced to turn power over to Yuan Shikai, who commanded the New Army and was Prime Minister under the Qing government, as part of the agreement to let the last Qing monarch abdicate (a decision Sun would later regret). Over the next few years, Yuan proceeded to abolish the national and provincial assemblies, and declared himself emperor in late 1915. Yuan's imperial ambitions were fiercely opposed by his subordinates; faced with the prospect of rebellion, he abdicated in March 1916, and died in June of that year.

Yuan's death in 1916 left a power vacuum in China; the republican government was all but shattered. This ushered in the Warlord Era, during which much of the country was ruled by shifting coalitions of competing provincial military leaders.

In 1919, the May Fourth Movement began as a response to the terms imposed on China by the Treaty of Versailles ending World War I, but quickly became a nationwide protest movement about the domestic situation in China. The protests were a moral success as the cabinet fell and China refused to sign the Treaty of Versailles, which had awarded German holdings to Japan. The New Culture Movement stimulated by the May Fourth Movement waxed strong throughout the 1920s and 1930s. According to Ebrey:

> "Nationalism, patriotism, progress, science, democracy, and freedom were the goals; imperialism, feudalism, warlordism, autocracy, patriarchy, and blind adherence to tradition were the enemies. Intellectuals struggled with how to be strong and modern and yet Chinese, how to preserve China as a political entity in the world of competing nations."[200]

The discrediting of liberal Western philosophy amongst leftist Chinese intellectuals led to more radical lines of thought inspired by the Russian Revolution, and supported by agents of the Comintern sent to China by Moscow. This created the seeds for the irreconcilable conflict between the left and right in China that would dominate Chinese history for the rest of the century.

Figure 56: *The flag of the Republic of China from 1928 to now.*

In the 1920s, Sun Yat-sen established a revolutionary base in south China, and set out to unite the fragmented nation. With assistance from the Soviet Union (itself fresh from Lenin's takeover), he entered into an alliance with the fledgling Communist Party of China. After Sun's death from cancer in 1925, one of his protégés, Chiang Kai-shek, seized control of the *Kuomintang* (Nationalist Party or KMT) and succeeded in bringing most of south and central China under its rule in a military campaign known as the Northern Expedition (1926–1927). Having defeated the warlords in south and central China by military force, Chiang was able to secure the nominal allegiance of the warlords in the North. In 1927, Chiang turned on the CPC and relentlessly chased the CPC armies and its leaders from their bases in southern and eastern China. In 1934, driven from their mountain bases such as the Chinese Soviet Republic, the CPC forces embarked on the Long March across China's most desolate terrain to the northwest, where they established a guerrilla base at Yan'an in Shaanxi Province. During the Long March, the communists reorganized under a new leader, Mao Zedong (Mao Tse-tung).

The bitter struggle between the KMT and the CPC continued, openly or clandestinely, through the 14-year-long Japanese occupation of various parts of the country (1931–1945). The two Chinese parties nominally formed a united front to oppose the Japanese in 1937, during the Second Sino-Japanese War (1937–1945), which became a part of World War II. Japanese forces committed numerous war atrocities against the civilian population, including biological warfare (see Unit 731) and the Three Alls Policy (*Sankō Sakusen*), the three alls being: *"Kill All, Burn All and Loot All"*.

Following the defeat of Japan in 1945, the war between the Nationalist government forces and the CPC resumed, after failed attempts at reconciliation and a negotiated settlement. By 1949, the CPC had established control over most of the country *(see Chinese Civil War)*. Westad says the Communists won the Civil War because they made fewer military mistakes than Chiang, and because in his search for a powerful centralized government, Chiang antagonized too many interest groups in China. Furthermore, his party was weakened in the war against the Japanese. Meanwhile, the Communists told different groups, such as peasants, exactly what they wanted to hear, and cloaked themselves in the cover of Chinese Nationalism.[201] During the civil war both the Nationalists and Communists carried out mass atrocities, with millions of non-combatants killed by both sides.[202] These included deaths from forced conscription and massacres.[203] When the Nationalist government forces were defeated by CPC forces in mainland China in 1949, the Nationalist government retreated to Taiwan with its forces, along with Chiang and most of the KMT leadership and a large number of their supporters; the Nationalist government had taken effective control of Taiwan at the end of WWII as part of the overall Japanese surrender, when Japanese troops in Taiwan surrendered to Republic of China troops.[204]

People's Republic of China (since 1949)

Major combat in the Chinese Civil War ended in 1949 with Kuomintang (KMT) pulling out of the mainland, with the government relocating to Taipei and maintaining control only over a few islands. The Communist Party of China was left in control of mainland China. On 1 October 1949, Mao Zedong proclaimed the People's Republic of China.[205] "Communist China" and "Red China" were two common names for the PRC.[206]

The PRC was shaped by a series of campaigns and five-year plans. The economic and social plan known as the Great Leap Forward caused an estimated 45 million deaths. Mao's government carried out mass executions of landowners, instituted collectivisation and implemented the Laogai camp system. Execution, deaths from forced labor and other atrocities resulted in millions of deaths under Mao. In 1966 Mao and his allies launched the Cultural Revolution, which continued until Mao's death a decade later. The Cultural Revolution, motivated by power struggles within the Party and a fear of the Soviet Union, led to a major upheaval in Chinese society.

In 1972, at the peak of the Sino-Soviet split, Mao and Zhou Enlai met US president Richard Nixon in Beijing to establish relations with the United States. In the same year, the PRC was admitted to the United Nations in place of the Republic of China, with permanent membership of the Security Council.

Figure 57: *The People's Liberation Army enters Beijing in the Pingjin Campaign*

Figure 58: *Chairman Mao Zedong proclaiming the establishment of the People's Republic of China in 1949.*

Figure 59: *The flag of the People's Republic of China since 1949.*

A power struggle followed Mao's death in 1976. The Gang of Four were arrested and blamed for the excesses of the Cultural Revolution, marking the end of a turbulent political era in China. Deng Xiaoping outmaneuvered Mao's anointed successor chairman Hua Guofeng, and gradually emerged as the *de facto* leader over the next few years.

Deng Xiaoping was the Paramount Leader of China from 1978 to 1992, although he never became the head of the party or state, and his influence within the Party led the country to significant economic reforms. The Communist Party subsequently loosened governmental control over citizens' personal lives and the communes were disbanded with many peasants receiving multiple land leases, which greatly increased incentives and agricultural production. In addition, there were many free market areas opened. The most successful free market areas was shenzhen. It is located in guangdong and the property tax free area still exists today. This turn of events marked China's transition from a planned economy to a mixed economy with an increasingly open market environment, a system termed by some as "market socialism", and officially by the Communist Party of China as "Socialism with Chinese characteristics". The PRC adopted its current constitution on 4 December 1982.

In 1989 the death of former general secretary Hu Yaobang helped to spark the Tiananmen Square protests of that year, during which students and others campaigned for several months, speaking out against corruption and in favour of greater political reform, including democratic rights and freedom of speech. However, they were eventually put down on 4 June when PLA troops and vehicles entered and forcibly cleared the square, with many fatalities. This event was widely reported, and brought worldwide condemnation and sanctions against the government.[207,208] A filmed incident involving the "tank man" was seen worldwide.

CPC general secretary and PRC President Jiang Zemin and PRC Premier Zhu Rongji, both former mayors of Shanghai, led post-Tiananmen PRC in the 1990s. Under Jiang and Zhu's ten years of administration, the PRC's economic performance pulled an estimated 150 million peasants out of poverty and sustained an average annual gross domestic product growth rate of 11.2%. The country formally joined the World Trade Organization in 2001.

Although the PRC needs economic growth to spur its development, the government began to worry that rapid economic growth was degrading the country's resources and environment. Another concern is that certain sectors of society are not sufficiently benefiting from the PRC's economic development; one example of this is the wide gap between urban and rural areas. As a result, under former CPC general secretary and President Hu Jintao and Premier Wen Jiabao, the PRC initiated policies to address issues of equitable distribution of resources, but the outcome was not known as of 2014[209]. More than 40 million farmers were displaced from their land, usually for economic development, contributing to 87,000 demonstrations and riots across China in 2005. For much of the PRC's population, living standards improved very substantially and freedom increased, but political controls remained tight and rural areas poor.

Further reading

<templatestyles src="Template:Refbegin/styles.css" />

Surveys

- Blunden, Caroline, and Mark Elvin. *Cultural Atlas of China* (2nd ed 1998) excerpt and text search[210]
- Dardess, John W. (2010). *Governing China, 150-1850*[211]. Hackett Publishing. ISBN 1-60384-311-6.<templatestyles src="Module:Citation/CS1/styles.css"></templatestyles>
- Eberhard, Wolfram. *A History of China* (1950; 4th edition, revised 1977), 380 pages' Google Book[212]
- Ebrey, Patricia Buckley (2010). *The Cambridge Illustrated History of China*. Cambridge: Cambridge University Press. ISBN 9780521196208.<templatestyles src="Module:Citation/CS1/styles.css"></templatestyles>

- Elvin, Mark. *The Pattern of the Chinese Past* (Stanford Up, 1973)
- Fairbank, John King and Goldman, Merle. *China: A New History.* 2nd ed. Harvard U. Press, (2006). 640 pp.
- Gernet, Jacques, J. R. Foster, and Charles Hartman. *A History of Chinese Civilization* (1996). One-volume survey.
- Hsu, Cho-yun. *China: A New Cultural History* (Columbia University Press; 2012) 612 pages; stress on China's encounters with successive waves of globalization.
- Hsü, Immanuel Chung-yueh. *The Rise of Modern China,* 6th ed. (Oxford University Press, 1999), highly detailed coverage of 1644–1999, in 1136pp.
- Huang, Ray. *China, a Macro History* (1997) 335pp. A personal, essayistic approach Questia online edition (by subscription[213]
- Keay, John. *China: A History* (2009), 642pp
- Franz, Michael. *China through the Ages: History of a Civilization.* (1986). 278pp; online edition Questia (by subscription[214]
- Mote, Frederick W. *Imperial China, 900–1800* Harvard University Press, 1999, 1,136 pages. Aauthoritative treatment of the Song, Yuan, Ming, and Qing dynasties.
- Perkins, Dorothy. *Encyclopedia of China: The Essential Reference to China, Its History and Culture.* Facts on File, 1999. 662 pp.
- Roberts, J. A. G. *A Concise History of China.* Harvard U. Press, 1999. 341 pp.
- Schoppa, R. Keith. *The Columbia Guide to Modern Chinese History.* Columbia U. Press, 2000. 356 pp. Questia online edition (by subscription[215]
- Spence, Jonathan D. *The Search for Modern China* (1999), 876pp; survey from 1644 to 1990s [[Questia[216]]] online edition (by subscription).
- Wang, Ke-wen, ed. *Modern China: An Encyclopedia of History, Culture, and Nationalism.* Garland, 1998. 442 pp.
- Wright, David Curtis. *History of China* (2001) 257pp; Questia online edition (by subscription)[217]
- Wills, Jr., John E. *Mountain of Fame: Portraits in Chinese History* (1994) Biographical essays on important figures.

Prehistory

- Chang, Kwang-chih. *The Archaeology of Ancient China,* Yale University Press, 1986.
- Discovery of residue from fermented beverage consumed up to 9,000 years ago in Jiahu, Henan Province, China. By Dr. Patrick E McGovern, University of Pennsylvania archaeochemist and colleagues from China, Great Britain and Germany.

- Zhu, Rixiang; Zhisheng An; Richard Potts; Kenneth A. Hoffman. "Magnetostratigraphic dating of early humans in China"[218] (PDF). Bibcode: 2003ESRv...61..341Z[219]. doi: 10.1016/S0012-8252(02)00132-0[220]. Retrieved 23 January 2011.<templatestyles src="Module:Citation/CS1/styles.css"></templatestyles>
- The Discovery of Early Pottery in China[221] by Zhang Chi, Department of Archaeology, Peking University, China.

Shang dynasty

- Durant, Stephen W. *The Cloudy Mirror: Tension and Conflict in the Writings of Sima Qian* (1995).

Qin

- Lewis, Mark Edward (2007). *The Early Chinese Empires: Qin and Han.* History of imperial China Series. Cambridge, Massachusetts: Belknap Press of Harvard University Press. ISBN 9780674024779.<templatestyles src="Module:Citation/CS1/styles.css"></templatestyles>

Han dynasty

- de Crespigny, Rafe. 1972. The Ch'iang Barbarians and the Empire of Han: A Study in Frontier Policy. *Papers on Far Eastern History* 16, Australian National University. Canberra.
- de Crespigny, Rafe. 1984. *Northern Frontier. The Policies and Strategies of the Later Han Empire.* Rafe de Crespigny. 1984. Faculty of Asian Studies, Australian National University. Canberra.
- de Crespigny, Rafe (1990). Chapter One from *Generals of the South: the Foundation and early history of the Three Kingdoms state of Wu.* "South China under the Later Han Dynasty"[222]. *Asian Studies Monographs, New Series No. 16.* Faculty of Asian Studies, The Australian National University, Canberra. Archived from the original[223] on 16 November 2010. Retrieved 23 January 2011.<templatestyles src="Module:Citation/CS1/styles.css"></templatestyles>
- de Crespigny, Rafe (1996). "Later Han Military Administration: An Outline of the Military Administration of the Later Han Empire"[224]. *Asian Studies Monographs, New Series No. 21* (Based on the Introduction to Emperor Huan and Emperor Ling being the Chronicle of Later Han for the years 189 to 220 AD as recorded in Chapters 59 to 69 of the Zizhi tongjian of Sima Guang ed.). Faculty of Asian Studies, The Australian National University. Archived from the original[225] on 28 May 2011. Retrieved 23 January 2011.<templatestyles src="Module:Citation/CS1/styles.css"></templatestyles>

- Dubs, Homer H. 1938–55. *The History of the Former Han Dynasty by Pan Ku.* (3 vol)
- Hill, John E. (2009) *Through the Jade Gate to Rome: A Study of the Silk Routes during the Later Han Dynasty, 1st to 2nd centuries CE.* <templatestyles src="Module:Citation/CS1/styles.css" />ISBN 978-1-4392-2134-1.
- Hulsewé, A. F. P. and Loewe, M. A. N., eds. *China in Central Asia: The Early Stage 125 B.C. – A.D. 23: an annotated translation of chapters 61 and 96 of the History of the Former Han Dynasty.* (1979)
- Twitchett, Denis and Loewe, Michael, eds. 1986. *The Cambridge History of China. Volume I. The Ch'in and Han Empires, 221 B.C. – a.d. 220.* Cambridge University Press.
- Yap, Joseph P. (2009) *Wars With the Xiongnu – A Translation From Zizhi tongjian*, AuthorHouse. <templatestyles src="Module:Citation/CS1/styles.css" />ISBN 1-4900-0604-4

Jin, the Sixteen Kingdoms, and the Northern and Southern dynasties

- de Crespigny, Rafe (1991). "The Three Kingdoms and Western Jin: A History of China in the Third Century AD"[226]. *East Asian History*. Faculty of Asian Studies, Australian National University, Canberra (1 June 1991, pp. 1–36, & no. 2 December 1991, pp. 143–164). Retrieved 23 January 2011.<templatestyles src="Module:Citation/CS1/styles.css"></templatestyles>
- Lewis, Mark Edward (2009). *China between Empires: The Northern and Southern Dynasties*. Cambridge, Massachusetts: Belknap Press of Harvard University Press. ISBN 9780674040151.<templatestyles src="Module:Citation/CS1/styles.css"></templatestyles>

Sui dynasty

- Wright, Arthur F. 1978. *The Sui Dynasty*. Alfred A. Knopf, New York. <templatestyles src="Module:Citation/CS1/styles.css" />ISBN 0-394-49187-4, <templatestyles src="Module:Citation/CS1/styles.css" />ISBN 0-394-32332-7 (pbk).

Tang dynasty

- Benn, Charles. 2002. *China's Golden Age: Everyday Life in the Tang Dynasty*. Oxford University Press. <templatestyles src="Module:Citation/CS1/styles.css" />ISBN 0-19-517665-0.

- Lewis, Mark Edward. 2012. *China's Cosmopolitan Empire: The Tang Dynasty* (2012). excerpt[227]; A standard scholarly survey.
- Schafer, Edward H. 1967. *The Vermilion Bird: T'ang Images of the South*. University of California Press, Berkeley and Los Angeles. Reprint 1985. <templatestyles src="Module:Citation/CS1/styles.css" />ISBN 0-520-05462-8.
- Shaffer, Lynda Norene. 1996. *Maritime Southeast Asia to 1500*. Armonk, New York, M.E. Sharpe, Inc. <templatestyles src="Module:Citation/CS1/styles.css" />ISBN 1-56324-144-7.
- Wang, Zhenping. 1991. "T'ang Maritime Trade Administration." Wang Zhenping. *Asia Major*, Third Series, Vol. IV, 1991, pp. 7–38.

Song dynasty

- Ebrey, Patricia. *The Inner Quarters: Marriage and the Lives of Chinese Women in the Sung Period* (1990)
- Gernet, , Jacques (1962). *Daily Life in China, on the Eve of the Mongol Invasion, 1250–1276*. translated by Wright, H. M. Stanford, CA: Stanford University Press. ISBN 0804707200.<templatestyles src="Module:Citation/CS1/styles.css"></templatestyles>
- Hymes, Robert, and Conrad Schirokauer, eds. *Ordering the World: Approaches to State and Society in Sung Dynasty China*, U of California Press, 1993; complete text online free[228]
- Kuhn, Dieter (2009). *The Age of Confucian Rule: The Song Transformation of China*. Cambridge, Massachusetts: Belknap Press of Harvard University Press. ISBN 9780674031463.<templatestyles src="Module:Citation/CS1/styles.css"></templatestyles>
- Shiba, Yoshinobu. 1970. *Commerce and Society in Sung China*. Originally published in Japanese as *So-dai sho-gyo—shi kenkyu-*. Tokyo, Kazama shobo-, 1968. Yoshinobu Shiba. Translation by Mark Elvin, Centre for Chinese Studies, University of Michigan.

Yuan dynasty

- Brook, Timothy (2010). *The Troubled Empire: China in the Yuan and Ming Dynasties*[229]. Cambridge, Massachusetts: Belknap Press of Harvard University Press. ISBN 978-0-674-04602-3.<templatestyles src="Module:Citation/CS1/styles.css"></templatestyles>

Ming dynasty

- Brook, Timothy. *The Confusions of Pleasure: Commerce and Culture in Ming China.* (1998).
- —— (2010). *The Troubled Empire: China in the Yuan and Ming Dynasties*[229]. Cambridge, Massachusetts: Belknap Press of Harvard University Press. ISBN 978-0-674-04602-3.<templatestyles src="Module:Citation/CS1/styles.css"></templatestyles> 329 pages. Focus on the impact of a Little Ice Age on the empire, as the empire, beginning with a sharp drop in temperatures in the 13th century during which time the Mongol leader Kubla Khan moved south into China.
- Dardess, John W. *A Ming Society: T'ai-ho County, Kiangsi, Fourteenth to Seventeenth Centuries.* (1983); uses advanced "new social history" complete text online free[230]
- Farmer, Edward. *Zhu Yuanzhang and Early Ming Legislation: The Reordering of Chinese Society Following the Era of Mongol Rule.* E.J. Brill, 1995.
- Goodrich, L. Carrington, and Chaoying Fang. *Dictionary of Ming Biography.* (1976).
- Huang, Ray. *1587, A Year of No Significance: The Ming Dynasty in Decline.* (1981).
- Mote, Frederick W., and Denis Twitchett, eds. *The Cambridge History of China. Vol. 7, part 1: The Ming Dynasty, 1368–1644* (1988). 1008 pp. excerpt and text search[231]
- ——*The Cambridge History of China. Vol. 8: The Ming Dynasty, 1368–1644, Part 2.* (1998). 1203 pp.
- Schneewind, Sarah. *A Tale of Two Melons: Emperor and Subject in Ming China.* (2006).
- Tsai, Shih-shan Henry. *Perpetual Happiness: The Ming Emperor Yongle.* (2001).

Qing dynasty

- Arthur W. Hummel. *Eminent Chinese of the Ch'ing Period (1644–1912).* (Washington: Library of Congress. Orientalia, Division; U.S. Government Printing Office, 1943). 2 vols. Reprinted: Berkshire, 2016. 800 still generally reliable biographical articles, a number of which are online: Qing Research Portal[232].
- Fairbank, John K. and Liu, Kwang-Ching, ed. *The Cambridge History of China. Vol. 2: Late Ch'ing, 1800–1911, Part 2.* Cambridge U. Press, 1980. 754 pp.
- Mann, Susan. *Precious Records: Women in China's Long Eighteenth Century* (1997)

- Naquin, Sysan, and Evelyn S. Rawski. *Chinese Society in the Eighteenth Century* (1989) excerpt and text search[233]
- Peterson, Willard J., ed. *The Cambridge History of China. Vol. 9, Part 1: The Ch'ing Dynasty to 1800.* Cambridge U. Press, 2002. 753 pp.
- Rawski, Evelyn S. *The Last Emperors: A Social History of Qing Imperial Institutions* (2001)
- Rowe, William T. (2009). *China's Last Empire: The Great Qing*[234]. Cambridge, Massachusetts: Harvard University Press. ISBN 9780674036123.<templatestyles src="Module:Citation/CS1/styles.css"></templatestyles>
- Smith, Richard J. (2015). *The Qing Dynasty and Traditional Chinese Culture*[235]. Lanham: Rowman & Littlefield. ISBN 978-1-4422-2194-9.<templatestyles src="Module:Citation/CS1/styles.css"></templatestyles>
- Struve, Lynn A., ed. *The Qing Formation in World-Historical Time.* (2004). 412 pp.
- Struve, Lynn A., ed. *Voices from the Ming-Qing Cataclysm: China in Tigers' Jaws* (1998)
- Yizhuang, Ding. "Reflections on the 'New Qing History' School in the United States," *Chinese Studies in History,* Winter 2009/2010, Vol. 43 Issue 2, pp 92–96.

Nationalist era (1912–present)

- Bergere, Marie-Claire. *Sun Yat-Sen* (1998), 480pp. Standard biography
- Boorman, Howard L., ed. *Biographical Dictionary of Republican China.* (Vol. I-IV and Index. 1967–1979). 600 short scholarly biographies excerpt and text search[236]
- Dreyer, Edward L. *China at War, 1901–1949.* (1995). 422 pp.
- Eastman Lloyd. *Seeds of Destruction: Nationalist China in War and Revolution, 1937– 1945.* (1984)
- Eastman Lloyd et al. *The Nationalist Era in China, 1927–1949* (1991)
- Ebrey, Patricia (1996), "Surnames and Han Chinese Identity", in Melissa J. Brown, *Negotiating Ethnicities in China and Taiwan*, Berkeley, CA: University of California Press, <templatestyles src="Module:Citation/CS1/styles.css" />ISBN 1557290482.
- Edmondson, Robert (2002), "The February 28 Incident and National Identity", in Stephane Corcuff, *Momories of the Future:National Identity Issues and the Search for a New Taiwan*, New York: M.E. Sharpe.
- Fairbank, John K., ed. *The Cambridge History of China, Vol. 12, Republican China 1912–1949. Part 1.* (1983) 1001 pp.

- Fairbank, John K. and Feuerwerker, Albert, eds. *The Cambridge History of China. Vol. 13: Republican China, 1912–1949, Part 2.* (1986). 1092 pp.
- Fogel, Joshua A. *The Nanjing Massacre in History and Historiography* (2000)
- Gordon, David M. "The China-Japan War, 1931–1945," *The Journal of Military History* v70#1 (2006) 137–182. Overview of important books and interpretations; online[237]
- Hsiung, James C. and Steven I. Levine, eds. *China's Bitter Victory: The War with Japan, 1937–1945* (1992), essays by scholars; Questia online edition (by subscription[238];
- Hsi-sheng, Ch'i. *Nationalist China at War: Military Defeats and Political Collapse, 1937–1945* (1982)
- Mitter, Rana. *Forgotten Ally: China's World War II, 1937–1945.* (Boston: Houghton Mifflin Harcourt, 2013). <templatestyles src="Module:Citation/CS1/styles.css" />ISBN 9780618894253.
- Manthorpe, Jonathan (2008), Forbidden Nation: A History of Taiwan, Palgrave Macmillan.
- Mitter, Rana. *A Bitter Revolution : China's Struggle with the Modern World.* (Oxford; New York: Oxford University Press, 2004). <templatestyles src="Module:Citation/CS1/styles.css" />ISBN 0192803417.
- Hung, Chang-tai. *War and Popular Culture: Resistance in Modern China, 1937–1945* (1994) complete text online free[239]
- Lary, Diana. *The Chinese People at War: Human Suffering and Social Transformation, 1937–1945* (2010)
- Rubinstein, Murray A., ed. *Taiwan: A New History* (2006), 560pp
- Shiroyama, Tomoko. *China during the Great Depression: Market, State, and the World Economy, 1929–1937* (2008)
- Singh, Gunjan. "Kuomintang, Democratization and the One-China Principle", in Sharma, Anita; Chakrabarti, Sreemati, *Taiwan Today*, Anthem Press, pp. 42–65 (2010) <templatestyles src="Module:Citation/CS1/styles.css" />ISBN 9780857289667.
- Shuyun, Sun. *The Long March: The True History of Communist China's Founding Myth* (2007)
- Taylor, Jay. *The Generalissimo: Chiang Kai-shek and the Struggle for Modern China.* (2009) <templatestyles src="Module:Citation/CS1/styles.css" />ISBN 978-0-674-03338-2
- Westad, Odd Arne. *Decisive Encounters: The Chinese Civil War, 1946–1950.* (2003). 413 pp. A standard history
- Wilson, Richard W. *Learning To Be Chinese: The Political Socialization of Children in Taiwan* (1970)

Communist era (1949–present)

- Barnouin, Barbara, and Yu Changgen. *Zhou Enlai: A Political Life* (2005)
- Chang, Jung and Jon Halliday. *Mao: The Unknown Story*, (2005), 814 pages, <templatestyles src="Module:Citation/CS1/styles.css" />ISBN 0-679-42271-4
- Davin, Delia (2013). *Mao: A Very Short Introduction*[240]. Oxford UP.<templatestyles src="Module:Citation/CS1/styles.css"></templatestyles>
- Dikötter, Frank. *The Tragedy of Liberation : A History of the Chinese Revolution, 1945–57.* (New York: Bloomsbury Press, 2013). <templatestyles src="Module:Citation/CS1/styles.css" />ISBN 9781620403471.
- Dikötter, Frank. *Mao's Great Famine: The History of China's Most Devastating Catastrophe, 1958–62.* (London: Bloomsbury, 2010). <templatestyles src="Module:Citation/CS1/styles.css" />ISBN 9780747595083.
- Dittmer, Lowell. *China's Continuous Revolution: The Post-Liberation Epoch, 1949–1981* (1989) online free[241].
- Gao, Wenqian (2007). *Zhou Enlai: The Last Perfect Revolutionary*. translated by Rand, Peter and Lawrence R. Sullivan. NY: Public Affairs. ISBN 978-1-58648-415-6.<templatestyles src="Module:Citation/CS1/styles.css"></templatestyles>. Both sympathetic and critical.
- Kirby, William C.; Ross, Robert S.; and Gong, Li, eds. *Normalization of U.S.-China Relations: An International History.* (2005). 376 pp.
- Li, Xiaobing. *A History of the Modern Chinese Army* (2007)
- MacFarquhar, Roderick and Fairbank, John K., eds. *The Cambridge History of China. Vol. 15: The People's Republic, Part 2: Revolutions within the Chinese Revolution, 1966–1982.* Cambridge U. Press, 1992. 1108 pp.
- Meisner, Maurice. *Mao's China and After: A History of the People's Republic,* 3rd ed. (Free Press, 1999), dense book with theoretical and political science approach.
- Pantsov, Alexander and Steven I. Levine. *Deng Xiaoping : A Revolutionary Life.* Oxford University Press, 2015). <templatestyles src="Module:Citation/CS1/styles.css" />ISBN 9780199392032.
- Pantsov, Alexander, With Steven I Levine. *Mao: The Real Story.* (New York: Simon & Schuster, 2012). <templatestyles src="Module:Citation/CS1/styles.css" />ISBN 9781451654479.
- Spence, Jonathan. *Mao Zedong* (1999)
- Walder, Andrew G. *China under Mao: A Revolution Derailed* (Harvard University Press, 2015) 413 pp. online review[242]
- Wang, Jing. *High Culture Fever: Politics, Aesthetics, and Ideology in Deng's China* (1996) complete text online free[243]

Cultural Revolution, 1966–76

- Clark, Paul. *The Chinese Cultural Revolution: A History* (2008), a favorable look at artistic production excerpt and text search[244]
- Esherick, Joseph W.; Pickowicz, Paul G.; and Walder, Andrew G., eds. *The Chinese Cultural Revolution as History.* (2006). 382 pp.
- Jian, Guo; Song, Yongyi; and Zhou, Yuan. *Historical Dictionary of the Chinese Cultural Revolution.* (2006). 433 pp.
- Richard Curt Kraus. *The Cultural Revolution: A Very Short Introduction.* (New York: Oxford University Press, Very Short Introductions Series, 2012). <templatestyles src="Module:Citation/CS1/styles.css" / >ISBN 9780199740550.
- MacFarquhar, Roderick and Fairbank, John K., eds. *The Cambridge History of China. Vol. 15: The People's Republic, Part 2: Revolutions within the Chinese Revolution, 1966–1982.* Cambridge U. Press, 1992. 1108 pp.
- MacFarquhar, Roderick and Michael Schoenhals. *Mao's Last Revolution.* (2006).
- MacFarquhar, Roderick. *The Origins of the Cultural Revolution. Vol. 3: The Coming of the Cataclysm, 1961–1966.* (1998). 733 pp.
- Yan, Jiaqi and Gao, Gao. *Turbulent Decade: A History of the Cultural Revolution.* (1996). 736 pp.

Economy and environment

- Chao, Kang. *Man and Land in Chinese History: An Economic Analysis* (Stanford UP, 1986)
- Chow, Gregory C. *China's Economic Transformation* (2nd ed. 2007)
- Elvin, Mark. *Retreat of the Elephants: An Environmental History of China.* (2004). 564 pp.
- Elvin, Mark and Liu, Ts'ui-jung, eds. *Sediments of Time: Environment and Society in Chinese History.* (1998). 820 pp.
- von Glahn, Richard. *The Economic History of China: From Antiquity to the Nineteenth Century* (Cambridge UP, 2016). 461 pp. online review[245]
- Ji, Zhaojin. *A History of Modern Shanghai Banking: The Rise and Decline of China's Finance Capitalism.* (2003. 325) pp.
- Naughton, Barry. *The Chinese Economy: Transitions and Growth* (2007)
- Rawski, Thomas G. and Lillian M. Li, eds. *Chinese History in Economic Perspective,* University of California Press, 1992 complete text online free[246]
- Sheehan, Jackie. *Chinese Workers: A New History.* Routledge, 1998. 269 pp.
- Stuart-Fox, Martin. *A Short History of China and Southeast Asia: Tribute, Trade and Influence.* (2003). 278 pp.

Women and gender

- Ebrey, Patricia. *The Inner Quarters: Marriage and the Lives of Chinese Women in the Sung Period* (1990)
- Hershatter, Gail, and Wang Zheng. "Chinese History: A Useful Category of Gender Analysis," *American Historical Review,* Dec 2008, Vol. 113 Issue 5, pp 1404–1421
- Hershatter, Gail. *Women in China's Long Twentieth Century* (2007), full text online[247]
- Hershatter, Gail, Emily Honig, Susan Mann, and Lisa Rofel, eds. *Guide to Women's Studies in China* (1998)
- Ko, Dorothy. *Teachers of Inner Chambers: Women and Culture in China, 1573–1722* (1994)
- Mann, Susan. *Precious Records: Women in China's Long Eighteenth Century* (1997)
- Wang, Shuo. "The 'New Social History' in China: The Development of Women's History," *History Teacher,* May 2006, Vol. 39 Issue 3, pp 315–323

Scholarly journals

- *Central Asian Survey*
- *Chinese Studies in History*[248]
- *East Asian History*[249]
- *Early Medieval China*[250]. Covers the period between the end of the Han and beginning of the Tang.
- *Journal of Modern Chinese History*[251]
- *Late Imperial China*
- *Modern China: An International Journal of History and Social Science*[252]
- *Sino-Japanese Studies*[253]
- *T'oung Pao: International Journal of Chinese Studies*

Bibliography

- Benjamin Elman, Classical Historiography For Chinese History[254], (November 2015) Princeton University. Extensive lists of sinological resources and bibliography.
- Cheng, Linsun (2009). *Berkshire Encyclopedia of China.* Great Barrington, Mass.: Berkshire Pub. Group. ISBN 9781933782683.<templatestyles src="Module:Citation/CS1/styles.css"></templatestyles>

- Hayford, Charles (1997). *China*. World Bibliograpical Series. Oxford, England; Santa Barbara, CA: Clio Press. ISBN 1851092358.<templatestyles src="Module:Citation/CS1/styles.css"></templatestyles>. Selective, annotated bibliography; up to 1995.
- Li, Xiaobing. *China at War: An Encyclopedia* (2012).
- Pong., David (2009). *Encyclopedia of Modern China*. Farmington Hills, MI: Charles Scribner's Sons/Gale Cengage Learning. ISBN 9780684315713.<templatestyles src="Module:Citation/CS1/styles.css"></templatestyles>
- Wilkinson, Endymion, *Chinese History: A New Manual*, Harvard University, Asia Center (for the Harvard-Yenching Institute), 2013, 1128p., <templatestyles src="Module:Citation/CS1/styles.css" />ISBN 978-0-674-06715-8. Supersedes Wilkinson (2000). Though aimed at research specialists, contains many useful summaries that will be useful for general readers.

External links

Wikimedia Commons has media related to *History of China*.

Wikivoyage has a travel guide for *Chinese Empire*.

- (in Chinese) Chinese Database[255] by Academia Sinica.
- Modernizing China[256] from the Dean Peter Krogh Foreign Affairs Digital Archives[257]
- (in Chinese) Manuscript and Graphics Database[258] by Academia Sinica.
- Ulrich Theobald, China Knowledge (2016)[259] Online encyclopaedia of traditional China, including literature, philosophy, art, and other themes.
- Chinese Text Project[260], texts and translations of historical Chinese works.
- *Yin Yu Tang: A Chinese Home*[261], an exploration of domestic Chinese architecture during the Qing dynasty.
- Cultural Revolution Propaganda Poster[262]
- China Rediscovers its Own History[263], a 100-minute lecture on Chinese history given by Yu Ying-shih, Emeritus Professor of East Asian Studies and History at Princeton University.
- Resources for Middle School students[264] (grades 5–9).
- China from the Inside[265], a 2006 PBS documentary.
- Ancient Asian World[266]

- History of China: Table of Contents[267] by the Chaos Group at the University of Maryland.

Medieval Japan

History of Japan

History of Japan
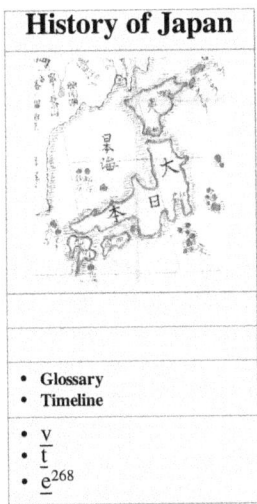
• Glossary • Timeline
• v • t • e[268]

Part of a series on the **Culture of Japan**
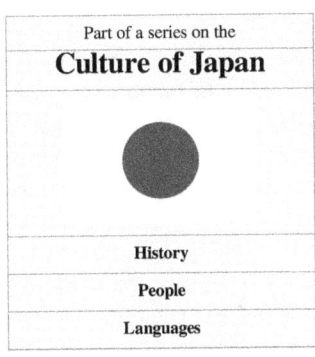
History
People
Languages

Cuisine

Festivals

- • Japan portal
- v
- t
- e[269]

The first human habitation in the Japanese archipelago has been traced to prehistoric times. The Jōmon period, named after its "cord-marked" pottery, was followed by the Yayoi in the first millennium BC, when new technologies were introduced from continental Asia. During this period, the first known written reference to Japan was recorded in the Chinese *Book of Han* in the first century AD. Between the fourth century and the ninth century, Japan's many kingdoms and tribes gradually came to be unified under a centralized government, nominally controlled by the Emperor. This imperial dynasty continues to reign over Japan. In 794, a new imperial capital was established at Heian-kyō (modern Kyoto), marking the beginning of the Heian period, which lasted until 1185. The Heian period is considered a golden age of classical Japanese culture. Japanese religious life from this time and onwards was a mix of native Shinto practices and Buddhism.

Over the following centuries the power of the Emperor and the imperial court gradually declined and passed to the military clans and their armies of samurai warriors. The Minamoto clan under Minamoto no Yoritomo emerged victorious from the Genpei War of 1180–85. After seizing power, Yoritomo set up his capital in Kamakura and took the title of *shōgun*. In 1274 and 1281, the Kamakura shogunate withstood two Mongol invasions, but in 1333 it was toppled by a rival claimant to the shogunate, ushering in the Muromachi period. During the Muromachi period regional warlords called *daimyōs* grew in power at the expense of the *shōgun*. Eventually, Japan descended into a period of civil war. Over the course of the late sixteenth century, Japan was reunified under the leadership of the *daimyō* Oda Nobunaga and his successor Toyotomi Hideyoshi. After Hideyoshi's death in 1598, Tokugawa Ieyasu came to power and was appointed *shōgun* by the Emperor. The Tokugawa shogunate, which governed from Edo (modern Tokyo), presided over a prosperous and peaceful era known as the Edo period (1600–1868). The Tokugawa shogunate imposed a strict class system on Japanese society and cut off almost all contact with the outside world.

Portugal and Japan started in 1543 their first affiliation, making the Portuguese the first Europeans to reach Japan by landing in the southern archipelago of Japan. The Netherlands were the first to establish trade relations with Japan, Japan–Netherlands relations dating back to 1609. The American Perry Expedition in 1853–54 more completely ended Japan's seclusion; this contributed to the fall of the shogunate and the return of power to the Emperor in 1868. The new national leadership of the following Meiji period transformed the isolated, feudal island country into an empire that closely followed Western models and became a great power. Although democracy developed and modern civilian culture prospered during the Taishō period (1912–26), Japan's powerful military had great autonomy and overruled Japan's civilian leaders in the 1920s and 1930s. The military invaded Manchuria in 1931, and from 1937 the conflict escalated into a prolonged war with China. Japan's attack on Pearl Harbor in December 1941 led to war with the United States and its allies. Japan's forces soon became overextended, but the military held out in spite of Allied air attacks that inflicted severe damage on population centers. Emperor Hirohito announced Japan's unconditional surrender on 15 August 1945, following the atomic bombings of Hiroshima and Nagasaki and the Soviet invasion of Manchuria.

The Allies occupied Japan until 1952, during which a new constitution was enacted in 1947 that transformed Japan into a constitutional monarchy. After 1955, Japan enjoyed very high economic growth, and became a world economic powerhouse. Since the 1990s, economic stagnation has been a major issue. An earthquake and tsunami in 2011 caused massive economic dislocations and a serious nuclear power disaster.

Geographical background

The mountainous Japanese archipelago stretches northeast to southwest 3,000 km off the east of the Asian continent at the convergence of four tectonic plates; it has about forty active volcanoes and experiences about 1,000 earthquakes a year. The steep, craggy mountains that cover two-thirds of its surface are prone to quick erosion from fast-flowing rivers and to mudslides. They thus have hampered internal travel and communication and driven the population to rely on transportation along coastal waters. There is a great variety to its regions' geographical features and weather patterns, with a rainy season in most parts in early summer. Volcanic soil that washes along the 13% of the area that makes up the coastal plains provides fertile land, and the mainly temperate climate allows long growing seasons, which with the diversity of flora and fauna provide rich resources able to support the density of the population.[270]

Overview

A commonly accepted periodization of Japanese history:

Dates	Period	Period	Subperiod	Main government
30,000–10,000 BC	Japanese Paleolithic			unknown
10,000–300 BC	Ancient Japan	Jōmon		
300 BC – 300 AD		Yayoi		
300–538		Kofun		Imperial government
538–710	Classical Japan	Asuka		
710–794		Nara		
794–1185		Heian		
1185–1333	Medieval Japan	Kamakura		Kamakura shogunate
1333–1336		Kenmu Restoration		Imperial government
1336–1392		Muromachi	Nanboku-chō period	Ashikaga shogunate
1392–1467				
1467–1573			Sengoku period	Ashikaga shogunate and *sengoku daimyōs*
1573–1603		Azuchi–Momoyama		Oda Nobunaga, Toyotomi Hideyoshi and Tokugawa Ieyasu
1603–1868	Early Modern Japan	Edo	Tokugawa period	Tokugawa shogunate
1868–1912	Modern Japan	Meiji	Pre-war	Imperial government
1912–1926		Taishō		
1926–1945		Shōwa (Prewar)		
1945–1952	Contemporary Japan	Shōwa (Occupied Post-war)	Post-war	GHQ/SCAP
1952–1989		Shōwa (Post-occupation)		Parliamentary democracy

| 1989–present | Heisei | | |

Prehistoric and ancient Japan

Paleolithic and Jōmon periods

Land bridges, during glacial periods when the world sea level is lower, have periodically linked the Japanese archipelago to the Asian continent via Sakhalin Island in the north and via the Ryukyu Islands and Taiwan in the south since the beginning of the current Quaternary glaciation 2.58 million years ago. There may also have been a land bridge to Korea in the southwest, though not in the 125,000 years or so since the start of the last interglacial. The Korea Strait was, however, quite narrow at the Last Glacial Maximum from 25,000 to 20,000 years BP. The earliest firm evidence of human habitation is of early Upper Paleolithic hunter-gatherers from 40,000 years ago, when Japan was separated from the continent. Edge-ground axes dating to 32–38,000 years ago, found in 224 sites in Honshu and Kyushu, are unlike anything found in neighbouring areas of continental Asia,[271] and have been proposed as evidence for the first *Homo sapiens* in Japan; watercraft appear to have been in use in this period. Radiocarbon dating has shown that the earliest fossils in Japan date back to around 32,000-27,000 years ago; for example in the case of Yamashita Cave 32,100 ± 1,000 BP, in Sakitari Cave cal 31,000–29,000 BP, in Shiraho Saonetabaru Cave c. 27,000 BP among others.

The Jōmon period of prehistoric Japan spans from about 12,000 BC[272] (in some cases dates as early as 14,500 BC are given[273]) to about 800 BC.[274] Japan was inhabited by a hunter-gatherer culture that reached a considerable degree of sedentism and cultural complexity. The name "cord-marked" was first applied by the American scholar Edward S. Morse who discovered shards of pottery in 1877 and subsequently translated it into Japanese as *jōmon*.[275] The pottery style characteristic of the first phases of Jōmon culture was decorated by impressing cords into the surface of wet clay.

Yayoi period

New technologies and modes of living took over from the Jōmon culture, spreading from northern Kyushu. The date of the change was until recently thought to be around 400 BC,[276,277] but radio-carbon evidence suggests a date up to 500 years earlier, between 1,000 and 800 BC. The period was named after a district in Tokyo where a new, unembellished style of pottery was discovered in 1884. Though hunting and foraging continued, the Yayoi period brought a new reliance on agriculture. Bronze and iron weapons and tools

Figure 60: *Jōmon period pottery*

Figure 61: *A Yayoi period bronze bell, third century AD*

were imported from China and Korea; such tools were later also produced in Japan.[278] The Yayoi period also saw the introduction of weaving and silk production,[279] glassmaking and new techniques of woodworking.

The Yayoi technologies originated on the Asian mainland. There is debate among scholars as to what extent their spread was accomplished by means of migration or simply a diffusion of ideas, or a combination of both. The migration theory is supported by genetic and linguistic studies.[280] Hanihara Kazurō has suggested that the annual immigrant influx from the continent ranged from 350 to 3,000.[281] Modern Japanese are genetically more similar to the Yayoi people than to the Jōmon people—though more so in southern Japan than in the north—whereas the Ainu bear significant resemblance to the Jōmon people.[282] It took time for the Yayoi people and their descendants to fully displace or intermix with the Jōmon, who continued to exist in northern Honshu until the eighth century AD.[283]

The population of Japan began to increase rapidly, perhaps with a 10-fold rise over the Jōmon. Calculations of the population size have varied from 1.5 to 4.5 million by the end of the Yayoi.[284] Skeletal remains from the late Jōmon period reveal a deterioration in already poor standards of health and nutrition, in contrast to Yayoi archaeological sites where there are large structures suggestive of grain storehouses. This change was accompanied by an increase in both the stratification of society and tribal warfare, indicated by segregated gravesites and military fortifications. Yoshinogari site, a large moated village of the period, began to be excavated by archaeologists in the late-1980s.[285]

During the Yayoi period, the Yayoi tribes gradually coalesced into a number of kingdoms. The earliest written work of history to mention Japan, the *Book of Han* completed around 82 AD, states that Japan, referred to as Wa, was divided into one hundred kingdoms. A later Chinese work of history, the *Wei Zhi*, states that by 240 AD one powerful kingdom had gained ascendancy over the others. According to the *Wei Zhi*, this kingdom was called Yamatai, though modern historians continue to debate its location and other aspects of its depiction in the *Wei Zhi*. Yamatai was said to have been ruled by the female monarch Himiko.[286]

Kofun period (c. 250–538)

During the subsequent Kofun period, most of Japan gradually unified under a single kingdom. The symbol of the growing power of Japan's new leaders was the *kofun* burial mounds they constructed from around 250 onwards.[287] Many were of massive scale, such as the Daisenryō Kofun, a 486 m-long keyhole-shaped burial mound that took huge teams of laborers fifteen years to complete.[288] The *kofun* were often surrounded by and filled with numerous *haniwa* clay sculptures, often in the shape of warriors and horses.

Figure 62: *Daisenryō Kofun, Osaka*

The center of the unified state was Yamato in the Kinai region of central Japan. The rulers of the Yamato state were a hereditary line of Emperors who still reign as the world's longest dynasty. The rulers of the Yamato extended their power across Japan through military conquest, but their preferred method of expansion was to convince local leaders to accept their authority in exchange for positions of influence in the government.[289] Many of the powerful local clans who joined the Yamato state became known as the *uji*.

These leaders sought and received formal diplomatic recognition from China, and Chinese accounts record five successive such leaders as the Five kings of Wa. Craftsmen and scholars from China and the Three Kingdoms of Korea played an important role in transmitting continental technologies and administrative skills to Japan during this period.[290]

Figure 63: *Territorial extent of Yamato court during the Kofun period*

Classical Japan

Asuka period (538–710)[291]

The Asuka period began in 538 AD with the introduction of the Buddhist religion from the Korean kingdom of Baekje.[292] Since then, Buddhism has coexisted with Japan's native Shinto religion, in what is today known as Shinbutsu-shūgō.[293] The period draws its name from the *de facto* imperial capital, Asuka, in the Kinai region.

The Buddhist Soga clan took over the government in 587 and controlled Japan from behind the scenes for nearly sixty years.[294] Prince Shōtoku, an advocate of Buddhism and of the Soga cause, who was of partial Soga descent, served as regent and *de facto* leader of Japan from 594 to 622. Shōtoku authored the Seventeen-article constitution, a Confucian-inspired code of conduct for officials and citizens, and attempted to introduce a merit-based civil service called the Cap and Rank System.[295] In 607, Shōtoku offered a subtle insult to China by opening his letter with the phrase, "The sovereign of the land where the sun rises is sending this mail to the sovereign of the land where the sun sets" as seen in the kanji characters for Japan (Nippon) thus indicating that sun's full strength originates with Japan and China receives the waning sun.[296] By 670 a variant of this expression, *Nihon*, established itself as the official name of the nation, which has persisted to this day.[297]

Figure 64: *Prince Shōtoku*

In 645, the Soga clan were overthrown in a coup launched by Prince Naka no Ōe and Fujiwara no Kamatari, the founder of the Fujiwara clan.[298] Their government devised and implemented the far-reaching Taika Reforms. The reforms nationalized all land in Japan, to be distributed equally among cultivators, and ordered the compilation of a household registry as the basis for a new system of taxation.[299] Subsequently, the Jinshin War of 672, a bloody conflict between Prince Ōama and his nephew Prince Ōtomo, two rivals to the throne, became a major catalyst for further administrative reforms. These reforms culminated with the promulgation of the Taihō Code, which consolidated existing statutes and established the structure of the central government and its subordinate local governments.[300] These legal reforms created the *ritsuryō* state, a system of Chinese-style centralized government that remained in place for half a millennium.

Nara period (710–794)

In 710, the government constructed a grandiose new capital at Heijō-kyō (modern Nara) modeled on Chang'an, the capital of the Chinese Tang dynasty. During this period, the first two books produced in Japan appeared: the *Kojiki* and *Nihon Shoki*,[301] which contain chronicles of legendary accounts of early Japan and its creation myth, which describes the imperial line as descendants of the gods.[302] The latter half of the eighth century saw the compilation of the *Man'yōshū*, widely considered the finest collection of Japanese poetry.[303]

During this period, Japan suffered a series of natural disasters, including wildfires, droughts, famines, and outbreaks of disease, such as a smallpox epidemic that killed over a quarter of the population.[304] Emperor Shōmu (r. 724–49) feared his lack of piousness had caused the trouble and so increased the government's promotion of Buddhism, including the construction of the temple Tōdai-ji.[305] The funds to build this temple were raised in part by the influential Buddhist monk Gyōki, and once completed it was used by the Chinese monk Ganjin as an ordination site.[306] Japan nevertheless entered a phase of population decline that continued well into the following Heian period.[307]

Heian period (794–1185)

In 784, the capital moved briefly to Nagaoka-kyō, then again in 794 to Heian-kyō (modern Kyoto), which remained the capital until 1868.[308] Political power within the court soon passed to the Fujiwara clan, a family of court nobles who grew increasingly close to the imperial family through intermarriage.[309] In 858, Fujiwara no Yoshifusa had himself declared *sesshō* ("regent") to the underage Emperor. His son Fujiwara no Mototsune created the office of *kampaku*, which could rule in the place of an adult reigning Emperor. Fujiwara

Figure 65: *Miniature model of Heian-kyō*

no Michinaga, a skilled statesman who became *kampaku* in 996, governed during the height of the Fujiwara clan's power[310] and had four of his daughters married to Japanese Emperors. The Fujiwara clan held on to power until 1086, when Emperor Shirakawa ceded the throne to his son Emperor Horikawa but continued to exercise political power, establishing the practice of cloistered rule,[311] by which the reigning Emperor would function as a figurehead while real power was held by a retired predecessor behind the scenes.[312]

Throughout the Heian period, the power of the imperial court declined. The court became so self-absorbed with power struggles, and with the artistic pursuits of court nobles, that it neglected the administration of government outside the capital. The nationalization of land undertaken as part of the *ritsuryō* state decayed as various noble families and religious orders succeeded in securing tax-exempt status for their private *shōen* manors. By the eleventh century, more land in Japan was controlled by *shōen* owners than by the central government. The imperial court was thus deprived of the tax revenue to pay for its national army. In response, the owners of the *shōen* set up their own armies of samurai warriors.[313] Two powerful noble families that had descended from branches of the imperial family,[314] the Taira and Minamoto clans, acquired large armies and many *shōen* outside the capital. The central government began to employ these two warrior clans to help suppress rebellions and piracy.[315] Although Japan's population stabilized during the late-Heian period after hundreds of years of decline,[316] this was accompanied by the growth of a new class of slaves composed of poor farmers, debtors, and criminals sold into bondage.

During the early Heian period, the imperial court successfully consolidated its control over the Emishi people of northern Honshu.[317] Ōtomo no Otomaro was the first man the court granted the title of *seii tai-shōgun* ("Great Barbarian Subduing General").[318] In 802, seii tai-shōgun Sakanoue no Tamuramaro subjugated the Emishi people, who were led by Aterui. By 1051, members of the Abe clan, who occupied key posts in the regional government, were openly defying the central authority. The court requested the Minamoto clan to engage the Abe clan, whom they defeated in the Former Nine Years War.[319] The court, thus, temporarily reasserted its authority in northern Japan. Following another civil war – the Later Three-Year War – Fujiwara no Kiyohira took full power; his family, the Northern Fujiwara, controlled northern Honshu for the next century from their capital Hiraizumi.[320]

Between 812–814 CE, a smallpox epidemic killed almost half of the Japanese population.

In 1156, a dispute over succession to the throne erupted and the two rival claimants (Emperor Go-Shirakawa and Emperor Sutoku) hired the Taira and Minamoto clans in the hopes of securing the throne by military force. During this war, the Taira clan led by Taira no Kiyomori defeated the Minamoto clan. Kiyomori used his victory to accumulate power for himself in Kyoto and even installed his own grandson Antoku as Emperor. The outcome of this war led to the rivalry between the Minamoto and Taira clans. As a result, the dispute and power struggle between both clans led to the Heiji Rebellion in 1160. In 1180, Taira no Kiyomori was challenged by an uprising led by Minamoto no Yoritomo, a member of the Minamoto clan whom Kiyomori had exiled to Kamakura.[321] Though Taira no Kiyomori died in 1181, the ensuing bloody Genpei War between the Taira and Minamoto families continued for another four years. The victory of the Minamoto clan was sealed in 1185, when a force commanded by Yoritomo's younger brother, Minamoto no Yoshitsune, scored a decisive victory at the naval Battle of Dan-no-ura. Yoritomo and his retainers, thus, became the *de facto* rulers of Japan.[322]

Heian culture

During the Heian period, the imperial court was a vibrant center of high art and culture.[323] Its literary accomplishments include the poetry collection *Kokinshū* and the *Tosa Diary*, both associated with the poet Ki no Tsurayuki, as well as Sei Shōnagon's collection of miscellany *The Pillow Book*,[324] and Murasaki Shikibu's *Tale of Genji*, considered the supreme masterpiece of Japanese literature.[325]

The development of the kana written syllabaries was part of a general trend of declining Chinese influence during the Heian period. The Japanese missions to Tang dynasty of China, which began in the year 630,[326] ended during the

Figure 66: *A handscroll painting dated c. 1130, illustrating a scene from the "Bamboo River" chapter of The Tale of Genji*

ninth century and thereafter more typically Japanese forms of art and poetry developed.[327] A major architectural achievement, apart from Heian-kyō itself, was the temple of Byōdō-in built in 1053 in Uji.[328]

Medieval Japan

Kamakura period (1185–1333)

Upon the consolidation of power, Minamoto no Yoritomo chose to rule in consort with the imperial court in Kyoto. Though Yoritomo set up his own government in Kamakura in the Kantō region located in eastern Japan, its power was legally authorized by the Imperial court in Kyoto in several occasions. In 1192, the Emperor declared Yoritomo *seii tai-shōgun* (征夷大将軍 ; *Eastern Barbarian Subduing Great General*), abbreviated *shōgun*.[329] Later (in Edo period), the word *bakufu* (幕府 ; originally means a general's house or office, literally a "tent office") came to be used to mean a government headed by a shogun. The English term *shogunate* refers to the *bakufu*.[330] Japan remained largely under military rule until 1868.[331]

Legitimacy was conferred on the shogunate by the Imperial court, but the shogunate were the *de facto* rulers of the country. The court maintained bureaucratic and religious functions, and the shogunate welcomed participation by members of the aristocratic class. The older institutions remained intact in a weakened form, and Kyoto remained the official capital. This system has been contrasted with the "simple warrior rule" of the later Muromachi period.

While the Ise branch of the Taira, which had fought against Yoritomo, was extinguished, other branches, as well as the Hōjō, Chiba, Hatakeyama and

Figure 67: *A samurai battling Mongol forces*

other families descended from the Taira, continued to thrive in eastern Japan, with some (notably the Hōjō) attaining high positions in the Kamakura shogunate.[332] WP:NOTRS Yoshitsune was initially harbored by Fujiwara no Hidehira, the grandson of Kiyohira and the de facto ruler of northern Honshu. In 1189, after Hidehira's death, his successor Yasuhira attempted to curry favor with Yoritomo by attacking Yoshitsune's home. Although Yoshitsune was killed, Yoritomo still invaded and conquered the Northern Fujiwara clan's territories.[333] In subsequent centuries, Yoshitsune would become a legendary figure, portrayed in countless works of literature as an idealized tragic hero.[334]

After Yoritomo's death in 1199, the office of shogun weakened. Behind the scenes, Yoritomo's wife Hōjō Masako became the true power behind the government. In 1203, her father, Hōjō Tokimasa, was appointed regent to the shogun, Yoritomo's son Minamoto no Sanetomo. Henceforth, the Minamoto shoguns became puppets of the Hōjō regents, who wielded actual power.[335]

The regime that Yoritomo had established, and which was kept in place by his successors, was decentralized and feudalistic in structure, in contrast with the earlier ritsuryō state. Yoritomo selected the provincial governors, known under the titles of *shugo* or *jitō*,[336] from among his close vassals, the *gokenin*. The Kamakura shogunate allowed its vassals to maintain their own armies and to administer law and order in their provinces on their own terms.[337]

In 1221, the retired Emperor Go-Toba instigated what became known as the Jōkyū War, a rebellion against the shogunate, in an attempt to restore political power to the court. The rebellion was a failure, and led to Go-Toba himself being exiled to Oki Island, along with two other Emperors, the retired Emperor Tsuchimikado and Emperor Juntoku, who were exiled to Tosa Province and Sado Island respectively.[338] The shogunate further consolidated its political power relative to the Kyoto aristocracy.[339]

The samurai armies of the whole nation were mobilized in 1274 and 1281 to confront two full-scale invasions launched by Kublai Khan of the Mongol Empire.[340] Though outnumbered by an enemy equipped with superior weaponry, the Japanese fought the Mongols to a standstill in Kyushu on both occasions until the Mongol fleet was destroyed by typhoons called *kamikaze*, meaning "divine wind". In spite of the Kamakura shogunate's victory, the defense so depleted its finances that it was unable to provide compensation to its vassals for their role in the victory. This had permanent negative consequences for the shogunate's relations with the samurai class.[341]

Discontent among the samurai proved decisive in ending the Kamakura shogunate. In 1333, Emperor Go-Daigo launched a rebellion in the hope of restoring full power to the imperial court. The shogunate sent General Ashikaga Takauji to quell the revolt, but Takauji and his men instead joined forces with Emperor Go-Daigo and overthrew the Kamakura shogunate.[342]

Japan nevertheless entered a period of prosperity and population growth starting around 1250. In rural areas, the greater use of iron tools and fertilizer, improved irrigation techniques, and double-cropping increased productivity and rural villages grew.[343] Fewer famines and epidemics allowed cities to grow and commerce to boom. Buddhism, which had been largely a religion of the elites, was brought to the masses by prominent monks, such as Hōnen (1133–1212), who established Pure Land Buddhism in Japan, and Nichiren (1222–82), who founded Nichiren Buddhism. Zen Buddhism spread widely among the samurai class.[344]

Literary developments of the late-Heian and Kamakura periods

Waka poetry flourished in the late Heian and early Kamakura periods.

The aristocrat Fujiwara no Shunzei was "the leading poet of [his] day"[345] and on a request from Emperor Go-Shirakawa compiled the *Senzai Wakashū* the seventh imperial collection.[346] Donald Keene noted that Shunzei was "the most eminent poet since Tsurayuki to have been charged with the compilation of an imperial collection".[347] The anthology, commissioned in 1183 but not completed until 1188, after the defeat of the Taira, contained poems by Taira adherents who had been officially denounced as enemies of the throne, as a gesture to calm the vengeful spirits of the Taira.[348] It also contained poems by thirty-three female poets, the most women recognized by any of the late-Heian imperial collections.[349] Teika, Shunzei's son,[350] would become even more important: his *Hyakunin Isshu* made him "the arbiter of the poetic tastes of most Japanese even as late as the twentieth century".[351] His later work copying manuscripts was of such importance that Keene noted that "what we know of the literature of Teika's day and earlier is mainly what he thought was worthy of preservation."[352] He also served on the committee that compiled the eighth imperial anthology, the *Shin Kokin Wakashū*,[353] and along with the itinerant monk Saigyō and Emperor Go-Toba, is considered one of the best poets represented in the collection.³⁵⁴ More poems by Saigyō were included in the collection than those of any other poet.³⁵⁵ and centuries later Matsuo Bashō selected him as the representative poet of the *waka* genre.³⁵⁶

The third shogun, Minamoto no Sanetomo, was the first distinctive new poet of the Kamakura period,³⁵⁷ and he studied the art under Teika's tutelage.³⁵⁸ Among Sanetomo's admirers include Kamo no Mabuchi³⁵⁹ and Saitō Mokichi.³⁶⁰

Zen monks were associated with the composition of poetry in Chinese,³⁶¹ and at least one Zen monk, Shōtetsu, was notable for his contributions to the *waka* medium.³⁶² After Shōtetsu, however, *waka* composition became an oddity until modern times.

The Kamakura period saw an explosion in the popularity of a new genre: the "war tale" (*gunki monogatari*), whose early representative works include the *Hōgen Monogatari*, *Heiji Monogatari* and *Heike Monogatari*.³⁶³ The latter work, which recounted the rise and fall of the Taira clan, has been described as "the Japanese epic", and the twentieth-century novelist and essayist Kafū Nagai called it "a unique and immortal Japanese *épopée*."³⁶⁴ These works were at least partly indebted to earlier Heian works such as the *Shōmonki* (ja:将門記) and *Mutsu Waki* (ja:陸奥話記), bare historical chronicles of battles fought against Taira no Masakado and the Earlier Nine Years' War, narrated in a non-literary style of classical Chinese as opposed to the mixed Sino-Japanese vernacular of the later Kamakura works.³⁶⁵

Muromachi period (1333–1568)

Takauji and many other samurai soon became dissatisfied with Emperor Go-Daigo's Kenmu Restoration, an ambitious attempt to monopolize power in the imperial court. Takauji rebelled after Go-Daigo refused to appoint him shogun. In 1338, Takauji captured Kyoto and installed a rival member of the imperial family to the throne, Emperor Kōmyō, who did appoint him shogun.³⁶⁶ Go-Daigo responded by fleeing to the southern city of Yoshino, where he set up a rival government. This ushered in a prolonged period of conflict between the Northern Court and the Southern Court.³⁶⁷

Takauji set up his shogunate in the Muromachi district of Kyoto. However, the shogunate was faced with the twin challenges of fighting the Southern Court and of maintaining its authority over its own subordinate governors. Like the Kamakura shogunate, the Muromachi shogunate appointed its allies to rule in the provinces, but these men increasingly styled themselves as feudal lords—called *daimyōs*—of their domains and often refused to obey the shogun.³⁶⁸ The Ashikaga shogun who was most successful at bringing the

Figure 68: *Portrait of Ashikaga Takauji*

country together was Takauji's grandson Ashikaga Yoshimitsu, who came to power in 1368 and remained influential until his death in 1408. Yoshimitsu expanded the power of the shogunate and in 1392, brokered a deal to bring the Northern and Southern Courts together and end the civil war. Henceforth, the shogunate kept the Emperor and his court under tight control.

During the final century of the Ashikaga shogunate the country descended into another, more violent period of civil war. This started in 1467 when the Ōnin War broke out over who would succeed the ruling shogun. The *daimyōs* each took sides and burned Kyoto to the ground while battling for their preferred candidate. By the time the succession was settled in 1477, the shogun had lost all power over the *daimyō*, who now ruled hundreds of independent states throughout Japan.[369] During this Warring States period, *daimyōs* fought among themselves for control of the country.[370] Some of the most powerful *daimyōs* of the era were Uesugi Kenshin, Takeda Shingen,[371] and Date Masamune.[372] One enduring symbol of this era was the ninja, skilled spies and assassins hired by *daimyōs*. Few definite historical facts are known about the secretive lifestyles of the ninja, who became the subject of many legends.[373] In addition to the *daimyōs*, rebellious peasants and "warrior monks" affiliated with Buddhist temples also raised their own armies.[374]

Amid this on-going anarchy, a Chinese ship was blown off course and landed in 1543 on the Japanese island of Tanegashima, just south of Kyushu. The

History of Japan

Figure 69: *Map showing the territories of major daimyō families around 1570*

Figure 70: *Crest used by the daimyō Uesugi Kenshin*

Figure 71: *Edo-period screen depicting the Battle of Sekigahara. It began on 21 October 1600 with a total of 160,000 men facing each other.*

three Portuguese traders on board were António Mota, Francisco Zeimoto, and presumably Fernão Mendes Pinto. They were the first Europeans to set foot in Japan.[375] Soon European traders would introduce many new items to Japan, most importantly the musket.[376] By 1556, the *daimyōs* were already using about 300,000 muskets in their armies.[377] The Europeans also brought Christianity, which soon came to have a substantial following in Japan. The Jesuit missionary Francis Xavier disembarked in Kyushu in 1549.

Muromachi culture

In spite of the war, Japan's relative economic prosperity, which had begun in the Kamakura period, continued well into the Muromachi period. By 1450 Japan's population stood at ten million, compared to six million at the end of the thirteenth century.[378] Commerce flourished, including considerable trade with China and Korea.[379] Because the *daimyōs* and other groups within Japan were minting their own coins, Japan began to transition from a barter-based to a currency-based economy.[380] During the period, some of Japan's most representative art forms developed, including ink wash painting, *ikebana* flower arrangement, the tea ceremony, Japanese gardening, *bonsai*, and *Noh* theater.[381] Though the eighth Ashikaga shogun, Yoshimasa, was an ineffectual political and military leader, he played a critical role in promoting these cultural developments.[382]

Early modern Japan

Azuchi–Momoyama period (1568–1600)

During the second half of the 17th century Japan gradually reunified under two powerful warlords, Oda Nobunaga and Toyotomi Hideyoshi. The period

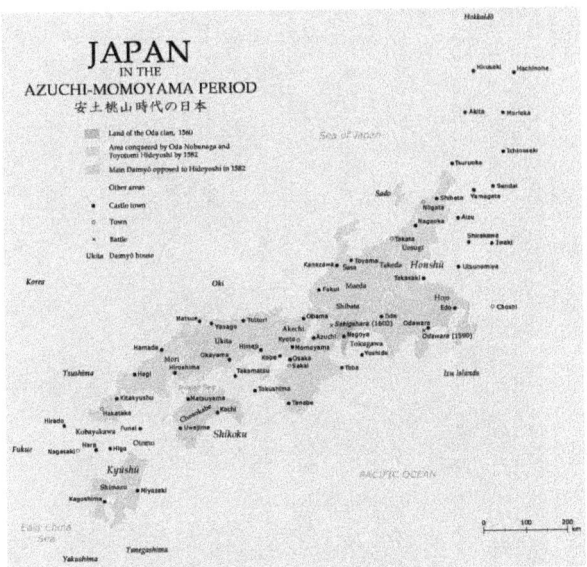

Figure 72: *Japan in 1582, territory conquered by Oda Nobunaga in grey*

takes its name from Nobunaga's headquarters, Azuchi Castle, and Hideyoshi's headquarters, Momoyama Castle.[383]

Nobunaga was the *daimyō* of the small province of Owari. He burst onto the scene suddenly in 1560 when, during the Battle of Okehazama, his army defeated a force several times its size led by the powerful *daimyō* Imagawa Yoshimoto.[384] Nobunaga was renowned for his strategic leadership and his ruthlessness. He encouraged Christianity to incite hatred toward his Buddhist enemies and to forge strong relationships with European arms merchants. He equipped his armies with muskets and trained them with innovative tactics.[385] He promoted talented men regardless of their social status, including his peasant servant Toyotomi Hideyoshi, who became one of his best generals.[386]

The Azuchi–Momoyama period began in 1568 when Nobunaga seized Kyoto and thus effectively brought an end to the Ashikaga shogunate. He was well on his way towards his goal of reuniting all Japan in 1582 when one of his own officers, Akechi Mitsuhide, killed him during an abrupt attack on his encampment. Hideyoshi avenged Nobunaga by crushing Akechi's uprising and emerged as Nobunaga's successor.[387] Hideyoshi completed the reunification of Japan by conquering Shikoku, Kyushu, and the lands of the Hōjō family in eastern Japan.[388] He launched sweeping changes to Japanese society, including the confiscation of swords from the peasantry, new restrictions

Figure 73: *Tokugawa Ieyasu*

on *daimyōs*, persecutions of Christians, a thorough land survey, and a new law effectively forbidding the peasants and samurai from changing their social class.[389] Hideyoshi's land survey designated all those who were cultivating the land as being "commoners", an act which effectively granted freedom to most of Japan's slaves.[390]

As Hideyoshi's power expanded he dreamed of conquering China and launched two massive invasions of Korea starting in 1592. Hideyoshi failed to defeat the Chinese and Korean armies on the Korean Peninsula and the war ended only after his death in 1598.

In the hope of founding a new dynasty, Hideyoshi had asked his most trusted subordinates to pledge loyalty to his infant son Toyotomi Hideyori. Despite this, almost immediately after Hideyoshi's death, war broke out between Hideyori's allies and those loyal to Tokugawa Ieyasu, a *daimyō* and a former ally of Hideyoshi.[391] Tokugawa Ieyasu won a decisive victory at the Battle of Sekigahara in 1600, ushering in 268 uninterrupted years of rule by the Tokugawa clan.[392]

Edo period (1600–1868)

The Edo period was characterized by relative peace and stability[393] under the tight control of the Tokugawa shogunate, which ruled from the eastern city

Figure 74: *Crest of the Tokugawa family*

of Edo (modern Tokyo).³⁹⁴ In 1603, Emperor Go-Yōzei declared Tokugawa Ieyasu *shōgun*, and Ieyasu abdicated two years later to groom his son as the second *shōgun* of what became a long dynasty.³⁹⁵ Nevertheless, it took time for the Tokugawas to consolidate their rule. In 1609, the *shōgun* gave the *daimyō* of Satsuma Domain permission to invade the Ryukyu Kingdom for perceived insults towards the shogunate; the Satsuma victory began 266 years of Ryukyu's dual subordination to Satsuma and China.³⁹⁶,³⁹⁷ Ieyasu led the Siege of Osaka that ended with the destruction of the Toyotomi clan in 1615.³⁹⁸ Soon after the shogunate promulgated the Laws for the Military Houses, which imposed tighter controls on the *daimyōs*,³⁹⁹ and the alternate attendance system, which required each *daimyō* to spend every other year in Edo.⁴⁰⁰ Even so, the *daimyōs* continued to maintain a significant degree of autonomy in their domains.⁴⁰¹ The central government of the shogunate in Edo, which quickly became the most populous city in the world, took counsel from a group of senior advisors known as *rōjū* and employed samurai as bureaucrats.⁴⁰² The Emperor in Kyoto was funded lavishly by the government but was allowed no political power.⁴⁰³

The Tokugawa shogunate went to great lengths to suppress social unrest. Harsh penalties, including crucifixion, beheading, and death by boiling, were decreed for even the most minor offenses, though criminals of high social class were often given the option of *seppuku* ("self-disembowelment"), an ancient form of suicide that now became ritualized. Christianity, which was seen as a potential threat, was gradually clamped down on until finally, after the Christian-led Shimabara Rebellion of 1638, the religion was completely outlawed.[404] To prevent further foreign ideas from sowing dissent, the third Tokugawa shogun, Iemitsu, implemented the *sakoku* ("closed country") isolationist policy under which Japanese people were not allowed to travel abroad, return from overseas, or build ocean-going vessels.[405] The only Europeans allowed on Japanese soil were the Dutch, who were granted a single trading post on the island of Dejima. China and Korea were the only other countries permitted to trade,[406] and many foreign books were banned from import.

During the first century of Tokugawa rule, Japan's population doubled to thirty million, due in large part to agricultural growth; the population remained stable for the rest of the period.[407] The shogunate's construction of roads, elimination of road and bridge tolls, and standardization of coinage promoted commercial expansion that also benefited the merchants and artisans of the cities.[408] City populations grew,[409] but almost ninety percent of the population continued to live in rural areas.[410] Both the inhabitants of cities and of rural communities would benefit from one of the most notable social changes of the Edo period: increased literacy and numeracy. The number of private schools greatly expanded, particularly those attached to temples and shrines, and raised literacy to thirty percent. This may have been the world's highest rate at the time[411] and drove a flourishing commercial publishing industry, which grew to produce hundreds of titles per year.[412] In the area of numeracy – approximated by an index measuring people's ability to report an exact rather than a rounded age (age-heaping method), and which level shows a strong correlation to later economic development of a country – Japan's level was comparable to that of north-west European countries, and moreover, Japan's index came close to the 100 percent mark throughout the nineteenth century. These high levels of both literacy and numeracy were part of the socio-economical foundation for Japan's strong growth rates during the following century.

Culture and philosophy

The Edo period was a time of prolific cultural output. Haiku, whose greatest master is generally considered Matsuo Bashō (1644–94),[413] rose as a major form of poetry. Forms of theatre developed, such as the flamboyant kabuki drama and *bunraku* puppet theatre, the latter of which reached its height of through the plays of Chikamatsu Monzaemon (1653–1725).[414] Members of the wealthy merchant class who patronized this poetry and theater were said to live hedonistic lives, which came to be called *ukiyo* ("floating world").[415] They often paid for the services of courtesans and geisha entertainers, most of whom also served as prostitutes in designated red-light districts such as Yoshiwara in Edo.[416] This lifestyle inspired *ukiyo-zōshi* popular novels and *ukiyo-e* art,

Figure 75: *Samurais could kill a commoner for the slightest insult and were widely feared by the Japanese population. Edo period, 1798*

the latter of which were often woodblock prints[417] that progressed to greater sophistication and use of multiple printed colors.[418]

Decline and fall of the shogunate

By the late eighteenth and early nineteenth centuries, the shogunate showed signs of weakening.[419] The dramatic growth of agriculture that had characterized the early Edo period had ended and the government handled the devastating Tenpō famines poorly. Peasant unrest grew and government revenues fell.[420] The shogunate cut the pay of the already financially distressed samurai, many of whom worked side jobs to make a living.[421] Discontented samurai were soon to play a major role in engineering the downfall of the Tokugawa shogunate.[422]

At the same time, the people drew inspiration from new ideas and fields of study. Dutch books brought into Japan stimulated interest in Western learning, called *rangaku* or "Dutch learning".[423] The physician Sugita Genpaku, for instance, used concepts from Western medicine to help spark a revolution in Japanese ideas of human anatomy.[424] The scholarly field of *kokugaku* or "National Learning", developed by scholars such as Motoori Norinaga and Hirata Atsutane, promoted what it asserted were native Japanese values. For

Figure 76: *Samurai of the Satsuma Domain during the Boshin War*

instance, it criticized the Chinese-style Neo-Confucianism advocated by the shogunate and emphasized the Emperor's divine authority, which the Shinto faith taught had its roots in Japan's mythic past, which was referred to as the "Age of the Gods".[425]

The arrival in 1853 of a fleet of American ships commanded by Commodore Matthew C. Perry threw Japan into turmoil. The US government aimed to end Japan's isolationist policies. The shogunate had no defense against Perry's gunboats and had to agree to his demands that American ships be permitted to acquire provisions and trade at Japanese ports. The US, Great Britain, Russia, and other Western powers imposed what became known as "unequal treaties" on Japan which stipulated that Japan must allow citizens of these countries to visit or reside on Japanese territory and must not levy tariffs on their imports or try them in Japanese courts.[426]

The shogunate's failure to oppose the Western powers angered many Japanese, particularly those of the southern domains of Chōshū and Satsuma.[427] Many samurai there, inspired by the nationalist doctrines of the kokugaku school, adopted the slogan of *sonnō jōi* ("revere the Emperor, expel the barbarians").[428] The two domains then went on to form an alliance. In August 1866, soon after becoming shogun, Tokugawa Yoshinobu, struggled to maintain power as civil unrest continued. In November 1867, Yoshinobu officially

Figure 77: *Emperor Meiji, the 122nd Emperor of Japan*

tendered his resignation to the Emperor and he formally stepped down ten days later.[429] The Chōshū and Satsuma domains in 1868 convinced the young Emperor Meiji and his advisors to issue a rescript calling for an end to the Tokugawa shogunate. The armies of Chōshū and Satsuma soon marched on Edo and the ensuing Boshin War led to the eventual fall of the shogunate.[430]

Modern Japan

Meiji period (1868–1912)

The Emperor was restored to nominal supreme power,[431] and in 1869, the imperial family moved to Edo, which was renamed Tokyo ("eastern capital").[432] However, the most powerful men in the government were former samurai from Chōshū and Satsuma rather than the Emperor, who was fifteen in 1868. These men, known as the Meiji oligarchs, oversaw the dramatic changes Japan would experience during this period.[433] The leaders of the Meiji government, who are regarded as some of the most successful statesmen in human history,[434] desired Japan to become a modern nation-state that could stand equal to the Western imperialist powers.[435] Among them were Ōkubo Toshimichi and Saigō Takamori from Satsuma, as well as Kido Takayoshi, Ito Hirobumi, and Yamagata Aritomo from Chōshū.

Political and social changes

The Meiji government abolished the Neo-Confucian class structure[436] and replaced the feudal domains of the *daimyōs* with prefectures. It instituted comprehensive tax reform and lifted the ban on Christianity. Major government priorities included the introduction of railways,[437] telegraph lines, and a universal education system.

The Meiji government promoted widespread Westernization[438] and hired hundreds of advisers from Western nations with expertise in such fields as education, mining, banking, law, military affairs, and transportation to remodel Japan's institutions.[439] The Japanese adopted the Gregorian calendar, Western clothing, and Western hairstyles.[440] One leading advocate of Westernization was the popular writer Fukuzawa Yukichi.[441] As part of its Westernization drive, the Meiji government enthusiastically sponsored the importation of Western science, above all medical science. In 1893, Kitasato Shibasaburō established the Institute for Infectious Diseases, which would soon become world-famous,[442] and in 1913, Hideyo Noguchi proved the link between syphilis and paresis.[443] Furthermore, the introduction of European literary styles to Japan sparked a boom in new works of prose fiction. Characteristic authors of the period included Futabatei Shimei and Mori Ōgai,[444] although the most famous of the Meiji era writers was Natsume Sōseki,[445] who wrote satirical, autobiographical, and psychological novels[446] combining both the older and newer styles.[447] Ichiyō Higuchi, a leading female author, took inspiration from earlier literary models of the Edo period.[448]

Government institutions developed rapidly in response to the Freedom and People's Rights Movement, a grassroots campaign demanding greater popular participation in politics. The leaders of this movement included Itagaki Taisuke and Ōkuma Shigenobu.[449] Itō Hirobumi, the first Prime Minister of Japan, responded by writing the Meiji Constitution, which was promulgated in 1889. The new constitution established an elected lower house, the House of Representatives, but its powers were restricted. Only two percent of the population were eligible to vote, and legislation proposed in the House required the support of the unelected upper house, the House of Peers. Both the cabinet of Japan and the Japanese military were directly responsible not to the elected legislature but to the Emperor. Concurrently, the Japanese government also developed a form of Japanese nationalism under which Shinto became the state religion and the Emperor was declared a living god.[450] Schools nationwide instilled patriotic values and loyalty to the Emperor.[451]

Figure 78: *Chinese generals surrendering to the Japanese in the Sino-Japanese War of 1894–1895*

Rise of imperialism and the military

In December 1871, a Ryukyuan ship was shipwrecked on Taiwan and the crew were massacred. In 1874, using the incident as a pretext, Japan launched a military expedition to Taiwan to assert their claims to the Ryukyu Islands. The expedition featured the first instance of the Japanese military ignoring the orders of the civilian government, as the expedition set sail after being ordered to postpone.[452]

Yamagata Aritomo, who was born a samurai in the Chōshū Domain, was a key force behind the modernization and enlargement of the Imperial Japanese Army, especially the introduction of national conscription.[453] The new army was put to use in 1877 to crush the Satsuma Rebellion of discontented samurai in southern Japan led by the former Meiji leader Saigo Takamori.[454]

The Japanese military played a key role in Japan's expansion abroad. The government believed that Japan had to acquire its own colonies to compete with the Western colonial powers. After consolidating its control over Hokkaido and annexing the Ryukyu Kingdom, it next turned its attention to China and Korea.[455] In 1894, Japanese and Chinese troops clashed in Korea, where they were both stationed to suppress the Donghak Rebellion. During the ensuing First Sino-Japanese War, Japan's highly motivated and well-led forces defeated the more numerous and better-equipped military of Qing China.[456] The island of Taiwan was thus ceded to Japan in 1895,[457] and Japan's government gained enough international prestige to allow Foreign Minister Mutsu Munemitsu to renegotiate the "unequal treaties".[458] In 1902 Japan signed an important military alliance with the British.[459]

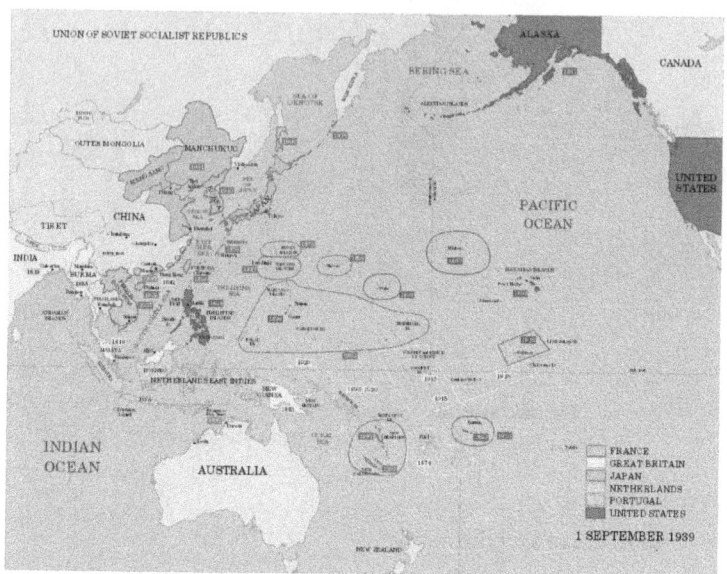

Figure 79: *Japanese Empire in 1939*

Japan next clashed with Russia, which was expanding its power in Asia. The Russo-Japanese War of 1904–05 ended with the dramatic Battle of Tsushima, which was another victory for Japan's military. Japan thus laid claim to Korea as a protectorate in 1905, followed by full annexation in 1910.[460]

Economic modernization and labor unrest

During the Meiji period, Japan underwent a rapid transition towards an industrial economy. Both the Japanese government and private entrepreneurs adopted Western technology and knowledge to create factories capable of producing a wide range of goods.[461] By the end of the period, the majority of Japan's exports were manufactured goods.[462] Some of Japan's most successful new businesses and industries constituted huge family-owned conglomerates called *zaibatsu*, such as Mitsubishi and Sumitomo.[463] The phenomenal industrial growth sparked rapid urbanization. The proportion of the population working in agriculture shrank from 75 percent in 1872 to 50 percent by 1920.[464]

Japan enjoyed solid economic growth at this time and most people lived longer and healthier lives. The population rose from 34 million in 1872 to 52 million in 1915.[465] Poor working conditions in factories led to growing labor unrest,[466] and many workers and intellectuals came to embrace socialist ideas.[467] The Meiji government responded with harsh suppression of dissent. Radical socialists plotted to assassinate the Emperor in the High Treason Incident of 1910, after which the Tokkō secret police force was established to root out left-wing agitators.[468] The government also introduced social legislation in 1911 setting maximum work hours and a minimum age for employment.[469]

Taishō period (1912–1926)

During the short reign of Emperor Taishō Japan developed stronger democratic institutions and grew in international power. The Taishō political crisis opened the period with mass protests and riots organized by Japanese political parties, which succeeded in forcing Katsura Tarō to resign as prime minister.[470] This and the rice riots of 1918 increased the power of Japan's political parties over the ruling oligarchy.[471] The Seiyūkai and Minseitō parties came to dominate politics by the end of the so-called "Taishō democracy" era.[472] The franchise for the House of Representatives had been gradually expanded since 1890,[473] and in 1925 universal male suffrage was introduced. However, in the same year the far-reaching Peace Preservation Law also passed, prescribing harsh penalties for political dissidents.[474]

Japan's participation in World War I on the side of the Allies sparked unprecedented economic growth and earned Japan new colonies in the South Pacific seized from Germany.[475] After the war Japan signed the Treaty of Versailles and enjoyed good international relations through its membership in the League of Nations and participation in international disarmament conferences.[476] The Great Kantō earthquake in September 1923 left over 100,000 dead, and combined with the resultant fires destroyed the homes of more than three million.[477]

The growth of popular prose fiction, which began during the Meiji period, continued into the Taishō period as literacy rates rose and book prices dropped.[478] Notable literary figures of the era included short story writer Ryūnosuke Akutagawa[479] and the novelist Haruo Satō. Jun'ichirō Tanizaki, described as "perhaps the most versatile literary figure of his day" by the historian Conrad Totman, produced many works during the Taishō period influenced by European literature, though his 1929 novel *Some Prefer Nettles* reflects deep appreciation for the virtues of traditional Japanese culture.[480] At the end of the Taishō period, Tarō Hirai, known by his penname Edogawa Ranpo, began writing popular mystery and crime stories.[481]

Figure 80: *The Empire of Japan in 1937*

Shōwa period (1926–1989)

Emperor Hirohito's sixty-three-year reign from 1926 to 1989 is the longest in recorded Japanese history.[482] The first twenty years were characterized by the rise of extreme nationalism and a series of expansionist wars. After suffering defeat in World War II, Japan was occupied by foreign powers for the first time in its history, and then re-emerged as a major world economic power.

Manchurian Incident and the Second Sino-Japanese War

Left-wing groups had been subject to violent suppression by the end of the Taishō period,[483] and radical right-wing groups, inspired by fascism and Japanese nationalism, rapidly grew in popularity.[484] The extreme right became influential throughout the Japanese government and society, notably within the Kwantung Army, a Japanese army stationed in China along the Japanese-owned South Manchuria Railroad.[485] During the Manchurian Incident of 1931, radical army officers bombed a small portion of the South Manchuria Railroad and, falsely attributing the attack to the Chinese, invaded Manchuria. The Kwantung Army conquered Manchuria and set up the puppet government of Manchukuo there without permission from the Japanese government. International criticism of Japan following the invasion led to Japan withdrawing from the League of Nations.[486]

Prime Minister Tsuyoshi Inukai of the Seiyūkai Party attempted to restrain the Kwantung Army and was assassinated in 1932 by right-wing extremists.

Figure 81: *Headquarters of South Manchuria Railway, Dalian, c. 1940*

Because of growing opposition within the Japanese military and the extreme right to party politicians, who they saw as corrupt and self-serving, Inukai was the last party politician to govern Japan in the pre-World War II era. In February 1936 young radical officers of the Imperial Japanese Army attempted a coup d'état. They assassinated many moderate politicians before the coup was suppressed.[487] In its wake the Japanese military consolidated its control over the political system and most political parties were abolished when the Imperial Rule Assistance Association was founded in 1940.[488]

Japan's expansionist vision grew increasingly bold. Many of Japan's political elite aspired to have Japan acquire new territory for resource extraction and settlement of surplus population.[489] These ambitions led to the outbreak of the Second Sino-Japanese War in 1937. After their victory in the Chinese capital, the Japanese military committed the infamous Nanking Massacre. The Japanese military failed to defeat the Chinese government led by Chiang Kai-shek and the war descended into a bloody stalemate that lasted until 1945.[490] Japan's stated war aim was to establish the Greater East Asia Co-Prosperity Sphere, a vast pan-Asian union under Japanese domination.[491] Hirohito's role in Japan's foreign wars remains a subject of controversy, with various historians portraying him as either a powerless figurehead or an enabler and supporter of Japanese militarism.[492]

The United States opposed Japan's invasion of China and responded with increasingly stringent economic sanctions intended to deprive Japan of the re-

Figure 82: *Japanese experts inspect the scene of the 'railway sabotage' on South Manchurian Railway, leading to the Mukden Incident and the Japanese occupation of Manchuria.*

sources to continue its war in China.[493] Japan reacted by forging an alliance with Germany and Italy in 1940, known as the Tripartite Pact, which worsened its relations with the US. In July 1941, the United States, the United Kingdom, and the Netherlands froze all Japanese assets when Japan completed its invasion of French Indochina by occupying the southern half of the country, further increasing tension in the Pacific.[494]

World War II

In late 1941, Japan's government, led by Prime Minister and General Hideki Tojo, decided to break the US-led embargo through force of arms.[495] On December 7, 1941, the Imperial Japanese Navy launched a surprise attack on the American fleet at Pearl Harbor, Hawaii. This brought the US into World War II on the side of the Allies. Japan then successfully invaded the Asian colonies of the United States, the United Kingdom, and the Netherlands, including the Philippines, Malaya, Hong Kong, Singapore, Burma, and the Dutch East Indies.[496]

In the early stages of the war, Japan scored victory after victory. The tide began to turn against Japan following the Battle of Midway in June 1942 and the subsequent Battle of Guadalcanal, in which Allied troops wrested the Solomon Islands from Japanese control.[497] During this period the Japanese military was responsible for such war crimes as mistreatment of prisoners of war, massacres of civilians, and the use of chemical and biological weapons.[498] The Japanese

Figure 83: *Planes from the Japanese aircraft carrier Shōkaku preparing the attack on Pearl Harbor*

military earned a reputation for fanaticism, often employing banzai charges and fighting almost to the last man against overwhelming odds.[499] In 1944 the Imperial Japanese Navy began deploying squadrons of *kamikaze* pilots who crashed their planes into enemy ships.[500]

Life in Japan became increasingly difficult for civilians due to stringent rationing of food, electrical outages, and a brutal crackdown on dissent.[501] In 1944 the US Army captured the island of Saipan, which allowed the United States to begin widespread bombing raids on the Japanese mainland.[502] These destroyed over half of the total area of Japan's major cities.[503] The Battle of Okinawa, fought between April and June 1945, was the largest naval operation of the war and left 77,166 Japanese soldiers and more than 140,000 Okinawans dead, suggesting that the planned invasion of mainland Japan would be even bloodier.[504,505] The Japanese superbattleship *Yamato* was sunk en route to aid in the Battle of Okinawa.[506]

However, on August 6, 1945, the US dropped an atomic bomb over Hiroshima, killing over 90,000 people. This was the first nuclear attack in history. On August 9 the Soviet Union declared war on Japan and invaded Manchukuo, and Nagasaki was struck by a second atomic bomb.[507] The unconditional surrender of Japan was announced by Emperor Hirohito and communicated to the Allies

Figure 84: *Atomic cloud over Hiroshima, 1945*

on August 14, and broadcast on national radio on the following day, marking the end of Imperial Japan's ultranationalist ideology, and was a major turning point in Japanese history.

Occupation of Japan

Japan experienced dramatic political and social transformation under the Allied occupation in 1945–1952. US General Douglas MacArthur, the Supreme Commander of Allied Powers, served as Japan's *de facto* leader and played a central role in implementing reforms, many inspired by the New Deal of the 1930s.[508]

The occupation sought to decentralize power in Japan by breaking up the *zaibatsu*, transferring ownership of agricultural land from landlords to tenant farmers,[509] and promoting labor unionism.[510] Other major goals were the demilitarization and democratization of Japan's government and society. Japan's military was disarmed,[511] its colonies were granted independence,[512] the Peace Preservation Law and Tokkō were abolished,[513] and the International Military Tribunal of the Far East tried war criminals.[514] The cabinet became responsible not to the Emperor but to the elected National Diet.[515] The Emperor was permitted to remain on the throne, but was ordered to renounce his claims to divinity, which had been a pillar of the State Shinto system.[516] Japan's new constitution came into effect in 1947 and guaranteed civil

Figure 85: *General MacArthur and Emperor Hirohito*

Figure 86: *The Japanese government releases members of the Japan Communist Party on October 10, 1945.*

Figure 87: *Shigeru Yoshida*

liberties, labor rights, and women's suffrage,[517] and through Article 9, Japan renounced its right to go to war with another nation.[518]

The San Francisco Peace Treaty of 1951 officially normalized relations between Japan and the United States. The occupation ended in 1952, although the US continued to administer a number of the Ryukyu Islands,[519] with Okinawa being the last to be returned in 1972.[520] The US continues to operate military bases throughout the Ryukyu Islands, mostly on Okinawa, as part of the US-Japan Security Treaty.[521,522]

Postwar growth and prosperity

Shigeru Yoshida served as prime minister in 1946–47 and 1948–54, and played a key role in guiding Japan through the occupation.[523] His policies, known as the Yoshida Doctrine, proposed that Japan should forge a tight relationship with the United States and focus on developing the economy rather than pursuing a proactive foreign policy.[524] Yoshida's Liberal Party merged in 1955 into the new Liberal Democratic Party (LDP),[525] which went on to dominate Japanese politics for the remainder of the Shōwa period.[526]

Although the Japanese economy was in bad shape in the immediate postwar years, an austerity program implemented in 1949 by finance expert Joseph Dodge ended inflation.[527] The Korean War (1950–53) was a major boon to

Figure 88: *US Secretary of State Dean Acheson signing the Treaty of Peace with Japan, September 8, 1951*

Japanese business.[528] In 1949 the Yoshida cabinet created the Ministry of International Trade and Industry (MITI) with a mission to promote economic growth through close cooperation between the government and big business. MITI sought successfully to promote manufacturing and heavy industry,[529] and encourage exports.[530] The factors behind Japan's postwar economic growth included technology and quality control techniques imported from the West, close economic and defense cooperation with the United States, non-tariff barriers to imports, restrictions on labor unionization, long work hours, and a generally favorable global economic environment.[531] Japanese corporations successfully retained a loyal and experienced workforce through the system of lifetime employment, which assured their employees a safe job.[532]

By 1955, the Japanese economy had grown beyond prewar levels,[533] and by 1968 it had become the second largest in the world. The GNP expanded at an annual rate of nearly 10% from 1956 until the 1973 oil crisis slowed growth to a still-rapid average annual rate of just over 4% until 1991.[534] Life expectancy rose and Japan's population increased to 123 million by 1990.[535] Ordinary Japanese people became wealthy enough to purchase a wide array of consumer goods. During this period, Japan became the world's largest manufacturer of automobiles and a leading producer of electronics.[536] Japan signed the Plaza Accord in 1985 to depreciate the US dollar against the yen and other currencies.

By the end of 1987, the Nikkei stock market index had doubled and the Tokyo Stock Exchange became the largest in the world. During the ensuing economic bubble, stock and real-estate loans grew rapidly.[537]

Japan became a member of the United Nations in 1956 and further cemented its international standing in 1964, when it hosted the Olympic Games in Tokyo.[538] Japan was a close ally of the United States during the Cold War, though this alliance did not have unanimous support from the Japanese people. As requested by the United States, Japan reconstituted its army in 1954 under the name Japan Self-Defense Forces (JSDF), though some Japanese insisted that the very existence of the JSDF was a violation of Article 9 of Japan's constitution.[539] In 1960, hundreds of thousands protested against amendments to the US-Japan Security Treaty.[540] Japan successfully normalized relations with the Soviet Union in 1956, despite an ongoing dispute over the ownership of the Kuril Islands,[541] and with South Korea in 1965, despite an ongoing dispute over the ownership of the islands of Liancourt Rocks.[542] In accordance with US policy, Japan recognized the Republic of China on Taiwan as the legitimate government of China after World War II, though Japan switched its recognition to the People's Republic of China in 1972.[543]

Among cultural developments, the immediate post-occupation period became a golden age for Japanese cinema.[544] The reasons for this include the abolition of government censorship, low film production costs, expanded access to new film techniques and technologies, and huge domestic audiences at a time when other forms of recreation were relatively scarce.[545]

Heisei period (1989–present)

Emperor Akihito's reign began upon the death of his father, Emperor Hirohito. The economic bubble popped in 1989, and stock and land prices plunged as Japan entered a deflationary spiral. Banks found themselves saddled with insurmountable debts that hindered economic recovery.[546] Stagnation worsened as the birthrate declined far below replacement level.[547] The 1990s are often referred to as Japan's Lost Decade.[548] Economic performance was frequently poor in the following decades and the stock market never returned to its pre-1989 highs.[549] Japan's system of lifetime employment largely collapsed and unemployment rates rose.[550] The faltering economy and several corruption scandals weakened the LDP's dominant political position. Japan was nevertheless governed by non-LDP prime ministers only in 1993–96[551] and 2009–12.

Japan's dealing with its war legacy has strained international relations. China and Korea have found official apologies, such as those of the Emperor in 1990 and the Murayama Statement of 1995, inadequate or insincere.[552] Nationalist politics have exacerbated this, such as denial of the Nanking Massacre

Figure 89: *Wreckage at a railway station destroyed during the 2011 earthquake and tsunami*

and other war crimes;[553] revisionist history textbooks, which have provoked protests in East Asia,[554] and frequent visits by Japanese politicians to Yasukuni Shrine, where convicted war criminals are enshrined.[555] Legislation in 2015 expanding the military's role overseas was criticized as a "war bill".

In spite of Japan's economic difficulties, this period also saw Japanese popular culture, including video games, anime, and manga, become worldwide phenomena, especially among young people.[556]

On March 11, 2011, one of the largest earthquakes recorded in Japan occurred in the northeast.[557] The resulting tsunami damaged the nuclear facilities in Fukushima, which experienced a nuclear meltdown and severe radiation leakage.[558] In the 21st century there have been increasing reports on the prevalence of sexlessness among the Japanese, including its byproducts such as a decreasing population, the increasing popularity of sexbots[559] and the *herbivore men* phenomenon.[560]

Social conditions

Social stratification in Japan became pronounced during the Yayoi period. Expanding trade and agriculture increased the wealth of society, which was increasingly monopolized by social elites. By 600 AD, a class structure had developed which included court aristocrats, the families of local magnates, commoners, and slaves.[561] Over 90% were commoners, who included farmers, merchants, and artisans.[562] During the late Heian period, the governing elite consisted of three classes. The traditional aristocracy shared power with Buddhist monks and samurai, though the latter became increasingly dominant in the Kamakura and Muromachi periods.[563] These periods witnessed the rise of the merchant class, which diversified into a greater variety of specialized occupations.[564]

Women initially held social and political equality with men, and archaeological evidence suggests a prehistorical preference for female rulers in western Japan. Female Emperors appear in recorded history until the Meiji Constitution declared strict male-only ascension in 1889.[565] Chinese Confucian-style patriarchy was first codified in the 7th–8th centuries with the *ritsuryō* system,[566] which introduced a patrilineal family register with a male head of household.[567] Women until then had held important roles in government which thereafter gradually diminished, though even in the late Heian period women wielded considerable court influence. Marital customs and many laws governing private property remained gender neutral.[568]

For reasons that are unclear to historians the status of women rapidly deteriorated from the fourteenth century and onwards.[569] Women of all social classes lost the right to own and inherit property and were increasingly viewed as inferior to men.[570] Hideyoshi's land survey of the 1590s further entrenched the status of men as dominant landholders.[571] During the US occupation following World War II, women gained legal equality with men,[572] but faced widespread workplace discrimination. A movement for women's rights led to the passage of an equal employment law in 1986, but by the 1990s women held only 10% of management positions.[573]

Hideyoshi's land survey of the 1590s designated all who cultivated the land as commoners, an act which granted effective freedom to most of Japan's slaves.

The Tokugawa shogunate rigidified long-existent class divisions,[574] placing most of the population into a Neo-Confucian hierarchy of four occupations, with the ruling elite at the top, followed by the peasants who made up 80% of the population, then artisans, and merchants at the bottom.[575] Court nobles,[576] clerics, outcasts, entertainers, and workers of the licensed quarters fell outside this structure.[577] Different legal codes applied to different classes, marriage between classes was prohibited, and towns were subdivided into different class areas.[574] The social stratification had little bearing on economic conditions: many samurai lived in poverty[577] and the wealth of the merchant class grew throughout the period as the commercial economy developed and urbanization grew.[578] The Edo-era social power structure proved untenable and gave way following the Meiji Restoration to one in which commercial power played an increasingly significant political role.[579]

Although all social classes were legally abolished at the start of the Meiji period, income inequality greatly increased.[580] New economic class divisions were

History of Japan

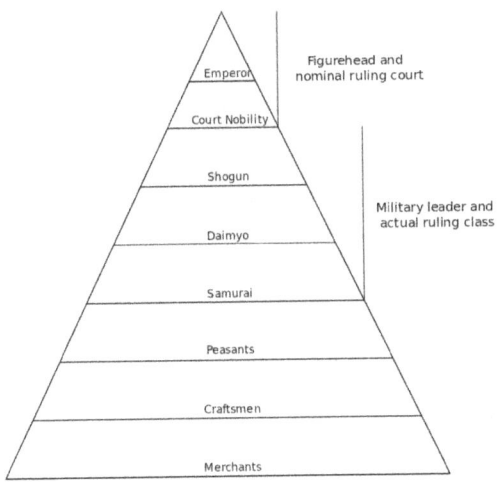

Figure 90: *Social structure of the Edo period*

formed between capitalist business owners who formed the new middle class, small shopkeepers of the old middle class, the working class in factories, rural landlords, and tenant farmers.[581] The great disparities of income between the classes dissipated during and after World War II, eventually declining to levels that were among the lowest in the industrialized world. Some postwar surveys indicated that up to 90% of Japanese self-identified as being middle class.[582]

Populations of workers in professions considered unclean, such as leatherworkers and those who handled the dead, developed in the 15th and 16th centuries into hereditary outcast communities.[583] These people, later called *burakumin*, fell outside the Edo-period class structure and suffered discrimination that lasted after the class system was abolished.[584] Though activism has improved the social conditions of those from *burakumin* backgrounds, discrimination in employment and education lingered into the 21st century.[585]

Books cited

- Batten, Bruce Loyd (2003). *To the Ends of Japan: Premodern Frontiers, Boundaries, and Interactions*[586]. Honolulu, HI: University of Hawaii Press. ISBN 978-0-8248-2447-1.<templatestyles src="Module:Citation/CS1/styles.css"></templatestyles>

- Bix, Hebert P. (2000). *Hirohito and the Making of Modern Japan*[587]. New York, NY: Harper Collins. ISBN 978-0-06-186047-8.<templatestyles src="Module:Citation/CS1/styles.css"></templatestyles>
- Coox, Alvin (1988). "The Pacific War," in *The Cambridge History of Japan: Volume 6*. Cambridge: Cambridge University Press.
- Deal, William E (2006). *Handbook to Life in Medieval and Early Modern Japan*. New York: Facts on File.
- Deal, William E and Ruppert, Brian Douglas (2015). *A Cultural History of Japanese Buddhism*. Chichester, West Sussex : Wiley Blackwell.
- Duus, Peter (2011). "Showa-era Japan and beyond," in Routledge Handbook of Japanese Culture and Society. New York: Routledge.
- Farris, William Wayne (2009). *Japan to 1600: A Social and Economic History*[588]. Honolulu, HI: University of Hawaii Press. ISBN 978-0-8248-3379-4.<templatestyles src="Module:Citation/CS1/styles.css"></templatestyles>
- Farris, William Wayne (1995). *Population, Disease, and Land in Early Japan, 645–900*[589]. Cambridge, Massachusetts: Harvard University Asia Center. ISBN 978-0-674-69005-9.<templatestyles src="Module:Citation/CS1/styles.css"></templatestyles>
- Feifer, George (1992). *Tennozan: The Battle of Okinawa and the Atomic Bomb*. New York: Ticknor & Fields.
- Frank, Richard (1999). *Downfall: The End of the Imperial Japanese Empire*[590]. New York, NY: Random House. ISBN 978-0-14-100146-3.<templatestyles src="Module:Citation/CS1/styles.css"></templatestyles>
- Gao, Bai (2009). "The Postwar Japanese Economy". In Tsutsui, William M. *A Companion to Japanese History*. John Wiley & Sons. pp. 299–314. ISBN 978-1-4051-9339-9.<templatestyles src="Module:Citation/CS1/styles.css"></templatestyles>
- Habu, Junko (2004). *Ancient Jomon of Japan*[591]. Cambridge, MA: Cambridge Press. ISBN 978-0-521-77670-7.<templatestyles src="Module:Citation/CS1/styles.css"></templatestyles>
- Hane, Mikiso (1991). *Premodern Japan: A Historical Survey*[592]. Boulder, CO: Westview Press. ISBN 978-0-8133-4970-1.<templatestyles src="Module:Citation/CS1/styles.css"></templatestyles>
- Hastings, Sally A. (2007). "Gender and Sexuality in Modern Japan," in *A Companion to Japanese History*. Malden, Massachusetts: Blackwell Publishing.
- Henshall, Kenneth (2012). *A History of Japan: From Stone Age to Superpower*[593]. London: Palgrave Macmillan. ISBN 978-0-230-34662-8.<templatestyles src="Module:Citation/CS1/styles.css"></

- Hunter, Janet (1984). *Concise Dictionary of Modern Japanese History*. Berkeley: University of California Press.
- Imamura, Keiji (1996). *Prehistoric Japan: New Perspectives on Insular East Asia*. Honolulu: University of Hawaii Press.
- Ito, Takatoshi (1992). *The Japanese Economy*. Cambridge, Massachusetts: MIT Press.
- Jansen, Marius (2000). *The Making of Modern Japan*. Cambridge, Massachusetts: Belknap Press of Harvard University.
- Kaner, Simon (2011). "The Archaeology of Religion and Ritual in the Japanese Archipelago," in *The Oxford Handbook of the Archaeology of Ritual and Religion*. Oxford: Oxford University Press.
- Keene, Donald (1998) [1984]. *A History of Japanese Literature, Vol. 3: Dawn to the West – Japanese Literature of the Modern Era (Fiction)* (paperback ed.). New York, NY: Columbia University Press. ISBN 978-0-231-11435-6.
- Keene, Donald (1999) [1993]. *A History of Japanese Literature, Vol. 1: Seeds in the Heart – Japanese Literature from Earliest Times to the Late Sixteenth Century* (paperback ed.). New York, NY: Columbia University Press. ISBN 978-0-231-11441-7.
- Kerr, George (1958). *Okinawa: History of an Island People*. Rutland, Vermont: Tuttle Company.
- Kidder, J. Edward (1993). "The Earliest Societies in Japan," in *The Cambridge History of Japan: Volume 1*. Cambridge: Cambridge University Press.
- Kumar, Ann (2008). *Globalizing the Prehistory of Japan: Language, Genes and Civilisation*. New York: Routledge.
- Large, Stephen S. (2007). "Oligarchy, Democracy, and Fascism," in *A Companion to Japanese History*. Malden, Massachusetts: Blackwell Publishing.
- Lauerman, Lynn (2002). *Science & Technology Almanac*. Westport, Connecticut: Greenwood Press.
- Mackie, Vera (2003). *Feminism in Modern Japan*. New York: Cambridge University Press.
- Maher, Kohn C. (1996). "North Kyushu Creole: A Language Contact Model for the Origins of Japanese," in *Multicultural Japan: Palaeolithic*

to Postmodern. New York: Cambridge University Press.
- Mason, RHP and Caiger, JG (1997). *A History of Japan*. Rutland, Vermont: Tuttle.
- Meyer, Milton W. (2009). *Japan: A Concise History*. Lanham, Maryland: Rowman & Littlefield.
- McClain, James L. (2002). *Japan: A Modern History*[594]. New York, NY: W. W. Norton & Company. ISBN 978-0-393-04156-9.<templatestyles src="Module:Citation/CS1/styles.css"></templatestyles>
- McCullough, William H. (1999). "The Heian Court, 794–1070," in *The Cambridge History of Japan: Volume 2*. Cambridge: Cambridge University Press.
- Moriguchi, Chiaki and Saez, Emmanuel (2010). "The Evolution of Income Concentration in Japan, 1886–2005," in *Top Incomes : A Global Perspective*. Oxford: Oxford University Press.
- Morton, W Scott and Olenike, J Kenneth (2004). *Japan: Its History and Culture*. New York: McGraw-Hill.
- Neary, Ian (2003). "*Burakumin* at the End of History". *Social Research*. **70** (1): 269–294. JSTOR 40971613[595].<templatestyles src="Module:Citation/CS1/styles.css"></templatestyles>
- Neary, Ian (2009). "Class and Social Stratification". In Tsutsui, William M. *A Companion to Japanese History*. John Wiley & Sons. pp. 389–406. ISBN 978-1-4051-9339-9.<templatestyles src="Module:Citation/CS1/styles.css"></templatestyles>
- Perkins, Dorothy (1991). *Encyclopedia of Japan*. New York: Facts on File.
- Perez, Louis G. (1998). *The History of Japan*[596]. Westport, CT: Greenwood Press. ISBN 978-0-313-30296-1.<templatestyles src="Module:Citation/CS1/styles.css"></templatestyles>
- Sansom, George (1958). *A History of Japan to 1334*[597]. Stanford, CA: Stanford University Press. ISBN 978-0-8047-0523-3.<templatestyles src="Module:Citation/CS1/styles.css"></templatestyles>
- Sanz, Nuria (2014). *Human origin sites and the World Heritage Convention in Asia*. UNESCO.<templatestyles src="Module:Citation/CS1/styles.css"></templatestyles>
- Schirokauer, Conrad (2013). *A Brief History of Chinese and Japanese Civilizations*. Boston: Wadsworth Cengage Learning.<templatestyles src="Module:Citation/CS1/styles.css"></templatestyles>
- Silberman, Neil Asher (2012). *The Oxford Companion to Archaeology*. New York: Oxford University Press.<templatestyles src="Module:Citation/CS1/styles.css"></templatestyles>
- Sims, Richard (2001). *Japanese Political History since the Meiji Renovation, 1868–2000*. New York: Palgrave.<templatestyles

- src="Module:Citation/CS1/styles.css"></templatestyles>
- Takeuchi, Rizo (1999). "The Rise of the Warriors," in *The Cambridge History of Japan: Volume 2.* Cambridge: Cambridge University Press.
- Togo, Kazuhiko (2005). *Japan's Foreign Policy 1945–2003: The Quest for a Proactive Policy.* Boston: Brill.<templatestyles src="Module:Citation/CS1/styles.css"></templatestyles>
- Tonomura, Hitomi (2007). "Women and Sexuality in Premodern Japan," in *A Companion to Japanese History.* Malden, Massachusetts: Blackwell Publishing.
- Totman, Conrad (2005). *A History of Japan*[598]. Malden, MA: Blackwell Publishing. ISBN 978-1-119-02235-0.<templatestyles src="Module:Citation/CS1/styles.css"></templatestyles>
- Wakita, Osamu (1991). "The social and economic consequences of unification". In Hall, John Whitney. *The Cambridge History of Japan.* **4**. Cambridge University Press. pp. 96–127. ISBN 978-0-521-22355-3.<templatestyles src="Module:Citation/CS1/styles.css"></templatestyles>
- Walker, Brett (2015). *A Concise History of Japan.* Cambridge: Cambridge University Press.
- Weston, Mark (2002). *Giants of Japan: The Lives of Japan's Greatest Men and Women*[599]. New York, NY: Kodansha. ISBN 978-0-9882259-4-7.<templatestyles src="Module:Citation/CS1/styles.css"></templatestyles>

Medieval Southeast Asia

History of Southeast Asia

Part of a series on the
History of Southeast Asia
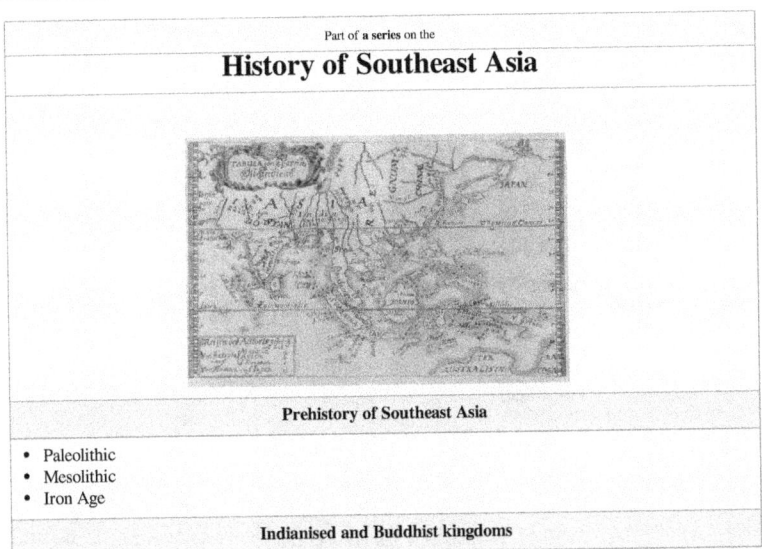
Prehistory of Southeast Asia
• Paleolithic • Mesolithic • Iron Age
Indianised and Buddhist kingdoms

- Hinduism in Southeast Asia
- Buddhism in Southeast Asia
- Java and Sumatra
  - Srivijaya
  - Majapahit
- Indochina
  - Angkor
  - Champa
  - Đại Việt
  - Lan Xang
  - Pagan
  - Sukhothai
- Philippines
  - Ma-i
  - Tondo
  - Rajahnate of Cebu
  - Madja-as
  - Rajahnate of Butuan

Decline of Hindu/Buddhist influence and sea trade

- Silk Road
- Spread of Islam
  - Islam in Southeast Asia
- Arrival of European traders
  - Portuguese discoveries
  - Spanish discoveries
  - Dutch discoveries
- Spread of Christianity

European colonialism

- Spanish Philippines
- Dutch Indonesia
- British Burma, Malaya and Borneo
- French Indochina
- Thailand
- Anglo-Burmese Wars
  - First Anglo-Burmese War
  - Second Anglo-Burmese War
  - Third Anglo-Burmese War
- Philippine Revolution
- Spanish–American War
  - Philippine–American War
  - American Philippines

World War II and decolonisation

- Japanese conquests
  - Empire of Japan
- End of World War II in Asia
- Indonesian National Revolution

Cold War

- Indochina Wars
- Malayan Emergency
- Thai insurgency
- Second Malayan Emergency
- Sarawak insurgency
- Indonesia–Malaysia confrontation
- Indonesian mass killings
- Philippine rebellion

Contemporary Southeast Asia
• Revolution and fall of Communism • ASEAN
Southeast Asia portal
• v • t • e[600]

The term *Southeast Asia* has been in use since World War II. The region has been further divided into two distinct sub-regions, Mainland Southeast Asia (or Indochina) that comprises the modern states of Vietnam, Laos, Cambodia, Thailand, Myanmar (Burma) and West Malaysia and Maritime Southeast Asia (or Insular Southeast Asia) that comprises the modern states of Indonesia, East Malaysia, Singapore, Philippines, East Timor, Brunei, Cocos (Keeling) Islands, and Christmas Island.

The earliest *Homo sapiens* presence in Mainland Southeast Asia can be traced back to 50,000 years ago and to at least 40,000 years ago in Maritime Southeast Asia. As early as 10,000 years ago, Hoabinhian settlers had developed a tradition and culture of distinct artefact and tool production. During the Neolithic, Austroasiatic peoples populated Indochina via land routes and sea-borne Austronesian immigrants preferably settled in insular Southeast Asia. The earliest agricultural societies that cultivated millet and wet-rice emerged around 1,700 BCE in the lowlands and river floodplains of Indochina.

The Phung Nguyen culture (modern northern Vietnam) and the Ban Chiang site (modern Thailand) account for the earliest use of copper by around 2,000 BCE, followed by the Dong Son culture, who by around 500 BCE had developed a highly sophisticated industry of bronze production and processing. Around the same time the first *Agrarian Kingdoms* emerged where territory was abundant and favourable, such as Funan at the lower Mekong and Van Lang in the Red River delta. Smaller and insular principalities increasingly engaged in and contributed to the rapidly expanding sea trade.

The history of Southeast Asia has been greatly influenced by its wide topographical diversity. Maritime Southeast Asia is apart from exceptions like Borneo and Sumatra a patchwork of recurring land-sea patterns on widely dispersed islands and archipelagos. A discontinuity, that admitted moderately sized thalassocratic states indifferent to territorial ambitions where growth and prosperity was associated with sea trade. Mainland Southeast Asia with a continuous, but rugged and difficult terrain provided the basis for the early Khmer and Mon civilisations. However, an extensive coastline and the south—and south-eastbound major river systems of the Irrawaddy, Salween, Chao Phraya,

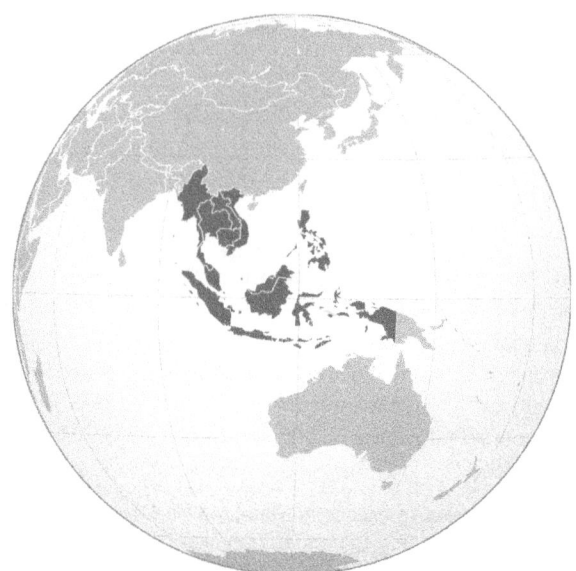

Figure 91:
Southeast Asia

Mekong, and Red River always have directed focus, local trade, socio-cultural and economic activities towards the Indian Ocean and the South China Sea.

Since around 100 BCE the Southeast Asian archipelago occupied a central position at the crossroads of the Indian Ocean and the South China Sea trading routes which immensely stimulated the economy and the influx of ideas promoted societal organisation and advance. Most local trading polities selectively adopted Indian Hindu elements of statecraft, religion, culture and administration during the early centuries of the common era, which marked the beginning of recorded history and the continuation of a characteristic cultural development. Chinese culture diffused more indirectly and sporadic as trade was based on land routes like the Silk Road. Long periods of Chinese isolationism and political relations that were confined to ritualistic tribute procedures prevented deep acculturation.

Buddhism, particularly in Indochina began to affect the political structure beginning in the 8th to 9th centuries. Islam ideas arrived in insular Southeast Asia as early as the 8th century, where the first Muslim societies emerged by the 13th century.

The era of European colonialism, early Modernity and the Cold War era revealed the reality of limited political significance for the various Southeast

Figure 92:
Borobudur in Java

Asian polities. Post-World War II national survival and progress required a modern state and a strong national identity. Most modern Southeast Asian countries enjoy a historically unprecedented degree of political freedom and self-determination and have embraced the practical concept of intergovernmental co-operation within the Association of Southeast Asian Nations.

Name

There are numerous ancient historic Asian designations for Southeast Asia, none are geographically consistent with each other. Names referring to Southeast Asia include *Suvarnabhumi* or *Sovannah Phoum* (*Golden Land*) and *Suvarnadvipa* (*Golden Islands*) in Indian tradition, the *Lands below the Winds* in Arabia and Persia, *Nanyang* (*South Seas*) to the Chinese and *Nanyo* in Japan. A 2nd-century world map created by Ptolemy of Alexandria names the Malay Peninsula as Avrea Chersonesvs, (Golden Peninsula).

The term Southeast Asia has been coined to designate the area of operation (the South East Asia Command, SEAC) for Anglo-American forces in the Pacific Theater of World War II from 1941 to 1945.

Human history
↑ Prehistory
Recorded history
Ancient

- Earliest records
- Africa
- Americas
- Oceania
- East Asia
- South Asia
- Southeast Asia
- Middle East
- Europe

Postclassical

- Africa
- Americas
- Oceania
- East Asia
- South Asia
- Southeast Asia
- Middle East
- Europe

Modern

- Early modern
- Late modern

See also

- Contemporary
- Modernity
- Futurology

↓ Future

- v
- t
- e[601]

Prehistory

Paleolithic

Anatomically modern human hunter-gatherer migration into Southeast Asia before 50,000 years ago has been confirmed by the combined fossil record of the region. These immigrants might have, to a certain extent, merged and reproduced with members of the archaic population of *Homo erectus*, as the fossil discoveries in the Tam Pa Ling Cave suggest. Data analysis of stone tool assemblages and fossil discoveries from Indonesia, Southern China, the Philippines, Sri Lanka and more recently Cambodia and Malaysia has established *Homo erectus* migration routes and episodes of presence as early as 120,000 years ago and even older isolated finds date back to 1.8 million years ago.[602,603] Java Man (*Homo erectus erectus*) and *Homo floresiensis* attest for a sustained regional presence and isolation, long enough for notable diversification of the species' specifics.

Figure 93: *Niah Cave entrance at sunset*

Ocean drops of up to 120 m (393.70 ft) below the present level during Pleistocene glacial periods revealed the vast lowlands known as Sundaland, enabling hunter-gatherer populations to freely access insular Southeast Asia via extensive terrestrial corridors. Modern human presence in the Niah cave on East Malaysia dates back to 40,000 years BP, although archaeological documentation of the early settlement period suggests only brief occupation phases. However, author Charles Higham argues that, despite glacial periods modern humans were able to cross the sea barrier beyond Java and Timor, who around 45,000 years ago left traces in the Ivane Valley in eastern New Guinea "at an altitude of 2,000 m (6,561.68 ft) exploiting yams and pandanus, hunting, and making stone tools between 43,000 and 49,000 years ago."

The oldest habitation discovered in the Philippines is located at the Tabon Caves and dates back to approximately 50,000 years BP. Items there found such as burial jars, earthenware, jade ornaments and other jewellery, stone tools, animal bones, and human fossils date back to 47,000 years BP. Unearthed human remains are approximately 24,000 years old.

Signs of an early tradition are discernible in the Hoabinhian, the name given to an industry and cultural continuity of stone tools and flaked cobble artefacts that appears around 10,000 BP in caves and rock shelters first described in *Hòa Bình*, Vietnam, later also documented in Terengganu, Malaysia, Sumatra, Thailand, Laos, Myanmar, Cambodia and Yunnan, southern China. Research emphasises considerable variations in quality and nature of the artefacts, influenced by region-specific environmental conditions and proximity and access to local resources. Remarkable is nonetheless that the Hoabinhian culture accounts for the first verified ritual burials in Southeast Asia.

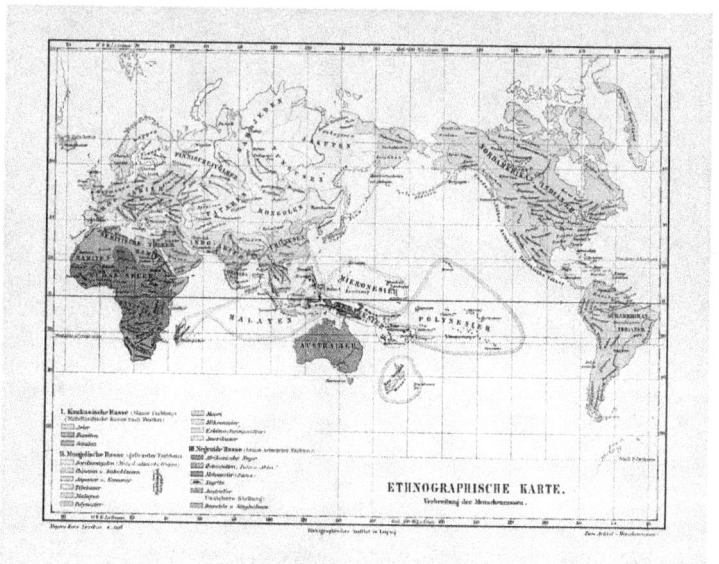

Figure 94: *Austronesian migration routes in the 4th edition of Meyers Konversations-Lexikon (1885–1892)*

Neolithic Migrations

The earliest *Homo sapiens* immigrants, loosely identified as *Australo-Melanesians*, *Aboriginal*, *Negritos* and *Hill Tribes* are associated with the occupation of caves, rock shelters and isolated upland regions in Vietnam, Thailand and the Philippines or on remote islands, such as the Andaman Islands and although displaced from the coasts and plains they are present in all regions for at least 30,000 years.

Subsequent Neolithic immigration waves are intensely debated considered dynamic and complex, and research has resorted to linguistic terms and argumentation for group identification and classification.

The Austroasiatic migration wave centred around the Mon and the Khmer, who originate in North-Eastern India arrive around 5000 BP and are identified with the settlement on the broad riverine floodplains of Burma, Indochina and Malaysia.

The origin, period and settlement pattern of the Austronesian immigrants, whose elusive branches would eventually be dispersed all over the islands between Madagascar and Oceania, has been for a long time interpreted on a linguistic basis, although more recent genetic research contradicts these ideas.

History of Southeast Asia 251

Figure 95: *Hypothetical map of Văn Lang (early 3rd century BCE)*

Certain is, these marine migrants were accomplished seafarers, who arrived on boats around 4,000 BP and soon dominated maritime Southeast Asia, populated the lowlands and coasts and pushed indigenous people of Indonesia, the Philippines or New Guinea to the interior regions.

Early agricultural societies

Territorial principalities in both Insular and Mainland Southeast Asia, characterised as *Agrarian kingdoms* had by around 500 BCE developed an economy based on surplus crop cultivation and moderate coastal trade of domestic natural products. Several states of the Malayan-Indonesian "thalassian" zone shared these characteristics with Indochinese polities like the Pyu city-states in the Irrawaddy river valley, Van Lang in the Red River delta and Funan around the lower Mekong. Văn Lang, founded in the 7th century BCE endured until 258 BCE under the rule of the Hồng Bàng dynasty, as part of the Đông Sơn culture eventually sustained a dense and organised population, that produced an elaborate Bronze Age industry.

Intensive wet-rice cultivation in an ideal climate enabled the farming communities to produce a regular crop surplus, that was used by the ruling elite to raise, command and pay work forces for public construction and maintenance projects such as canals and fortifications.

Though millet and rice cultivation was introduced around 2000 BCE, hunting and gathering remained an important aspect of food provision, in particular in forested and mountainous inland areas. Many tribal communities of the aboriginal Australo-Melanesian settlers continued the lifestyle of mixed sustenance until the modern era.

Two layer hypothesis

Between around 1,700 and 1,000 BC people settled in the Southeast Asian lowlands as wet-rice and millet farming techniques from the Yangtze River valley were adopted. Author and archaeologist Charles Higham suggests in his work *"Hunter-Gatherers in Southeast Asia: From Prehistory to the Present"* "the indigenous hunter-gatherers integrated with intrusive Neolithic communities and, while losing their cultural identity, contributed their genes to the present population of Southeast Asia." or alternatively the "hunter-gatherers withdrew to rainforest refugia and, through selective pressures inherent in such an environment, survived as the small-bodied, dark-skinned humans found to this day in the Philippines, Peninsular Malaysia and Thailand, and the Andaman Islands." Unfortunately the Two layer hypothesis, based on the human occupation of mainland Southeast Asia during two distinct periods by two separate racial groups is only applicable when you know who really was involved in this integration process. Immigration from China alongside the introduction of farming occurred and DNA testing calls for revision of Neolithic migrations.

Bronze Age Southeast Asia

Earliest known copper and bronze production in Southeast Asia has been found at the site of Ban Chiang in North-east Thailand and among the Phung Nguyen culture of northern Vietnam around 2000 BCE.

The Dong Son culture established a tradition of bronze production and the manufacture of ever more refined bronze and iron objects, such as plows, axes and sickles with shaft holes, socketed arrow and spearheads and small ornamented items. By about 500 BCE large and delicately decorated bronze drums of remarkable quality, that weighed more than 70 kg (150 lb) were produced in the laborious lost-wax casting process. This industry of highly sophisticated metal processing has been developed locally bare of Chinese or Indian influence. Historians relate these achievements to the presence of well organised, centralised and hierarchical communities and a large population.

Pottery Culture

Between 1,000 BCE and 100 CE the Sa Huỳnh culture flourished along the south-central coast of Vietnam.[604] Ceramic jar burial sites, that included grave goods have been discovered at various sites along the entire territory. Among large, thin-walled, terracotta jars, ornamented and colourised cooking pots,

Figure 96:
Dong Son drum

Figure 97: *Buni clay pottery*

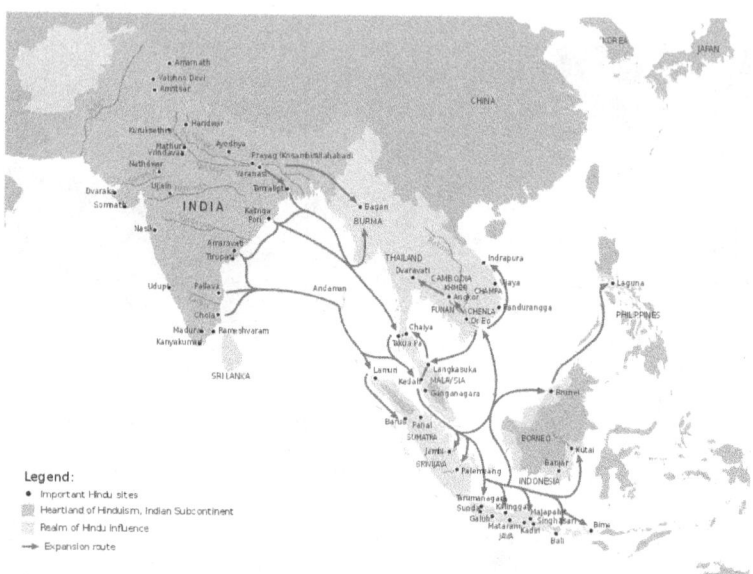

Figure 98: *Expansion of Hinduism in Southeast Asia*

glass items, jade earrings and metal objects had been deposited near the rivers and at the coast.

The Buni culture is the name given to another early independent centre of refined pottery production that has been well documented on the basis of excavated burial gifts, deposited between 400 BCE and 100 CE in coastal northwestern Java. The objects and artefacts of the Buni tradition are known for their originality and remarkable quality of incised and geometric decors. Its resemblance to the Sa Huỳnh culture and the fact that it represents the earliest *Indian Rouletted Ware* recorded in Southeast Asia are subject of ongoing research.

Early historical era

Indianised kingdoms

Since around 500 B.C. Asia's expanding land and maritime trade had led to socio-economic interaction and cultural stimulation and diffusion of mainly Hindu beliefs into the regional cosmology of Southeast Asia. Iron Age trade expansion caused regional geostrategic remodelling. Southeast Asia was now situated in the central area of convergence of the Indian and the East Asian

Figure 99: *Shiva statue, Champa (modern Vietnam)*

maritime trade routes, the basis for economic and cultural growth. The concept of the *Indianised kingdoms*, a term coined by George Coedès, describes Southeast Asian principalities that since the early common era as a result of prolonged interaction had incorporated central aspects of Indian institutions, religion, statecraft, administration, culture, epigraphy, writing and architecture.[605]

The earliest Hindu kingdoms emerged in Sumatra and Java, followed by mainland polities such as Funan and Champa. Selective adoption of Indian civilisation elements and individual suitable adaption stimulated the emergence of centralised states and development of highly organised societies. Ambitious local leaders realised the benefits of Hindu worship. Rule in accord with universal moral principles represented in the concept of the devaraja was more appealing than the Chinese concept of intermediaries.

The exact nature, process and extent of Indian influence upon the civilisations of the region is still fiercely debated by contemporary scholars. Debated are most claims over whether it was Indian merchants, Brahmins, nobles or Southeast Asian mariner-merchants who played a central role in bringing Indian conceptions to Southeast Asia. Debated is the depth of the influence of traditions for the people. Whereas early 20th-century scholars emphasised the thorough Indianisation of Southeast Asia, more recent authors argued that this influence was very limited and affected only a small section of the elite.

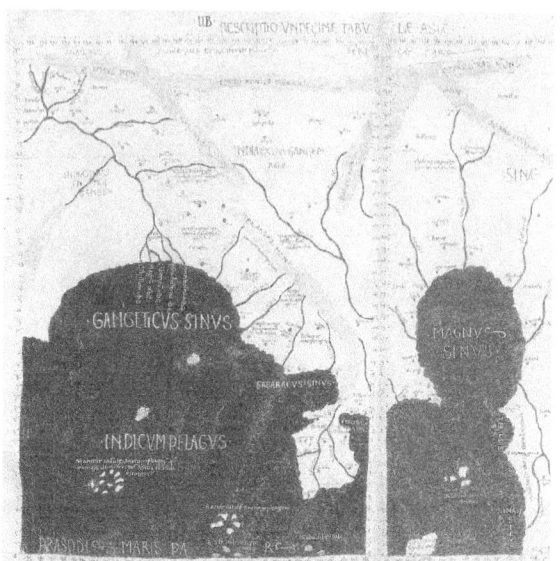

Figure 100: *Detail of Asia in Ptolemy's world map. Gulf of the Ganges left, Southeast Asian peninsula in the centre written as Avrea Chersonesvs, China Sea right, with "Sinae" (China).*

Sea trade from China to India passed Champa, Funan at the Mekong Delta, proceeded along the coast to the Isthmus of Kra, portaged across the narrow and transhipped for distribution in India. This trading link boosted the development of Funan, its successor Chenla and the Malayan states of Langkasuka on the eastern and Kedah on the western coast.

Numerous coastal communities in maritime Southeast Asia adopted Hindu and Buddhist cultural and religious elements from India and developed complex polities ruled by native dynasties. Early Hindu kingdoms in Indonesia are 4th century Kutai that rose in East Kalimantan, Tarumanagara in West Java and Kalingga in Central Java.

Early relations with China

Earliest attested trading contacts existed between Southeast Asia and the Chinese Shang dynasty (around 1600 BCE to around 1046 BCE), when cowry shells served as currency. Various natural products, such as ivory, rhinoceros horn, tortoise shells, pearls and birds' feathers found their way to Luoyang the capital of the Zhou dynasty, that lasted from 1050 to 771 BCE. Although

History of Southeast Asia

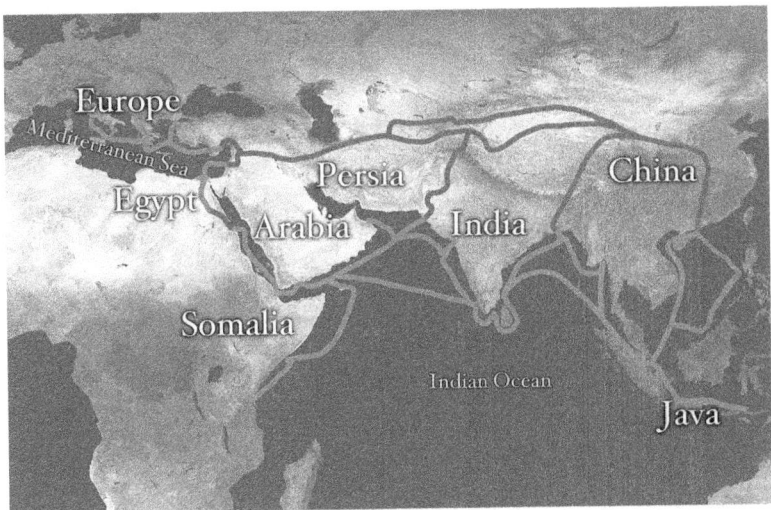

Figure 101: *Major trading routes in the pre-colonial Eastern Hemisphere*

knowledge about port localities and shipping lanes is very limited, it is assumed that most of this exchange took place on land routes and only a small percentage was shipped "on coastal vessels crewed by Malay and Yue traders".

Military conquests during the short lived Han dynasty brought a number of foreign peoples within the Chinese empire when the Imperial Chinese tributary system began to evolve under Han rule. This tributary system was based on the Chinese worldview, that had developed under the Shang dynasty, in which China is deemed the center and apogee of culture and civilisation, the *Middle kingdom* (Zhōngguó), surrounded by several layers of increasingly barbarous peoples. Contact with Southeast Asia steadily increased by the end of the Han period.

Spread of Buddhism

Local rulers have most benefited from the introduction of Hinduism during the early common era as it greatly enhanced the legitimacy of their reign. Historians increasingly argue, that the process of Hindu religious diffusion must be attributed to the initiative of the local chieftains. Buddhist teachings, that almost simultaneously arrived in Southeast Asia developed during the subsequent centuries an exalted distinction and eventually came to be perceived as more appealing to the demands of the general population, a belief system and philosophy that addresses concrete human affairs. Emperor Ashoka initiated

Figure 102: *Borobudur stupa, central Java (9th century)*

the tradition to send trained monks and missionaries abroad who spread Buddhism, that includes a sizeable body of literature, oral traditions, iconography, art and offers guidance as it seeks to solve central existential questions with emphasis on individual effort and conduct.

Between the 5th and the 13th century Buddhism flourished in Southeast Asia. By the 8th century the Buddhist Srivijaya kingdom emerged as a major trading power in central Maritime Southeast Asia and around the same period the Shailendra dynasty of Java extensively promoted Buddhist art that found its strongest expression in the vast Borobudur monument. After the establishment of a new royal dynasty of provincial origin in the Khmer Empire the first Buddhist kings emerged during the 11th century. Mahayana Buddhist ideas from India where the original Theravada Buddhism had already been replaced centuries ago took hold first in Southeast Asia. However, a pure form of Theravada Buddhist teachings had been preserved in Sri Lanka since the 3rd century. Pilgrims and wandering monks from Sri Lanka introduced Theravada Buddhism in the Pagan Empire of Burma, the Siamese Sukhothai Kingdom in Laos, the Lower Mekong Basin during Cambodia's dark ages and further into Vietnam and Insular Southeast Asia.

History of Southeast Asia

Figure 103: *Angkor Wat, Khmer Empire (12th century)*

Figure 104: *The Laguna Copperplate Inscription, Philippines (c. 900 CE)*

Medieval history

Srivijaya on Sumatra island had developed into the dominant power of Maritime Southeast Asia by the 5th century. Its capital Palembang became a major seaport and functioned as an entrepot on the Spice Route between India and China. Srivijaya was also a notable centre of Vajrayana Buddhist learning and influence. Around the 6th century CE, Malay merchants began sailing to Srivijaya where goods were transhipped directly on Sumatran ports. The winds of the Northeast Monsoon during October to December prevented sailing ships to proceed directly from the Indian Ocean to the South China Sea. The third system involved direct trade between the Indian and Chinese coasts during the Southwest Monsoon season. Srivijaya's wealth and influence faded when changes in nautical technology in the 10th century enabled Chinese and Indian merchants to ship cargo directly between their countries and also enabled the Chola state in southern India to carry out a series of destructive attacks on Srivijaya's possessions, ending Palembang's entrepot function.

From the 7th to 15th centuries Sumatra was ruled by kaleidoscope of Buddhist kingdoms, from Kantoli, Srivijaya, Malayu, Pannai and Dharmasraya kingdom. Most of its history from the 6th to 13th centuries, Sumatra was dominated by Srivijaya empire.

After the fall of Tarumanagara, West Java was ruled by Sunda Kingdom. While Central and Eastern Java was dominated by a kaleidoscope of competing agrarian kingdoms including the Sailendras, Mataram, Kediri, Singhasari, and finally Majapahit. In the 8th to 9th centuries, the Sailendra dynasty that ruled Medang i Bhumi Mataram kingdom built numbers massive monuments in Central Java, includes Sewu and Borobudur temple.

In the Philippines, the Laguna Copperplate Inscription dating from 900 CE relates a granted debt from a *Maginoo* caste nobleman named *Namwaran* who lived in the historic Tondo which is now part of Manila area. This document mentions a leader of Medang in Java.

The Khmer Empire effectively dominated all Mainland Southeast Asia from the early 9th until the 15th century, during which time they developed a sophisticated monumental architecture of most exquisite expression and mastery of composition at Angkor. The distinct culture of the kingdom of Dvaravati first appears in records around the 6th century. By the 10th century, Dvaravati had come under the influence of the Khmer Empire and by the 12th century Thai tribes had conquered the Chao Phraya River valley of modern-day central Thailand and established the local Sukhothai Kingdom in the 13th century and the Ayutthaya Kingdom in the 14th century.

According to the Nagarakertagama, around the 13th century, Majapahit's vassal states spread throughout much of today's Indonesia, making it the largest empire ever to exist in Southeast Asia. The empire declined in the 15th century after the rise of Islamic states in coastal Java, Malay peninsula and Sumatra.

Figure 105: *Minaret of the Menara Kudus Mosque, a Majapahit-style red brick tower with Mogul-style building in the background*

Spread of Islam

By the eight century, less than 200 years after the establishment of Islam in Arabia, the first traders and merchants who adhered to Mohammad's prophecies reportedly appeared in Maritime Southeast Asia. Certain is also, that Islam did not play a notable role anywhere in the archipelago or Indochina before the 13th century. As it happened, widespread and gradual replacement of Hinduism by Theravada Buddhism reflected a popular desire for a more personal, introvert spirituality acquired through individual ritual activities and effort.

In addressing the issue of how Islam was introduced into Southeast Asia, most historians have elaborated various scenarios along an Arabia to India and India to Southeast Asia sequence. Opinions vary on the identity and method of the agent. Either Arabian traders and scholars, who did not live or settle in India arrived directly in island Southeast Asia, or Arab traders, that had been settling in coastal India and Sri Lanka for generations. Muslim traders from India (Gujarat), converts of South Asian descend and ethnicity are variously considered as to have played a major role.

A number of sources propose the South China Sea as another "route" of Islam introduction. Arguments for this hypothesis include:

- Extensive trade between Arabia and China before the 10th century is well documented and has been corroborated by archaeological evidence (see: Belitung shipwreck).

Figure 106: *Portuguese illustration of Malays of Malacca, 1540. Malacca sultanate played a significant role in spreading Islamic faith in the region*

- During the Mongol conquest and the subsequent rule of the Yuan dynasty (1271–1368) hundreds of thousands of Muslims entered China. In Yunnan Islam was propagated and commonly embraced.
- The *Kufic Grave Stones* in Champa are indices of an early and permanent Islamic community in Indochina. The founder of the Demak Sultanate was of Sino-Javanese origin.
- Hui mariner Zheng He proposed ancient Chinese architecture as to be the stylistic basis for the oldest Javanese mosques during his 15th-century visit of Demak, Banten and the Panjunan Masjid in Cirebon.

In a 2013 EU publication of the *European Commission Forum* an inclusive attitude is being maintained: "Islam spread in Southeast Asia via Muslims of diverse ethnic and cultural origins, from Middle Easterners, Arabs and Persians, to Indians, and even Chinese, all of whom followed the great commercial routes of the epoch."

Research has several answers as to what caused the distinct syncretic (its modern expression is cultural Islam, as opposed to Middle Eastern and North African political Islam) Islam in Southeast Asia, that allowed the continuation and inclusion of elements and ritual practices of Hinduism, Buddhism and ancient Pan-East Asian Animism. Most principalities had developed highly distinctive cultures as a result of centuries of active participation in the cultural interchange and by borrowing from the flow of ideas that criss-crossed the archipelago, coming from across the Indian Ocean in the west and the South China Sea in the east. Cultural and institutional adoption was a creative and selective process, in which foreign elements were incorporated into a local synthesis.

Unlike some other "Islamised" regions like North Africa, Iberia, the Middle East and later northern India, Islamic faith in Southeast Asia was not enforced in the wake of victorious territorial conquests, but followed trade routes as with the Islamisation of Turkic Central Asia, sub-Saharan Africa, southern India, north west China.

The idea of equality (before God) for the *Ummat* (the people of God) and a personal religious effort through regular prayer was more appealing to the average person than the perceived fatalism of the Hindu pandemonium. However, Islam also taught obedience and submission, which guaranteed that the social structure of a converted people or political entity hardly saw any fundamental changes.

There are various records of lay Muslim missionaries, scholars and mystics, particularly Sufis who were most active in bringing about a peaceful proselytisation. Java, for example "received Islam by nine very active men", who were referred to as *"Wali Sanga"* (*Nine Saints*), although the historical identity of such people is almost impossible to determine. The foundation of the first Islamic kingdom in Sumatra, the Samudera Pasai Sultanate took place during the 13th century.

Nagore Shahul Hamid (1504–1570), the "Qadir Wali" was a popular protector of sailors and seafarers. A simple ritual practice was maintained by Tamil Muslims in his shrine on the coast south of Madras. He attracted pilgrims from Malaysia, Indonesia, Sri Lanka and anyone else who sought his aid.

Islam and its notion of exclusivity and finality is incompatible with all other religions and the Chinese concept of heavenly harmony and the Son of Heaven as the enforcer. The integration in the traditional East Asian tributary system with China at the centre Muslim Malays and Indonesians exacted a pragmatic approach of cultural Islam in diplomatic relations with China.

The conversion of the remnants of the Buddhist Srivijaya empire, that once controlled trade in much of Southeast Asia and in particular the Strait of Malacca, marked a strategic turning point as this act turned the Strait into an Islamic water. With the fall of Srivijaya the way was open for effective and widespread proselytisation and the establishment of Muslim trading centres. Modern Malays view the Sultanate of Malacca, which existed from the 15th to the early 16th century as the first political entity of contemporary Malaysia.

Chinese treasure voyages

By the end of the 14th century Ming China had conquered Yunnan in the South, yet had lost control of the Silk Road after the fall of the Mongol Yuan dynasty. The ruling Yongle Emperor resolved to focus on the Indian Ocean sea routes seeking to consolidate the ancient Imperial Tributary System, establish greater diplomatic and military presence and widen the Chinese sphere of influence. He ordered the construction of a huge trade and representation fleet that, between 1405 and 1433, undertook several voyages into Southeast Asia, to India, the Persian Gulf and as far as East Africa. Under the leadership of Zheng He hundreds of naval vessels of then unparalleled size, grandeur and technological advancement and manned by sizeable military contingents, ambassadors, merchants, artists and scholars repeatedly visited several major Southeast Asian principalities. The individual fleets engaged in a number of clashes with pirates and occasionally supported various royal contenders. However, pro-expansionist voices at the court in Peking lost influence after the 1450s and the voyages were discontinued. The protraction of the ritualistic ceremonies and scanty travels of emissaries in the Tributary System alone was not sufficient to develop firm and lasting Chinese commercial and political influence in the region especially during the impending onset of highly competitive global trade.

Early modern era

European colonisation

The earliest Europeans to have visited Southeast Asia were Marco Polo during the 13th century in the service of Kublai Khan and Niccolò de' Conti during the early 15th century. Regular and momentous voyages only began in the 16th century after the arrival of the Portuguese, who actively sought direct and competitive trade. They were usually accompanied by missionaries, who hoped to promote Christianity.

Portugal was the first European power to establish a bridgehead on the lucrative maritime Southeast Asia trade route, with the conquest of the Sultanate of Malacca in 1511. The Netherlands and Spain followed and soon superseded Portugal as the main European powers in the region. In 1599, Spain began to colonise the Philippines. In 1619, acting through the Dutch East India Company, the Dutch took the city of Sunda Kelapa, renamed it Batavia (now Jakarta) as a base for trading and expansion into the other parts of Java and the surrounding territory. In 1641, the Dutch took Malacca from the Portuguese.[606] Economic opportunities attracted Overseas Chinese to the region in great numbers. In 1775, the Lanfang Republic, possibly the first republic in

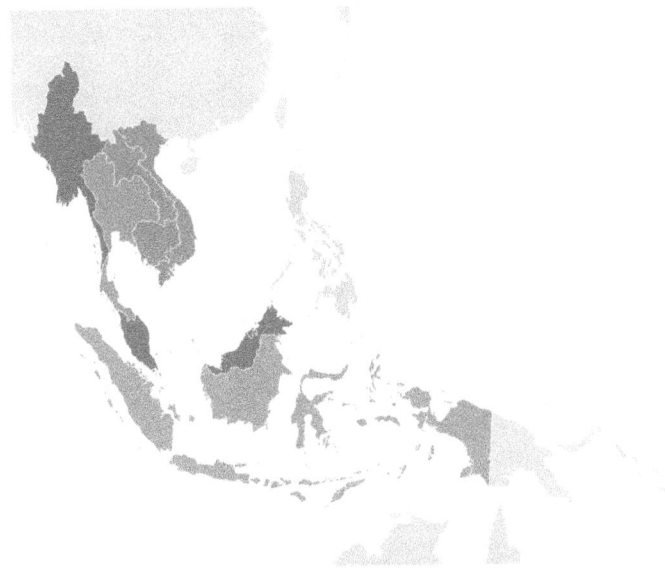

Figure 107: *European colonisation of Southeast Asia.*
Legend:
France
Netherlands
Portugal
Spain
United Kingdom

the region, was established in West Kalimantan, Indonesia, as a tributary state of the Qing Empire; the republic lasted until 1884, when it fell under Dutch occupation as Qing influence waned.[607]

Englishmen of the United Kingdom, in the guise of the Honourable East India Company led by Josiah Child, had little interest or impact in the region, and were effectively expelled following the Siam–England war (1687). Britain, in the guise of the British East India Company, turned their attention to the Bay of Bengal following the Peace with France and Spain (1783). During the conflicts, Britain had struggled for naval superiority with the French, and the need of good harbours became evident. Penang Island had been brought to the attention of the Government of India by Francis Light. In 1786, the settlement of George Town was founded at the northeastern tip of Penang Island by Captain Francis Light, under the administration of Sir John Macpherson; this marked the beginning of British expansion into the Malay Peninsula.[608]

Figure 108: *Portrait of Afonso de Albuquerque, the first European to conquer a part of Southeast Asia of Malacca.*

The British also temporarily possessed Dutch territories during the Napoleonic Wars; and Spanish areas in the Seven Years' War. In 1819, Stamford Raffles established Singapore as a key trading post for Britain in their rivalry with the Dutch. However, their rivalry cooled in 1824 when an Anglo-Dutch treaty demarcated their respective interests in Southeast Asia. British rule in Burma began with the first Anglo-Burmese War (1824–1826).

Early United States entry into what was then called the East Indies (usually in reference to the Malay Archipelago) was low key. In 1795, a secret voyage for pepper set sail from Salem, Massachusetts on an 18-month voyage that returned with a bulk cargo of pepper, the first to be so imported into the country, which sold at the extraordinary profit of seven hundred per cent. In 1831, the merchantman *Friendship* of Salem returned to report the ship had been plundered, and the first officer and two crewmen murdered in Sumatra. The Anglo-Dutch Treaty of 1824 obligated the Dutch to ensure the safety of shipping and overland trade in and around Aceh, who accordingly sent the Royal Netherlands East Indies Army on the punitive expedition of 1831. President Andrew Jackson also ordered America's first Sumatran punitive expedition of 1832, which was followed by a punitive expedition in 1838. The *Friendship* incident thus afforded the Dutch a reason to take over Ache; and Jackson, to dispatch diplomatist Edmund Roberts, who in 1833 secured the Roberts Treaty with Siam. In 1856 negotiations for amendment of this treaty, Townsend Harris stated the position of the United States:

> The United States does not hold any possessions in the East, nor does it desire any. The form of government forbids the holding of colonies. The United States therefore cannot be an object of jealousy to any Eastern Power. Peaceful commercial relations, which give as well as receive benefits, is what the President wishes to establish with Siam, and such is the object of my mission.

From the end of the 1850s onwards, while the attention of the United States shifted to maintaining their union, the pace of European colonisation shifted to a significantly higher gear.

This phenomenon, denoted New Imperialism, saw the conquest of nearly all Southeast Asian territories by the colonial powers. The Dutch East India Company and British East India Company were dissolved by their respective governments, who took over the direct administration of the colonies. Only Thailand was spared the experience of foreign rule, though Thailand, too, was greatly affected by the power politics of the Western powers. The Monthon reforms of the late 19th Century continuing up till around 1910, imposed a Westernised form of government on the country's partially independent cities called Mueang, such that the country could be said to have successfully colonised itself. Western powers did, however, continue to interfere in both internal and external affairs.

By 1913, the British had occupied Burma, Malaya and the northern Borneo territories, the French controlled Indochina, the Dutch ruled the Netherlands East Indies while Portugal managed to hold on to Portuguese Timor. In the Philippines, the 1872 Cavite Mutiny was a precursor to the Philippine Revolution (1896–1898). When the Spanish–American War began in Cuba in 1898, Filipino revolutionaries declared Philippine independence and established the First Philippine Republic the following year. In the Treaty of Paris of 1898 that ended the war with Spain, the United States gained the Philippines and other territories; in refusing to recognise the nascent republic, America effectively reversed her position of 1856. This led directly to the Philippine–American War, in which the First Republic was defeated; wars followed with the Republic of Zamboanga, the Republic of Negros and the Republic of Katagalugan, all of which were also defeated.

Colonial rule had had a profound effect on Southeast Asia. While the colonial powers profited much from the region's vast resources and large market, colonial rule did develop the region to a varying extent. Commercial agriculture, mining and an export based economy developed rapidly during this period.

Figure 109: *Japanese imperial army entering Manila, January 1942.*

The introduction Christianity bought by the colonist also have profound effect in the societal change.

Increased labour demand resulted in mass immigration, especially from British India and China, which brought about massive demographic change. The institutions for a modern nation state like a state bureaucracy, courts of law, print media and to a smaller extent, modern education, sowed the seeds of the fledgling nationalist movements in the colonial territories. In the inter-war years, these nationalist movements grew and often clashed with the colonial authorities when they demanded self-determination.

20th-century Southeast Asia

Japanese invasion and occupations

In September 1940, following the Fall of France and pursuant to the Pacific war goals of Imperial Japan, the Japanese Imperial Army invaded Vichy French Indochina, which ended in the abortive Japanese coup de main in French Indochina of 9 March 1945. On 5 January 1941, Thailand launched the Franco-Thai War, ended on 9 May 1941 by a Japanese-imposed treaty signed in Tokyo.[609] On 7/8 December, Japan's entry into World War II began with the invasion of Thailand, the only invaded country to maintain nominal independence, due to her political and military alliance with the Japanese—on 10 May 1942, her northwestern Payap Army invaded Burma during the Burma

Figure 110: *Combat operations at Ia Drang Valley, during Vietnam War, November 1965.*

Campaign. From 1941 until war's end, Japanese occupied Cambodia, Malaya, and the Philippines, which ended in independence movements. Japanese occupation of the Philippines led to the forming of the Second Philippine Republic, formally dissolved in Tokyo on 17 August 1945. Also on 17 August, a proclamation of Indonesian Independence was read at the conclusion of Japanese occupation of the Dutch East Indies since March 1942.

Post-war decolonisation

With the rejuvenated nationalist movements in wait, the Europeans returned to a very different Southeast Asia after World War II. Indonesia declared independence on 17 August 1945 and subsequently fought a bitter war against the returning Dutch; the Philippines was granted independence by the United States in 1946; Burma secured their independence from Britain in 1948, and the French were driven from Indochina in 1954 after a bitterly fought war (the Indochina War) against the Vietnamese nationalists. The United Nations provided a forum for nationalism, post-independent self-definition, nation-building and the acquisition of territorial integrity for many newly independent nations.

During the Cold War, countering the threat of communism was a major theme in the decolonisation process. After suppressing the communist insurrection during the Malayan Emergency from 1948 to 1960, Britain granted independence to Malaya and later, Singapore, Sabah and Sarawak in 1957 and 1963 respectively within the framework of the Federation of Malaysia. In one of the most bloody single incidents of violence in Cold War Southeast Asia, General Suharto seized power in Indonesia in 1965 and initiated a massacre of approximately 500,000 alleged members of the Communist Party of Indonesia (PKI).

Following the independence of the Indochina states with the battle of Dien Bien Phu, North Vietnamese attempts to conquer South Vietnam resulted in the Vietnam War. The conflict spread to Laos and Cambodia and heavy intervention from the United States. By the war's end in 1975, all these countries were controlled by communist parties. After the communist victory, two wars between communist states—the Cambodian–Vietnamese War of 1975–89 and the Sino-Vietnamese War of 1979—were fought in the region. The victory of the Khmer Rouge in Cambodia resulted in the Cambodian Genocide.[610,611]

In 1975, Portuguese rule ended in East Timor. However, independence was short-lived as Indonesia annexed the territory soon after. However, after more than 20 years of fighting Indonesia, East Timor won its independence and was recognised by the UN in 2002. Finally, Britain ended its protectorate of the Sultanate of Brunei in 1984, marking the end of European rule in Southeast Asia.

Contemporary Southeast Asia

Modern Southeast Asia has been characterised by high economic growth by most countries and closer regional integration. Indonesia, Malaysia, the Philippines, Singapore and Thailand have traditionally experienced high growth and are commonly recognised as the more developed countries of the region. As of late, Vietnam too had been experiencing an economic boom. However, Myanmar, Cambodia, Laos and the newly independent East Timor are still lagging economically.

On 8 August 1967, the Association of Southeast Asian Nations (ASEAN) was founded by Thailand, Indonesia, Malaysia, Singapore, and the Philippines. Since Cambodian admission into the union in 1999, East Timor is the only Southeast Asian country that is not part of ASEAN, although plans are under way for eventual membership. The association aims to enhance co-operation among Southeast Asian community. ASEAN Free Trade Area has been established to encourage greater trade among ASEAN members. ASEAN has also been a front runner in greater integration of Asia-Pacific region through East Asia Summits.

Figure 111: *ASEAN members' flags in Jakarta.*

Bibliography

- Dennell, Robin (2010). "'Out of Africa I': Current Problems and Future Prospects". In Fleagle, John G.; et al. *Out of Africa I: The First Hominin Colonization of Eurasia*. Vertebrate Paleobiology and Paleoanthropology Series. Dordrecht: Springer. pp. 247–74. ISBN 978-90-481-9036-2.<templatestyles src="Module:Citation/CS1/styles.css"></templatestyles>
- Morwood, M. J. (2003). "Revised age for Mojokerto 1, an early *Homo erectus* cranium from East Java, Indonesia"[612]. *Australian Archaeology*. **57**: 1–4. Archived from the original[613] on 10 March 2014. Retrieved 10 March 2014.<templatestyles src="Module:Citation/CS1/styles.css"></templatestyles>.
- Swisher, C. C. (1994). "Age of the earliest known hominin in Java, Indonesia". *Science*. **263** (5150): 1118–21. doi: 10.1126/science.8108729[614]. PMID 8108729[615].<templatestyles src="Module:Citation/CS1/styles.css"></templatestyles>
- Holt, Peter Malcolm; Lewis, Bernard (1977). *The Cambridge History of Islam*. Cambridge University Press. p. 21. ISBN 0-521-29137-2.<templatestyles src="Module:Citation/CS1/styles.css"></templatestyles> pg.123-125

- von Glahn, Richard (27 December 1996). *Fountain of Fortune: Money and Monetary Policy in China, 1000-1700*. University of California Press. ISBN 978-0-520-91745-3.<templatestyles src="Module:Citation/CS1/styles.css"></templatestyles>
- Reid, Anthony (9 May 1990). *Southeast Asia in the Age of Commerce, 1450-1680: The Lands Below the Winds*. Yale University Press. ISBN 978-0-300-04750-9.<templatestyles src="Module:Citation/CS1/styles.css"></templatestyles>

Further reading

<templatestyles src="Template:Refbegin/styles.css" />

- Cœdès, George (1968). Walter F. Vella, ed. *The Indianized States of Southeast Asia*. trans.Susan Brown Cowing. University of Hawaii Press. ISBN 978-0-8248-0368-1.<templatestyles src="Module:Citation/CS1/styles.css"></templatestyles>
- Lokesh, Chandra, & International Academy of Indian Culture. (2000). Society and culture of Southeast Asia: Continuities and changes. New Delhi: International Academy of Indian Culture and Aditya Prakashan.
- Daigorō Chihara (1996). *Hindu-Buddhist Architecture in Southeast Asia*[616]. BRILL. ISBN 90-04-10512-3.<templatestyles src="Module:Citation/CS1/styles.css"></templatestyles>
- Peter Church (3 February 2012). *A Short History of South-East Asia*[617]. John Wiley & Sons. ISBN 978-1-118-35044-7.<templatestyles src="Module:Citation/CS1/styles.css"></templatestyles>
- George Cœdès (1968). *The Indianized States of South-East Asia*[618]. University of Hawaii Press. ISBN 978-0-8248-0368-1.<templatestyles src="Module:Citation/CS1/styles.css"></templatestyles>
- Charles Alfred Fisher (1964). *South-east Asia: a social, economic, and political geography*[619]. Methuen.<templatestyles src="Module:Citation/CS1/styles.css"></templatestyles>
- Bernard Philippe Groslier (1962). *The art of Indochina: including Thailand, Vietnam, Laos and Cambodia*[620]. Crown Publishers.<templatestyles src="Module:Citation/CS1/styles.css"></templatestyles>
- D.G.E. Hall (1966). *A History of South-East Asia*[621].<templatestyles src="Module:Citation/CS1/styles.css"></templatestyles>
- Daniel George Edward Hall; Phút Tấn Nguyễn (1968). *Đông Nam Á sử lược*[622]. Pacific Northwest Trading Company.<templatestyles src="Module:Citation/CS1/styles.css"></templatestyles>

- Kenneth R. Hall (28 December 2010). *A History of Early Southeast Asia: Maritime Trade and Societal Development, 100–1500*[623]. Rowman & Littlefield Publishers. ISBN 978-0-7425-6762-7.
- Virginia Matheson Hooker (2003). *A Short History of Malaysia: Linking East and West*[624]. Allen & Unwin. ISBN 978-1-86448-955-2.
- Michael C. Howard (23 February 2012). *Transnationalism in Ancient and Medieval Societies: The Role of Cross-Border Trade and Travel*[625]. McFarland. ISBN 978-0-7864-9033-2.
- Victor T. King (2008). *The Sociology of Southeast Asia: Transformations in a Developing Region*[626]. NIAS Press. ISBN 978-87-91114-60-1.
- Paul Michel Munoz (2006). *Early Kingdoms of the Indonesian Archipelago and the Malay Peninsula*[627]. National Book Network. ISBN 978-981-4155-67-0.
- D. R. SarDesai (2003). *Southeast Asia, Past and Present*[628]. Westview Press. ISBN 978-0-8133-4143-9.
- Heidhues, Mary Somer. "'Southeast Asia: A Concise History" ISBN 0-500-28303-6
- Majumdar, R.C. (1979). *India and South-East Asia*. I.S.P.Q.S. History and Archaeology Series Vol. 6. ISBN 81-7018-046-5.
- Ooi, Keat Gin, ed. (2004). *Southeast Asia: A Historical Encyclopedia, from Angkor Wat to East Timor, Volume 1*[629] (illustrated ed.). ABC-CLIO. ISBN 1576077705. Retrieved 24 April 2014.
- Guy, John (1986). Guy, John, ed. *Oriental trade ceramics in South-East Asia, ninth to sixteenth centuries: with a catalogue of Chinese, Vietnamese and Thai wares in Australian collections*[630] (illustrated, revised ed.). Oxford University Press.
- David G. Marr; Anthony Crothers Milner (1986). *Southeast Asia in the 9th to 14th Centuries*[631]. Institute of Southeast Asian Studies. ISBN 978-9971-988-39-5.

- Osborne, Milton. *Southeast Asia. An introductory history.* <templatestyles src="Module:Citation/CS1/styles.css" />ISBN 1-86508-390-9
- Jan M. Pluvier (1995). *Historical Atlas of South-East Asia*[632]. E.J. Brill. ISBN 978-90-04-10238-5.<templatestyles src="Module:Citation/CS1/styles.css"></templatestyles>
- Anthony Reid (1 August 2000). *Charting the Shape of Early Modern Southeast Asia*[633]. Silkworm Books. ISBN 978-1-63041-481-8.<templatestyles src="Module:Citation/CS1/styles.css"></templatestyles>
- Scott, James C., The Art of Not Being Governed: An Anarchist History of Upland Southeast Asia (Yale Agrarian Studies Series), 464 pages, Yale University Press (30 September 2009), <templatestyles src="Module:Citation/CS1/styles.css" />ISBN 0300152280, <templatestyles src="Module:Citation/CS1/styles.css" />ISBN 978-0300152289
- Tarling, Nicholas (ed). *The Cambridge history of Southeast Asia* Vol I-IV. <templatestyles src="Module:Citation/CS1/styles.css" />ISBN 0-521-66369-5
- R. C. Majumdar, Study of Sanskrit in South-East Asia
- R. C. Majumdar, *India and South-East Asia*, I.S.P.Q.S. History and Archaeology Series Vol. 6, 1979, <templatestyles src="Module:Citation/CS1/styles.css" />ISBN 81-7018-046-5.
- Paul Michel Munoz (2006). *Early Kingdoms of the Indonesian Archipelago and the Malay Peninsula.* Editions Didier Millet. ISBN 981-4155-67-5.<templatestyles src="Module:Citation/CS1/styles.css"></templatestyles>
- Reid, Anthony (1993). *Southeast Asia in the Age of Commerce, 1450-1680: Expansion and crisis, Volume 2*[634]. Volume 2 of Southeast Asia in the Age of Commerce, 1450-1680 (illustrated ed.). Yale University Press. ISBN 0300054122. Retrieved 24 April 2014.<templatestyles src="Module:Citation/CS1/styles.css"></templatestyles>
- Reid, Anthony; Alilunas-Rodgers, Kristine, eds. (1996). *Sojourners and Settlers: Histories of Southeast China and the Chinese*[635]. Contributor Kristine Alilunas-Rodgers (illustrated, reprint ed.). University of Hawaii Press. ISBN 0824824466. Retrieved 24 April 2014.<templatestyles src="Module:Citation/CS1/styles.css"></templatestyles>
- Edward H. Schafer (1963). *The Golden Peaches of Samarkand: A Study of T'ang Exotics*[636]. University of California Press. GGKEY:XZ70D3XUH9A.<templatestyles src="Module:Citation/CS1/styles.css"></templatestyles>
- Paz, Victor; Solheim, II, Wilhelm G., eds. (2004). *Southeast Asian Archaeology: Wilhelm G. Solheim II Festschrift*[637] (illustrated ed.). University of the Philippines Press. ISBN 9715424511. Retrieved 24

- April 2014.<templatestyles src="Module:Citation/CS1/styles.css"></templatestyles>
- Yule, Paul. *The Bronze Age Metalwork of India*. Prähistorische Bronzefunde XX,8, Munich, 1985, <templatestyles src="Module:Citation/CS1/styles.css" />ISBN 3 406 30440 0.
- Demeter, F.; Shackelford, L. L.; Bacon, A.-M.; Duringer, P.; Westaway, K.; Sayavongkhamdy, T.; Braga, J.; Sichanthongtip, P.; Khamdalavong, P.; Ponche, J.-L.; Wang, H.; Lundstrom, C.; Patole-Edoumba, E.; Karpoff, A.-M. (20 August 2012). "Anatomically modern human in Southeast Asia (Laos) by 46 ka"[638]. *Proceedings of the National Academy of Sciences*. **109** (36): 14375–14380. doi: 10.1073/pnas.1208104109[639]. PMC 3437904[640].<templatestyles src="Module:Citation/CS1/styles.css"></templatestyles>
- Marwick, Ben (January 2008). "Stone artefacts and recent research in the archaeology of mainland Southeast Asian hunter-gatherers"[641]. *Before Farming*. **2008** (4): 1–19. doi: 10.3828/bfarm.2008.4.1[642].<templatestyles src="Module:Citation/CS1/styles.css"></templatestyles>
- *The South East Asian Review*[643]. Institute of South East Asian Studies. 1995.<templatestyles src="Module:Citation/CS1/styles.css"></templatestyles>
- *Southeast Asia*[644]. Lonely Planet. 15 September 2010. ISBN 978-1-74220-377-5.<templatestyles src="Module:Citation/CS1/styles.css"></templatestyles>
- *Tri thức Đông Nam Á*[645]. Nhà xuất bản Chính trị quốc gia. 2008. pp. 208–.<templatestyles src="Module:Citation/CS1/styles.css"></templatestyles>
- *Thailandia*[646]. Touring Editore. 2005. ISBN 978-88-365-3327-5.<templatestyles src="Module:Citation/CS1/styles.css"></templatestyles>

Further reading

- Reid, Anthony. *A History of Southeast Asia: Critical Crossroads* (Blackwell History of the World, 2015)

External links

- A Short History of China and Southeast Asia.pdf[647]
- Ancient Southeast Asia Throbbing Blood Tube[648]
- Wikiversity – Department of Southeast Asian History
- 雲南・東南アジアに関する漢籍史料[649]

- Citizenship and Democratization in Southeast Asia[650]
- Democracy and Citizen Politics in East Asia[651]

Appendix

References

[1] Stearns 2011, p. 68.
[2] Stearns 2011, p. 65.
[3] Stearns 2011, p. 66.
[4] Stearns 2011, p. 43.
[5] Stearns 2011, p. 44.
[6] Stearns 2011, p. 42.
[7] Stearns 2011, p. 45.
[8] Stearns 2011, p. 270, Chapter 12.
[9] Stearns 2011, pp. 271–272, Chapter 12.
[10] Stearns 2011, p. 273, Chapter 12.
[11] Stearns 2011, p. 274, Chapter 12.
[12] Stearns 2011, p. 327, Chapter 14.
[13] Bowman 2000, pp. 124–137.
[14] Stearns et al. 2011, pp. 291–301.
[15] Stearns et al. 2011, pp. 296.
[16] Stearns 2011, p. 503, Chapter 22.
[17] Stearns 2011, p. 504, Chapter 22.
[18] Stearns 2011, p. 505, Chapter 22.
[19] Stearns 2011, p. 507, Chapter 22.
[20] Stearns 2011, p. 339, Chapter 15.
[21] Stearns 2011, p. 508, Chapter 22.
[22] Stearns 2011, p. 509, Chapter 22.
[23] Stearns 2011, p. 510, Chapter 22.
[24] https://books.google.com/books?id=cYoHOqC7Yx4C
[25] https://www.amazon.com/History-Christianity-Asia-Vol-1500-1900/dp/1570757011/ref=tmm_pap_swatch_0?_encoding=UTF8&qid=1519541778&sr=1-1
[26] https://www.amazon.com/History-Asia-Rhoads-Murphey/dp/0205168558/
[27] *Out of Africa.* http://www.amnh.org/exhibitions/past-exhibitions/human-origins/the-history-of-human-evolution/out-of-africa American Museum of Natural History. Retrieved April 23, 2014.
[28] *Evolutionary Tree Information.* http://humanorigins.si.edu/evidence/human-fossils/species/homo-erectus Human Origins. Smithsonian Institution. Retrieved April 23, 2014.
[29] Rightmire & Lordkipanidze 2010, p. 242.
[30] Dennell 2010, pp. 247–48, 266.
[31]
[32] *Homo erectus.* http://www.nhm.ac.uk/nature-online/life/human-origins/early-human-family/homo-erectus/index.html London: Natural History Museum. Retrieved April 23, 2014.
[33]
[34] *New Migrants.* http://www.amnh.org/exhibitions/past-exhibitions/human-origins/the-history-of-human-evolution/new-migrants American Museum of Natural History. Retrieved April 23, 2014.
[35] A previous theory, the "multiregional continuity theory", held that the Asian *Homo sapiens* evolved from the Asian *Homo erectus*. This has been disproved by DNA findings which show that all living humans descended from a common African ancestor who lived within the past 200,000 years. The *Homo erectus* species then ceased to exist.
[36] *Expansion of Homo Sapiens* http://www.amnh.org/exhibitions/past-exhibitions/human-origins/the-history-of-human-evolution/expansion-of-homo-sapiens American Museum of Natural History. Retrieved April 23, 2014.
[37]

[38] *By Land and Sea.* http://www.amnh.org/exhibitions/past-exhibitions/human-origins/one-human-species/by-land-and-by-sea American Museum of Natural History. Retrieved April 23, 2014.
[39] *Steppes into Asia.* http://www.amnh.org/exhibitions/past-exhibitions/human-origins/one-human-species/steppes-into-asia American Museum of Natural History. Retrieved April 23, 2014.
[40] *Life During the Ice Age.* http://www.amnh.org/exhibitions/past-exhibitions/human-origins/the-history-of-human-evolution/life-during-the-ice-age American Museum of Natural History. Retrieved April 23, 2014.
[41] Woods (2010), p. 87.
[42] Bagley (1999), pp. 181–182.
[43] Keightley (1999), pp. 235–237.
[44] Krishnamurti (2003), p. 22.
[45] p. 204
[46] Pollock (2003), p. 60.
[47] , pp. 121–122.
[48] //en.wikipedia.org/w/index.php?title=Template:Prehistoric_Asia_by_region&action=edit
[49] Rightmire & Lordkipanidze 2010, p. 241.
[50] Marshall Cavendish, *World and Its Peoples: Eastern and Southern Asia.* https://www.questia.com/read/120464266 New York: Marshall Cavendish. **1**. 2007. p. 30.
[51] Marshall Cavendish, *World and Its Peoples: Eastern and Southern Asia.* https://www.questia.com/read/120464266 New York: Marshall Cavendish. **1**. 2007. pp. 30-31.
[52] Marshall Cavendish, *World and Its Peoples: Eastern and Southern Asia.* https://www.questia.com/read/120464266 New York: Marshall Cavendish. **1**. 2007. pp. 31-36.
[53] Tchernov 1987.
[54] Dennell 2007, pp. 41 and 55–58.
[55] Swisher et al. 1994; Dennell 2010, p. 262.
[56] Dennell 2010, p. 266, citing Morwood et al. 2003.
[57] *Spreading through Asia.* http://www.amnh.org/exhibitions/past-exhibitions/human-origins/the-history-of-human-evolution/spreading-through-asia American Museum of Natural History. Retrieved April 23, 2014.
[58] https://web.archive.org/web/20140310154453/https://www.library.uq.edu.au/ojs/index.php/aa/article/view/526/1690
[59] https://www.library.uq.edu.au/ojs/index.php/aa/article/view/526/1690
[60] //doi.org/10.1126%2Fscience.8108729
[61] //www.ncbi.nlm.nih.gov/pubmed/8108729
[62] //en.wikipedia.org/w/index.php?title=Template:Ancient_Near_East_topics&action=edit
[63] Samuel Noah Kramer, *History Begins at Sumer*, (tr. Mendelson, F. A., Moscow, 1963).
[64] //en.wikipedia.org/w/index.php?title=Template:Human_history&action=edit
[65] Sumer and the Sumerians, by Harriet E. W. Crawford, p 69
[66] Sumer and the Sumerians, by Harriet E. W. Crawford, p 75
[67] //en.wikipedia.org/w/index.php?title=Template:Bronze_Age&action=edit
[68] Amorite http://concise.britannica.com/ebc/article-9007224/Amorites *Encyclopædia Britannica*
[69] James P. Mallory, "Kuro-Araxes Culture", *Encyclopedia of Indo-European Culture*, Fitzroy Dearborn, 1997.
[70] See page 9. http://www.jaas.org/edocs/v18n2/Parpola-identity_Article%20-Final.pdf
[71] A convenient table of sea peoples in hieroglyphics, transliteration and English is given in the dissertation of Woodhuizen, 2006, who developed it from works of Kitchen cited there.
[72] As noted by Gardiner V.1 p.196, other texts have UNIQ-hiero-0-874b6c040acd5a2b-QINU ḫ3ty.w "foreign-peoples"; both terms can refer to the concept of "foreigners" as well. Zangger in the external link below expresses a commonly held view that "sea peoples" does not translate this and other expressions but is an academic innovation. The Woudhuizen dissertation and the Morris paper identify Gaston Maspero as the first to use the term "peuples de la mer" in 1881.
[73] Gardiner V.1 p.196.
[74] Manassa p.55.
[75] Line 52. The inscription is shown in Manassa p.55 plate 12.

[76] Several articles in Oren.
[77] See A. Stoia and the other essays in M.L. Stig Sørensen and R. Thomas, eds., *The Bronze Age—Iron Age Transition in Europe* (Oxford) 1989, and T.H. Wertime and J.D. Muhly, *The Coming of the Age of Iron* (New Haven) 1980.
[78] //en.wikipedia.org/w/index.php?title=Template:Iron_Age&action=edit
[79] Assyrian Eponym List http://www.livius.org/li-ln/limmu/limmu_1c.html
[80] Tadmor, H. (1994). *The Inscriptions of Tiglath-Pileser III, King of Assyria.* pp.29
[81] Hawkins, John David; 1982a. "Neo-Hittite States in Syria and Anatolia" in *Cambridge Ancient History* (2nd ed.) 3.1: 372-441. Also: Hawkins, John David; 1995. "The Political Geography of North Syria and South-East Anatolia in the Neo-Assyrian Period" in *Neo-Assyrian Geography*, Mario Liverani (ed.), Università di Roma "La Sapienza", Dipartimento di Scienze storiche, archeologiche e anthropologiche dell'Antichità, Quaderni di Geografia Storica 5: Roma: Sargon srl, 87-101.
[82] *Urartu* article, Columbia Electronic Encyclopedia, 2007 http://encyclopedia2.thefreedictionary.com/Urartu
[83] Full translation of the Behistun Inscription
[84] https://books.google.com/books?id=Gt1jTpXAThwC&printsec=frontcover
[85] http://libmma.contentdm.oclc.org/cdm/compoundobject/collection/p15324coll10/id/33948
[86] http://ancientneareast.tripod.com/index.html
[87] http://vicinooriente.selfip.com/
[88] http://www.ancientneareast.net/
[89] https://web.archive.org/web/20050304014027/http://www.asia.si.edu/collections/results.cfm?group=Ancient%20Near%20East
[90] https://web.archive.org/web/20100828102017/http://www.asia.si.edu/visitor/archives.htm
[91] https://web.archive.org/web/20080708194356/http://www.archaeowiki.org/
[92] http://www.etana.org
[93] http://content.lib.washington.edu/neareastweb/index.html
[94] http://www.near-east-images.blogspot.com/
[95] http://www.anthropology.uw.edu.pl/
[96] //en.wikipedia.org/w/index.php?title=Template:Human_history&action=edit
[97] Robin Wright, *Sacred Rage: The Wrath of Militant Islam*, p. 65–66
[98] interview by Robin Wright of UK Foreign Secretary (at the time) Lord Carrington in November 1981, *Sacred Rage: The Wrath of Militant Islam* by Robin Wright, Simon and Schuster, (1985), p. 67
[99] Midant-Reynes, Béatrix. *The Prehistory of Egypt: From the First Egyptians to the First Kings.* Oxford: Blackwell Publishers.
[100] //en.wikipedia.org/w/index.php?title=Template:Ancient_Near_East_topics&action=edit
[101] http://www.ancient.eu/akkad/
[102] Egypt (page 102) https://books.google.com/books?id=rXmdAAAAQBAJ&pg=PA102
[103] The Inheritance of Rome https://books.google.com/books?id=yDiDfipV4AIC&pg=PT461
[104] , for the Byzantine–Sasanian rivalry and its cultural/religious overtones.
[105] , for the Byzantine–Sasanian struggle with Aksum and Himyar, as well as the territorial wars and focus on trade.
[106] Wawro 2008, pp. 112–115, for Byzantine territory, Sasanian invasions, Heraclius' success at repelling invasion, and the exhaustion of both states.
[107] , for the replacement of the Sasanian king by Heraclius.
[108] Stearns et al. 2011, p. 138.
[109] Hourani 2013, The world into which the Arabs came, for Arabian migrations, the Lakhmids & Ghassanids, and religious diversity.
[110] Subhi Y. Labib (1969), "Capitalism in Medieval Islam", *The Journal of Economic History* **29** (1), p. 79–96 [80].
[111] Stearns et al. 2011, p. 171.
[112] Stearns et al. 2011, p. 159.
[113] Wawro 2008, pp. 146–149.
[114] Guzman 1985, pp. 230–233.
[115] Quataert 2000.

[116] Mansfield & Pelham 2013, pp. 141–147.
[117] Dr. Tofallis, Kypros, *A History of Cyprus*, p.98 (2002)
[118] Matthew F. Jacobs, " World War I: A War (and Peace?) for the Middle East https://doi.org/10.1093/dh/dhu031" *Diplomatic History*) (2014) 38#4: 776–785.
[119] Justin McCarthy, *The Population of Palestine* 1990
[120] Lewis 1995, pp. 348–350.
[121] Elizabeth Monroe, *Britain's Moment in the Middle East, 1914-1956* (1963) online https://www.questia.com/library/954023/britain-s-moment-in-the-middle-east-1914-1956
[122] Watson, Peter (2006). *Ideas: A History of Thought and Invention, from Fire to Freud*. New York: Harper Perennial. p. 1096.
[123] Bergen, Peter, *Holy War Inc.*, Free Press, (2001), p.68
[124] https://books.google.com/books?id=imw_KFD5bsQC&pg=PR7
[125] http://www.illinoismedieval.org/EMS/EMSpdf/V2/V2Guzman.pdf
[126] https://books.google.com/books?id=irtb55WDsjMC
[127] https://books.google.com/books?id=lZ5TAQAAQBAJ
[128] https://www.questia.com/library/954023/britain-s-moment-in-the-middle-east-1914-1956
[129] https://books.google.com/books?id=T1jR39OM_hsC
[130] http://www.qdl.qa/en/articles-from-our-experts
[131] http://repository.library.georgetown.edu/handle/10822/552622
[132] http://www.healthguidance.org/entry/6308/1/Ancient-Civilizations--Mesopotamia.html
[133] https://www.webcitation.org/6KKWk56jd?url=http://www.aina.org/brief.html
[134] http://gulf2000.columbia.edu/images/maps/MidEast_Cultural_Historical_Zones_lg.png
[135] //en.wikipedia.org/w/index.php?title=Template:Human_history&action=edit
[136] O'Connell, Robert L.: "Soul of the Sword.", page 51. The Free Press, New York, 2002
[137] . Jane Qiu, The Surprisingly Early Settlement of the Tibetan Plateau https://www.scientificamerican.com/article/the-surprisingly-early-settlement-of-the-tibetan-plateau/, *Scientific American, 1 March 2017*.
[138] R. Spencer Wells et al., The Eurasian Heartland: A continental perspective on Y-chromosome diversity http://hpgl.stanford.edu/publications/PNAS_2001_v98_p10244.pdf
[139] von Le Coq, Albert. (1913). *Chotscho: Facsimile-Wiedergaben der Wichtigeren Funde der Ersten Königlich Preussischen Expedition nach Turfan in Ost-Turkistan* http://dsr.nii.ac.jp/toyobunko/LFc-42/V-1/page/0003.html.en. Berlin: Dietrich Reimer (Ernst Vohsen), im Auftrage der Gernalverwaltung der Königlichen Museen aus Mitteln des Baessler-Institutes, Tafel 19 http://dsr.nii.ac.jp/toyobunko/VIII-1-B-31/V-1/page-hr/0107.html.en. (Accessed 3 September 2016).
[140] Gasparini, Mariachiara. " A Mathematic Expression of Art: Sino-Iranian and Uighur Textile Interactions and the Turfan Textile Collection in Berlin, http://heiup.uni-heidelberg.de/journals/index.php/transcultural/article/view/12313/8711#_edn32" in Rudolf G. Wagner and Monica Juneja (eds), *Transcultural Studies*, Ruprecht-Karls Universität Heidelberg, No 1 (2014), pp 134–163. See also . (Accessed 3 September 2016.)
[141] Hansen, Valerie (2012), *The Silk Road: A New History*, Oxford University Press, p. 98, .
[142] Christoph Baumer "The History of Central Asia – The Age of the Silk Roads (Volume 2); PART I: EARLY EMPIRES AND KINGDOMS IN EAST CENTRAL ASIA 1. The Xiongnu, the First Steppe Nomad Empire"
[143] Herodotus, IV, 83–144 http://www.perseus.tufts.edu/cgi-bin///ptext?doc=Perseus%3Atext%3A1999.01.0126&layout=&loc=4.83.1
[144] http://www.turks.org.uk/ A Journey of a Thousand Years
[145] Hann (2008). *Community matters in Xinjiang*. p52
[146] Includes only citizens of the PRC. Does not include members of the People's Liberation Army in active service. Source: 2000年人口普查中国民族人口资料，民族出版社，2003/9 ()
[147] Martha Brill Olcott. *Central Asia's New States*
[148] https://web.archive.org/web/20100113160437/http://www.wilsoncenter.org/index.cfm?fuseaction=wq.essay&essay_id=545818
[149] http://www.unesco.org/culture/asia/index-en.html
[150] https://web.archive.org
[151] https//web.archive.org

[152] https//web.archive.org
[153] http//www.iranica.com
[154] https//web.archive.org
[155] http://www.csen.org/?
[156] //doi.org/10.1080%2F03068370500456819
[157] http://www.perseus.tufts.edu/cgi-bin/ptext?doc=Perseus:text:1999.01.0125:book=1:chapter=1:section=0
[158] //doi.org/10.2277%2F0521497817
[159] //doi.org/10.1080%2F713660015
[160] https://web.archive.org/web/20121215042300/http://repository.library.georgetown.edu/handle/10822/552518
[161] https://web.archive.org/web/20160115205405/https://repository.library.georgetown.edu/handle/10822/552494
[162] Keay, 155 "... the history of what used to be called 'medieval' India ..."; Harle, 9 "I have eschewed the term 'medieval', meaningless in the Indian context, for the years from c. 950 to c. 1300 ..."
[163] Ahmed, xviii
[164] Keay, 155 "... the history of what used to be called 'medieval' India ..."
[165] Rowland, 273
[166] Examples: Farooqui; Radhey Shyam Chaurasia, *History of Medieval India: From 1000 A.D. to 1707 A.D.*, 2002, google books https://books.google.co.uk/books?isbn=8126901233; Satish Chandra, *Medieval India: From Sultanat to the Mughals*, 2004 (2 vols), google books https://books.google.co.uk/books?isbn=8124110646; Upinder Singh, *A History of Ancient and Early Medieval India: From the Stone Age to the 12th century*, 2008, google books https://books.google.co.uk/books?isbn=813171120X
[167] A Textbook of Historiography, 500 B.C. to A.D. 2000 By E. Sreedharan, p. 457, referencing Peter Hardy
[168] Rowland, 273; Stein, 105
[169] Not for Burjor Avari, who ends "ancient India" at 1200. Avari, 2
[170] For architecture, see Michell, 87-88. For "classical hinduism", see the note at Outline of ancient India.
[171] Keay, xxii-xxiii
[172] Keay, xx-xxi
[173] https://books.google.co.uk/books?id=WTaTDAAAQBAJ&printsec=frontcover
[174] https://books.google.co.uk/books?id=sxhAtCflwOMC&printsec=frontcover
[175] https://web.archive.org/web/20070929125948/http://persian.packhum.org/persian/index.jsp?serv=pf&file=80201010&ct=0
[176] https://web.archive.org/web/20070929132016/http://persian.packhum.org/persian/index.jsp
[177] https://books.google.com/books?id=nyYslywJUE8C&printsec=frontcover&source=gbs_ge_summary_r&cad=0#v=onepage&q&f=false
[178] //en.wikipedia.org/w/index.php?title=Template:History_of_China&action=edit
[179] William G. Boltz, Early Chinese Writing, World Archaeology, Vol. 17, No. 3, Early Writing Systems. (Feb., 1986), pp. 420–436 (436).
[180] David N. Keightley, "Art, Ancestors, and the Origins of Writing in China", *Representations*, No. 56, Special Issue: The New Erudition. (Autumn, 1996), pp.68–95 (68).
[181] *Cradles of Civilization-China: Ancient Culture, Modern Land*, Robert E. Murowchick, gen. ed. Norman: University of Oklahoma Press, 1994
[182] Qiu Xigui (2000). *Chinese Writing*. English translation of 文字學概論 by Gilbert L. Mattos and Jerry Norman. Early China Special Monograph Series No. 4. Berkeley: The Society for the Study of Early China and the Institute of East Asian Studies, University of California, Berkeley.
[183] *Leadership Strategies, Economic Activity, and Interregional Interaction: Social Complexity in Northeast China*, pp. 89
[184] Higham, Charles. 1996. *The Bronze Age of Southeast Asia*
[185] Liana Chua, Mark Elliott, *Distributed Objects: Meaning and Mattering after Alfred Gell* (2013), p. 83 https://books.google.ch/books?id=yVZFAAAAQBAJ&pg=PA83

[186] "Bronze Age China" http://www.nga.gov/exhibitions/chbro_bron.shtm. National Gallery of Art. Retrieved 11 July 2013.

[187] Scripts found on Erlitou pottery https://web.archive.org/web/20050213035644/http://www.gog.com.cn/gz/art0402/ca615230.htm (written in Simplified Chinese)

[188] 《史记·殷本纪》：帝陽甲崩，弟盤庚立，是為帝盤庚。帝盤庚之時，殷已都河北，盤庚渡河南，復居成湯之故居，乃五遷，無定處。殷民咨胥皆怨，不欲徙。盤庚乃告諭諸侯大臣曰：「昔高后成湯與爾之先祖俱定天下，法則可修。捨而弗勉，何以成德！」乃遂涉河南，治亳，行湯之政，然後百姓由寧，殷道復興。諸侯來朝，以其遵成湯之德也。

[189] *Nature* The 2,300-year-old matrix is the world's oldest decimal multiplication table http://www.nature.com/news/ancient-times-table-hidden-in-chinese-bamboo-strips-1.14482

[190] Bodde 1986, p. 84

[191] , pp. 234–236

[192] Ban Chao http://www.britannica.com/EBchecked/topic/440601/Ban-Chao, Britannica Online Encyclopedia

[193] Mark Edward Lewis, *China's Cosmopolitan Empire: The Tang Dynasty* (2012). excerpt https://www.amazon.com/Chinas-Cosmopolitan-Empire-Dynasty-Imperial/dp/0674064011/.

[194] Ebrey 1999, p. 127.

[195] Kiang 1999, p. 12.

[196] Mark Edward Lewis, *China's Cosmopolitan Empire: The Tang Dynasty* (2012). p. 1

[197] "China > History > The Ming dynasty > Political history > The dynastic succession", *Encyclopædia Britannica Online*, 2007

[198] John M. Roberts (1997). *A Short History of the World* https://books.google.com/books?id=3QZXvUhGwhAC. Oxford University Press. p. 272.

[199] Philip Kuhn, *Rebellion and its Enemies in Late Imperial China: Militarization and Social Structure, 1796–1864* (1970) ch 6

[200] Patricia Buckley Ebrey, *Cambridge Illustrated History of China* (1996) p 271

[201] Odd Arne Westad, *Restless Empire: China and the World Since 1750* (2012) p 291

[202] Rummel, Rudolph (1994), Death by Government.

[203] Valentino, Benjamin A. Final solutions: mass killing and genocide in the twentieth century Cornell University Press. December 8, 2005. p88

[204] Surrender Order of the Imperial General Headquarters of Japan http://www.taiwandocuments.org/ghq.htm, 2 September 1945, "(a) The senior Japanese commanders and all ground, sea, air, and auxiliary forces within China (excluding Manchuria), Formosa, and French Indochina north of 16 degrees north latitude shall surrender to Generalissimo Chiang Kai-shek."

[205] The Chinese people have stood up http://www.isop.ucla.edu/eas/documents/mao490921.htm. UCLA Center for East Asian Studies. Retrieved 16 April 2006.

[206] Smith, Joseph; and Davis, Simon. [2005] (2005). The A to Z of the Cold War. Issue 28 of *Historical dictionaries of war, revolution, and civil unrest*. Volume 8 of *A to Z guides*. Scarecrow Press publisher. , .

[207] Youngs, R. *The European Union and the Promotion of Democracy*. Oxford University Press, 2002.

[208] Carroll, J. M. *A Concise History of Hong Kong*. Rowman & Littlefield, 2007.

[209] //en.wikipedia.org/w/index.php?title=History_of_China&action=edit

[210] https://www.amazon.com/Cultural-Atlas-China/dp/0816038147/

[211] https//books.google.com

[212] https://books.google.com/books?id=mUofeN6WW_IC&printsec=frontcover&dq=editions:ISBN160303420X#v=onepage&q=editions%3AISBN160303420X&f=false

[213] https://www.questia.com/library/book/china-a-macro-history-by-ray-huang.jsp

[214] https://www.questia.com/library/book/china-through-the-ages-history-of-a-civilization-by-franz-michael.jsp

[215] https://www.questia.com/library/book/the-columbia-guide-to-modern-chinese-history-by-r-keith-schoppa.jsp

[216] https://www.questia.com/read/98946348

[217] https://www.questia.com/library/book/the-history-of-china-by-david-curtis-wright-john-e-findling-frank-w-thackeray.jsp

[218] http://www.paleomag.net/members/rixiangzhu/Earth-Sci%20Review.pdf

[219] http://adsabs.harvard.edu/abs/2003ESRv...61..341Z
[220] //doi.org/10.1016%2FS0012-8252%2802%2900132-0
[221] https://web.archive.org/web/20070614011439/http://arheologija.ff.uni-lj.si/documenta/pdf29/29chi.pdf
[222] https://web.archive.org/web/20101116113351/http://www.anu.edu.au/asianstudies/decrespigny/south_china.html
[223] http://www.anu.edu.au/asianstudies/decrespigny/south_china.html
[224] https://web.archive.org/web/20110528225757/http://www.anu.edu.au/asianstudies/decrespigny/mil_org.html
[225] http://www.anu.edu.au/asianstudies/decrespigny/mil_org.html
[226] http://www.anu.edu.au/asianstudies/decrespigny/3KWJin.html
[227] https://www.amazon.com/Chinas-Cosmopolitan-Empire-Dynasty-Imperial/dp/0674064011/
[228] http://content.cdlib.org/ark:/13030/ft1000031p/?&query=&brand=ucpress
[229] https://books.google.com/books?id=b80ePdTYWXoC
[230] http://content.cdlib.org/ark:/13030/ft2s2004qh/?&query=&brand=ucpress
[231] https://books.google.com/books?id=tyhT9SZRLS8C
[232] http://www.daicing.info/
[233] https://www.amazon.com/Chinese-Society-Eighteenth-Century-Naquin/dp/0300046022/
[234] https://books.google.com/books?id=KN7Awmzx2PAC&printsec=
[235] https://books.google.com/books?id=RhmaCgAAQBAJ
[236] https://books.google.com/books?id=r3AJFusMHJwC
[237] http://muse.jhu.edu/login?auth=0&type=summary&url=/journals/journal_of_military_history/v070/70.1gordon.html
[238] https://www.questia.com/library/book/chinas-bitter-victory-the-war-with-japan-1937-1945-by-james-c-hsiung-steven-i-levine.jsp
[239] http://content.cdlib.org/ark:/13030/ft829008m5/?&query=&brand=ucpress
[240] https://books.google.com/books?id=GfShg2lD8Y4C
[241] http://content.cdlib.org/ark:/13030/ft3q2nb24q/?&query=&brand=ucpress
[242] https://www.h-net.org/reviews/showrev.php?id=43955
[243] http://content.cdlib.org/ark:/13030/ft0489n683/?&query=&brand=ucpress
[244] https://www.amazon.com/dp/0521875153
[245] http://eh.net/?s=von+Glahn%2C
[246] http://content.cdlib.org/ark:/13030/ft6489p0n6/?&query=&brand=ucpress
[247] http://escholarship.org/uc/gaia_gaia_books
[248] http://www.tandfonline.com/toc/mcsh20/current
[249] http://www.eastasianhistory.org/
[250] https://web.archive.org/web/20060719230513/http://www.aall.ufl.edu/EMC/
[251] http://tandfonline.com/rmoh
[252] http://mcx.sagepub.com/
[253] http://chinajapan.org/
[254] https://web.archive.org/web/20160422202728/http://www.princeton.edu/chinese-historiography/index.xml
[255] http://www.ihp.sinica.edu.tw/database/index.htm
[256] http://repository.library.georgetown.edu/handle/10822/552524
[257] https://web.archive.org/web/20160115205405/https://repository.library.georgetown.edu/handle/10822/552494
[258] http://saturn.ihp.sinica.edu.tw/~wenwu/ww.htm
[259] https://web.archive.org/web/20121129203455/http://www.chinaknowledge.de/History/history.htm
[260] http://chinese.dsturgeon.net/
[261] http://pem.org/yinyutang/
[262] https://www.webcitation.org/query?url=http://www.geocities.com/crmaozedong/index.html&date=2009-10-25+17:56:42
[263] https://www.loc.gov/today/cyberlc/feature_wdesc.php?rec=4043
[264] https://web.archive.org/web/20080105233305/http://sd71.bc.ca/sd71/school/courtmid/Library/subject_resources/socials/CHINA.htm

[265] https://www.pbs.org/kqed/chinainside/
[266] http://www.automaticfreeweb.com/index.cfm?s=ancientasianworld
[267] http://www-chaos.umd.edu/history/toc.html
[268] //en.wikipedia.org/w/index.php?title=Template:History_of_Japan&action=edit
[269] //en.wikipedia.org/w/index.php?title=Template:Culture_of_Japan&action=edit
[270] Schirokauer 2013, pp. 128–130.
[271] Sanz, 157–159.
[272] Jomon Fantasy: Resketching Japan's Prehistory http://web-japan.org/trends00/honbun/tj990615.html. June 22, 1999.
[273] Habu, 42.
[274] Silberman et al., 154–155.
[275] Kidder, 59.
[276] Batten, 60.
[277] Kumar, 1.
[278] Imamura, 168–170.
[279] Kaner, 462.
[280]
[281] Maher, 40.
[282] Henshall, 11–12.
[283] Henshall, 13.
[284] Farris, 3.
[285] Song-Nai Rhee et al., "Korean Contributions to Agriculture, Technology, and State Formation in Japan", *Asian Perspectives*, Fall 2007, 431.
[286] Henshall, 14–15.
[287] Henshall, 15–16.
[288] Totman, 102.
[289] Henshall, 16, 22.
[290]
[291] The dates of the Asuka period are not widely agreed upon, with some historians, particularly art historians, dividing the period 538–710 into two or more periods. Others take a later start date for the Asuka period, for example starting it in 592 with the accession of Empress Suiko.
[292] *Kodansha Encyclopedia of Japan Volume One* (New York: Kodansha, 1983), 104–106.
[293] Perez, 16, 18.
[294] Totman, 106.
[295] Henshall, 18–19.
[296] Weston, 127.
[297] Song-Nai Rhee et al., "Korean Contributions to Agriculture, Technology, and State Formation in Japan", *Asian Perspectives*, Fall 2007, 445.
[298] Totman, 107–108.
[299] Sansom, 57.
[300] Sansom, 68.
[301] Henshall, 24.
[302] Henshall, 56.
[303] Keene 1999: 85, 89.
[304] Totman, 140–142.
[305] Henshall, 26.
[306] Deal and Ruppert, 63–64.
[307] Farris, 59.
[308] Sansom, 99.
[309] Henshall, 29–30.
[310] Totman, 149–151.
[311] Keene 1999 : 306.
[312] Totman, 151–152.
[313] Perez, 25–26.
[314] Henshall, 31.
[315] Totman, 153.

[316] Farris, 87.
[317] McCullough, 30–31.
[318] Meyer, 62.
[319] Sansom, 249–250.
[320] Takeuchi, 675–677.
[321] Henshall, 31–32.
[322] Henshall, 33–34.
[323] Henshall, 28.
[324] Totman, 186–187.
[325] Keene 1999: 477–478.
[326] Meyer, Milton W., page 44.
[327] Henshall, 30.
[328] Totman, 183.
[329] Henshall, 34–35.
[330] Perkins, 20.
[331] Weston, 139.
[332] *MyPaedia* article "Heishi".
[333] Weston, 135–136.
[334] Keene 1999 : 892–893, 897.
[335] Weston, 137–138.
[336] Henshall, 35–36.
[337] Perez, 28–29.
[338] Keene 1999 : 672, 831.
[339] Totman, 156.
[340] Sansom, 441–442.
[341] Henshall, 39–40.
[342] Henshall, 40–41.
[343] Farris, 144–145.
[344] Perez, 32–33.
[345] Keene 1999 : 321.
[346] Keene 1999 : 320.
[347] Keene 1999 : 323.
[348] Keene 1999 : 321–322.
[349] Keene 1999 : 324.
[350] Keene 1999 : 650–651.
[351] Keene 1999 : 674.
[352] Keene 1999 : 673–674.
[353] Keene 1999 : 657.
[354] Keene 1999 : 643.
[355] Keene 1999 : 680.
[356] Keene 1999 : 681.
[357] Keene 1999 : 700.
[358] Keene 1999 : 700–701.
[359] Keene 1999 : 702–703.
[360] Keene 1999 : 701.
[361] Keene 1999 : 736.
[362] Keene 1999 : 735–736.
[363] Keene 1999 : 617, 629.
[364] Keene 1999 : 637; Keene 1998 : 415.
[365] Keene 1999 : 613–615.
[366] Henshall, 41.
[367] Henshall, 43–44.
[368] Perez, 37.
[369] Totman, 240–241.
[370] Perez, 46.

[371] Stephen Turnbull and Richard Hook, *Samurai Commanders (1)* (Oxford: Osprey, 2005), 53–54.
[372] Stephen Turnbull and Richard Hook, *Samurai Commanders (2)* (Oxford: Osprey, 2005), 50.
[373] Louis Perez, "Ninja," in *Japan at War : An Encyclopedia*, ed. Louis Perez (Santa Barbara, California: ABC-CLIO, 2013), 277–278.
[374] Perez, 39, 41.
[375] Henshall, 45.
[376] Perez, 46–47.
[377] Farris, 166.
[378]
[379] Farris, 152.
[380] Perez, 40.
[381] Perez, 43–45.
[382] Harold Bolitho, "Book Review: Yoshimasa and the Silver Pavilion," *The Journal of Asian Studies*, August 2004, 799–800.
[383] *Kodansha Encyclopedia of Japan Volume One* (New York: Kodansha, 1983), 126.
[384] Henshall, 46.
[385] Perez, 48–49.
[386] Weston, 141–143.
[387] Henshall, 47–48.
[388] Farris, 192.
[389] Perez, 51–52.
[390] Farris, 193.
[391] Henshall, 50.
[392] Hane, 133.
[393] Perez, 72.
[394] Henshall, 53–54.
[395] Henshall, 54–55.
[396] Turnbull, Stephen. *The Samurai Capture a King: Okinawa 1609*. Osprey Publishing, 2009. Pp 13.
[397] Kerr, 162–167.
[398] Totman, 297.
[399] McClain, 26–27.
[400] Henshall, 57–58.
[401] Perez, 62–63.
[402] Totman, 308.
[403] Perez, 60.
[404] Henshall, 60.
[405] Martha Chaiklin, "Sakoku (1633–1854)", in *Japan at War: An Encyclopedia*, ed. Louis Perez (Santa Barbara, California: ABC-CLIO, 2013), 356–357.
[406] Henshall, 61.
[407] Totman, 317, 337.
[408] Totman, 319–320, 322.
[409] Jansen, 116–117.
[410] Perez, 67.
[411] Henshall, 64.
[412] Jansen, 163–164.
[413] Hane, 213–214
[414] Hane, 203–204.
[415] Hane, 200.
[416] Henshall, 66.
[417] Hane, 201–202.
[418] Deal, 296.
[419] Henshall, 68–69.
[420] Totman, 367–369.
[421] McClain, 123–124, 128.

[422] Sims, 8–9.
[423] Perez, 79–80.
[424] Walker, 149–151.
[425] Hane, 168–169.
[426] Perez, 84–85.
[427] Henshall, 70.
[428] Totman, 380, 382.
[429] Takano, p. 256.
[430] Henshall, 71, 236.
[431] Henshall, 75.
[432] Henshall, 78.
[433] Morton and Olenike, 171.
[434] Weston, 172–173.
[435] Henshall, 75–76, 217.
[436] Henshall, 79–89.
[437] W. Dean Kinzley, "Merging Lines: Organising Japan's National Railroad, 1906–1914", *Journal of Transport History*, 27#2 (2006)
[438] Totman, 401.
[439] Henshall, 84–85.
[440] Henshall, 81.
[441] Henshall, 83.
[442] Totman, 460–461.
[443] Lauerman, 421.
[444] Totman, 464–465.
[445] Henshall, 103.
[446] Weston, 254–255.
[447] Totman, 466.
[448] Mason and Caiger, 315.
[449] Henshall, 85–92.
[450] Bix, 27, 30.
[451] F.H. Hinsley, ed. *The New Cambridge Modern History, Vol. 11: Material Progress and World-Wide Problems, 1870–98* (1962) contents http://library.mpib-berlin.mpg.de/toc/z2010_334.pdf pp 464–86
[452] Kerr, 356–360.
[453] Perez, 98.
[454] Henshall, 80.
[455] Totman, 422–424.
[456] Perez, 118–119.
[457] Perez, 120.
[458] Perez, 115, 121.
[459] Perez, 122.
[460] Henshall, 96–97.
[461] Henshall, 99–100.
[462]
[463] Perez, 102–103.
[464] Hunter, 3.
[465] Totman, 403–404, 431.
[466] Totman, 440–442.
[467] Totman, 452–453.
[468] Perez, 134.
[469] Totman, 443.
[470] Henshall, 108–109.
[471] Perez, 135–136.
[472] Meyer, 179, 193.
[473] Large, 160.
[474] Perez, 138.

[475] Totman, 471, 488–489.
[476] Henshall, 111.
[477] Henshall, 110.
[478] Totman, 520.
[479] Totman, 525.
[480] Totman, 522–523.
[481] Totman, 524.
[482] Totman, 583.
[483] Sims, 139.
[484] Sims, 179–180.
[485] Perez, 139–140.
[486] Henshall, 114–115.
[487] Henshall, 115–116.
[488] McClain, 454.
[489] Henshall, 119–120.
[490] Henshall, 122–123.
[491] Henshall, 123–124.
[492] Weston, 201–203.
[493] Totman, 553–554.
[494] Totman, 555–556.
[495] Henshall, 124–126.
[496] Henshall, 129–130.
[497] Henshall, 132–133.
[498] Henshall, 131–132, 135.
[499] Frank, 28–29.
[500] Henshall, 134.
[501] Perez, 147–148.
[502] Morton and Olenike, 188.
[503] Totman, 562.
[504] "The Cornerstone of Peace." Kyushu-Okinawa Summit 2000: Okinawa G8 Summit Host Preparation Council, 2000. Accessed 9 Dec 2012.
[505] Feifer, xi, 446–463.
[506] Coox, 368.
[507] Henshall, 136–137.
[508] Henshall, 142–143.
[509] Perez, 151–152.
[510] Henshall, 144.
[511] Perez, 150–151.
[512] Totman, 570.
[513] Mackie, 121.
[514] Henshall, 145–146.
[515] Totman, 571.
[516] Henshall, 147–148.
[517] Henshall, 150.
[518] Henshall, 145.
[519] Henshall, 158.
[520] Klein, Thomas. "The Ryukyus on the Eve of Reversion". *Pacific Affairs*. Vol. 45, No. 1 (Spring, 1972). Pp120.
[521] 沖口県の基地の現状 http://www.pref.okinawa.jp/kititaisaku/GEN.pdf, Okinawa Prefectural Government
[522] 沖に所在する在日米軍施設・区域 http://www.clearing.mod.go.jp/hakusho_data/2006/2006/html/i4262000.html, Japan Ministry of Defense
[523] Perez, 156–157, 162.
[524] Perez, 159.
[525] Perez, 163.
[526] Henshall, 163.

[527] Henshall, 154–155.
[528] Henshall, 156–157.
[529] Henshall, 159–160.
[530] Perez, 169.
[531] Henshall, 161–162.
[532] Henshall, 162, 166, 182.
[533] Totman, 576.
[534] Gao 2009, p. 303.
[535] Totman, 584–585.
[536] Henshall, 160–161.
[537] Gao 2009, p. 305.
[538] Henshall, 167.
[539] Ito, 60.
[540] Totman, 580–581.
[541] Togo, 234–235.
[542] Togo, 162–163.
[543] Togo, 126–128.
[544] Perez, 177–178.
[545] Totman, 669.
[546] Henshall, 181–182.
[547] Henshall, 185–187.
[548] Meyer, 250.
[549] Totman, 678.
[550] Henshall, 182–183.
[551] Henshall, 189–190.
[552] Henshall, 199.
[553] Henshall, 199–201.
[554] Henshall, 197–198.
[555] Henshall, 191.
[556] Henshall, 204.
[557] Ugai, Yagi & Wakai 2012, p. 140.
[558] Henshall, 187–188.
[559] Lee, Jason. "Robotic Evolution." Sex Robots. Palgrave Macmillan, Cham, 2017. 1–17.
[560] Kawanishi, Yuko. Mental Health Challenges Facing Contemporary Japanese Society. Brill, 2009.
[561] Farris, 26.
[562]
[563] Farris, 152, 181.
[564] Farris, 152, 157.
[565] Tonomura, 352.
[566] Tonomura, 351.
[567] Tonomura, 353–354.
[568] Tonomura, 354–355.
[569] Farris, 162–163.
[570] Farris, 159–160.
[571] Tonomura, 360.
[572] Hastings, 379.
[573] Totman, 614–615.
[574] Wakita 1991, p. 123.
[575] Neary 2009, p. 390.
[576] Henshall 2012, p. 56.
[577] Neary 2009, p. 391.
[578] Neary 2009, p. 392.
[579] Neary 2009, p. 393.
[580] Moriguchi and Saez, 80, 88.
[581] Neary, 397.

[582] Duus, 21.
[583] Neary 2003, p. 269.
[584] Neary 2003, p. 270.
[585] Neary 2003, p. 271.
[586] https://books.google.com/books?id=fRs3Qdya40QC
[587] https://books.google.com/books?id=zjmVltzm1kYC
[588] https://books.google.com/books?id=oEkewem1LBYC
[589] https://books.google.com/books?id=5dmxY_HIWp8C
[590] https://books.google.com/books?id=MwnqPgAACAAJ
[591] https://books.google.com/books?id=vGnAbTyTynsC
[592] https://books.google.com/books?id=jgJHBAAAQBAJ
[593] https://books.google.com/books?id=vD76fF5hqf8C
[594] https://books.google.com/books?id=obYhbzN-dY0C
[595] //www.jstor.org/stable/40971613
[596] https://books.google.com/books?id=ahYF-A3oylkC
[597] https://books.google.com/books?id=t2c4t4yw21gC
[598] https://books.google.com/books?id=QBGGBAAAQBAJ
[599] https://books.google.com/books?id=Hr2soAEACAAJ
[600] //en.wikipedia.org/w/index.php?title=Template:History_of_Southeast_Asia&action=edit
[601] //en.wikipedia.org/w/index.php?title=Template:Human_history&action=edit
[602] Swisher 1994; 2010, p. 123; Dennell 2010, p. 262.
[603] Dennell 2010, p. 266, citing Morwood 2003
[604] John N. Miksic, Geok Yian Goh, Sue O Connor – *Rethinking Cultural Resource Management in Southeast Asia* 2011 Page 251 "This site dates from the fifth to first century BCE and it is one of the earliest sites of the Sa Huỳnh culture in Thu Bồn Valley (Reinecke et al. 2002, 153–216); 2) Lai Nghi is a prehistoric cemetery richly equipped with iron tools and weapons, ..."
[605] National Library of Australia. Asia's French Connection : George Coedes and the Coedes Collection http://www.nla.gov.au/asian/form/coedes2.html
[606] *For fifty or sixty years, the Portuguese enjoyed the exclusive trade to China and Japan. In 1717, and again in 1732, the Chinese government offered to make Macao the emporium for all foreign trade, and to receive all duties on imports; but, by a strange infatuation, the Portuguese government refused, and its decline is dated from that period.* (Roberts, 2007 PDF image 173 p. 166)
[607] Other experiments in republicanism in adjacent regions were the Japanese Republic of Ezo (1869) and the Republic of Taiwan (1895).
[608] Company agent John_Crawfurd used the census taken in 1824 for a statistical analysis of the relative economic prowess of the peoples there, giving special attention to the Chinese: *The Chinese amount to 8595, and are landowners, field-labourers, mechanics of almost every description, shopkeepers, and general merchants. They are all from the two provinces of Canton and Fo-kien, and three-fourths of them from the latter. About five-sixths of the whole number are unmarried men, in the prime of life : so that, in fact, the Chinese population, in point of effective labour, may be estimated as equivalent to an ordinary population of above 37,000, and, as will afterwards be shown, to a numerical Malay population of more than 80,000!* (Crawfurd image 48. p.30)
[609] Vichy versus Asia: The Franco-Siamese War of 1941 http://www.ww2f.com/topic/12620-vichy-versus-asia-the-franco-siamese-war-of-1941/
[610] Frey, Rebecca Joyce (2009). *Genocide and International Justice*.
[611] Olson, James S.; Roberts, Randy (2008). *Where the Domino Fell: America and Vietnam 1945–1995* (5th ed.). Malden, Massachusetts: Blackwell Publishing
[612] https://web.archive.org/web/20140310154453/https://www.library.uq.edu.au/ojs/index.php/aa/article/view/526/1690
[613] https://www.library.uq.edu.au/ojs/index.php/aa/article/view/526/1690
[614] //doi.org/10.1126%2Fscience.8108729
[615] //www.ncbi.nlm.nih.gov/pubmed/8108729
[616] https://books.google.com/?id=wiUTOanLClcC
[617] https://books.google.com/?id=8S5PXyWMEeAC

[618] https://books.google.com/?id=iDyJBFTdiwoC
[619] https://books.google.com/books?id=LLhAAAAAMAAJ
[620] https://books.google.com/books?id=T9mfAAAAMAAJ
[621] https://books.google.com/books?id=_U21B4ExmpAC
[622] https://books.google.com/books?id=caMLAAAAIAAJ
[623] https://books.google.com/?id=fjsEn3w4TPgC
[624] https://books.google.com/?id=6F7xthSLFNEC
[625] https://books.google.com/?id=6QPWXrCCzBIC
[626] https://books.google.com/?id=54s1JHO69OMC
[627] https://books.google.com/books?id=NqwuAQAAIAAJ
[628] https://books.google.com/?id=S4Ci1E4ydgoC&dq=Rajendra+Chola+zulkarnain
[629] https://books.google.com/?id=QKgraWbb7yoC
[630] https://books.google.com/books?id=GxrrAAAAMAAJ
[631] https://books.google.com/?id=Lon7gmj040MC&printsec=frontcover#v=onepage&q&f=false
[632] https://books.google.com/books?id=gzRtAAAAMAAJ
[633] https://books.google.com/?id=YNMGBAAAQBAJ
[634] https://books.google.com/?id=vxgHExnla4MC
[635] https://books.google.com/?id=YFIGVqZ9ZKsC
[636] https://books.google.com/?id=9Z7cZ77SqEQC
[637] https://books.google.com/books?id=fj1mAAAAMAAJ
[638] http://www.pnas.org/content/109/36/14375.short
[639] //doi.org/10.1073%2Fpnas.1208104109
[640] //www.ncbi.nlm.nih.gov/pmc/articles/PMC3437904
[641] https//scholar.google.com
[642] //doi.org/10.3828%2Fbfarm.2008.4.1
[643] https://books.google.com/books?id=NRFXAAAAMAAJ
[644] https://books.google.com/?id=eTuUboxIQTsC
[645] https://books.google.com/?id=wZZPAQAAMAAJ&pg=PA208
[646] https://books.google.com/?id=23_Qzobeu4wC
[647] https://www.researchgate.net/file.PostFileLoader.html?id...assetKey...
[648] https://web.archive.org/web/20050413155545/http://www.i3pep.org/archives/2004/11/18/ancient-southeast-asia/
[649] http://toyoshi.lit.nagoya-u.ac.jp/maruha/kanseki
[650] http://booksandjournals.brillonline.com/content/books/9789004329669
[651] http://www.asianbarometer.org/publications/fcec32f13ab256a0262837fe2466c134.pdf

Article Sources and Contributors

The sources listed for each article provide more detailed licensing information including the copyright status, the copyright owner, and the license conditions.

History of Asia *Source:* https://en.wikipedia.org/w/index.php?oldid=862735183 *License:* Creative Commons Attribution-Share Alike 3.0 *Contributors:* A520, Adavidb, Aggerdon, Allens, Anpanman, Arjayay, Armundo bokan, Art LaPella, BD2412, Bgwhite, Billinghurst, Bongwarrior, Botteville, Bsherr, Citizen Canine, Citobun, ClueBot NG, Cold Season, DBigXray, DaGizza, Dawnseeker2000, Dbachmann, DePiep, DemocraticLuntz, DerHexer, Discospinster, Dolescum, Dyieri, Edgar181, Elockid, Ermahgerd9, Excirial, Folantin, Forever49x, GenQuest, Genstorm555, Gilliam, GoingBatty, Grafen, GreenC, Guoguo12, Hanif Al Husaini, Hmains, Ilikeqwertyuiop, InvaderCito, JLincoln, JaconaFrere, Jarble, Jprg1966, Juro2351, Kanguole, Khanate General, Khazar2, L Manju, LilHelpa, Llywrch, Lotje, LuK3, Lugia2453, Madalibi, Magioladitis, Malerisch, Marcocapelle, Marechal Ney, Materialscientist, Me, Myself, and I are Here, Meganesia, Milktaco, Mr Stephen, MutchyMan112, Ohconfucius, Phenolla, Philg88, Pierre.Guirguis, Pinethicket, Prof. Mc, Prrrrecious, Realhistorybuff, RegentsPark, Rizome∼enwiki, Rjensen, Rockstar2217, Rsrikanth05, Rubbish computer, Rurik the Varangian, Serols, ShelfSkewed, Skylark2008, Snowmanradio, Sunriseshore, SwitchLink, TAnthony, Tdslk, Tentinator, The Human Trumpet Solo, The Transhumanist, The Wonkers, TheConduqtor, TheNano7474, TheTimesAreAChanging, Timmyshin, Topbanana, Trappist the monk, Tsuaa, Tuanminh01, Tylernaut314, Vadoff, Valyop, Vatasura, Vctrbarbieri, Wavelength, Widr, Wishva de Silva, Young gee 1525, 207 anonymous edits 1

Prehistoric Asia *Source:* https://en.wikipedia.org/w/index.php?oldid=861867901 *License:* Creative Commons Attribution-Share Alike 3.0 *Contributors:* Acampbell70, Arjayay, Auric, BD2412, CaroleHenson, Cattus, Chris the speller, Cnilep, Coin945, Cold Season, Dbachmann, Dmitri Lytov, Dt Mos Ios, EuroCarGT, Fraenir, Garyyao1216, GoingBatty, Herbgold, Hmains, IacobusAmor, Indian Chronicles, J04n, Jahani65, Jarble, Kvng, LouisAragon, Madalibi, Meteor sandwich yum, Northamerica1000, Onceinawhile, R'n'B, Rjwilmsi, Rsrikanth05, Shwetha, Trappist the monk, Victor falk, Vsmith, Wavelength, Wbm1058, Wikiuser13, Wikiworkbot2.0, Wuzh, Wwikix, Xyzzyplugh, 14 anonymous edits 27

Ancient Near East *Source:* https://en.wikipedia.org/w/index.php?oldid=863995692 *License:* Creative Commons Attribution-Share Alike 3.0 *Contributors:* 4twentybruh69, A. Parrot, A8UDI, Agrso, Alan Liefting, Alansohn, Anadrev, Anonymous233388, Arminden, BD2412, Bender235, Bihco, Bluberrybuttermilkpancakes, Botteville, Carlog3, Carlon, Categorystuff, Chackerian, ChrisGualtieri, Christov01, Chzz, ClueBot NG, Colonies Chris, Corgame3, Cush, Dbachmann, Dewritech, Dimadick, Dmitri Lytov, Edgars2007, Egsan Bacon, Eno Lirpa, Excirial, Fang 23, Fitzburgh, Fixer88, Florian Blaschke, Flyer22 Reborn, Frietjes, Fullstop, GPRutter, Gabbe, General Ization, Generalboss3, Girth Summit, Glevum, Graham87, Greater LBN, Greyshark09, Hamiltonmj1983, Hattar393, Hertz1888, Hi2010, Hmains, Hmainsbot1, HyeProfile, Icarusgeek, Ijon, In ictu oculi, InverseHypercube, Iritscen, Iry-Hor, Izzedine, JLincoln, Jagged 85, Jayjg, JesseW900, Jim1138, Johnbod, Kalamkaar, Kantknow, Koakhtzvigad, Krakkos, Kukkulanum, Kwamikagami, Largoplazo, LilHelpa, LlywelynII, Look2See1, LouisAragon, Marcocapelle, Mccapra, Me, Myself, and I are Here, Meganesia, Modernist, Natg 19, Neutrality, Obtund, Olaffpomona, Olympic god, Orangesaft, Orser67, Phlegat, Pikiwyn, Rarevogel, Reade, Reddi, Referencearchivist, Rewhitley, Ribbentrop, Rich Farmbrough, Ricky81682, Ronhjones, Sam Sailor, Samwingkit, Sardanaphalus, SereneRain, Sir Bronx, Snoji, StAnselm, Steinedons, Sunriseshore, Supbonkers, Syncategoremata, TFighterPilot, Tachs, Tahc, Tajotep, The PIPE, The Thing That Should Not Be, Thegreatluigi, Tiamut, Tom.Reding, Trappist the monk, Triggerhippie4, Uruiamme, Vasiliy Faronov, Vbrm, WANAX, Wario-Man, Wikiklrsc, WilliamDigiCol, Woohookitty, Wufei05, Yerpo, Yoninah, Zoeperkoe, ZxxZxxZ, Περίεργος, אשכנזישע־יידן, 157 anonymous edits 39

History of the Middle East *Source:* https://en.wikipedia.org/w/index.php?oldid=863289179 *License:* Creative Commons Attribution-Share Alike 3.0 *Contributors:* A412, A520, Ace of Raves, Acjelen, Addihockey10 (automated), Againme, Ammodramus, Anadrev, Antiqueight, Arulns, BD2412, Bender235, Binksternet, Booyahhayoob, Carl.bunderson, Chamboz, Chris the speller, Citizen Canine, Clairehallstrom, ClueBot NG, Colonies Chris, Crispulop, DadaNeem, DarioTW, Darjeelingblend, Dawnseeker2000, Dbachmann, Dcirovic, Deli nk, Denisarona, Diannaa, Doncram, Donner60, Doug Weller, Elman Həsənli, Excesses, Excirial, Farawahar, Fayenatic london, Flyer22 Reborn, Freckles93, Frietjes, FunkMonk, Ginsuloft, Giraffedata, Grandia01, GreenC, Greyshark09, Guy1890, GünniX, Haeinous, Hakkıselimöztürk, Hfghfhfhffgfgfdgfdg, Hmains, Ilikemennow01, Interpréteur, IronGargoyle, Isaac Rabinovitch, Ithinkicahn, J04n, JLincoln, Jodosma, Jorjulio, Joy, Jprg1966, Kamran the Great, Karafs, Kathovo, Ketiltrout, Kinghamnt, Koavf, Ktr101, LWG, Lightwynne, LouisAragon, Loupiotte, Lugia2453, Magioladitis, Marine2323, Materialscientist, Matthew Fennell, Maurice Carbonaro, Michaeldsuarez, Mild Bill Hiccup, Mogism, Mrmatiko, Neutrality, Niceguyedc, NintendoFTW, OnBeyondZebrax, Onceinawhile, PWilkinson, Palindromedairy, Piguy101, Qwerty Binary, Qzd, R'n'B, Right The Wrongs, Rjensen, RoslynSKP, Runehelmet, SUM1, Sanya3, Sbb, SchreiberBike, Shaibalahmar, Skizzik, SnowFire, Spitzak, Srednuas Lenoroc, SwaggerKing1738, The Transhumanist, The.Chaldeans, TheRandomMaria, TheTimesAreAChanging, Timoteoharvey, Triggerhippie4, Trust Is All You Need, Ullierlich, Vcessayist, Watisfictie, Wavelength, Wbm1058, Whizz40, Widr, Wikipelli, Yair rand, YourLifeBeginsHere, Yusufrocks123, Zg111383, הורון, יניב, 201 anonymous edits 55

History of Central Asia *Source:* https://en.wikipedia.org/w/index.php?oldid=863195201 *License:* Creative Commons Attribution-Share Alike 3.0 *Contributors:* A-MAN, Ace of Raves, Adamv88, Adamwebb175, After Midnight, Aherunar, Aivazovsky, Akhil Bakshi, Alcherin, AllGloryToTheHypnotoad, Anadrev, Ancientsteppe, AnnaFrance, Arthur Rubin, Atethnekos, Axeman89, BD2412, BTLizard, Baristarim, Beagel, Bender235, Benjamin Trovato, Bundeslagr, Certes, Cewale, Chamboz, Charles Matthews, CharlotteWebb, Chewings72, Chris the speller, Citation bot 1, Citizen Canine, Clarifer, ClueBot NG, Cold Season, CommonsDelinker, Conscious, Conservative321, Cplakidas, DVdm, Dawnseeker2000, Dbachmann, Dcattell, Dmitri Lytov, Docmojo, Drienstra, Dyieri, East718, Enerelt, Ermahgerd9, EyeSerene, Ezhiki, FakirNL, Fanx, Fraenir, Francis Tyers, Freyr35, Frietjes, Gadfium, Gadget850, Gan Yucheng, Geoffg, Gralo, GravityIsForSuckers, Green Giant, Greg Grahame, Ground Zero, GünniX, Hajatvrc, Halq So'zi, Hmains, Hux, Interpréteur, Iridescent, Irishpunktom, Jac40490, Jagged 85, Jebba, Jeltz, Jimjamjak, Jncraton, Joseon Empire, Just a guy from the KP, K6ka, KEO144000, Kanguole, KazakhPol, Kdammers, KentJR, KevinOB, Khanate General, Khoikhoi, Kintetsubuffalo, KnowledgeOfSelf, Ksyrie, Kungfuadam, Kuru, LarryJeff, LouisAragon, Luna Santin, Madalibi, Magyar from Ural, Mana Excalibur, Marcocapelle, Marskell, Martin Peter Clarke, Materialscientist, Maximajorian Viridio, McSnath, Mccapra, Melamed katz, Mgaved, Minerva2, Mira3z, MisfitToys, Modify, Monsieurdl, Moonsell, Mudwater, Mxater, Mystiq0, Navops47, NeoJay, Neurolysis, Niceguyedc, Noren, Ntsimp, Nymf, ONUnicorn, Omicronpersei8, Otebig, Pazkyle, PericlesofAthens, Peter Isotalo, Pinethicket, R'n'B, Ran, Raul654, Rich Farmbrough, Rigadoun, Rjwilmsi, Rune.welsh, Rzybow, SUM1, Sam Blacketer, SandyGeorgia, Sangjinhwa, Saturne160, SchreiberBike, Shanes, Sharofat Arabi, Sikandarji, SimonP, Sjock, Skyfiler, SophieHadifz, Spschmidt27615, Srose, Stellmach, Stemonitis, Streetsk8ta4life, Suto, Sweetsavant, Sze cavalry01, Tech77, The Transhumanist, The Way, Themightyquill, Tobby72, Tombseye, Triesto, Ufwuct, Unschool, Verbum Veritas, VoABot II, Vsmith, Wall5625, Wario-Man, WereSpielChequers, Widr, WilyD, Woohookitty, Xcrem, YUL89YYZ, Yannismarou, Zaparojdik, Zeroordie6002, 124 anonymous edits 89

Medieval India *Source:* https://en.wikipedia.org/w/index.php?oldid=862596572 *License:* Creative Commons Attribution-Share Alike 3.0 *Contributors:* 10metreh, Acaiber, Adam9007, Adzz, Akshay0412, Antrocent, Arcade81, Arjayay, AtticTapestry, Ayman shariff, BD2412, Bentogoa, Capankajsmilyo, Certes, Chandra.shreya, ClueBot NG, Daiyusha, Dbachmann, Delusion23, Denisarona, Dthomsen8, ESP6502, Edward, Ekabhishek, Fez Cap 12, Fixer88, Flinders Petrie, Floatjon, FxdhMxdh, Gauravvaid0, Ginsuloft, Highpeaks35, I.am.viji, Imad bahadur, JaGa, JackintheBox, John of Reading, Johnbod, Jonesey95, Just4edit, Look2See1, Lor, Maestro2016, Malcolma, Marcocapelle, Marek69, Murgh Krahi, NewEnglandYankee, Oshwah, PRVVGP, PlyrStar93, Qefqef, QuartierLatin1968, Quinton Feldberg, Risto hot sir, SamanthaAnderson12, Seaphoto, Serols, Shyamsunder, Sideways713, Singhalkartik72, Skylark2008, Sunriseshore, Suparnawiki123, Tachs, Tarique012, Tinku Sinha, Tompop888, Tournesol, Ugog Nizdast, Utcursch, Viscious81, Widr, WikiDan61, Wikiuser13, Worldbruce, Xander009, Yintan, 136 anonymous edits 119

History of China *Source:* https://en.wikipedia.org/w/index.php?oldid=864460914 *License:* Creative Commons Attribution-Share Alike 3.0 *Contributors:* Alvin Lee, Argento Surfer, Arkuat, Berting Li, BlackRanger88, Certes, Chrrev, Citizen Canine, Coconut1002, Darthkenobi0, Dawnseeker2000, Dbachmann, Dr.Holmes, Dr.Koo, Dr.O'brian, Editthat1, EricABCAT, Esiymbro, Finnusertop, FuzhouneseMinpride, Geographyinitiative, Hairy Dude, Highpeaks35, Hzh, Infinenoi, InvictaHOG, Isquen, JJMC89, Jacbourg, Kanguole, KaoruTsi, L293D, Lawrencekhoo, LifanDefense, Livven, LlywelynII, LuciferZH, Mandruss, Me, Myself, and I are Here, Meyjes, Miracle dream, Moonriddengirl, Moxy, MrOllie, Narky Blert, Natg 19, Ogress, Omnipaedista, PericlesofAthens, Quark1005, Quyenjan, R3venans, Rainbow.Weaver.Tani, Redstar766, Rich Farmbrough, Rodw, Seasonsinthesun, Selfworm, Spirit of Eagle, Sunriseshore, Tamaru7, The Professor (Time Lord), Tuntable, Underbar dk, WOSlinker, Wandrative, Whaterss, Wikievil666, Wtlwiki 125

History of Japan *Source:* https://en.wikipedia.org/w/index.php?oldid=864448687 *License:* Creative Commons Attribution-Share Alike 3.0 *Contributors:* 1997kB, A Great Catholic Person, Abcdefghijklmnopqrstuvwxyz1234567891021, Alex Shih, Alpacasucker69, Anthony Appleyard, Biridiancity, Brian poole, Broccoli and Coffee, Byteflush, C.Fred, CAPTAIN RAJU, CLCStudent, CV9933, Chewings72, Chloe.allsion, Citizen Canine, Ckulsen, ClueBot NG, Coldh678, CommonsDelinker, Craic Den, Curly Turkey, Davidf13, Dawnseeker2000, Donner60, Dr.K., Dr.Koo, Drewmutt, El C, EthanMagnuson, Evilgras, Excirial, Flyer22 Reborn, Fortunatestars, Frem3, Gilliam, Grammarian3.14159265359, Gulumeemee, Hijiri88, Historyifjaoan, I JethroBT, Ira Leviton, IronGargoyle, Isquen, Jassamine's tree, Jim jimson5, Jim1138, Joefromrandb, Johnny162, Jondel, Junior5a, JustAMuggle, Katie lt3, Keiiri, Kieranboss212, Kintetsubuffalo, Kuru, KylieTastic, Laodah, Laszlo Panaflex, Lennart97, LilHelpa, Lkfitz, Lopesave21, Manofcolor, Maplestrip, Materialscientist, MelbourneStar, Meyjes, Miki Filigranski, Moncrief, Mondo Beer, Mvhaha, NMaia, Nakashchit, Narky Blert, Nishidani, NottNott, Obergruppenführer Burger, Omaemona1982, Oshwah, Paintspot, Paisley Liverpool, PizzaMan, Poohpooh817, Portugalcanuck, Power∼enwiki, Qzd, RA0808, Rjensen, Rjwilmsi, Serols, Shenme, Simplexity22, Sol Pacificus, Strident40, Thecakelies, Tim!, ToBeFree, Tobby72, Tomurtogo, Vivexdino, Wintereu, XIIIfromTOKYO, Yamowatago, Yourworstnightmare69, Yoyi ling, Zawl, 142 anonymous edits 195

History of Southeast Asia *Source:* https://en.wikipedia.org/w/index.php?oldid=863217617 *License:* Creative Commons Attribution-Share Alike 3.0 *Contributors:* AbigailAbernathy, Acayl, Adam9007, Anadrev, Andreas Philopater, BD2412, Bender235, Blaylockjam10, Brutannica, Ccxlslr98, ChrisGualtieri, Citizen Canine, ClueBot NG, Cold Season, Collector143, CommonsDelinker, Comtebenoit, Console2, Cookingtheworld, Cowlibob, Darwgon0801, David.moreno72, Dawnseeker2000, Dbachmann, Dcirovic, Diannaa, Dl2000, Doyley, ERAGON, Ergative rlt, Ermahgerd9, Excirial, Facts707,

Flyer22 Reborn, Fraenir, Gilliam, Gourami Watcher, Graeme Bartlett, GreenC, Gunkarta, Hanif Al Husaini, Hmains, Hmainsbot1, Interpréteur, JaconaFrere, Jameshfisher, Jann Arlie, Jdcomix, Jodosma, John of Reading, Jprg1966, Juxlos, Jytdog, KING31423, Keith D, Khazar2, Kimjonghuy, KylieTastic, Liflon, LittleWink, Lrncohen3, M-le-mot-dit, MRD2014, Macofe, Magioladitis, Marcus Cyron, Maximajorian Viridio, Miguel raul, Milktaco, Minna Sora no Shita, Modulus12, Muffin Wizard, MusikAnimal, Ng Pey Shih 07, Nobiscis, Pawyilee, Pghod, Pmccawley, PohranicniStraze, Quinxorin, Rumilo Santiago, SchreiberBike, Shannonkhod, Shhhhwwww!!, SilkTork, Spiderjerky, Sunriseshore, That man baby, Theparties, Tim!, Victor falk, Vnonymous, Vítor, Wbm1058, Wikirictor, Williamteoh97, Z. PUPU, 73 anonymous edits 243

Image Sources, Licenses and Contributors

The sources listed for each image provide more detailed licensing information including the copyright status, the copyright owner, and the license conditions.

Figure 1 *Source:* https://en.wikipedia.org/w/index.php?title=File:Chinese_silk,_4th_Century_BC.JPG *License:* Public Domain *Contributors:* PericlesofAthens 2

Figure 2 *Source:* https://en.wikipedia.org/w/index.php?title=File:SeidenstrasseGMT.JPG *License:* Creative Commons Attribution-Sharealike 3.0 *Contributors:* Kelvin Case 7

Figure 3 *Source:* https://en.wikipedia.org/w/index.php?title=File:Buddhist_Expansion.svg *Contributors:* Artoxx, Currda, Gunkarta, Journalman-Manila 11

Figure 4 *Source:* https://en.wikipedia.org/w/index.php?title=File:Battle_of_Talas.png *Contributors:* User:Seasonsinthesun 12

Figure 5 *Source:* https://en.wikipedia.org/w/index.php?title=File:Route_of_Marco_Polo.png *Contributors:* User:Seasonsinthesun 14

Figure 6 *Source:* https://en.wikipedia.org/w/index.php?title=File:Shotoku_Taishi.jpg *License:* Creative Commons Attribution-Sharealike 3.0 *Contributors:* PHGCOM 15

Figure 7 *Source:* https://en.wikipedia.org/w/index.php?title=File:Modern_Asia_(1796).tif *License:* Public Domain *Contributors:* Cirt, Kaldari, Mattes, Roland zh, SarahStierch, ZxxZxxZ 18

Figure 8 *Source:* https://en.wikipedia.org/w/index.php?title=File:Fort_St._George,_Chennai.jpg *License:* Public Domain *Contributors:* User:Jappalang 20

Figure 9 *Source:* https://en.wikipedia.org/w/index.php?title=File:Schall-von-bell.jpg *License:* Public Domain *Contributors:* Cherubino, Daderot, Mattes, Nishanshaman, Raymond, Thib Phil, Vmenkov 20

Figure 10 *Source:* https://en.wikipedia.org/w/index.php?title=File:Batavia,_C._de_Jonghe_(1740).jpg *License:* Public Domain *Contributors:* Bennylin, BotMultichill, Elekhh, Fentener van Vlissingen, HyperGaruda, Ilse@～commonswiki, Jed, Kameraad Pjotr, Taks～commonswiki, Vysotsky, WereSpielChequers 21

Figure 11 *Source:* https://en.wikipedia.org/w/index.php?title=File:Asia_(late_19th_century-_early_20th_century).jpg *Contributors:* User:Philipandrew 24

Figure 12 *Source:* https://en.wikipedia.org/w/index.php?title=File:Asiacolour.PNG *License:* Creative Commons Attribution-Sharealike 1.0 *Contributors:* Geekdiva, Globe-trotter, MGA73bot2, OgreBot 2 28

Figure 13 *Source:* https://en.wikipedia.org/w/index.php?title=File:Homo_Georgicus_IMG_2921.JPG *License:* Public Domain *Contributors:* Bogomolov.PL, Geekdiva, Kilom691, Nachosan, Rama, TMZ 1111 29

Figure 14 *Source:* https://en.wikipedia.org/w/index.php?title=File:Homo_erectus_pekinensis_-_archeaeological.png *Contributors:* User:Cicero Moraes 29

Figure 15 *Source:* https://en.wikipedia.org/w/index.php?title=File:Human_spreading_over_history.png *License:* Public Domain *Contributors:* KVDP 30

Image *Source:* https//en.wikipedia.org *License:* GNU Free Documentation License *Contributors:* sailko 32

Figure 16 *Source:* https://en.wikipedia.org/w/index.php?title=File:Dolmen_fr_Godavari_district,_Andhra_Pradesh,_India_(KVHAAs_Månadsblad_1880_s09_fig7).jpg *License:* Public Domain *Contributors:* James Fergusson (1808-1886) 36

Image *Source:* https://en.wikipedia.org/w/index.php?title=File:Babylonlion.JPG *License:* Public Domain *Contributors:* Attar-Aram syria, Chaos, Hama Rock, Jarekt, Jbribeiro1, Meno25, Slowking4, Thiotrix, Wst 39

Figure 17 *Source:* https://en.wikipedia.org/w/index.php?title=File:Ancient_Orient.png *License:* Public domain *Contributors:* Dbachmann at en.wikipedia 41

Image *Source:* https://en.wikipedia.org/w/index.php?title=File:Folder_Hexagonal_Icon.svg *License:* GNU Free Documentation License *Contributors:* Anomie, Jo-Jo Eumerus, Mifter 45

Image *Source:* https://en.wikipedia.org/w/index.php?title=File:Commons-logo.svg *License:* logo *Contributors:* Anomie, Callanecc, CambridgeBayWeather, Jo-Jo Eumerus, RHaworth 45

Image *Source:* https://en.wikipedia.org/w/index.php?title=File:Portal-puzzle.svg *License:* Public Domain *Contributors:* Anomie, Jo-Jo Eumerus, Topbanana 45

Figure 18 *Source:* https://en.wikipedia.org/w/index.php?title=File:Middle_East_geographic.jpg *License:* Public Domain *Contributors:* Denniss, Hashekemist, Red devil 666, Rex, Saperaud～commonswiki, Timeshifter, Zaccarias, 2 anonymous edits 57

Figure 19 *Source:* https://en.wikipedia.org/w/index.php?title=File:NearEast3.png *License:* Creative Commons Attribution-Sharealike 3.0 *Contributors:* User:Kmusser 58

Figure 20 *Source:* https://en.wikipedia.org/w/index.php?title=File:Semitic_languages.svg *License:* Public Domain *Contributors:* Rafy 59

Image *Source:* https://en.wikipedia.org/w/index.php?title=File:Ancient_Egypt_Wings.svg *License:* Creative Commons Attribution-Share Alike *Contributors:* Jeff Dahl 61

Figure 21 *Source:* https://en.wikipedia.org/w/index.php?title=File:Cherub_plaque_Louvre_MRR245_n2.jpg *License:* Public Domain *Contributors:* User:Jastrow 67

Figure 22 *Source:* https://en.wikipedia.org/w/index.php?title=File:Map_of_expansion_of_Caliphate.svg *License:* Public Domain *Contributors:* DieBuche 68

Figure 23 *Source:* https://en.wikipedia.org/w/index.php?title=File:Interior_de_la_mezquita_de_Córdoba.jpg *License:* Creative Commons Attribution-Sharealike 3.0 *Contributors:* User:Alvaraujo 69

Figure 24 *Source:* https://en.wikipedia.org/w/index.php?title=File:OttomanEmpire1590.png *License:* GNU Free Documentation License *Contributors:* Magog the Ogre, Renato de carvalho ferreira 72

Figure 25 *Source:* https://en.wikipedia.org/w/index.php?title=File:I_Selim.jpg *License:* Public Domain *Contributors:* Ottoman miniature painter 73

Figure 26 *Source:* https://en.wikipedia.org/w/index.php?title=File:C)_Armenian_Girl,_Druse,_Inhabitant_of_Damascus.jpg *License:* Public Domain *Contributors:* THE HISTORY OF COSTUME By Braun & Schneider 73

Figure 27 *Source:* https://en.wikipedia.org/w/index.php?title=File:Arabia_1914.png *License:* Creative Commons Attribution-Sharealike 3.0 *Contributors:* User:Underlying lk 74

Figure 28 *Source:* https://en.wikipedia.org/w/index.php?title=File:Atatürk.jpg *Contributors:* Ceroles, Danyalov～commonswiki, Denisutku, Docu, E4024, FSII, Fastily, Hiddenhauser, Jcb, Karedefter, Kürschner, Man vyi, Place Clichy, Rateslines～commonswiki, Stefan2, Takabeg, Thuresson, Toter Alter Mann, Ullierlich, Zzyzx11, とある白い猫, 1 anonymous edits 76

Figure 29 *Source:* https://en.wikipedia.org/w/index.php?title=File:The_Middle_East.ogv *License:* Public Domain *Contributors:* National Archives 80

Figure 30 *Source:* https://en.wikipedia.org/w/index.php?title=File:Begin,_Carter_and_Sadat_at_Camp_David_1978.jpg *License:* Public Domain *Contributors:* Fitz-Patrick, Bill, photographer 81

Figure 31 *Source:* https://en.wikipedia.org/w/index.php?title=File:MiddleEast.png *License:* Public Domain *Contributors:* US-Government ... 83

Figure 32 *Source:* https://en.wikipedia.org/w/index.php?title=File:Map_of_Central_Asia.png *License:* Creative Commons Attribution-Share Alike *Contributors:* User:Cacahuate 90

Image *Source:* https://en.wikipedia.org/w/index.php?title=File:UrumqiWarrior.jpg *License:* Public Domain *Contributors:* Ismoon (talk) 23:05, 20 December 2012 (UTC) 91

Image *Source:* https://en.wikipedia.org/w/index.php?title=File:BactrianZoroastrian.jpg *License:* Public Domain *Contributors:* Artacoana, P4K1T0 91

Image *Source:* https://en.wikipedia.org/w/index.php?title=File:Sogdian-fragment-ca._700_AD.jpg *License:* Public Domain *Contributors:* Unknown Sogdian weaver. Photo from brochure. 92

Image *Source:* https//en.wikipedia.org *License:* Creative Commons Zero *Contributors:* User:Daderot 92

Figure 33 *Source:* https://en.wikipedia.org/w/index.php?title=File:Tetradrachm_Eukratides.jpg *License:* Public Domain *Contributors:* User PHG on en.wikipedia 94

Figure 34 *Source:* https://en.wikipedia.org/w/index.php?title=File:Afrasiab_-_details_from_The_Ambassadors'_Painting_3_-_great_procession.JPG *License:* Creative Commons Attribution-Sharealike 3.0 *Contributors:* User:Faqscl 94

Figure 35 *Source:* https://en.wikipedia.org/w/index.php?title=File:Central_Asian_Buddhist_Monks.jpeg *Contributors:* of the paintings - Unknown. Of the book, Albert von Le Coq. 95

Figure 36 *Source:* https://en.wikipedia.org/w/index.php?title=File:Gilt_silver_jar_with_pattern_of_dancing_horses.jpg *License:* Public Domain *Contributors:* User Mountain on zh.wikipedia 97

Figure 37 *Source:* https//en.wikipedia.org *License:* GNU Free Documentation License *Contributors:* sailko 98

Figure 38 *Source:* https://en.wikipedia.org/w/index.php?title=File:Lions,_soie_polychrome_sogdienne,_Asie_centrale.jpg *License:* Public Domain *Contributors:* Aschroet, OgreBot 2, PericlesofAthens, Yann ... 100
Figure 39 *Source:* https://en.wikipedia.org/w/index.php?title=File:Central_Asian_trade_routes.jpg *License:* Public Domain *Contributors:* Grtek, Ignacio Icke, MGA73bot2, Martin H., Rilegator, Rosemania, Warburg, Zykasaa ... 101
Figure 40 *Source:* https://en.wikipedia.org/w/index.php?title=File:Genghis_Khan_empire-en.svg *License:* Creative Commons Attribution-Sharealike 2.5 *Contributors:* User:Historicair ... 102
Figure 41 *Source:* https://en.wikipedia.org/w/index.php?title=File:Turkmen_man_with_camel.jpg *Contributors:* Digital rendering for the Library of Congress by Walter Frankhauser / WalterStudio ... 104
Figure 42 *Source:* https://en.wikipedia.org/w/index.php?title=File:Wassilij_Wassiljewitsch_Wereschtschagin_002.jpg *License:* Public Domain *Contributors:* Aavindraa, Abraham, Andres rojas22～commonswiki, BotMultichill, Botaurus, Emijrp, File Upload Bot (Eloquence), Off-shell, Revent, Shakko, Wmpearl, Zhuyifei1999, Владислав Резвый, Радион ... 105
Figure 43 *Source:* https://en.wikipedia.org/w/index.php?title=File:Prokudin-Gorskii-21.jpg *License:* Public Domain *Contributors:* , digital rendering for the Library of Congress by Walter Frankhauser / WalterStudio ... 106
Figure 44 *Source:* https://en.wikipedia.org/w/index.php?title=File:Central_Asia_-_political_map_2008.svg *License:* Creative Commons Attribution-Sharealike 3.0 *Contributors:* derivative work: Themightyquill (talk) Central_Asia_-_political_map_-_2000.svg: *derivative work: Themightyquill (talk) ... 113
Image *Source:* https://en.wikipedia.org/w/index.php?title=File:Wikiquote-logo.svg *License:* Public Domain *Contributors:* Rei-artur ... 124
Image *Source:* https://en.wikipedia.org/w/index.php?title=File:Padlock-silver.svg *Contributors:* AzaToth, BotMultichill, BotMultichillT, Gurch, Jarekt, Kallerna, Multichill, Perhelion, Rd232, Riana, Sarang, Siebrand, Steinsplitter, 4 anonymous edits ... 125
Figure 45 *Source:* https://en.wikipedia.org/w/index.php?title=File:□□□□□_□□.jpg *Contributors:* User:Tonloe5533 ... 127
Figure 46 *Source:* https://en.wikipedia.org/w/index.php?title=File:Territories_of_Dynasties_in_China.gif *License:* GNU Free Documentation License *Contributors:* Ian Kiu ... 127
Figure 47 *Source:* https://en.wikipedia.org/w/index.php?title=File:Timeline_of_Chinese_History.jpg *Contributors:* User:LifanDefense ... 128
Image *Source:* https://en.wikipedia.org/w/index.php?title=File:History_of_China.png *License:* Copyrighted free use *Contributors:* Original: Chong-Dae Probably zh:User:地狱牌咖啡壶 ... 125
Image *Source:* https://en.wikipedia.org/w/index.php?title=File:Linharaptor_exquistus.jpg *License:* Creative Commons Attribution-Sharealike 2.0 *Contributors:* ★Kumiko★ from Tokyo, Japan ... 129
Image *Source:* https://en.wikipedia.org/w/index.php?title=File:Tarbocosmo.jpg *License:* Creative Commons Attribution-Sharealike 3.0 *Contributors:* User:Veritastemplarius ... 129
Image *Source:* https://en.wikipedia.org/w/index.php?title=File:National_Museum_of_China_2014.02.01_14-43-38.jpg *License:* Creative Commons Attribution-Sharealike 3.0,2.5,2.0,1.0 *Contributors:* Zhangzhugang ... 130
Image *Source:* https://en.wikipedia.org/w/index.php?title=File:Bone_Arrowheads,_Jiahu_site.jpg *License:* Creative Commons Attribution-Sharealike 3.0 *Contributors:* User:幽灵巴尼 ... 130
Image *Source:* https//en.wikipedia.org *License:* Creative Commons Attribution-Sharealike 3.0 *Contributors:* User:LukeLOU ... 130
Image *Source:* https://en.wikipedia.org/w/index.php?title=File:Hemudu_Site_Museum,_2017-08-12_36.jpg *Contributors:* User:Siyuwj ... 130
Image *Source:* https://en.wikipedia.org/w/index.php?title=File:CMOC_Treasures_of_Ancient_China_exhibit_-_jade_disk.jpg *License:* Creative Commons Attribution-Sharealike 2.5 *Contributors:* Editor at Large ... 131
Image *Source:* https://en.wikipedia.org/w/index.php?title=File:CMOC_Treasures_of_Ancient_China_exhibit_-_bronze_jue.jpg *License:* Creative Commons Attribution-Sharealike 2.5 *Contributors:* Editor at Large ... 131
Image *Source:* https://en.wikipedia.org/w/index.php?title=File:Shang_dynasty.svg *License:* Creative Commons Attribution-Sharealike 3.0 *Contributors:* Lamassu Design Gurdjieff (talk) ... 132
Image *Source:* https://en.wikipedia.org/w/index.php?title=File:Oracle_bones_pit.JPG *License:* Creative Commons Attribution 2.0 *Contributors:* Chez Cåsver (Xuan Che) ... 132
Image *Source:* https://en.wikipedia.org/w/index.php?title=File:□□□□□□□,_2017-09-17.jpg *Contributors:* User:Siyuwj ... 132
Image *Source:* https://en.wikipedia.org/w/index.php?title=File:Ritual_Wine_Vessel_(Guang),_13th-11th_century_B.C.E._Bronze,_72.163a-b.jpg *Contributors:* Tracield ... 133
Image *Source:* https://en.wikipedia.org/w/index.php?title=File:Bronze_square_ding_(cauldron)_with_human_faces.jpg *License:* Creative Commons Attribution-Share Alike *Contributors:* smartneddy from FLICKR ... 133
Image *Source:* https://en.wikipedia.org/w/index.php?title=File:Dinastia_shang,_tipode_ding_biansato,_xiii-xii_sec._ac.JPG *License:* GNU Free Documentation License *Contributors:* sailko ... 133
Image *Source:* https://en.wikipedia.org/w/index.php?title=File:CMOC_Treasures_of_Ancient_China_exhibit_-_bronze_battle_axe.jpg *License:* Creative Commons Attribution-Sharealike 2.5 *Contributors:* Editor at Large ... 133
Image *Source:* https://en.wikipedia.org/w/index.php?title=File:Zhou_dynasty_1000_BC.png *License:* Creative Commons Attribution-ShareAlike 3.0 Unported *Contributors:* Territories_of_Dynasties_in_China.gif: Ian Kiu ... 134
Image *Source:* https://en.wikipedia.org/w/index.php?title=File:Wuwangfuchaimao.JPG *License:* Public Domain *Contributors:* fmwang ... 134
Image *Source:* https://en.wikipedia.org/w/index.php?title=File:You_with_zigzag_thunder_pattern.jpg *License:* GNU Free Documentation License *Contributors:* BotMultichill, Hiart, Ismoon, Kanguole, Lilyu, Lithoderm, MGA73bot2, Mountain, Petropoxy (Lithoderm Proxy), ProfZ, 1 anonymous edits ... 135
Image *Source:* https://en.wikipedia.org/w/index.php?title=File:Periodo_primavera_e_autunno,_ascia_o_alabarca_(ge),_V_sec._ac..JPG *License:* GNU Free Documentation License *Contributors:* sailko ... 135
Image *Source:* https://en.wikipedia.org/w/index.php?title=File:Five_Hegemons.png *Contributors:* User:Seasonsinthesun ... 135
Image *Source:* https://en.wikipedia.org/w/index.php?title=File:Linzi_sewer_2010_06_06.jpg *License:* Creative Commons Attribution-Sharealike 3.0 *Contributors:* Rolfmueller ... 136
Image *Source:* https://en.wikipedia.org/w/index.php?title=File:Sword_of_Goujian,_Hubei_Provincial_Museum,_2015-04-06_07.jpg *Contributors:* User:Siyuwj ... 136
Image *Source:* https://en.wikipedia.org/w/index.php?title=File:Sun_Gao_Bianzhong,_picture4.jpg *License:* Creative Commons Zero *Contributors:* User:Huangdan2060 ... 136
Image *Source:* https://en.wikipedia.org/w/index.php?title=File:Streitende-Reiche2.jpg *License:* Public Domain *Contributors:* Firespeaker, LlywelynII, Malus Catulus, Saperaud～commonswiki, Sarang, Zykasaa, 1 anonymous edits ... 137
Image *Source:* https//en.wikipedia.org *License:* Creative Commons Zero *Contributors:* User:Huangdan2060 ... 137
Image *Source:* https://en.wikipedia.org/w/index.php?title=File:Bi_with_two_dragons_and_grain_pattern.jpg *License:* GNU Free Documentation License *Contributors:* Cold Season, Hiart, KTo288, Lilyu, MGA73bot2, Mountain, PericlesofAthens, 1 anonymous edits ... 137
Image *Source:* https://en.wikipedia.org/w/index.php?title=File:Crystal_Cup(Warring_States_Period)_in_Hangzhou_Museum.JPG *License:* Creative Commons Attribution-Sharealike 3.0 *Contributors:* User:LukeLOU ... 137
Image *Source:* https://en.wikipedia.org/w/index.php?title=File:Qin_empire_210_BCE.jpg *License:* GNU Free Documentation License *Contributors:* User:Yu Ninjie ... 139
Image *Source:* https://en.wikipedia.org/w/index.php?title=File:Terracotta_Army-China2.jpg *License:* GNU Free Documentation License *Contributors:* see source ... 139
Image *Source:* https://en.wikipedia.org/w/index.php?title=File:□□□□□1.JPG *License:* Creative Commons Attribution-Sharealike 3.0 *Contributors:* User:蒋亦炯 ... 139
Image *Source:* https://en.wikipedia.org/w/index.php?title=File:Great_wall_of_qi_2008_07_14.jpg *License:* Creative Commons Attribution-Sharealike 3.0 *Contributors:* Rolfmueller ... 139
Image *Source:* https://en.wikipedia.org/w/index.php?title=File:Terrakotta_general_2010.jpg *License:* Creative Commons Attribution-Sharealike 3.0 *Contributors:* Holger.Ellgaard ... 140
Image *Source:* https://en.wikipedia.org/w/index.php?title=File:Terrakottaarmén-13.jpg *License:* Public Domain *Contributors:* Aschroet, Dcastor 140
Image *Source:* https://en.wikipedia.org/w/index.php?title=File:Han_map.jpg *License:* GNU Free Documentation License *Contributors:* User Yuninjie on en.wikipedia ... 141
Image *Source:* https://en.wikipedia.org/w/index.php?title=File:Summer_Vacation_2007,_263,_Watchtower_In_The_Morning_Light,_Dunhuang,_Gansu_Province.jpg *License:* Creative Commons Attribution 2.0 *Contributors:* The Real Bear ... 141
Image *Source:* https://en.wikipedia.org/w/index.php?title=File:Western_Han_Mawangdui_Silk_Map.JPG *License:* Public Domain *Contributors:* Anonymous ancient Chinese cartographer ... 141
Image *Source:* https://en.wikipedia.org/w/index.php?title=File:Dahuting_mural,_Eastern_Han_Dynasty.jpg *License:* Public Domain *Contributors:* PericlesofAthens ... 141
Figure 48 *Source:* https://en.wikipedia.org/w/index.php?title=File:Han_Expansion.png *Contributors:* User:Seasonsinthesun ... 142
Image *Source:* https://en.wikipedia.org/w/index.php?title=File:China_qing_blue.JPG *License:* Creative Commons Attribution 2.0 *Contributors:* Rosemania ... 143
Image *Source:* https://en.wikipedia.org/w/index.php?title=File:Bronze_mirror_with_painted_designs,_Western_Han.jpg *License:* Public Domain *Contributors:* Anonymous artist ... 143

Image *Source*: https://en.wikipedia.org/w/index.php?title=File:Warring_States_or_Western_Han_crossbow.jpg *License*: Creative Commons Attribution-Share Alike *Contributors*: Gary Lee Todd 143
Image *Source*: https://en.wikipedia.org/w/index.php?title=File:Warring_States_or_Western_Han_crossbow2.jpg *License*: Creative Commons Attribution-Share Alike *Contributors*: Gary Lee Todd 144
Figure 49 *Source*: https://en.wikipedia.org/w/index.php?title=File:□□□□.jpg *Contributors*: User:三猪 145
Image *Source*: https://en.wikipedia.org/w/index.php?title=File:China_5.jpg *License*: GNU Free Documentation License *Contributors*: Yu Ninjie 145
Image *Source*: https://en.wikipedia.org/w/index.php?title=File:Cao_Wei_Dynasty_fresco,_Luoyang.jpg *License*: Creative Commons Attribution-Share Alike *Contributors*: Gary Lee Todd 145
Image *Source*: https://en.wikipedia.org/w/index.php?title=File:Western_Jeun_Dynasty_280_CE.png *License*: GNU Free Documentation License *Contributors*: Ian Kiu 146
Image *Source*: https://en.wikipedia.org/w/index.php?title=File:Majishan_entire_hill_20090226.jpg *License*: Creative Commons Attribution-Sharealike 3.0 *Contributors*: MarsmanRom 146
Image *Source*: https://en.wikipedia.org/w/index.php?title=File:P-leshenfu.jpg *License*: Public Domain *Contributors*: 顓愷之 146
Image *Source*: https://en.wikipedia.org/w/index.php?title=File:China400ce.png *License*: Creative Commons Attribution-Sharealike 3.0 *Contributors*: User:Javierfv1212 146
Image *Source*: https://en.wikipedia.org/w/index.php?title=File:Southern_and_Northern_Dynasties_440_CE.png *License*: Creative Commons Attribution 3.0 *Contributors*: Ian Kiu 147
Image *Source*: https://en.wikipedia.org/w/index.php?title=File:Hanging_Monastery_02.JPG *License*: Creative Commons Attribution-Sharealike 3.0 *Contributors*: User:Nicor 147
Image *Source*: https://en.wikipedia.org/w/index.php?title=File:Yungang5_2010.JPG *License*: Creative Commons Attribution-Share Alike *Contributors*: Sfu 147
Image *Source*: https://en.wikipedia.org/w/index.php?title=File:Jiucenglou_of_Mogao_Caves.jpg *License*: Creative Commons Attribution-Sharealike 3.0 *Contributors*: 慕尼黑啤酒 148
Image *Source*: https://en.wikipedia.org/w/index.php?title=File:Cheui_Dynasty_581_CE.png *License*: Creative Commons Attribution 3.0 *Contributors*: Ian Kiu 148
Image *Source*: https://en.wikipedia.org/w/index.php?title=File:1400□□□□□_zhao_zhou_qiao_-_panoramio.jpg *License*: Creative Commons Attribution-Sharealike 3.0 *Contributors*: そらみみ 148
Image *Source*: https://en.wikipedia.org/w/index.php?title=File:Tianlongshan_Grotto_-_Manshan_Pavillion,_Taiyuan,_Shanxi.JPG *Contributors*: User:Underbar dk 149
Image *Source*: https://en.wikipedia.org/w/index.php?title=File:Sui_Yangdi_Tang.jpg *License*: Public Domain *Contributors*: HéctorTabaré, Japalang, Jarekt, Jonathan Groß, Leyo, Lx 121, Morio, Shizhao, Zolo, ITrate, 白布飄揚, 4 anonymous edits 149
Image *Source*: https://en.wikipedia.org/w/index.php?title=File:Tang_Dynasty_circa_700_CE.png *License*: GNU Free Documentation License *Contributors*: Ian Kiu 150
Image *Source*: https://en.wikipedia.org/w/index.php?title=File:□□_□□_□□□□_-_panoramio.jpg *License*: Creative Commons Attribution-Sharealike 3.0 *Contributors*: Underbar dk 150
Image *Source*: https://en.wikipedia.org/w/index.php?title=File:□□□□□□Luo_Yang_Dragon_Gate_Grottoes_-_panoramio_(9).jpg *License*: Creative Commons Attribution-Sharealike 3.0 *Contributors*: N509FZ, Underbar dk 150
Image *Source*: https://en.wikipedia.org/w/index.php?title=File:Dunhuang_star_map.jpg *License*: Public Domain *Contributors*: Brian J. Ford . 150
Figure 50 *Source*: https://en.wikipedia.org/w/index.php?title=File:Tang_Protectorates.png *Contributors*: User:Seasonsinthesun 151
Image *Source*: https://en.wikipedia.org/w/index.php?title=File:□□□_□□□□_□□□□_02.jpg *Contributors*: -revi, Eggmoon, HappyMidnight, Ismoon, Jcb 152
Image *Source*: https://en.wikipedia.org/w/index.php?title=File:Dali_Santa_11.JPG *License*: Public Domain *Contributors*: Brücke-Osteuropa . 152
Image *Source*: https://en.wikipedia.org/w/index.php?title=File:□□□□.jpg *License*: Creative Commons Attribution-Sharealike 3.0 *Contributors*: User:Smwy09 153
Image *Source*: https://en.wikipedia.org/w/index.php?title=File:Xi'anwildgoosepagoda2.JPG *License*: Public Domain *Contributors*: Guucancat 153
Image *Source*: https://en.wikipedia.org/w/index.php?title=File:Quanzhou_Kaiyuan_Si_20120229-43.jpg *License*: Creative Commons Attribution-Share Alike *Contributors*: Zhangzhugang 154
Image *Source*: https://en.wikipedia.org/w/index.php?title=File:Gongchen_bagoda.JPG *License*: Creative Commons Attribution-Sharealike 3.0 *Contributors*: Dirrival 154
Image *Source*: https://en.wikipedia.org/w/index.php?title=File:Five_Dynasties_Ten_Kingdoms_923_CE.png *License*: Creative Commons Attribution 3.0 *Contributors*: Ian Kiu 154
Image *Source*: https://en.wikipedia.org/w/index.php?title=File:YunYanSiPagoda.jpg *License*: Creative Commons Attribution-Sharealike 3.0 *Contributors*: Sjschen 155
Image *Source*: https://en.wikipedia.org/w/index.php?title=File:096_20100911_bt_shanghai_museum_(4986578699).jpg *License*: Creative Commons Attribution 2.0 *Contributors*: Bill Taroli 155
Image *Source*: https://en.wikipedia.org/w/index.php?title=File:Gu_Hongzhong_15.jpg *License*: Public Domain *Contributors*: Eugene a . 155
Image *Source*: https://en.wikipedia.org/w/index.php?title=File:China_-_Song_Dynasty-en.svg *License*: Creative Commons Attribution-Sharealike 3.0 *Contributors*: User:Kanguole, User:LiDaobing, User:Mozzan 156
Image *Source*: https://en.wikipedia.org/w/index.php?title=File:Song-Bodhisattva1.jpg *License*: Creative Commons Attribution-Sharealike 2.5 *Contributors*: Louis le Grand 156
Image *Source*: https://en.wikipedia.org/w/index.php?title=File:Chinese_Gunpowder_Formula.JPG *License*: Public Domain *Contributors*: PericlesofAthens 156
Image *Source*: https://en.wikipedia.org/w/index.php?title=File:Very_large_crouching_tiger_cannon.jpg *License*: Public Domain *Contributors*: User:Yprpyup 156
Image *Source*: https://en.wikipedia.org/w/index.php?title=File:Dingzhou_Liaodi_Pagoda_3.jpg *License*: Creative Commons Attribution-ShareAlike 3.0 Unported *Contributors*: User:Zeus1234 157
Image *Source*: https://en.wikipedia.org/w/index.php?title=File:People's_Republic_of_China_Beijing_Tianningsi_Tianing_Temple_David_McBride_Photography-0045_02.jpg *Contributors*: User:Davidmcbride 157
Image *Source*: https://en.wikipedia.org/w/index.php?title=File:Hohhot_White_Pagoda_Ta_2.jpg *License*: Creative Commons Attribution-Sharealike 3.0 *Contributors*: User:BabelStone 157
Image *Source*: https://en.wikipedia.org/w/index.php?title=File:Poyang_Yongfu_Si_Ta_2017.11.25_10-04-37.jpg *License*: GNU Free Documentation License *Contributors*: Zhangzhugang 158
Image *Source*: https://en.wikipedia.org/w/index.php?title=File:Suzhou_(December_8,_2015)_-_16.jpg *Contributors*: User:Another Believer . 159
Image *Source*: https://en.wikipedia.org/w/index.php?title=File:□□□_Jingzhou_Pagoda.JPG *Contributors*: User:Inhorw 159
Image *Source*: https://en.wikipedia.org/w/index.php?title=File:Northern_Chaoyang_Pagoda_06_2015-09.jpg *Contributors*: User:猫猫的日记本 159
Image *Source*: https://en.wikipedia.org/w/index.php?title=File:Song_Dynasty_Hydraulic_Mill_for_Grain.JPG *License*: Public Domain *Contributors*: PericlesofAthens 159
Image *Source*: https://en.wikipedia.org/w/index.php?title=File:□□□□.jpg *License*: Public Domain *Contributors*: User Zhuwq on zh.wikipedia . 160
Image *Source*: https://en.wikipedia.org/w/index.php?title=File:Qingming_Festival_2.jpg *License*: Public Domain *Contributors*: HéctorTabaré, KTo288, Li39391O8, Missvain, PericlesofAthens, Rsteen 160
Image *Source*: https://en.wikipedia.org/w/index.php?title=File:Leifeng_Pagoda_in_the_Southern_Song_Dynasty_by_Li_Song.jpg *License*: Public Domain *Contributors*: 三猪, 猫猫的日记本 160
Image *Source*: https://en.wikipedia.org/w/index.php?title=File:Miaoyingsi_baita.jpg *License*: GNU Free Documentation License *Contributors*: user:yongxinge 161
Image *Source*: https://en.wikipedia.org/w/index.php?title=File:Deva_King_of_the_East.jpg *License*: Creative Commons Attribution-Sharealike 3.0 *Contributors*: BabelStone 161
Image *Source*: https://en.wikipedia.org/w/index.php?title=File:Yuan_chinese_gun.jpg *License*: Creative Commons Attribution-Sharealike 3.0,2,2.5,2.0,1.0 *Contributors*: Ytrottier 161
Image *Source*: https://en.wikipedia.org/w/index.php?title=File:Yuan_dynasty_banknote_with_its_printing_plate_1287.jpg *License*: Creative Commons Attribution-Sharealike 3.0 *Contributors*: PHGCOM 161
Figure 51 *Source*: https://en.wikipedia.org/w/index.php?title=File:MongolMap.png *License*: Public Domain *Contributors*: Los Angeles County Museum of Art 162
Image *Source*: https://en.wikipedia.org/w/index.php?title=File:The_Observatory,_Dengfeng,_2015-09-24_08.jpg *Contributors*: User:Siyuwj . 163
Image *Source*: https://en.wikipedia.org/w/index.php?title=File:□□□□_-_panoramio.jpg *License*: Creative Commons Attribution-Sharealike 3.0 *Contributors*: 三猪 163
Image *Source*: https://en.wikipedia.org/w/index.php?title=File:□□□□.jpg *License*: Creative Commons Attribution-Sharealike 3.0 *Contributors*: User:Redpipe 164
Image *Source*: https://en.wikipedia.org/w/index.php?title=File:Zhao_guan_Tower_2011-10.JPG *License*: Creative Commons Attribution-Sharealike 3.0 *Contributors*: 猫猫的日记本 164

Image *Source:* https://en.wikipedia.org/w/index.php?title=File:Dongyang_Luzhai_2015.05.24_15-53-48.jpg *License:* GNU Free Documentation License *Contributors:* Zhangzhugang ... 165
Image *Source:* https://en.wikipedia.org/w/index.php?title=File:XiAn_CityWall_DiLou.jpg *Contributors:* Fanghong, HéctorTabaré, Matt314, Saperaud～commonswiki, Sl ... 165
Image *Source:* https://en.wikipedia.org/w/index.php?title=File:Fenghuang_old_town.JPG *License:* GNU Free Documentation License *Contributors:* 韩笃一 ... 165
Image *Source:* https://en.wikipedia.org/w/index.php?title=File:Yixian_Hongcun_2016.09.09_17-27-03.jpg *License:* GNU Free Documentation License *Contributors:* Zhangzhugang ... 165
Image *Source:* https://en.wikipedia.org/w/index.php?title=File:Xinye-9.jpg *Contributors:* User:PromoteMyCity ... 166
Figure 52 *Source:* https://en.wikipedia.org/w/index.php?title=File:Nieuhof-Ambassade-vers-la-Chine-1665_0789.tif *Contributors:* Hansmuller, Steinsplitter ... 166
Image *Source:* https://en.wikipedia.org/w/index.php?title=File:Haihui_Temple_(Shanxi).JPG *Contributors:* User:Underbar dk ... 166
Image *Source:* https://en.wikipedia.org/w/index.php?title=File:Jining_Chongjue_Si_Tieta_2015.08.13_17-18-45.jpg *License:* GNU Free Documentation License *Contributors:* Zhangzhugang ... 167
Image *Source:* https://en.wikipedia.org/w/index.php?title=File:Lin_Liang-Eagles.jpg *License:* Public Domain *Contributors:* Choufanging, Jann, Sevilledade, Shakko, Stout256, Zolo ... 168
Image *Source:* https://en.wikipedia.org/w/index.php?title=File:Bian_Jingzhao-Snow_Plum_and_Twin_Cranes.jpg *License:* Public Domain *Contributors:* Deerstop, Elkost, Ismoon, Jann, Jarble, Shakko, Stout256, 1 anonymous edits ... 169
Image *Source:* https://en.wikipedia.org/w/index.php?title=File:Carte_generale_de_l'Empire_Chinois_et_du_Japon_(1836).jpg *License:* Public Domain *Contributors:* Brue, Adrien Hubert, 1786-1832; Picquet, C. ... 170
Image *Source:* https://en.wikipedia.org/w/index.php?title=File:Museum_für_Ostasiatische_Kunst_Dahlem_Berlin_Mai_2006_041.jpg *License:* Public Domain *Contributors:* Gryffindor ... 170
Image *Source:* https://en.wikipedia.org/w/index.php?title=File:MilitaryCostumeEmperorKienLong1736-1796.jpg *License:* Creative Commons Attribution-Sharealike 3.0,2.5,2.0,1.0 *Contributors:* PHGCOM ... 170
Image *Source:* https://en.wikipedia.org/w/index.php?title=File:Chinese_Geomantic_Compass_c._1760,_National_Maritime_Museum.JPG *Contributors:* User:Victoria C ... 170
Image *Source:* https://en.wikipedia.org/w/index.php?title=File:߀߀߀߀߀߀.jpg *License:* Creative Commons Attribution-Sharealike 2.0 *Contributors:* Morio, Sgsg, Shizhao, Zhangzhugang ... 170
Image *Source:* https://en.wikipedia.org/w/index.php?title=File:Putuo_Zongcheng_Temple.jpg *License:* Creative Commons Attribution-Share Alike *Contributors:* Gisling ... 171
Image *Source:* https://en.wikipedia.org/w/index.php?title=File:߀߀߀߀߀_-_panoramio_(14).jpg *License:* Creative Commons Attribution 3.0 *Contributors:* Perumalism, そらみみ ... 171
Image *Source:* https://en.wikipedia.org/w/index.php?title=File:߀߀߀_߀߀_߀߀.jpg *License:* User:三猪 ... 171
Image *Source:* https://en.wikipedia.org/w/index.php?title=File:߀߀.jpg *License:* Creative Commons Attribution-Sharealike 3.0 *Contributors:* User:Shizhao ... 171
Figure 53 *Source:* https://en.wikipedia.org/w/index.php?title=File:Portrait_of_the_Qianlong_Emperor_in_Court_Dress.jpg *Contributors:* Daderot, Ecummenic, Gryffindor, Ismoon, Jdx, Leyo, Louis le Grand～commonswiki, Morio, Qingprof, 4 anonymous edits ... 173
Figure 54 *Source:* https://en.wikipedia.org/w/index.php?title=File:Li_Hung_Chang_in_1896.jpg *License:* Public Domain *Contributors:* Russell & Sons ... 173
Figure 55 *Source:* https://en.wikipedia.org/w/index.php?title=File:Xinhai_Revolution_in_Shanghai.jpg *License:* Public Domain *Contributors:* Mt-Bell, Olybrius, Sgsg, Zolo ... 175
Image *Source:* https://en.wikipedia.org/w/index.php?title=File:Sunyatsen1.jpg *License:* Public Domain *Contributors:* Militaryace ... 176
Image *Source:* https://en.wikipedia.org/w/index.php?title=File:Yuan_Shikai2.jpg *License:* Public Domain *Contributors:* OgreBot 2, Sgsg ... 176
Figure 56 *Source:* https://en.wikipedia.org/w/index.php?title=File:Flag_of_the_Republic_of_China.svg *License:* Public Domain *Contributors:* User:SKopp ... 177
Figure 57 *Source:* https://en.wikipedia.org/w/index.php?title=File:PLA_Enters_Peking.jpg *Contributors:* ContinentalAve, File Upload Bot (Magnus Manske), NumbiGate, OgreBot 2, ShinePhantom, Shizhao ... 179
Figure 58 *Source:* https://en.wikipedia.org/w/index.php?title=File:Mao_proclaiming_the_establishment_of_the_PRC_in_1949.jpg *License:* Public Domain *Contributors:* 侯波 Hou Bo 侯波回忆：我去天安门城楼拍摄开国大典 (英)(1) ... 179
Figure 59 *Source:* https://en.wikipedia.org/w/index.php?title=File:Flag_of_the_People's_Republic_of_China.svg *License:* Public Domain *Contributors:* Drawn by User:SKopp, redrawn by User:Denelson83 and User:Zscout370 Recode by cs:User:-xfi- (code), User:Shizhao (colors ... 180
Image *Source:* https://en.wikipedia.org/w/index.php?title=File:Wikivoyage-Logo-v3-icon.svg *License:* Creative Commons Attribution-Sharealike 3.0 *Contributors:* User:AleXXw ... 192
Image *Source:* https://en.wikipedia.org/w/index.php?title=File:Kailchiranzu1806.jpg *License:* Public Domain *Contributors:* Greenland4, Gryffindor, Lssrn, Pekachu, ロリ, 1 anonymous edits ... 195
Image *Source:* https://en.wikipedia.org/w/index.php?title=File:Flag_of_Japan.svg *License:* Public Domain *Contributors:* Anomie, Jo-Jo Eumerus ... 195
Figure 60 *Source:* https://en.wikipedia.org/w/index.php?title=File:JarWithSpiralsFinalJomonKamegaokaStyle.jpg *License:* Creative Commons Attribution-ShareAlike 3.0 Unported *Contributors:* PHGCOM ... 200
Figure 61 *Source:* https://en.wikipedia.org/w/index.php?title=File:DotakuBronzeBellLateYayoi3rdCenturyCE.jpg *License:* Creative Commons Attribution-ShareAlike 3.0 Unported *Contributors:* PHGCOM ... 200
Figure 62 *Source:* https://en.wikipedia.org/w/index.php?title=File:NintokuTomb.jpg *Contributors:* Ministry of Land, Infrastructure and Transport Government of Japan & moja resized ... 202
Figure 63 *Source:* https://en.wikipedia.org/w/index.php?title=File:Yamato_en.png *License:* GNU Free Documentation License *Contributors:* Alexandrin, Copydays, Forestfarmer, Geofrog, MGA73bot2, Mps2, 丁 ... 203
Image *Source:* https://en.wikipedia.org/w/index.php?title=File:Nihon.png *License:* Creative Commons Attribution-ShareAlike 3.0 *Contributors:* Nihongo_Horizontal.svg: *derivative work: Yurko Nihongo.svg: To SVG by OsamaK from Image:Nihongo.png was basd from . der ... 204
Figure 64 *Source:* https://en.wikipedia.org/w/index.php?title=File:Prince_Shotoku.jpg *License:* Public Domain *Contributors:* Apalsola, Ismoon, Kintetsubuffalo, Koresdcine, OceanSound, Ras57, ReijiYamashina, 2 anonymous edits ... 204
Figure 65 *Source:* https://en.wikipedia.org/w/index.php?title=File:߀߀߀߀߀.jpg *License:* Public Domain *Contributors:* Wikiwikiyarou ... 206
Figure 66 *Source:* https://en.wikipedia.org/w/index.php?title=File:Genji_emaki_TAKEKAWA.jpg *License:* Public Domain *Contributors:* Imperial court in Kyoto ... 208
Figure 67 *Source:* https://en.wikipedia.org/w/index.php?title=File:Mōko_Shūrai_Ekotoba.jpg *License:* Public Domain *Contributors:* Allforrous, Aotake, BotMultichill, MathieuMD, Phoenix7777, Usiwakamaru, Worldantiques, 1 anonymous edits ... 209
Figure 68 *Source:* https://en.wikipedia.org/w/index.php?title=File:Ashikaga_Takauji.JPG *License:* Public Domain *Contributors:* Urashimataro ... 213
Figure 69 *Source:* https://en.wikipedia.org/w/index.php?title=File:Map_Japan_Genki1-en.svg *License:* Public Domain *Contributors:* User:Ro4444 ... 213
Figure 70 *Source:* https://en.wikipedia.org/w/index.php?title=File:Japanese_Crest_Uesugi_Sasa.svg *License:* Creative Commons Attribution-ShareAlike 3.0,2.5,2.0,1.0 *Contributors:* Mukai ... 213
Figure 71 *Source:* https://en.wikipedia.org/w/index.php?title=File:Sekigahara_Kassen_Byōbu-zu_(Gifu_History_Museum).jpg *License:* Public Domain *Contributors:* Collection of The City of Gifu Museum of History ... 214
Figure 72 *Source:* https://en.wikipedia.org/w/index.php?title=File:Azuchimomoyama-japan.png *License:* Creative Commons Attribution-ShareAlike 3.0 Unported *Contributors:* Zakuragi ... 215
Figure 73 *Source:* https://en.wikipedia.org/w/index.php?title=File:Tokugawa_Ieyasu2.JPG *License:* Public Domain *Contributors:* Boneyard90, Colibrix, DIREKTOR, Grampus, Grandiose, Ihimutefu, M-sho-gun, Scientia.asiae, Tokorokoko, WikiWisePowder, ラッチキング ... 216
Figure 74 *Source:* https://en.wikipedia.org/w/index.php?title=File:Tokugawa_family_crest.svg *License:* Public Domain *Contributors:* User:Jak, User:Lemon-s ... 217
Figure 75 *Source:* https://en.wikipedia.org/w/index.php?title=File:Satsuma-samurai-during-boshin-war-period.jpg *License:* Public Domain *Contributors:* 山東京伝 ... 219
Figure 76 *Source:* https://en.wikipedia.org/w/index.php?title=File:Meiji_tenno1.jpg *License:* Public Domain *Contributors:* Baronnet, Brad101, Catfisheye, Clusternote, Gryffindor, Horeki, Infrogmation, JMCC1, KTo288, Kl8333x9～commonswiki, Lecen, Morio, Pinkville, Quibik, Scewing, Svajcr, Takabeg, Thib Phil, Tomomarusan, Un1c0s bot～commonswiki, Worldantiques, Xhienne, 2 anonymous edits ... 220
Figure 77 *Source:* https://en.wikipedia.org/w/index.php?title=File:Meiji_tenno1.jpg *License:* Public Domain *Contributors:* Artist: Eduardo Chiossone (1833–98); Photographer: Maruki Riyō (also misspelt as Maruki Toshiaki) UNIQ-ref-4-874b6c040ac ... 221
Figure 78 *Source:* https://en.wikipedia.org/w/index.php?title=File:Generals_Pyongyang_MigitaToshihide_October1894.jpg *License:* Public Domain *Contributors:* Migita Toshihide ... 223
Figure 79 *Source:* https://en.wikipedia.org/w/index.php?title=File:Pacific_Area_-_The_Imperial_Powers_1939_-_Map.svg *License:* derivative work: Emok (talk) World2Hires_filled_mercator.svg: Emok Image:Pacific_Area_-_The_Imperial_Powers_1939_-_Map.j ... 224
Figure 80 *Source:* https://en.wikipedia.org/w/index.php?title=File:1937_Japan_VP8.webm *License:* Creative Commons Attribution-Sharealike 3.0 *Contributors:* User:Runawaysquash ... 226

297

Figure 81 *Source:* https://en.wikipedia.org/w/index.php?title=File:Mantetsu_Honsha.jpg *License:* Public Domain *Contributors:* South Manchuria Railway Co. ... 227

Figure 82 *Source:* https://en.wikipedia.org/w/index.php?title=File:193109_mukden_incident_railway_sabotage.jpg *License:* Public Domain *Contributors:* BrokenSphere, Chamarasca, DonatoD, Ingolfson, Kl833x9~commonswiki, Man yyi, Takabeg ... 228

Figure 83 *Source:* https://en.wikipedia.org/w/index.php?title=File:Carrier_shokaku.jpg *License:* Public Domain *Contributors:* , the original photograph was captured on Attu in 1943. ... 229

Figure 84 *Source:* https://en.wikipedia.org/w/index.php?title=File:Atomic_cloud_over_Hiroshima_-_NARA_542192_-_Edit.jpg *License:* Public Domain *Contributors:* Retouched by: Mmxx ... 230

Figure 85 *Source:* https://en.wikipedia.org/w/index.php?title=File:Macarthur_hirohito.jpg *License:* Public Domain *Contributors:* Bellerophon5685, BrokenSegue, Catsmeat, Docu, Esemono, Hawkeye7, Hohum, Infrogmation, Makthorpe, Materialscientist, Morio, Shika ryouse shomei, あばさ一 ... 231

Figure 86 *Source:* https://en.wikipedia.org/w/index.php?title=File:Release_of_Communist.JPG *License:* Public Domain *Contributors:* User:あばさ一 ... 231

Figure 87 *Source:* https://en.wikipedia.org/w/index.php?title=File:Shigeru_Yoshida_smiling2.jpg *License:* Public Domain *Contributors:* Aschroet, WTCA ... 232

Figure 88 *Source:* https://en.wikipedia.org/w/index.php?title=File:Treaty_of_peace_with_japan.jpg *License:* Creative Commons Attribution 2.0 *Contributors:* U.S. Department of State ... 233

Figure 89 *Source:* https://en.wikipedia.org/w/index.php?title=File:Shinchi_Sta_20110404.jpg *License:* Creative Commons Attribution-Sharealike 3.0,2.5,2.0,1.0 *Contributors:* Kuha455405 ... 235

Figure 90 *Source:* https://en.wikipedia.org/w/index.php?title=File:Edo_social_structure.svg *Contributors:* User:TheInfernoX ... 237

Image *Source:* https://en.wikipedia.org/w/index.php?title=File:CasparSchmalkalden_AsiaMap.jpg *License:* Public Domain *Contributors:* 1989, Aschroet, BotMultichill, BotMultichillT, Steffen Löwe Gera ... 241

Image *Source:* https://en.wikipedia.org/w/index.php?title=File:Location_Southeast_Asia.svg *Contributors:* user:Serg!o 243

Figure 91 *Source:* https://en.wikipedia.org/w/index.php?title=File:Southeast_Asia_(orthographic_projection).svg *License:* Creative Commons Attribution-Sharealike 3.0 *Contributors:* Huaiwei, Keepscases, NicoScribe, Sarang, TUBS, 白布飄扬, 1 anonymous edits ... 245

Figure 92 *Source:* https://en.wikipedia.org/w/index.php?title=File:Borobudur-Nothwest-view.jpg *License:* Creative Commons Attribution-Sharealike 3.0 *Contributors:* User:Gunkarta ... 246

Figure 93 *Source:* https://en.wikipedia.org/w/index.php?title=File:The_main_entrance_to_the_Niah_Caves_at_sunset..jpg *License:* Creative Commons Attribution-Sharealike 3.0 *Contributors:* User:Starlightchild ... 247

Figure 94 *Source:* https://en.wikipedia.org/w/index.php?title=File:Meyers_b11_s0476a.jpg *License:* Public Domain *Contributors:* de/Herrmann Julius Meyer, son of Joseph Meyer ... 249

Figure 95 *Source:* https://en.wikipedia.org/w/index.php?title=File:Bản_đồ_Văn_Lang_&_Nam_Cương.JPG *License:* Creative Commons Zero *Contributors:* User:I Love Triệu Đà ... 250

Figure 96 *Source:* https://en.wikipedia.org/w/index.php?title=File:Trong_dong_Dong_Son.jpg *License:* Creative Commons Attribution-Sharealike 3.0 *Contributors:* Grenouille vert ... 251

Figure 97 *Source:* https://en.wikipedia.org/w/index.php?title=File:Buni_Culture_Pottery_2.jpg *Contributors:* User:Gunkarta ... 253

Figure 98 *Source:* https://en.wikipedia.org/w/index.php?title=File:Hinduism_Expansion_in_Asia.svg *Contributors:* User:Gunkarta ... 254

Figure 99 *Source:* https//en.wikipedia.org *License:* GNU Free Documentation License *Contributors:* sailko ... 255

Figure 100 *Source:* https://en.wikipedia.org/w/index.php?title=File:Ptolemy_Asia_detail.jpg *License:* Public Domain *Contributors:* Bibi Saint-Pol, BotAdventures, Botteville, Fconaway, Flamarande~commonswiki, Green Giant, Lliura, LlywelynII, Marcus Cyron, Mattes, Mediatus, PericlesofAthens, Snek01, Stassats, Un1c0s bot~commonswiki, Wieralee ... 256

Figure 101 *Source:* https://en.wikipedia.org/w/index.php?title=File:Silk_route_copy.jpg *Contributors:* ... 257

Figure 102 *Source:* https://en.wikipedia.org/w/index.php?title=File:Stupa_Borobudur.jpg *License:* GNU Free Documentation License *Contributors:* Original uploader was Gunawan Kartapranata at en.wikipedia ... 258

Figure 103 *Source:* https://en.wikipedia.org/w/index.php?title=File:Angkor_Wat.jpg *License:* Creative Commons Attribution-Share Alike *Contributors:* Bjørn Christian Tørrissen ... 259

Figure 104 *Source:* https://en.wikipedia.org/w/index.php?title=File:Inskripsyon_sa_Binatbat_na_Tanso_ng_Laguna.jpg *Contributors:* User:Darwgon0801 ... 259

Figure 105 *Source:* https://en.wikipedia.org/w/index.php?title=File:Masjid_Menara_Kudus.jpg *License:* Creative Commons Zero *Contributors:* User:PL09Puryono ... 261

Figure 106 *Source:* https://en.wikipedia.org/w/index.php?title=File:Malays_from_the_Malacca_Sultanate_Codice_Casanatense.jpg *License:* Creative Commons Zero *Contributors:* Joseolgon, Wareno ... 262

Figure 107 *Source:* https://en.wikipedia.org/w/index.php?title=File:European_colonisation_of_Southeast_Asia.png *License:* GNU Free Documentation License *Contributors:* Rumilo Santiago ... 265

Figure 108 *Source:* https://en.wikipedia.org/w/index.php?title=File:Retrato_de_Afonso_de_Albuquerque_(após_1545)_-_Autor_desconhecido.png *License:* Public Domain *Contributors:* Aschroet, Joseolgon, JotaCartas, N.Português, RickMorais ... 266

Figure 109 *Source:* https://en.wikipedia.org/w/index.php?title=File:Japanese_light_tanks_moving_toward_Manila.jpg *License:* Public Domain *Contributors:* Japanese military ... 268

Figure 110 *Source:* https://en.wikipedia.org/w/index.php?title=File:Bruce_Crandall's_UH-1D.jpg *License:* Public Domain *Contributors:* United States Army ... 269

Figure 111 *Source:* https://en.wikipedia.org/w/index.php?title=File:ASEAN_Nations_Flags_in_Jakarta_3.jpg *License:* Creative Commons Attribution-Sharealike 3.0 *Contributors:* Gunawan Kartapranata ... 271

License

Creative Commons Attribution-Share Alike 3.0
//creativecommons.org/licenses/by-sa/3.0/

Index

-stan, 33

Abbasid, 101
Abbasid architecture, 70
Abbasid Caliphate, 9, 12
Abbasid caliphs, 72
Abdul Hamid II, 75
Abdullah I of Jordan, 78
Abe clan, 207
Above mean sea level, 36
Abrahamic religions, 4, 60
Abu Kamal, 48
Abu Salabikh, 31
Academia Sinica, 192
Achaemenid Empire, 4, 39, 41, 43, 51, 62, 65, 95
Achaemenid Persia, 50, 56
Adad-nirari II, 50
Adam Schall, 21
Aden Protectorate, 74
Administrative divisions of the Peoples Republic of China, 138
Admiral, 160
Adnanite, 59
Adolf Hitler, 79
Aegean Bronze Age, 45
Aegean civilization, 49
Aegean civilizations, 50
Afghanistan, 5, 33, 51, 84, 91, 96, 106
Afonso de Albuquerque, 266
Afrasiab painting, 94
Afrasiyab (Samarkand), 94
African Plate, 60
Afsharids, 72
Aftermath, 99
Aftermath of World War II, 247
Age of Discovery, 169, 244
Age of the Gods, 220
Agriculture, 41, 63
Ahiram, 31
Ahmed Hassan al-Bakr, 82
Ahom Kingdom, 121
Ainu people, 201
Air raids on Japan, 197, 229

Akechi Mitsuhide, 215
Akihito, 234
Akkad (city), 46
Akkadian, 40, 60, 62
Akkadian Empire, 39, 42, 46, 62, 63
Akkadian language, 31, 50
Alabaster, 92
Al-Andalus, 68
Alans, 101
Al-Aqsa Mosque, 70
Albania, 72
Albert Hourani, 85
Albert von Le Coq, 95
Alexander the Great, 4, 65, 96
Alexandria, 65, 247
Alexandria Eschate, 96
Algeria, 57, 74, 77
Alimqul, 105
All empires at their greatest extent, 172
Allies of World War I, 76, 225
Allies of World War II, 197, 228
Along the River During Qingming Festival, 160
Along the River During the Qingming Festival, 127, 160
Al-Qaida, 84
Alvin Coox, 238
American Civil War, 107
Amman Citadel Inscription, 31
Ammonite language, 31
Amorite, 46–48
Anatolia, 2, 9, 31, 39, 40, 47–50, 58, 62, 66, 68, 71
Anatolian languages, 48
Anatomically modern human, 34, 248
Anbar campaign (2013–14), 58
Ancient Carthage, 64
Ancient Chinese coinage, 149
Ancient Egypt, 39, 40, 45, 49, 62
Ancient history, 40, 44, 50, 55, 59, 89, 247
Ancient iron production, 50
Ancient Israel, 39, 62
Ancient Linzi, 136
Ancient Near East, 39, **39**, 44, 45, 55, 61, 89, 93, 248

Ancient Rome, 65
Andaman Islands, 250
Andhra Pradesh, 121
Andrew Jackson, 266
Andronovo culture, 93
An embassy from the East-India Company, 166
Angkor, 260
Angkor Wat, 259
Anglo-Burmese Wars, 244
Anglo-Dutch Treaty of 1824, 266
Anglo-Egyptian treaty of 1936, 79
Anglo-Iraqi War, 79
Anglo-Japanese Alliance, 223
Anglo-Maratha Wars, 122
Anglo-Sikh wars, 122
Anglo-Soviet invasion of Iran, 79
Anime, 235
Animism, 262
Anji Bridge, 149
Ankh, 61
An Lushan Rebellion, 153
Anshan (Persia), 46
An Shi Rebellion, 100
Anthony Reid (academic), 272
Antiquity, 44, 55, 89, 248
Anti-Western sentiment, 80
António Mota, 214
Anuradhapura, 32
Anwar Sadat, 81, 82
Anxi Protectorate, 99
Anyang, 133
Apennine culture, 45
Aq Qoyunlu, 72
Arab, 9, 68, 100
Arab–Byzantine wars, 9, 68, 263
Arab–Israeli conflict, 24
Arabia, 46, 247, 261
Arabian Desert, 59
Arabian Peninsula, 31, 40, 42, 60, 79, 100
Arabian plate, 59, 60
Arabic, 60
Arab nationalism, 77, 79, 82
Arab Revolt, 77
Arab socialism, 81
Arab Spring, 58, 85
Aral Sea, 115, 152
Aramaean, 49
Aramaeans, 48
Aramaic, 50, 52, 60
Aramaic language, 31, 40, 50, 58, 62
Aram (Biblical region), 48
Aram-Damascus, 64
Aramean, 43
Aramean flag, 61
Archaeology, 35
Archaic Greece, 43

Architecture, 9, 69
Arctic Ocean, 27
Arid, 90
Ariel Sharon, 84
Aristotle, 70
Armenia, 40, 47, 51, 66
Armenian Highland, 33, 51
Armenian Highlands, 40
Armenian nationalism, 77
Armenian people, 42
Armenians, 48
Arsenical bronze, 45
Arthur F. Wright, 184
Arthur W. Hummel, Sr., 186
Article 9 of the Japanese Constitution, 232
Artifact (archaeology), 36
Aryan, 93
ASEAN, 271
ASEAN Free Trade Area, 270
Ashikaga shogunate, 198
Ashikaga Takauji, 210, 212
Ashikaga Yoshimasa, 214
Ashikaga Yoshimitsu, 212
Ashina Helu, 99
Ashkhabad, 106
Ashoka, 5, 257
Ashurbanipal, 51
Ashur-uballit I, 47
Asia, 27, 33, 162
Asia Minor, 31, 40, 47, 50, 51
Askar Akayev, 112
Asorestan, 65
Assam, 5, 121
Assemblage (archaeology), 248
Association for Asian Studies, 118
Association of Southeast Asian Nations, 245, 247, 270
Assyria, 33, 39, 42, 46, 47, 49, 51, 62, 65
Assyrian Empire, 46, 56, 64
Assyrian flag, 61
Assyrian law, 40, 63
Assyrian nationalism, 77
Assyrian people, 42, 63, 65, 78
Assyriology, 40, 62
Astronomy, 41, 63
Asuka period, 15, 198
Asuka, Yamato, 203
Atatürks Reforms, 77
Ateas, 96
Aterui, 207
Atlantic Bronze Age, 45
Atomic bombings of Hiroshima and Nagasaki, 197
Attack on Pearl Harbor, 197, 228
Australia, 18, 37
Australoid race, 250, 252

Austria-Hungary, 77
Austroasiatic languages, 245, 250
Austronesian languages, 35, 245, 250
Awan dynasty, 31
Ayutthaya Kingdom, 260
Ayuwang Pagoda, 164
Azerbaijan, 40, 114
Azuchi Castle, 215
Azuchi–Momoyama period, 198

Baath Party, 82
Babur, 122
Babylon, 46
Babylonia, 39, 43, 47, 49–51, 62, 63
Babylonian astronomy, 40, 63
Babylonian captivity, 52
Babylonian law, 40, 63
Babylonian literature, 40, 62
Babylonian mathematics, 40, 63
Babylonian mythology, 40, 62
Bactria, 4, 92, 96
Bactria-Margiana Archaeological Complex, 93
Badami, 120
Baekje, 17, 203
Baghdad, 68
Bahrain, 57, 84
Bahubali, 120
Baikonur Cosmodrome, 109
Baiyue, 144
Bakufu, 208
Bakumatsu, 197
Baku-Tbilisi-Ceyhan pipeline, 113
Balance of power (international relations), 69, 77
Balfour Declaration, 78
Balkans, 56, 66, 72
Balkan Wars, 74
Balochistan, 5
Bamboo Annals, 126, 132
Ban Chao, 144
Ban Chiang, 245, 252
Banesh, 46
Banister Fletcher, 52
Banpo, 34, 130, 131
Banten, 262
Banzai charge, 229
Bao-chi, 34
Barbarian, 257
Barley, 93
Barter, 63
Bashar al-Assad, 82
Basmachi, 107
Basra, 83
Battle of Ain Jalut, 71
Battle of Bạch Đằng (938), 155
Battle of Caishi, 160

Battle of Dagu Forts (1900), 174
Battle of Dan-no-ura, 207
Battle of Dien Bien Phu, 270
Battle of Gaoliang River, 157
Battle of Guadalcanal, 228
Battle of Lake Poyang, 165
Battle of Langfang, 174
Battle of Liaoluo Bay, 169
Battle of Manzikert, 71
Battle of Maysalun, 79
Battle of Midway, 228
Battle of Mingtiao, 132
Battle of Muye, 135
Battle of Nanking, 227
Battle of Okehazama, 215
Battle of Okinawa, 229
Battle of Peking (1900), 174
Battle of Saipan, 229
Battle of Sekigahara, 214, 216
Battle of Talas, 12, 100
Battle of Tangdao, 160
Battle of Tientsin, 174
Battle of Tours, 68
Battle of Tsushima, 224
Battle of Tumu Fortress, 168
Battle of Tunmen, 169
Battle of Yamen, 161
Bay of Bengal, 265
Beaker culture, 45
Bedouin, 9, 59, 66
Before present, 60
Behistun inscription, 31
Beijing, 14, 28, 161, 162, 166, 167
Beisi Pagoda, 159
Beiyang Fleet, 174
Belitung shipwreck, 261
Belur, Karnataka, 121
Bengal, 10, 120
Bengal Sultanate, 121
Benjamin Elman, 191
Bernard Lewis, 86, 271
Bezeklik Thousand Buddha Caves, 95
Bhikkhu, 151
Bianjing, 156
Bian Jingzhao, 169
Bible, 51
Biblical Hebrew, 40, 62
Bi (jade), 131
Bill Clinton, 84
Bill Richardson, 113
Bison, 30
Black pepper, 266
Black Sea, 27, 33, 51
Blade (archaeology), 30
Blue eyes, 91, 95
Bodhisattva, 156

Bolshevik, 108
Bonsai, 214
Book of Han, 196, 201
Book of Wei (魏書), 201
Borneo, 30, 245, 267
Borobudur, 247, 258, 260
Boshin War, 221
Bosnia Eyalet, 72
Bow and arrow, 101
Boxer Protocol, 174
Boxer Rebellion, 174
Brahmaputra, 121
Britains imperial century (1815–1914), 265
British Borneo, 244
British East India Company, 122
British Empire, 41, 42, 76, 80, 172
British Hong Kong, 228
British India, 105, 106, 119, 121, 268
British Iron Age, 50
British Library, 87
British Malaya, 228, 244, 267
British occupation of Manila, 266
British Raj, 23
British Residency of the Persian Gulf, 74
British rule in Burma, 228, 244, 266
Brocade, 92
Bronze, 131, 245
Bronze Age, 3, 39, 41, 42, 45, 48, 50, 58, 62, 93, 132, 251
Bronze Age Anatolia, 45
Bronze Age Britain, 45
Bronze Age Caucasus, 45
Bronze Age China, 34
Bronze Age collapse, 39, 43, 49, 50, 62
Bronze Age Europe, 45
Bronze Age India, 45
Bronze Age Levant, 45
Bronze Age literature, 45
Bronze Age Mesopotamia, 45
Bronze Age sword, 45
Bronze Age writing, 45
Brunei, 37, 245, 270
Buddhism, 4, 11, 147, 148, 203, 205, 262
Buddhism in Japan, 196
Buddhism in Southeast Asia, 244
Buddhist, 120
Buddhist art, 258
Buddhist monk, 95
Buffer state, 106
Bukhara, 100, 106
Bukharan Jews, 114
Bulgaria, 51, 74
Buni culture, 253, 254
Bunraku, 218
Burakumin, 237
Bureaucracy, 128

Burma, 37, 121, 245, 267
Burma Campaign, 269
Burning of books and burying of scholars, 139
Burton Stein, 119
Bushido, 16
Byōdō-in, 208
Byzantine Empire, 9, 43, 56, 65, 66, 68, 71
Byzantine–Sasanian War of 602–628, 9, 68

Cabinet of Japan, 230
Cai Lun, 145
Cairo, 79
Caliph, 9, 68
Caliphate, 9, 68, 77, 100
Calligraphy, 140
Cambodia, 37, 245, 249, 270
Cambodian–Vietnamese War, 270
Cambodian Genocide, 270
Cambridge University Press, 117, 241
Canaan, 31, 45–47
Canegrate culture, 45
Cannibalism, 22
Cao Cao, 146
Cao Wei, 125, 145, 146
Capitalism, 74
Capture of Malacca (1511), 266
Carchemish, 48, 51
Career with the East India Company, 265
Carian language, 31
Carthage, 43
Caspian Sea, 27, 33, 113, 144
Catacomb culture, 45
Cataphract, 158
Category:Bronze Age, 45
Category:History of Southeast Asia, 243
Category:Japan, 195
Caucasian race, 95
Caucasus, 27, 29, 33, 47, 50, 51, 58
Caucasus Mountains, 1, 27, 33, 51
Cavalry, 98, 157
Cavite Mutiny, 267
C:Category:Dahuting Tomb murals, 141
Celibacy, 235
Cemetery H culture, 45
Cenozoic, 60
Cenozoic Era, 60
Centaur, 91
CENTO, 24
Central Asia, 7, 33, 36, 51, 90, 122, 165
Central Asian Revolt, 107
Central Asian Survey, 191
Central Committee of the Communist Party of China, 25
Central Europe, 50
Central Intelligence Agency, 84
Centralized government, 4, 41, 63

Ceramic Mesolithic, 92
Cereal, 61
Ceyhan River, 48
Chabi, 14
Chagatai Khanate, 102
Chalcolithic, 3, 42, 45, 92
Chalukya dynasty, 10
Champa, 244, 255, 256, 262
Chandragupta Maurya, 5
Changan, 100, 149, 150, 153, 205
Changqing District, 139
Changsha, 141
Changshan, 172
Chanyu, 95
Chanyuan Treaty, 157
Chao (currency), 163
Chaoyang, Liaoning, 159
Chariot, 45, 92, 93
Charles Higham (archaeologist), 249, 252
Chemistry, 70
Chen Dynasty, 8, 148, 149
Chengdu, 158
Chenla, 256
Cheras, 5
Chiang Kai-shek, 25, 177, 227
Chiba clan, 208
Chikamatsu Monzaemon, 218
Chimkent, 105
China, 1, 31, 90, 145, 179, 249, 268
China proper, 134, 142, 155, 156, 162
China Seas, 158
Chinese Bronze Age, 33
Chinese bronze inscriptions, 31
Chinese bronzes, 135
Chinese characters, 132, 142, 172
Chinese Civil War, 108, 129, 178
Chinese domination of Vietnam, 155
Chinese dragon, 143
Chinese dynasty, 162
Chinese economic reform, 180
Chinese historiography, 50, 126
Chinese History: A New Manual, 192
Chinese language, 5, 6
Chinese literature, 128
Chinese mythology, 132
Chinese philosophy, 128
Chinese Soviet Republic, 177
Chokusenshū, 210
Chola dynasty, 260
Chola Empire, 120, 121
Chola navy, 10
Cholas, 5, 10
Chong Shen Monastery, 153
Chongzhen Emperor, 22, 171
Chopper (archaeology), 28
Chōshū Domain, 220

Cho-yun Hsu, 182
Christianity, 264
Christianity in Asia, 244
Christianity in the Middle East, 60
Christmas Island, 245
Chronology of the ancient Near East, 39, 62
Chu–Han Contention, 142
Church bell, 76
Church of the East, 65
Church service, 76
Chu River, 107
Cilicia, 48
Cinema of Japan, 234
Cirebon, 262
Cishan culture, 2, 34
CITEREF2010, 290
CITEREFBagley1999, 278
CITEREFBowman2000, 277
CITEREFDennell2007, 278
CITEREFDennell2010, 277, 278, 290
CITEREFEbrey1999, 282
CITEREFGao2009, 289
CITEREFGuzman1985, 279
CITEREFHenshall2012, 289
CITEREFHourani2013, 279
CITEREFKeightley1999, 278
CITEREFKiang1999, 282
CITEREFKrishnamurti2003, 278
CITEREFLewis1995, 280
CITEREFMansfieldPelham2013, 280
CITEREFMorwood2003, 290
CITEREFMorwoodOSullivanSusan-
    toAziz2003, 278
CITEREFNeary2003, 290
CITEREFNeary2009, 289
CITEREFPollock2003, 278
CITEREFQuataert2000, 279
CITEREFRightmireLordkipanidze2010, 277,
    278
CITEREFSchirokauer2013, 284
CITEREFStearns2011, 277
CITEREFStearnsAdasSchwartzGilbert2011,
    277, 279
CITEREFSwisher1994, 290
CITEREFSwisherCurtisJacobGetty1994, 278
CITEREFTchernov1987, 278
CITEREFUgaiYagiWakai2012, 289
CITEREFWakita1991, 289
CITEREFWawro2008, 279
CITEREFWoods2010, 278
Cities of the ancient Near East, 63
City state, 59
City-state, 96
Civilization, 40, 46, 63, 128
Civil war, 162

Classical antiquity, 33, 43, 44, 50, 51, 55, 64, 89, 248
Cloistered rule, 206
Cloud Platform at Juyong Pass, 161
Cocos (Keeling) Islands, 245
Coin, 158
Cold War, 24, 57, 58, 81, 234, 244, 246, 269
Collectivisation, 178
Colonialism, 246
Colony, 64
Columbia University Press, 26, 239
Commandery (China), 138
Committee of Union and Progress, 75
Common Era, 8, 34
Commons:Category:Bronze Age, 45
Commons:Category:History of China, 192
Commons:Category:History of the Middle East, 87
Commonwealth of the Philippines, 228
Communism, 82, 269
Communist insurgency in Malaysia (1968–89), 244
Communist insurgency in Sarawak, 244
Communist insurgency in Thailand, 244
Communist party, 76
Communist Party of China, 177, 178
Communist Party of Indonesia, 270
Communist Party of the Soviet Union, 91
Company rule in India, 265
Compass, 158
Composite bow, 101
Comprador, 22
Confucian, 203
Confucianism, 6, 137, 142, 147
Confucius, 6, 137
Conquest dynasty, 162, 163, 171
Conquest of Kucha, 99
Conquest of the Western Turks, 99
Conrad Totman, 241
Consort clan, 144, 145
Constantinople, 65, 74
Constitutional monarchy, 197
Constitution of Japan, 197, 230
Constitution of the Peoples Republic of China, 180
Contemporary history, 44, 56, 89, 248
Continent, 27
Control of fire by early humans, 34
Copper Age, 42
Cotton, 107
Covert operations, 84
Cowry, 256
CPP–NPA–NDF rebellion, 244
Cradle of civilization, 40, 55, 62, 63, 128
Cradles of civilization, 41
Crimean War, 41

Cronyism, 84
Crossbow, 144
Crude oil, 77
Crusades, 69
Crystal, 137
Cultural assimilation, 129
Cultural Muslim, 262
Cultural Revolution, 109, 178
Culture of ancient Rome, 65
Culture of China, 128
Culture of Japan, 195, 196
Cuneiform, 31
Cuneiform law, 40, 63
Cuneiform script, 40, 45, 62
Currency, 63
Cycladic civilization, 45
Cypriot intercommunal violence, 82
Cyprus, 40, 49, 76, 80
Cyprus Convention, 76
Cyprus dispute, 82
Cyrillic, 108
Cyrus the Great, 4, 51

Dadiwan culture, 130
Dagestan, 51
Daimyō, 196, 198, 211
Daisenryō Kofun, 201

Đại Việt, 244

Dalian, 227
Dali Town, 153
Damaidi, 130
Damascus, 78
Danube, 72
Dao County, 130
Daoguang Emperor, 23
Darius I, 4
Dark Age, 49
Dark Ages in history, 49
Dark ages of Cambodia, 258
Date Masamune, 212
Dean Acheson, 233
Dean Peter Krogh Foreign Affairs Digital Archives, 87
Death, 244
Death toll, 153
Deccan Plateau, 121
Decimal multiplication table, 138
Decolonisation, 269
De facto, 129
Definition by South Asian Studies programs, 36
Deir ez-Zor, 48
Dejima, 218
Delhi, 121
Delhi Sultanate, 120, 121

Delia Davin, 189
Demak, Demak, 262
Demak Sultanate, 262
Dengfeng Observatory, 163
Deng Xiaoping, 180
Desinicization, 98
Destruction of opium at Humen, 23
Devagiri, 121
Devaraja, 255
Dharmasraya, 260
Diadem, 91
Di (Five Barbarians), 147
Dinghai, 160
Ding (vessel), 133
Disputed statement, 47, 84
Dissolution of the Soviet Union, 83
Divination, 52
Divinity, 52
Division of labor, 63
Division of the Mongol Empire, 161, 162
Djemal Pasha, 75
Dmanisi, 27, 29
DNA, 30, 277
DNA marker, 30
Dnieper, 96
Dnieper-Donets culture, 92
Dodecanese, 56, 74
Dolmen, 36
Domestication of the horse, 92, 97, 152
Donald Keene, 210, 239
Donald Rumsfeld, 84
Donghak Rebellion, 223
Dong Son culture, 245, 252

Đông Sơn culture, 251

Dong Son drum, 253
Dōtaku, 200
Double-cropping, 210
Douglas MacArthur, 230
Drainage basin, 114
Dromedary, 104
Druze, 60
Du Fu, 152
Dujiangyan, 139
Duke of Zhou, 135
Dungan revolt (1862–1877), 109, 174
Dunhuang, 99, 141
Dunhuang map, 150
Dutch East India Company, 35
Dutch East India Company (17th – 18th century), 264
Dutch East Indies, 228, 244
Dutch expedition on the west coast of Sumatra, 266
Dutch Formosa, 169

Dvaravati, 260
Dynasties in Chinese history, 34, 126, 127, 129, 167
Dzungar people, 107
Dzungars, 104

Earlier Nine Years War, 211
Early Bronze Age, 42, 45, 46
Early Bronze Age I, 42
Early Bronze Age II, 42
Early Bronze Age III, 42
Early Bronze Age IV, 42
Early Chalcolithic, 42
Early Dynastic Period of Egypt, 42
Early Dynastic Period of Sumer, 42
Early historical era, 44, 55, 89, 248
Early history of Burma, 32, 37
Early history of Cambodia, 32, 37
Early history of Kedah, 256
Early human migrations, 60
Early Iron Age, 49, 50
Early modern period, 44, 56, 89, 119, 246, 248
Early Muslim conquests, 263
East Asia, 1, 27, 33, 45, 50, 162
East Asian Bronze Age, 32
East Asia Summit, 270
East China Sea, 160
Eastern Anatolia Region, 40
Eastern Chalukya, 10
Eastern Chalukyas, 120
Eastern Ganga dynasty, 10, 121
Eastern Han, 125
Eastern Han dynasty, 141, 144
Eastern Hemisphere, 257
Eastern Iranian people, 95
Eastern Jin Dynasty, 147
Eastern Mediterranean, 56, 65
Eastern Wei, 148
Eastern world, 8, 18
Eastern Wu, 125, 146
Eastern Zhou, 125
East Godavari district, 36
East India Company, 265
East Indies, 266
East Malaysia, 245, 249
East Timor, 37, 245, 270
East Turkestan, 104
Ebla, 64
Eblaite language, 31
Ebla tablets, 31
Ecbatana, 51
Economic history of China, 126
Economic system, 61
Economy of Japan, 197
Economy of the Song dynasty, 158
Edessa, 65

Edict of Milan, 60
Edicts of Ashoka, 32
Edirne, 75
Edmund Roberts (diplomat), 266
Edo, 197, 217
Edogawa Ranpo, 225
Edo Neo-Confucianism, 236
Edo period, 197, 198, 214, 219
Edward S. Morse, 199
Egypt, 10, 39, 49–51, 58, 62, 66, 81
Egyptian Middle Kingdom, 43
Egyptian mythology, 40, 62
Egyptian Revolution of 1919, 78
Egypt (Roman province), 65
Eight Banners, 22, 172, 174
Eighteen Songs of a Nomad Flute, 160
Eight-Nation Alliance, 174
Elam, 3, 39, 40, 45, 46, 62
Elamite Cuneiform, 46
Elamite language, 31, 40, 46, 62
Elamites, 46
Ellora, 120
Eminent Chinese of the Ching Period, 186
Emirate of Bukhara, 106
Emirate of Nejd and Hasa, 74
Emirate of Sicily, 69
Emirate of Transjordan, 78
Emishi, 207
Emperor Antoku, 207
Emperor Gaozong of Tang, 99
Emperor Gaozu of Han, 142
Emperor Gaozu of Tang, 12, 150
Emperor Go-Daigo, 210
Emperor Go-Shirakawa, 207, 210
Emperor Go-Toba, 209, 211
Emperor Go-Yōzei, 217
Emperor Guangwu of Han, 144
Emperor Horikawa, 206
Emperor Jing of Han, 143
Emperor Juntoku, 209
Emperor Kanmu, 16
Emperor Kōmyō, 211
Emperor Meiji, 221
Emperor Ming of Han, 144
Emperor of China, 128, 150, 161
Emperor of Japan, 196, 198, 221
Emperor Shirakawa, 206
Emperor Shōmu, 205
Emperor Sutoku, 207
Emperor Taishō, 225
Emperor Taizong of Song, 157
Emperor Taizong of Tang, 150
Emperor Taizongs campaign against Tuyuhun, 99
Emperor Taizongs campaign against Xueyantuo, 99

Emperor Taizu of Song, 155, 156
Emperor Tenji, 205
Emperor Tsuchimikado, 209
Emperor Wen of Han, 143
Emperor Wen of Sui, 12, 149
Emperor Wu of Han, 7, 143, 144
Emperor Xuanzong of Tang, 13, 152
Emperor Yang of Sui, 12
Emperor Yuan of Jin, 147
Emperor Zhang of Han, 144
Empire, 121
Empire of Harsha, 120
Empire of Japan, 197, 198, 244, 268
Empires, 41
Empress Dowager Cixi, 174
Empress regnant, 152
Empress Suiko, 284
En:Bibcode, 183
En:Digital object identifier, 38, 116, 117, 183, 271, 275
End of World War II in Asia, 244
End time, 4
Endymion Wilkinson, 192
Energy security, 114
Enheduanna, 63
En:JSTOR, 240
En:PubMed Central, 275
Entrepot, 259
Enver Pasha, 75, 77
Eocene, 60
Equal-field system, 149, 152, 205
Eridu, 46
Erligang culture, 45, 133
Erlitou culture, 45, 131, 132
Ernst Herzfeld, 53
Esen Tayisi, 168
Ethnic Malay, 262
Ethnic religion, 60
Ethnoreligious, 60
Euclid, 70
Eucratides I, 94
Eunuch, 19
Eunuchs, 153
Euphrates, 46–48, 56, 59, 66
Eurasia, 27, 90
Eurasian Plate, 60
Europe, 33, 51, 90
European colonisation of Southeast Asia, 244
European ethnic groups, 264
Excavations, 53

Faber and Faber, 85
Failed state, 129
Faisal I of Iraq, 78
Fall of France, 268
Fall of the Soviet Union, 58

Fall of the Western Roman Empire, 65
Fara period, 31
Faravahar, 61
Far East, 41
Fars Province, 40
Fasting, 70
Fatalism, 263
Fatimid caliph, 70
February 26 Incident, 227
Federation of Malaya, 270
Federation of Malaysia, 270
Fenghuang, 143
Fenghuang County, 165
Fergana Valley, 93
Fernão Mendes Pinto, 214
Ferrous metallurgy, 131
Fertile Crescent, 39, 59, 62, 64, 67
Feudalism, 5, 135
File:BezeklikSogdianMerchants.jpg, 95
Final stages, 144
Firearm, 90, 160
First Anglo-Burmese War, 244, 266
First Balkan War, 75
First Bulgarian Empire, 68
First Constitutional Era, 75
First Crusade, 9, 71
First East Turkestan Republic, 108
First Intermediate Period of Egypt, 42
First Opium War, 23, 172
First Philippine Republic, 267
First Sino-Japanese War, 42, 174, 223
First Sumatran expedition, 266
First World War, 107
Fishing, 61
Five Barbarians, 90, 147
Five Dynasties and Ten Kingdoms period, 13, 126, 153, 155
Five kings of Wa, 202
Five Pillars of Islam, 70
Five-year plans of the Peoples Republic of China, 178
Flores, 37
Foot binding, 13
Forbidden City, 22, 168
Foreign government advisors in Meiji Japan, 222
Former Nine Years War, 207
Formosa, 282
Fortifications of Xian, 165
Fort St George, 20
Fossils, 199
Four Classes, 197
Four Garrisons of Anxi, 99
Four Heavenly Kings, 161
Four occupations, 236
Fourth Chinese domination of Vietnam, 168

France, 265, 267, 269
Francis Light, 265
Francis Xavier, 214
Franco-Thai War, 268
Franks, 68
Freedom and Accord Party, 75
Freedom and Peoples Rights Movement, 222
French Indochina, 23, 244, 282
Friendship (1830s), 266
Fubing, 98
Fubing system, 149, 152
Fujian, 169
Fujiwara clan, 16, 205
Fujiwara no Hidehira, 209
Fujiwara no Kamatari, 205
Fujiwara no Kiyohira, 207
Fujiwara no Michinaga, 206
Fujiwara no Mototsune, 205
Fujiwara no Shunzei, 210
Fujiwara no Teika, 210
Fujiwara no Yasuhira, 209
Fujiwara no Yoshifusa, 205
Fukushima Daiichi nuclear disaster, 197, 235
Fukuzawa Yukichi, 222
Full translation of the Behistun Inscription, 279
Funan (Southeast Asia), 245, 251
Futabatei Shimei, 222
Future, 44, 56, 89, 248
Futures studies, 44, 56, 89, 248
Fuyan Cave, 130

Gajapati Kingdom, 121
Galen, 70
Gallipoli Campaign, 77
Gamal Abdel Nasser, 81
Gang of Four, 180
Ganjin, 205
Gansu, 34, 100, 157
Gansu province, 148
Gaocheng District, 131
Gas, 114
Gaselee Expedition, 174
Gaston Maspero, 278
Gaussian elimination, 142
Gaza City, 49
Gaza Strip, 85
Geisha, 218
General judgment, 4
Genetic history of Europe, 92
Genghis Khan, 10, 102, 161
Genpei War, 17, 196, 207
Geoffrey Wawro, 86
Geography, 35
Geography of Asia, 90
Geology, 35
George Bailey Sansom, 240

George Coedès, 255
George Cœdès, 272
George H. W. Bush, 83
George Town, Penang, 265
George W. Bush, 84
Georgia (country), 27, 29, 33, 40
Geostrategy, 254
Gerzeh, 42
Gezer calendar, 31
Ghassanids, 67
Ghassulian, 42
Giant Wild Goose Pagoda, 153
Gilding, 92, 97, 152
Giraffe, 28
Glossary of Japanese history, 195
Gnosticism, 60
Goa, 23
Göbekli Tepe, 44
Gobi Desert, 1, 129
Goguryeo, 17
Goguryeo–Sui War, 149
Gojoseon, 45
Gokenin, 209
Göktürk, 95, 97, 99
Golasecca culture, 45
Golden Chersonese, 247
Golden Era (1946–1982), 83
Golden Sun Bird, 133
Governor-General, 106
Grand Canal (China), 149, 151, 162
Grand Secretariat, 167
Greater East Asia Co-Prosperity Sphere, 227
Great Game, 23
Great Karnak Inscription, 49
Great Leap Forward, 109, 178
Great power, 197
Great Wall of China, 140, 149, 155, 170
Great Wall of Qi, 139
Greco-Bactrian Kingdom, 91, 94, 96
Greco-Buddhism, 96
Greco-Persian Wars, 52
Greece, 4, 51, 72, 74
Greek city states, 52
Greek culture, 65
Greek Cypriots, 82
Greek Dark Ages, 43
Greek historiography, 50
Greek language, 60
Greek mythology, 91
Greenwood Press, 240
Gregorian calendar, 222
Gross national product, 233
Guangdong, 138, 169
Guangdong Provincial Museum, 169
Guang (vessel), 133
Guangxi, 138

Guangxu Emperor, 174
Guangzhou, 19, 151, 153
Guangzhou massacre, 153
Gu Hongzhong, 155
Gujarat, 121, 261
Gulf of İskenderun, 48
Gulf War, 83
Gun, 2
Gunki monogatari, 211
Gunpowder, 2, 103, 156, 160
Gupta Empire, 5, 120
Guzel Maitdinova, 115
Gyōki, 205
Gyokuon-hōsō, 230

Hadhramaut, 74
Hafez al-Assad, 82
Haijin, 169
Haiku, 218
Hajj, 70
Halebidu, 121
Hallstatt culture, 45
Hamadan, 51
Hamidian Massacres, 42, 75
Hammurabi, 48
Hampi, 121
Han campaign against Dian, 144
Han campaigns against Minyue, 144
Han Chinese, 109, 129, 139, 142, 153, 155, 163
Han Dynasty, 7, 96, 125, 128, 142, 257
Han–Nanyue War, 144
Han–Xiongnu War, 95, 143
Hanfu, 141, 145, 172
Hanging Monastery, 147
Hangzhou, 137, 158, 161, 163
Haniwa, 201
Hans Hildebrand, 36
Han Xizai, 155
Haplogroup F-M89, 61
Haplogroup IJ, 61
Haplogroup J1, 60
Haplogroup J2, 60
Haplogroup J-P209, 60
Harappa, 3
Harran, 51
Harris Treaty of 1856 with Siam, 267
Harsha, 10, 120
Haruo Satō (novelist), 225
Harvard University Asia Center, 238
Hatakeyama clan, 208
Hattusa, 31
Hattusas, 49
Hattusili I, 31, 47
Hayasa-Azzi, 43
Heaven, 4, 52

Hebei, 2, 34, 95, 131
Hebrew, 61
Hebrew language, 31
Hegemony, 136
Heian-kyō, 16, 196, 205, 206
Heian period, 16, 196, 198, 205
Heiji Monogatari, 211
Heiji Rebellion, 207
Heijō-kyō, 205
Heisei period, 199
Hejaz, 9, 59, 70
Hejaz Vilayet, 74
Hekla 3 eruption, 43
Hell, 4
Hellenistic art, 91
Hellenistic civilization, 91, 96
Hellenistic period, 4, 43
Hellenization, 66
Hemudu culture, 130
Henan, 34, 131, 133, 141
Hephthalite Empire, 96
Hephthalites, 102
Heraclius, 66
Herbert P. Bix, 238
Herbivore men, 235
Heresy, 65
Herodotus, 95
Hezbollah, 85
Hideki Tojo, 228
Hideyo Noguchi, 222
High Commissioner, 76
High Middle Ages, 163
High Treason Incident, 225
Himachal Pradesh, 121
Himalayas, 1, 5, 36
Himiko, 201
Himyarite Kingdom, 66
Hindu, 121, 246
Hindu-Arabic numeral system, 70
Hinduism, 3, 4, 70, 261, 262
Hinduism in Southeast Asia, 244
Hindu Kush, 36
Hippocrates, 70
Hira, 67
Hiraizumi, 207
Hirata Atsutane, 219
Hirohito, 197, 226, 234
Hiroshima, 229
Historical capitals of China, 162
Historiography, 50
Historiography of early Islam, 119
History, 265
History of Anatolia, 64
History of anatomy, 9, 70
History of Asia, **1**
History of astronomy, 9, 70

History of Central Asia, **89**
History of China, 119, 125, **125**
History of Chinese art, 126
History of East Asia, 44, 55, 89, 248
History of education in China, 126
History of Egypt, 65
History of elementary algebra, 9, 70
History of ethics, 9, 70
History of geometry, 9, 70
History of Germans in Russia, Ukraine and the Soviet Union, 110
History of gunpowder, 156
History of Hong Kong (1800s–1930s), 172
History of independent Mongolia, 113
History of Iran, 9, 40, 66
History of Islam, 261
History of Japan, 195, **195**
History of Manila, 260
History of medicine, 9, 70
History of Oceania, 44, 55, 89, 248
History of Roman Catholicism in Japan, 214
History of science and technology in China, 126
History of silk, 100
History of Southeast Asia, 243, **243**
History of Thailand, 267
History of the Hittites, 47
History of the Jews in Central Asia, 114
History of the Middle East, 40, **55**, 63
History of the Peoples Republic of China, 126
History of the Philippines (1521–1898), 264, 267
History of the world, 44, 55, 89, 247
History of writing, 44, 55, 63, 89, 248
Hittite Empire, 47–49, 51
Hittite language, 31, 40, 62
Hittite Middle Kingdom, 43
Hittite mythology, 40, 62
Hittite New Kingdom, 43
Hittite Old Kingdom, 43
Hittites, 39, 47–49, 62
Hittite texts, 40, 62
Hoabinhian, 245, 249
Hōgen Monogatari, 211
Hōgen Rebellion, 207
Hōjō clan, 208, 209
Hōjō Masako, 209
Hōjō Tokimasa, 209
Hokkaido, 223
Holy Land, 69, 71
Holy Roman Empire, 9, 71
Homo, 28
Homo erectus, 27, 28, 60, 129, 248
Homo erectus georgicus, 27, 29
Homo ergaster, 27
Homo floresiensis, 37, 248

Homo heidelbergensis, 28
Homo sapiens, 27, 30, 92
Hōnen, 210
Hồng Bàng dynasty, 251
Hongcun, 165
Hong Kong, 23
Hong Taiji, 169
Hongwu Emperor, 18, 165–167
Hong Xiuquan, 172
Honourable East India Company, 265
Honshu, 16, 199
Horn of Africa, 59
House of Peers (Japan), 222
House of Representatives (Japan), 222
House of the Huangcheng Chancellor, 171
Hoysala Empire, 121
Hua Guofeng, 180
Huai River, 158, 160
Huang Chao Rebellion, 153
Huang-Lao, 143
Hui people, 262
Hu Jintao, 181
Humanity Declaration, 230
Human sacrifice, 6
Human Y-chromosome DNA haplogroup, 60
Hunan, 130
Hundred Days Reform, 174
Hundred Schools of Thought, 137, 143
Hungary, 72
Huns, 5, 90, 102
Hunter-gatherer, 61, 199
Hurrian, 47, 48
Hurrian language, 31, 40, 62
Hurrians, 39, 48, 62
Hussein bin Ali, Sharif of Mecca, 77
Hu Yaobang, 180
Hyakunin Isshu, 210
Hyperinflation, 163

Ibn Saud, 78
Ichiyō Higuchi, 222
Idolatry, 66
Iemitsu, 218
Ikebana, 214
Ilam Province, 46
Ili River, 107
Ilkhanate, 71
Imagawa Yoshimoto, 215
Imperial China, 50
Imperial Chinese tributary system, 151, 157, 169, 257, 264
Imperial Commissioner (China), 23
Imperial examination, 140, 149, 151
Imperial House of Japan, 15, 196, 205
Imperial Japan, 24
Imperial Japanese Army, 223

Imperial Rule Assistance Association, 227
Incendiary device, 160
India, 1, 2, 7, 32, 37, 151, 246, 261
Indian Independence Act 1947, 121
Indianised kingdoms, 243
Indian Ocean, 19, 27, 36, 158, 246, 260, 263
Indian Ocean trade, 254
Indian Plate, 36
Indian subcontinent, 36, 119, 122
Indo-Aryans, 48
Indo-Aryan superstrate in Mitanni, 48
Indochina, 37, 245, 260, 262, 267, 269, 270
Indochina War, 269
Indochina Wars, 244
Indo-European languages, 48, 92
Indo-Greek Kingdom, 96
Indo-Iranian languages, 93
Indo-Iranians, 93
Indonesia, 37, 245, 265, 269, 270
Indonesia–Malaysia confrontation, 244
Indonesian invasion of East Timor, 270
Indonesian mass killings of 1965–1966, 244, 270
Indonesian National Revolution, 244, 269
Indonesian occupation of East Timor, 270
Indus River, 4
Industrialisation, 91
Industrial revolution, 74
Indus Valley Civilization, 3, 45
In Japan, 234
Ink wash painting, 214
Inner Mongolia, 98, 104
Insular Government of the Philippine Islands, 244
Insular Southeast Asia, 245
Insurance, 158
International military intervention against ISIL, 85
International Military Tribunal of the Far East, 230
International Standard Book Number, 26, 37, 38, 52, 85, 86, 115–118, 122–124, 181, 183–192, 237–241, 271–275
In the United Kingdom, 265
Invasion of French Indochina, 228
Invasion of Ryukyu, 217
Iran, 9, 31, 40, 46, 50, 66, 114
Iran–Iraq War, 82
Iranian Peoples, 46, 51
Iranian plateau, 46, 51
Iranian religions, 60
Iranian Revolution, 58, 81
Iraq, 9, 31, 40, 48, 50, 51, 63, 66, 78, 81
Iraqi Civil War (2014–present), 85
Iraqi revolt against the British, 79
Iron Age, 39, 41, 43, 45, 50, 58, 62, 243

Iron Age Anatolia, 50
Iron Age Caucasus, 50
Iron Age Europe, 50
Iron Age I A, 43
Iron Age I B, 43
Iron Age II, 43
Iron Age II A, 43
Iron Age II B, 43
Iron Age II C, 43
Iron Age in South Asia, 50
Iron Age Levant, 50
Iron Age metallurgy, 50
Iron Age Scandinavia, 50
Iron Age Southeastern Europe, 50
Iron metallurgy in Africa, 50
Irrawaddy river, 251
Irrigation, 3, 22, 59
Ise Heishi, 208
Ishuwa, 47
Isin, 46
Islam, 9, 68
Islamic fundamentalism, 81
Islamic Golden Age, 9
Islamic revival, 58
Islamic scholars, 75
Islamic State of Iraq and the Levant, 58, 85
Islamic terrorism, 81
Islam in Southeast Asia, 244, 262
Islamism, 58, 84, 262
Islamist, 114
Island country, 197
Ismailism, 60
Israel, 40, 49, 51, 57, 114
Israeli Declaration of Independence, 80
Israelite, 61
Israelites, 52
Israeli West Bank barrier, 85
Isshi Incident, 205
Isthmus of Kra, 256
Itagaki Taisuke, 222
Itō Hirobumi, 222
Ivory, 256

Jabal Shammar, 74
Jack Sasson, 52
Jacques Gernet, 117
Jadid, 107
Jadunath Sarkar, 123
Jagannath Temple, Puri, 121
Jakarta, 264, 271
Japan, 196
Japan Communist Party, 231
Japan during World War I, 225
Japanese aircraft carrier Shōkaku, 229
Japanese archipelago, 196, 197, 199
Japanese asset price bubble, 234

Japanese battleship Yamato, 229
Japanese coup de main in French Indochina, 268
Japanese creation myth, 205
Japanese cuisine, 196
Japanese Empire, 224
Japanese festivals, 196
Japanese garden, 214
Japanese history textbook controversies, 235
Japanese Imperial Army, 268
Japanese invasion of French Indochina, 268
Japanese invasion of Manchuria, 197
Japanese invasions of Korea (1592–98), 169, 216
Japanese language, 199
Japanese nationalism, 222
Japanese occupation of Cambodia, 269
Japanese occupation of Malaya, 269
Japanese occupation of the Dutch East Indies, 269
Japanese Paleolithic, 35, 196, 198
Japanese people, 195
Japanese popular culture, 235
Japanese post-war economic miracle, 24, 197
Japanese war crimes, 177
Japan–Korea Treaty of 1905, 224
Japan–Korea Treaty of 1910, 224
Japan–Netherlands relations, 197
Japan Self-Defense Forces, 234
Java, 28, 37, 247, 249, 258, 260, 263
Java (island), 260, 264
Java Man, 28, 248
Ja:将門記, 211
Ja:陸奥話記, 211
Jayaatu Khan Tugh Temür, 163
Jerry Norman (sinologist), 281
Jerusalem, 9, 71
Jesuit, 21, 214
Jesuit China missions, 21
Jewish exodus from Arab and Muslim countries, 80
Jewish state, 79
Jiahu, 130
Jiahu symbols, 131, 132
Jiajing Emperor, 169
Jiajing wokou raids, 169
Jiangsu Province, 159
Jiang Zemin, 181
Jiankang, 148
Jiaozi (currency), 158
Jiedushi, 153
Jie people, 147
Jimmy Carter, 81
Jinan, 139
Jin dynasty (1115–1234), 13, 126, 157, 158, 160, 162

Jin dynasty (265–420), 8, 125, 126, 146
Jin–Song Wars, 13, 158
Jingkang Incident, 158
Jin Ping Mei, 19
Jinshin War, 205
Ji (polearm), 135
Jiroft civilization, 45
Jitō, 209
Jizzakh, 106
Johan Nieuhof, 166
John Esposito, 85
John Keay, 120, 122
John K. Fairbank, 182
John Whitney Hall, 241
Jokhang, 100
Jōkyū War, 209
Jōmon, 35
Jōmon people, 201
Jōmon period, 45, 196, 198, 200
Jōmon pottery, 199
Jordan, 40, 51
Jordan River, 79
Jordan River Valley, 35
Joseon dynasty, 169
Joseph Dodge, 232
Joseph Stalin, 109
Joshua A. Fogel, 188
Journey to the West, 19
Jue (vessel), 131
Junichirō Tanizaki, 225
Junk (ship), 19, 23, 160
Jurchen campaigns against the Song dynasty, 158
Jurchen people, 13, 158, 169, 171

Kabuki, 218
Kadesh (Syria), 47
Kafū Nagai, 211
Kaidu–Kublai war, 162
Kaifeng, 127, 156–158
Kaiyuan Temple (Quanzhou), 154
Kakatiya dynasty, 121
Kalachuris of Tripuri, 120
Kalinga (historical region), 121
Kalingga, 256
Kamakura, 196, 208
Kamakura, Kanagawa, 17
Kamakura period, 17, 198
Kamakura shogunate, 17, 196, 198
Kami, 205
Kamianka-Dniprovska, 96
Kamikaze, 229
Kamikaze (typhoon), 210
Kamo no Mabuchi, 211
Kampaku, 205
Kana, 207

Kanbun, 211
Kangxi Dictionary, 172
Kangxi Emperor, 22, 172
Kanhadade Prabandha, 124
Kannada, 120
Kannadiga, 121
Kannauj, 10
Kanshi (poetry), 211
Kantoli, 260
Kantō region, 208
Karakorum, 71
Karakum Desert, 1
Karasahr, 99
Karnataka, 120, 121
Kashgar, 107
Kassites, 47
Katana, 16
Katsura Tarō, 225
Kazakh Autonomous Soviet Socialist Republic, 108
Kazakhstan, 33, 91
Kebaran culture, 44
Kediri Kingdom, 260
Kegare, 237
Kenesary Kasimov, 105
Kenmu Restoration, 198, 211
Khabur (Tigris), 47
Khagan, 71, 99, 162
Khalid ibn al-Walid, 9, 68
Khamag Mongol, 162
Khanate of Bukhara, 103
Khanate of Khiva, 103, 106
Khanate of Kokand, 103, 104, 106
Khanates, 105
Khanbaliq, 14, 162, 165
Khan (title), 102
Khitan people, 13, 156
Khitans, 98
Khiva, 105
Khmer Empire, 244, 258–260
Khmer people, 245
Khmer Rouge, 270
Khosrau II, 67
Khujand, 106
Khuzestan, 46, 82
Khvalynskoye gas field, 114
Khwarezmid Empire, 102
Kido Takayoshi, 221
Kinai, 202, 203
Kingdom of Aksum, 66
Kingdom of Ammon, 64
Kingdom of Edom, 64
Kingdom of Egypt, 79
Kingdom of Funan, 256
Kingdom of Iraq, 78
Kingdom of Israel (Samaria), 43, 64

Kingdom of Israel (united monarchy), 43, 47
Kingdom of Jerusalem, 9, 71
Kingdom of Judah, 43, 64
Kingdom of Moab, 64
Kingdom of Mysore, 122
Kingdom of Pergamon, 43
Kingdom of Qocho, 95
Kingdom of Tungning, 172
Kingdom (politics), 51
King of Iraq, 78
King Wu of Zhou, 135
Ki no Tsurayuki, 207, 210
Kirghiz Autonomous Socialist Soviet Republic (1920–1925), 108
Kiri-sute gomen, 219
Kitasato Shibasaburō, 222
Kizzuwatna, 48
Kodansha, 241
Kofun, 201
Kofun period, 198
Kojiki, 205
Kokand, 107
Kokinshū, 207
Kokugaku, 219
Konark Sun Temple, 121
Korea, 7, 169, 199
Korean Peninsula, 35, 149
Korean War, 24, 25, 232
Korla, 107
Koseki, 236
Koxinga, 169, 172
Krasnovodsk, 107
Kublai Khan, 14, 161, 209
Kucha, 99
Kuomintang, 177, 178
Kura-Araxes culture, 33, 48
Kurdish people, 78
Kurdistan, 48
Kurgan hypothesis, 92
Kuril Islands, 234
Kuril Islands dispute, 234
Kurmangazy field, 114
Kushan Empire, 5, 96
Kushan Kingdom, 96
Kutai, 256
Kuwait, 40, 57, 82, 84
Kwantung Army, 226
Kyoto, 196, 205
Kyrgyz Autonomous Oblast, 108
Kyrgyz people, 112
Kyrgyzstan, 33, 91
Kyushu, 199, 215

Lady-in-waiting, 16
Laguna Copperplate Inscription, 259, 260
Lake Van, 51

Lakhmids, 67
Land bridge, 199
Land of Israel, 2
Lanfang Republic, 264
Langkasuka, 256
Language and dialect, 60
Language family, 48
Language isolate, 46
Languages of Japan, 195
Lantian Man, 130
Lan Xang, 244
Laogai, 178
Laos, 37, 245, 249, 270
Laozi, 6
Lao Zi, 137
Largest naval battle in history, 165
Larsa, 46
Last Glacial Maximum, 92, 199
Late Bronze Age, 43, 49, 50
Late Bronze Age collapse, 45
Late Bronze Age I, 43
Late Bronze Age II A, 43
Late Bronze Age II B, 43
Late Chalcolithic, 42
Late Chinese Empire, 107
Late Hōjō clan, 215
Late Imperial China (journal), 191
Late modern period, 44, 56, 89, 248
Late Period of ancient Egypt, 64
Later Han (Five Dynasties), 155
Later Jin (Five Dynasties), 155, 157
Later Liang (Five Dynasties), 155
Later Tang, 155
Later Three-Year War, 207
Later Zhou, 155
Latin script, 77
Law, 41
Law code, 63
Laws for the Military Houses, 217
League of Nations, 225
League of Nations mandate, 78
Lebanese Civil War, 84
Lebanon, 2, 40, 51, 56, 66, 74, 78
Legal history of China, 126
Legalism (Chinese philosophy), 6, 137, 139
Leifeng Pagoda, 160
Levant, 35, 39, 40, 47, 49, 59, 62, 64, 66
Levantine corridor, 60
Levee, 22
Liancourt Rocks, 234
Liancourt Rocks dispute, 234
Liang dynasty, 148
Liang Shidu, 98
Liangzhu culture, 131
Liaodi Pagoda, 157
Liao dynasty, 13, 126, 155–159

Liaoning, 138
Liaoning Province, 159
Li Bai, 152
Liberal Democratic Party (Japan), 232
Liberal Party (Japan, 1945), 232
Libya, 51, 56, 57, 74, 77, 80
Libyan Civil War (2011–present), 85
Li Hongzhang, 173
Lin Biao, 25
Linguistic history of China, 126
Linheraptor, 129
Lin Liang, 168
Lin Tinggui, 160
Lin Zexu, 23
Li Song (painter), 160
List of Bronze Age sites in China, 33
List of campaigns of the Communist Party of China, 178
List of Chalcolithic cultures of China, 33
List of earthquakes in Japan, 235
List of ethnic groups in China, 162
List of largest cities throughout history, 150, 158
List of Mongol rulers, 161
List of Neolithic cultures of China, 33, 125
List of Paleolithic sites in China, 33
List of Rajput dynasties and states, 121
List of territories occupied by Imperial Japan, 244
List of tributaries of Imperial China, 169
Lithic core, 28, 36
Lithic flake, 28, 36
Liu Song dynasty, 148
Li Zicheng, 170, 171
Longman, 26
Long March, 177
Longmen Grottoes, 150
Longshan culture, 34, 131
Lop County, 91
Lord Liverpool, 76
Lost Decade (Japan), 197, 234
Lost-wax casting, 252
Lower Egypt, 64
Lower Xiajiadian culture, 131
Luoyang, 136, 144, 145, 149, 153, 256
Luwian, 48
Luwian language, 50
Lydian language, 31

Macao, 290
Macau, 19, 23, 169
Macedon, 96
Macedonian Empire, 41, 43, 65
Madagascar, 250
Madhya Pradesh, 121
Madja-as, 244

Madras, 20, 263
Maghreb, 58
Maginoo, 260
Magnetostratigraphy, 129
Maharaja, 122
Maharaja Sri-Gupta, 5
Maharashtra, 120, 122
Mahayana Buddhist, 258
Ma-i, 244
Mainland China, 129, 178
Mainland Southeast Asia, 37, 245
Maize, 19
Majapahit, 244, 260
Majiayao culture, 45, 131
Makarios III, 80
Malacca, 262, 264
Malacca sultanate, 262
Malatya, 47, 51
Malayan Emergency, 244, 270
Malay Archipelago, 266
Malayization, 262
Malay Peninsula, 247, 265
Malays (ethnic group), 257
Malaysia, 37, 249, 263, 270
Mammoth, 30
Manchu conquest of China, 22
Manchukuo, 226
Manchu people, 17, 22, 169–171
Manchuria, 34, 156, 169
Manchurian Incident, 226
Mandaeans, 60
Mandarin, 5
Mandate of Heaven, 5, 16, 128, 135, 144
Mandatory Palestine, 78
Manga, 235
Manichaeism, 96
Manila, 268
Manyōshū, 205
Mao: The Unknown Story, 189
Mao Zedong, 25, 177–179
Mapmaking, 70
Maratha Empire, 122
Marco Polo, 163, 264
Mari, Syria, 31, 48
Maritime Silk Route, 158
Maritime Southeast Asia, 37, 245, 256, 264
Maritime trade, 264
Market economy, 19
Market socialism, 180
Mark Weston, 241
Marriage alliances, 99
Mathematics, 1, 41, 63
Matsuo Bashō, 211, 218
Matteo Ricci, 21
Matthew C. Perry, 220
Maurice Meisner, 189

Maurya Empire, 5
May Fourth Movement, 176
Mecca, 67, 77
Medang, 260
Medang Kingdom, 260
Medes, 39, 40, 43, 51, 56, 62, 65, 95
Media history of China, 126
Medieval historiography, 50
Medieval history, 44, 55, 89, 248
Medieval India, **119**, 124
Medieval Near East, 44, 55, 89, 248
Medina, 67
Mediterranean, 50, 59
Mediterranean Basin, 64, 68
Mediterranean Sea, 68
Megaannum, 27
Megiddo (place), 47
Meiji Constitution, 222, 236
Meiji government, 221, 222
Meiji oligarchy, 197, 221
Meiji period, 197, 198
Meiji Restoration, 197
Mekong, 245, 251
Mekong Delta, 256
Melayu Kingdom, 260
Melid, 48
Memorial to the throne, 167
Menachem Begin, 81
Menara Kudus Mosque, 261
Mercury (element), 92, 140
Merneptah, 49
Merv, 106
Mesha Stele, 31
Mesolithic, 243
Mesopotamia, 1, 2, 31, 39, 40, 42, 45–48, 51, 56, 59, 62–64, 66
Mesopotamian mythology, 40, 62
Meteoric iron, 131
Meyers Konversations-Lexikon, 250
Miaoying Temple, 161
Michael Adas, 26
Michel Aflaq, 82
Microlith, 30
Middle Ages, 9, 44, 55, 68, 69, 89, 119, 248
Middle Assyrian Empire, 43
Middle Assyrian period, 50
Middle Bronze Age, 42
Middle Bronze Age I, 42
Middle Bronze Age II A, 43
Middle Bronze Age II B, 43
Middle Bronze Age II C, 43
Middle Class, 60
Middle East, 1, 9, 27, 35, 40, 42, 50, 55, 113, 262
Middle Elamite period, 43
Middle Indo-Aryan, 32

Middle Kingdom of Egypt, 64
Middle Kingdoms of India, 44, 50, 55, 89, 248
Mike Morwood, 38, 271
Mikhail Annenkov, 106
Mikhail Chernyayev, 106
Mikhail Skobelev, 106
Military history, 160
Military history of China (pre-1911), 126
Millet, 130, 245
Minamoto clan, 17, 196, 206
Minamoto no Sanetomo, 209, 211
Minamoto no Yoritomo, 196, 207, 208
Minamoto no Yoshitsune, 207
Minaret, 261
Ming dynasty, 126, 165–167, 169–172, 264
Ming–Hồ War, 168
Ming Great Wall, 168
Ministry of International Trade and Industry, 233
Minoan civilization, 43, 45
Minoan eruption, 43
Mitanni, 43, 47, 48
Mitsubishi, 224
Moabite language, 31
Modern history, 44, 55, 89, 248
Modern history of Cyprus, 82
Modernity, 44, 56, 89, 248
Modun Chanyu, 95
Mogao Caves, 148
Moghulistan, 168
Mohenjo-daro, 3
Mohism, 137
Mojokerto, 37
Momoyama Castle, 215
Möngke Khan, 71
Mongol conquest, 158
Mongol conquest of the Jin dynasty, 158
Mongol conquest of the Song dynasty, 158, 161, 162
Mongol conquests, 10
Mongol Empire, 10, 56, 71, 95, 102, 162, 163, 165, 209
Mongolia, 91, 98, 107, 156, 162, 165, 172
Mongolian Peoples Republic, 108
Mongolian Steppe, 163
Mongol invasions and conquests, 102
Mongol invasions of Japan, 162, 196, 209
Mongol invasions of Vietnam, 162
Mongols, 90, 93, 147, 162
Mongols in China, 162
Monotheism, 4
Mon people, 245
Monsoon, 260
Monthon, 267
Mori Ōgai, 222
Mosque, 70, 114, 262

317

Mosque–Cathedral of Córdoba, 70
Motif (textile arts), 100
Motif (visual arts), 91
Motoori Norinaga, 219
Mount Elbrus, 33
Mudan incident, 223
Mueang, 267
Mughal Empire, 17, 119, 122
Muhammad, 68, 77
Muhammad in Medina, 9
Mujahideen, 84
Multiregional origin of modern humans, 277
Mumun Pottery Period, 45
Murasaki Shikibu, 16, 207
Murayama Statement, 234
Muromachi period, 196, 198
Muscovy, 103
Musket, 214
Muslim, 107
Muslim conquest in the Indian subcontinent, 11
Muslim conquest of Persia, 9, 65, 68
Muslim conquest of Syria, 68
Muslim conquest of the Maghreb, 68, 263
Muslim conquests, 9, 41, 43, 60, 68
Muslim conquests of the Indian subcontinent, 263
Mustafa Kemal Atatürk, 76
Mutsu Munemitsu, 223
Mutsu Waki, 211
Mutual intelligibility, 60
Myanmar, 245, 249, 270
Mycenae, 49
Mycenaean Greece, 43, 45, 49
MyPaedia, 285

Nabatean kingdom, 64
Nabonidus, 51
Nabopolassar, 51
Nadir Shah, 104
Nagaoka-kyō, 205
Nagarakertagama, 260
Nagasaki, 229
Nagore Shahul Hamid, 263
Najd, 59
Nanban trade, 214
Nanboku-chō period, 198
Nanjing, 147, 166, 167, 175
Nanjing Road, 175
Nanking, 108, 227
Nanking Massacre, 227
Nanking Massacre denial, 234
Nanyang (region), 247
Nanyo (Japanese mandated territory), 225
Nanyue, 141
Napoleonic Wars, 266
Naram-Sin of Akkad, 31

Nara, Nara, 16, 205
Nara period, 16, 151, 198
Narva culture, 92
Nasr ibn Sayyar, 100
National Diet, 230
National epic, 211
National Gallery of Art, 282
Nationalism, 268
Nationalization, 77
National Palace Museum, 168
Nation state, 268
Natsume Sōseki, 222
Natufian culture, 44
Naval history of China, 126
Nayak dynasty, 122
Neanderthal, 34
Near East, 9, 27, 35, 41, 49, 55–57, 65
Near Eastern archaeology, 40
Nebuchadrezzar II, 51
Negritos, 250
Neo-Assyrian Empire, 39, 43, 49, 50, 56, 62, 64
Neo-Babylonian Empire, 39, 43, 51, 62, 65
Neo-Confucian, 160
Neo-Confucianism, 11, 13, 19, 167
Neo-Elamite period, 43
Neo-Hittite, 43, 47–49
Neo-Hittite kingdoms, 50
Neo-Hittite states, 39, 62
Neolithic, 33, 34, 47, 126, 130, 245, 250
Neolithic Revolution, 58
Neolithic signs in China, 130
Nephrite, 254
Netherlands, 264, 265
Netherlands East Indies, 267
New Army, 176
New Culture Movement, 176
New Deal, 230
New Guinea, 37, 249
New Guinea Highlands, 249
New Holland (Australia), 18
New Imperialism, 267
New Kingdom of Egypt, 43, 64
New Qing History, 187
Niah National Park, 30, 249
Nian Rebellion, 107, 174
Niccolò de Conti, 264
Nichiren, 210
Nichiren Buddhism, 210
Nihon Shoki, 205
Nikita Khrushchev, 25
Nikkei 225, 234
Nile, 59, 61
Nile River, 59
Nile valley, 64
Nineteenth dynasty of Egypt, 49

Nineveh, 51
Ningxia, 157
Ninja, 212
Nishiki-e, 219
Niu–Li factional strife, 153
Noh, 214
Nomad, 90, 97, 152
Nomadic, 59
Nomadic empire, 156
Nomadic empires, 96
Nomadism, 93
Nordic Bronze Age, 45
Normans, 69
North Africa, 262
North Asia, 27, 33
North China, 156
North China Plain, 34, 157
Northern Africa, 57, 58
Northern and Southern dynasties, 126
Northern Expedition, 177
Northern Fujiwara, 207
Northern Qi, 148
Northern Song, 960–1126, 126
Northern Song Dynasty, 156, 158
Northern Wei, 148
Northern Yuan dynasty, 165, 169
Northern Zhou, 148, 149
Northern Zhou Dynasty, 8
North Jakarta, 21
North Korea, 25
North Vietnam, 25, 270
Noun, 265
Novel, 164
Novocherkassk culture, 50
Nuclear testing, 115
Nurhaci, 22, 169, 171
Nursultan Nazarbayev, 114

Occupation of Japan, 197, 198
Oceania, 250
Ochre Coloured Pottery culture, 45
Oda Nobunaga, 197, 198, 214
Odisha, 121
Oiran, 218
Oirats, 168
Oki Island, 209

Ōkubo Toshimichi, 221
Ōkuma Shigenobu, 222

Old Chinese, 31, 34
Old Elamite period, 42
Old Kingdom of Egypt, 42, 64
Old North Arabian, 31
Old Persian, 31
Old South Arabian, 31

Oligocene, 60
Omen, 52
One-China policy, 129

Ōnin War, 212

OPEC, 57, 77
Operation Barbarossa, 110
Operation Cyclone, 84
Operation Downfall, 229
Opium, 23, 172
Optics, 70
Oracle bone, 31, 133
Ordos Desert, 98
Orenburg, 105, 107
Orissa, India, 121
Osaka Prefecture, 202
Osama bin Laden, 83, 84
Oslo Peace Accords, 84
Ostrich, 28

Ōtomo no Otomaro, 207

Ottoman Empire, 17, 35, 42, 56, 71, 74, 76
Ottoman–German Alliance, 77
Ottoman general election, 1908, 75
Ottoman Parliament, 75
Ottoman Turkish alphabet, 77
Ottoman Turks, 10, 71
Outcast (person), 237
Outline of ancient India, 120, 281
Outline of South Asian history, 44, 55, 89, 248
Out of Africa theory, 30
Overseas Chinese, 264
Overthrow of Sukarno, 270
Owari Province, 215
Oxford University Press, 85
Oxus, 104, 106

Pacific Ocean, 27, 152
Pacific War, 197, 247
Paddle wheel, 160
Paddy field, 245
Pagan Empire, 258
Pagan Kingdom, 244
Pakistan, 5, 36, 51
Palace economy, 49
Pala Empire, 10, 120
Palaeontology, 35
Palembang, 259
Paleolithic, 199, 243
Paleozoic, 60
Palermo, 69
Palestine Liberation Organization, 82
Palestine (region), 40, 66, 78
Palestinian refugee, 80

Palgrave Macmillan, 238
Pallava, 10
Pallava dynasty, 120
Pamir Mountains, 99
Pamirs, 144
Pan-Arabism, 57
Pan-Asian, 227
Pandanus, 249
Pandya dynasty, 5
Pandyas, 10
Pan-Islamism, 108
Pan-Islamist, 58
Panjakent, 98
Pannai, 260
Panthay Rebellion, 174
Pan-Turkism, 108
Paper currency, 163
Papermaking, 145
Paper money, 159
Paramount Leader, 180
Paresis, 222
Parthia, 40
Parthian Empire, 4, 43, 65, 96
Parthian language, 32
Particular judgment, 4
Partition of the Empire, 65
Pasargadae, 53
Pastoralism, 59
Pax Mongolica, 162
Pax Romana, 7
Pax Sinica, 142, 150
PBS, 192
Peace Preservation Law, 225
Peace with France and Spain, 265
Peanut, 19
Peasant, 144
Peiligang culture, 130, 131
Peking Man, 28, 29, 34, 130
Penang Island, 265
Penghu, 169
Penguin Books, 86
Peoples commune, 180
Peoples Liberation Army, 25, 179, 181, 280
Peoples Republic of China, 25, 33, 108, 115, 129, 234
Peopling of the Americas, 92
Per capita, 57
Perestroika, 112
Periodization, 42, 198
Perry Expedition, 197
Persepolis, 53
Persia, 24, 39, 46, 62, 106, 247
Persian Constitutional Revolution, 75
Persian Empire, 51, 96
Persian Gulf, 56, 57, 59, 74, 114, 264
Persian Gulf states, 83

Persian language, 33
Persian people, 93
Peter Holt (historian), 271
Peter I of Russia, 105
Peter Stearns, 26, 86
Petroleum, 56, 77
Phanerozoic, 60
Pharaoh, 56, 64
Phayap Army, 268
Philip II of Macedon, 96
Philippine Declaration of Independence, 267
Philippine–American War, 244, 267
Philippine Revolution, 244, 267
Philippines, 37, 245, 249, 260, 270
Phoenicia, 39, 42, 43, 59, 62, 64
Phoenician language, 31, 40, 62
Phoenician languages, 50
Phrygia, 43
Phrygian language, 31
Phrygians, 47
Phung Nguyen culture, 245, 252
Pingjin Campaign, 179
Pinyin, 5
Plague (disease), 164
Plate tectonics, 37
Plaza Accord, 233
Pleistocene, 249
Political parties, 76
Polychrome, 100
Polymath, 145
Pontic-Caspian steppe, 92
Pope Urban II, 71
Porcelain, 22, 170
Porcelain Tower, 166
Portal:Bronze Age, 45
Portal:Japan, 196
Portal:Southeast Asia, 245
Portugal, 264, 265, 267
Portuguese discoveries, 244
Portuguese People, 214
Portuguese Timor, 267
Post-classical history, 44, 55, 89, 248
Post-occupation Japan, 198
Post-war Japan, 198
Potala Palace, 171
Potters wheel, 63
Pottery, 254
Pottery Neolithic, 44
Prakrit, 32
Precipitation, 59
Pre-Columbian era, 44, 55, 89, 248
Predynastic Egypt, 42
Prefecture, 138
Prefectures of Japan, 222
Prehistoric Arabia, 32
Prehistoric Armenia, 32, 33

Prehistoric art, 30
Prehistoric Asia, **27**, 32
Prehistoric Azerbaijan, 32
Prehistoric Beifudi site, 2
Prehistoric China, 32, 33
Prehistoric Georgia, 32, 33
Prehistoric India, 36
Prehistoric Indonesia, 32, 37
Prehistoric Japan, 32, 35
Prehistoric Korea, 32, 33, 35
Prehistoric Malaysia, 32, 37
Prehistoric Siberia, 32
Prehistoric Tamil Nadu, 32, 36
Prehistoric Thailand, 32, 37
Prehistory, 44, 55, 89, 247, 248
Prehistory of Central Asia, 32
Prehistory of Iran, 32
Prehistory of Sri Lanka, 32, 36
Prehistory of Taiwan, 32, 33, 35
Prehistory of the Philippines, 32, 37
Prehistory of the Southern Levant, 32
Prehistory of Tibet, 32, 33
Prehistory of Xinjiang, 32, 33
Pre-pottery Neolithic A, 44
Pre-pottery Neolithic B, 44
Pre-pottery Neolithic C, 44
President of the Peoples Republic of China, 25
President of the Republic of China, 176
Press censorship, 76
Prime Minister of Japan, 222
Prince Bekovitch-Cherkassky, 105
Princely States, 106, 121
Prince Ōama, 205
Prince Ōtomo, 205
Prince Shōtoku, 15, 203
Princess Wencheng, 99
Princeton University Press, 116
Principality, 255
Proclamation of Indonesian Independence, 269
Professional revolutionaries, 25
Protectorate, 106
Protectorate of the Western Regions, 96
Protodynastic Period of Egypt, 42
Proto-Elamite, 42, 46
Protohistory, 45
Proto-Indo-Europeans, 93
Proto-writing, 130, 132
Provisional Government of the Republic of China (1912), 175
Ptolemaic Egypt, 64
Ptolemaic Kingdom, 43
Ptolemy, 70, 247, 256
PubMed Identifier, 38, 271
Punjab region, 96, 122
Punti–Hakka Clan Wars, 174
Pure Land Buddhism, 13, 210

Putuo Zongcheng Temple, 171
Puyi, 176
Pyu city-states, 251

Q82972, 192
Qara Khitai, 158
Qatar, 57, 84
Qatar Digital Library, 87
Qatna, 48
Qiang (historical people), 147
Qiang people, 147
Qianlong Emperor, 104, 172, 173
Qiao Family Compound, 171
Qijia culture, 45
Qin Dynasty, 6, 125, 128, 142
Qing China, 223
Qing conquest of the Ming, 172
Qing Dynasty, 17, 22, 90, 104, 107–109, 126, 129, 139, 169, 171
Qing dynasty (1644–1912), 172
Qing Empire, 265
Qinghai, 100
Qin Shi Huang, 6, 128, 138, 139
Qin Shi Huang Di, 139
Qin (state), 136
Qins wars of unification, 128
Qiu Xigui, 281
Quanzhou, 163
Quaternary glaciation, 199
Queue (hairstyle), 172
Quixotism, 105
Qu (poetry), 164
Quran, 114
Qutayba ibn Muslim, 100
Quwê, 51

Radiocarbon dating, 130, 199
Rafe de Crespigny, 183
Rainy season, 198
Raja, 120
Rajahnate of Butuan, 244
Rajahnate of Cebu, 244
Raja Raja Chola, 10
Rajasthan, 121
Rajendra Chola, 10
Rajput, 11, 121
Ramadan, 70
Ramesses III, 49
Rammed earth, 141
Rana Mitter, 188
Random House, 238
Rangaku, 219
Ranjit Singh, 122
Rashidun army, 9, 68
Rashidun Caliphate, 9, 68
Rashtrakuta dynasty, 120

321

Rattanakosin Kingdom (1782–1932), 244
R. C. Majumdar, 123, 274
R.C. Majumdar, 273
Reagan Doctrine, 84
Recorded history, 27, 44, 55, 89, 247
Records of the Grand Historian, 126, 132, 134
Reddy dynasty, 121
Red hair, 95
Red River delta, 245, 251
Red Sea, 60, 66
Region, 36, 40
Relief, 143
Religion, 41
Renaissance of the 12th century, 69
Republic, 264
Republic of China, 234
Republic of China (1912-1949), 129
Republic of China (1912–1949), 109, 126
Republic of China (1912–49), 108, 175
Republic of Ezo, 290
Republic of Negros, 267
Republic of Novgorod, 103
Republic of Taiwan (1895), 290
Republic of Turkey, 77
Republic of Venice, 163
Republic of Zamboanga, 267
Rescript, 221
Revolt of the Three Feudatories, 172
Revolutionary wave, 58, 85
Revolutions of 1989, 245
Rhinoceros, 256
Rhinoceroses, 28
Rice riots of 1918, 225
Richard Nelson Frye, 50
Richard Nixon, 178
Rikken Minseitō, 225
Ritsuryō, 205, 206, 236
Riwat, 36
Road map for peace, 85
Robin Dennell, 37, 271
Rock carvings, 61
Rōjū, 217
Romance of the Three Kingdoms, 146
Roman Empire, 4, 43, 65
Roman historiography, 50
Romania, 49, 74
Romano-Chinese relations, 145
Roman-Persian Wars, 43, 65
Roman Republic, 56, 65
Royal Netherlands East Indies Army, 266
Russia, 25, 33, 82
Russian archaeology, 92
Russian conquest of Siberia, 33
Russian Empire, 17, 90, 106
Russian Far East, 33
Russian Federation, 33

Russian Revolution of 1917, 91, 107
Russian Turkestan, 106
Russo-Japanese War, 224
Ryukyu Islands, 199, 223
Ryukyu Kingdom, 217
Ryūnosuke Akutagawa, 225

Saad Zaghloul, 78
Sabah, 270
Saber-toothed tiger, 28
Saddam Hussein, 81, 82
Saddle, 101
Sado Island, 209
Safavids, 56, 72
Sahara, 61
Sa Huỳnh, 290
Sa Huỳnh culture, 252, 254
Saigō Takamori, 221
Saigyō, 211
Sailendra, 260
Sailendra dynasty, 260
Saitō Mokichi, 211
Saka, 93
Sakanoue no Tamuramaro, 207
Sakay, 267
Sakhalin, 199
Sakoku, 197, 218
Saladin, 9, 71
Salafism, 58
Salah al-Din al-Bitar, 82
Salah Jadid, 82
Salt in Chinese history, 153
Samanid, 102
Samanids, 101
Samara culture, 92
Samaritans, 60
Samarkand, 94, 106
Samarra, 53
Sampul tapestry, 91
Samudera Pasai Sultanate, 263
Samuel Noah Kramer, 278
Samurai, 16, 196, 206
San Francisco Peace Treaty, 232
Sangiran, 37
Sankin-kōtai, 217
Sanqu, 164
Sanskrit, 3, 153
Sanxingdui, 131, 134
Sanxingdui culture, 133
Sarawak, 270
Sargon of Akkad, 63
Sargon the Great, 46
Sarira, 151
Sasanian Empire, 9, 66
Sassanian Empire, 9, 68
Sassanid, 4

Sassanid dynasty, 96
Sassanid Empire, 4, 43, 65
Sassanid Persia, 56
Satellite state, 91
Satsuma Domain, 217, 220
Satsuma Rebellion, 223
Saudi Arabia, 51, 57, 77, 78, 114
Scholar-bureaucrats, 151
Scholar official, 23
Scholar-official, 140, 164
Scholar-officials, 128
Science and technology of the Han dynasty, 145
Scientific revolution, 70
Scythia, 93
Scythians, 51, 96, 101
Sea peoples, 43, 49
SEATO, 24
Secession, 25
Second Anglo-Burmese War, 244
Second Battle of Tamao, 169
Second Constitutional Era, 75
Second East Turkestan Republic, 109
Second East Turkistan Republic, 108
Second Intermediate Period of Egypt, 43
Second Intifada, 84
Second Philippine Republic, 269
Second Sino-Japanese War, 25, 177, 197, 227
Second Sumatran expedition, 266
Second World War, 24, 109
Sedentism, 199
Sei Shōnagon, 207
Seiyūkai, 225
Seleucid, 4, 65
Seleucid Empire, 4, 43, 96
Self-determination, 268
Self-Strengthening Movement, 174
Selim I, 72
Selim the Grim, 73
Seljuk Turks, 102
Seljuq Empire, 9, 68
Seljuq Turks, 9, 56, 70
Semitic language, 46, 59
Semitic languages, 48
Semitic people, 59
Semu, 163
Sena dynasty, 121
Sengoku period, 196, 198, 212
Senzai Wakashū, 210
Seppuku, 217
September 11, 2001 attacks, 84
September 11 attacks, 83
Serbia, 74
Serfdom, 17, 164
Serhetabad, 106
Sesshō, 205

Seuna (Yadava) dynasty, 121
Seventeen-article constitution, 15, 203
Seven Years War, 266
Several, 136
Sewu, 260
Seymour Expedition, 174
S. Frederick Starr, 115
Shaanxi, 34, 157
Shaanxi History Museum, 161
Shabak people, 60
Shailendra dynasty, 258
Shandong, 139
Shang, 135
Shang dynasty, 34, 125, 126, 133, 256
Shanghai Cooperation Organization, 115
Shanhai Pass, 170
Shanxi, 147, 164, 171
Shatuo, 153, 155
Shell money, 256
Shelter (building), 30
Sheng Shicai, 108
Shen Kuo, 159
Sherd, 199
Shia, 81, 84
Shia Islam, 60
Shigeru Yoshida, 232
Shijiazhuang, 131
Shikoku, 215
Shimabara Rebellion, 218
Shinbutsu-shūgō, 203
Shin Kokin Wakashū, 210
Shinto, 196, 203
Shipment, 158
Shiraho Saonetabaru Cave Ruins, 199
Shiva, 255
Shōen, 206
Shōgun, 196, 208, 217
Shogunate, 17
Shōji, 16
Shōmonki, 211
Shōtetsu, 211
Shōwa period, 198
Shugo, 209
Shu Han, 125, 146
Shulaveri-Shomu culture, 33
Shun Dynasty, 22
Shunzhi Emperor, 172
Shuruppak, 31
Shūshin koyō, 233
Shu (state), 131
Siamese-American Treaty of Amity and Commerce, 267
Siam–England war (1687), 265
Siberia, 1, 5, 30, 33, 92, 107
Sichuan, 131, 138
Sick man of Europe, 74

Siege engine, 160
Siege of Baghdad (1258), 10
Siege of Constantinople (717–18), 68
Siege of Osaka, 217
Siege of the International Legations, 174
Sikh Empire, 122
Silk, 2, 6, 92, 141, 145
Silk Road, 2, 7, 11, 93, 96, 103, 115, 141, 143, 144, 148, 151, 162, 244
Silk Road transmission of Buddhism, 243
Silla, 17
Silver, 92
Sima Guang, 160
Sima Qian, 132
Simplified Chinese, 282
Sinai and Palestine Campaign, 78
Sindh, 11
Singapore, 37, 245, 266, 270
Singapore in the Straits Settlements, 228
Singhasari, 260
Sinicization, 147, 155–157, 163
Sinify, 148
Sino-Dutch conflicts, 169
Sino-Russian border conflicts, 172
Sino-Soviet split, 178
Sino-Vietnamese War, 270
Sir John Macpherson, 1st Baronet, 265
Siwa culture, 45
Six-Day War, 57, 81
Six Dynasties, 8
Sixteen Kingdoms, 126, 147
Sixteen Prefectures, 155, 157
Skhul and Qafzeh hominids, 30
Slavery, 63
Slavery in Japan, 216, 236
Small Wild Goose Pagoda, 153
Socialism with Chinese characteristics, 180
Social stratification, 41, 63, 201
Soga clan, 203
Sogdia, 92, 94, 95, 98, 100
Sogdiana, 93
Solomon Islands, 228
Some Prefer Nettles, 225
Song dynasty, 13, 126, 127, 155, 156, 160, 162, 167
Songtsän Gampo, 99
Sonnō jōi, 220
Sōrin, 167
South Asia, 1, 30, 36, 261
South Asian Stone Age, 32
South Caucasus, 33, 51
South China Sea, 6, 19, 246, 260, 261, 263
Southeast asia, 10, 27, 30, 37, 245, 246, 254, 255, 261
Southeast Asia, 243
South East Asia Command, 247

South-East Asian theatre of World War II, 244
Southeastern China, 149
Southern and Northern Dynasties, 8
Southern Ming dynasty, 172
Southern Qi, 148
Southern Song, 1127–1279, 126
Southern Song dynasty, 13, 158, 160, 162
South India, 121
South Manchuria Railroad, 226
South Vietnam, 270
Southward expansion of the Han dynasty, 144
Soviet Central Asia, 108
Soviet–Afghan War, 84
Soviet–Japanese Joint Declaration of 1956, 234
Soviet invasion of Afghanistan, 24
Soviet invasion of Manchuria, 197, 229
Soviet Jews, 82
Soviet Union, 24, 80, 82, 108, 177, 178, 229
Spain, 264, 265
Spanish East Indies, 23, 244
Spanish–American War, 244, 267
Spear of Fuchai, 134
Special Envoy, 113
Spice Route, 259
Spirituality, 52
Spoked wheel, 92
Spread of Islam in Southeast Asia, 244
Spring and Autumn Annals, 136, 138
Spring and Autumn period, 125, 128, 136
Sri Lanka, 32, 261
Srivijaya, 244, 258–260, 263
Srubna culture, 45
Stamford Raffles, 266
Standing army, 152
Stanford University Press, 240
State of Israel, 79
State (polity), 95
State Shinto, 222
Statistical analysis, 290
Steppe, 1, 90, 99
Stirrup, 101
Strait of Malacca, 263
Stuart B. Schwartz, 26
Stupa, 164, 258
Subartu, 47
Su Dingfang, 99
Suez Canal, 79
Sufism, 263
Sugita Genpaku, 219
Suicide bombing, 84
Sui Dynasty, 12, 126, 149
Sukhothai Kingdom, 244, 258, 260
Sultanate of Malacca, 263, 264
Sumatra, 245, 249, 259, 260
Sumer, 3, 39, 41, 42, 45, 46, 48, 62, 63
Sumerian language, 31, 40, 62

Sumerian literature, 40, 62
Sumero-Akkadian, 42
Sumitomo, 224
Summer Palace, 171
Sunda Kelapa, 264
Sunda Kingdom, 260
Sundaland, 249
Sun Tzu, 137
Sun Yat-sen, 175, 176
Supreme Commander for the Allied Powers, 198
Supreme Commander of Allied Powers, 230
Surrender of Japan, 197, 229
Susa, 46
Su Song, 159
Suvarnabhumi, 247
Suvarnadvipa, 247
Suzhou, 159
Sweet Dew incident, 153
Sweet potatoes, 19
Sword of Goujian, 136
Sykes–Picot Agreement, 78
Syncretism, 262
Syphilis, 222
Syria, 2, 31, 40, 46–51, 66, 78
Syriac Christians, 65
Syria–Lebanon Campaign, 79
Syrian Civil War, 85
System of linear equations, 142

Tabal, 48, 51
Tabon Caves, 249
Taihang Mountains, 2
Taihō Code, 205
Taika Reform, 15, 205
Taipei, 178
Taiping Rebellion, 107, 172
Taira clan, 17, 206
Taira no Kiyomori, 207
Taira no Masakado, 211
Taishō period, 197, 198
Taishō political crisis, 225
Taiwan, 25, 172, 178, 199
Taiwanese aborigines, 35
Taiwan expedition of 1874, 223
Taixue, 143
Tajik Civil War, 112
Tajikistan, 33, 91, 92, 98, 114
Tajik SSR, 108
Takeda Shingen, 212
Takhti-Sangin, 92
Talaat Pasha, 75
Taliban, 84
Tamilakam, 5
Tamil language, 32
Tamil Nadu, 120

Tamils, 263
Tam Pa Ling Cave, 248
Tanegashima, 212
Tang campaign against Karakhoja, 99
Tang campaign against the oasis states, 99
Tang campaigns against Karasahr, 99
Tang campaigns against the Western Turks, 99
Tang dynasty, 12, 95, 97, 100, 126, 150, 160, 205, 207
Tang dynasty in Inner Asia, 151
Tang poetry, 150, 152, 154
Tangut people, 157
Tangzhuang, 172
Tank man, 181
Tanzimat, 75
Taoism, 6, 137, 147
Taoist, 148
Taotie, 143
Tarbosaurus, 129
Tarim Basin, 99
Tarumanagara, 256
Tashkent, 106, 112
Tashkent Soviet, 107
Taurus Mountains, 48
Tea ceremony, 214
Tel Halaf, 2
Telugu people, 120, 121
Template:Ancient Near East topics, 40, 63
Template:Bronze Age, 45
Template:Culture of Japan, 196
Template:History of China, 126
Template:History of Japan, 195
Template:History of Southeast Asia, 245
Template:Human history, 44, 56, 89, 248
Template:Iron Age, 50
Template:Prehistoric Asia by region, 32
Template talk:Ancient Near East topics, 40, 63
Template talk:Bronze Age, 45
Template talk:Culture of Japan, 196
Template talk:History of China, 126
Template talk:History of Japan, 195
Template talk:History of Southeast Asia, 245
Template talk:Human history, 44, 56, 89, 248
Template talk:Iron Age, 50
Template talk:Prehistoric Asia by region, 32
Tenpō famine, 219
Terengganu, 249
Terracotta Army, 139, 140
Thailand, 24, 37, 245, 249, 270
Thailand in World War II, 268
Thalassocracy, 64, 245
The Cambridge History of Islam, 271
The enemy of my enemy is my friend, 79
The Great Game, 105
The History and Culture of the Indian People, 123

The History of India as told by its own Historians, 123
The History of India, as Told by Its Own Historians. The Muhammadan Period, 123
The Jin Period, 90
The Nine Chapters on the Mathematical Art, 142
The occupation, 269
Theocracy, 81
The Pillow Book, 207
Theravada Buddhism, 258, 261
The Tale of Genji, 16, 207, 208
The Tale of the Heike, 211
The Teaching Company, 86
The Travels of Marco Polo, 163
Third Anglo-Burmese War, 244
Third Battle of Nanking, 174
Third Chinese domination of Vietnam, 155
Third Dynasty of Ur, 42
Thrace, 51
Three Alls Policy, 177
Three Departments and Six Ministries, 149, 151
Three Kingdoms, 8, 125, 146
Three Kingdoms of Korea, 202, 203
Three Pagodas, 153
Tiananmen Square protests of 1989, 180
Tianlongshan Grottoes, 149
Tianning Temple (Beijing), 157
Tibet, 129, 171
Tibetan Empire, 99
Tibetan Kingdom, 99
Tibetan Plateau, 92, 132
Tibetans, 147
Tiglath-Pileser I, 47
Tiglath-Pileser III, 50
Tigris, 59
Tigris–Euphrates river system, 67
Timeline of Chinese history, 126
Timeline of Japanese history, 195
Timor, 249
Timothy Brook, 164, 186
Timur, 10, 71, 102
Tish-atal, 31
TLV mirror, 143
Tocharians, 93, 95
Tōdai-ji, 205
Tokubetsu Kōtō Keisatsu, 225
Tokugawa clan, 216
Tokugawa Ieyasu, 197, 198, 216
Tokugawa shogunate, 197, 198, 216
Tokugawa Yoshinobu, 220
Tokyo, 197, 221
Tokyo Stock Exchange, 234
Tomahawk (axe), 131
Tondo (historical polity), 244, 260
Tortoise, 256
Tosa Diary, 207
Tosa Province, 209
Toung Pao, 191
Toyotomi clan, 217
Toyotomi Hideyori, 216
Toyotomi Hideyoshi, 197, 198, 214
Trade, 63
Trade route, 49, 101
Trade unions, 76
Trade with China and the East Indies, 266
Traditional accounts, 144
Trans-Aral Railway, 107
Transcaspia, 106
Transcaspian Railway, 107
Transhipped, 256
Transhumance, 93
Transition from Sui to Tang, 99, 149
Transoxiana, 90
Trans-Siberian Railway, 24
Treasure voyages, 19, 167, 168, 264
Treaty of Mutual Cooperation and Security between the United States and Japan, 232, 234
Treaty of Nanking, 23, 172
Treaty of Nerchinsk, 172
Treaty of Paris (1898), 267
Treaty of San Francisco, 233
Treaty of Versailles, 176, 225
Treaty on Basic Relations between Japan and the Republic of Korea, 234
Trebuchet, 156, 160
Trialeti culture, 33
Tributary state, 265
Tripartite Pact, 228
Troy, 49
Troy VII, 43
Tsepon W. D. Shakabpa, 99
Tsinghua Bamboo Slips, 138
Tsuyoshi Inukai, 226
Tuen Mun, 169
Tulip Revolution, 112
Tumulus culture, 45
Tundra, 1
Tunisia, 74
Turco-Mongol, 122
Turfan, 95, 97
Turgesh, 100
Turkestan, 105
Turkestan Autonomous Soviet Socialist Republic, 108
Turkestan-Siberia Railway, 107
Turkey, 4, 9, 31, 40, 48, 51, 66, 114
Turkic expansion, 97
Turkic people, 147
Turkic peoples, 56, 90, 93, 97

Turkish alphabet, 77
Turkish Cypriots, 82
Turkish invasion of Cyprus, 82
Turkish National Movement, 76
Turkish people, 114
Turkish War of Independence, 76
Turkmenistan, 33, 91, 104
Turkmen people, 78, 104
Turkmen SSR, 108
Turks in the Tang military, 98
Turpan, 95
Twelve Level Cap and Rank System, 203
Twentieth dynasty of Egypt, 49
Twenty-fifth dynasty of Egypt, 50
Two layer hypothesis, 252

Ubaid period, 3, 42, 45, 46
Ubeidiya, 35
Uesugi Kenshin, 212, 213
Ugarit, 31, 43, 47, 49, 64
Ugaritic language, 31
Uji (clan), 202
Uji, Kyoto, 208
Ukiyo, 218
Ukiyo-e, 218
Ukiyo-zōshi, 218
Ukraine, 82, 105
Umayyad, 68
Umayyad architecture, 70
Umayyad Caliphate, 9, 68
Umayyad conquest of Hispania, 68, 263
Unequal treaties, 172, 220
UNESCO, 115
UNESCO World Heritage site, 121
Unetice culture, 45
Unilateral Declaration of Egyptian Independence, 79
Unit 731, 177
United Arab Emirates, 57, 84
United Kingdom, 105, 265
United Nations, 57, 79, 80, 83, 84, 234, 269
United Nations General Assembly, 82
United Nations General Assembly Resolution 2758, 178
United Nations General Assembly Resolution 3379, 82
United Nations General Assembly Resolution 4686, 82
United States, 266, 270
United States Civil Administration of the Ryukyu Islands, 232
United States foreign policy in the Middle East, 80
United States invasion of Afghanistan, 84
Universal male suffrage, 225
University of Hawaii Press, 237, 238

Upper and Lower Egypt, 56
Upper class, 60
Upper Egypt, 64
Uprising of the Five Barbarians, 147
Ural Mountains, 27
Urartian language, 40, 62
Urartu, 33, 39, 43, 51, 62
Urkesh, 31
Urnfield culture, 45
Uruk, 45
Uruk period, 42, 45, 46
USS Cole bombing, 84
Uttaranchal, 121
Uttar Pradesh, 121
Uyghur people, 97
Uzbekistan, 33, 91, 112
Uzbek SSR, 108

Vajrayana, 259
Van Lang, 245, 251
Văn Lang, 251
Vardhana dynasty, 120
Varieties of Arabic, 60
Varkhuman, 94
Vasily Bartold, 116
Vassal, 22
Vedas, 3
Vedic period, 3
Video gaming in Japan, 235
Vienna, 42
Vietnam, 3, 6, 7, 12, 37, 155, 245, 249, 252, 255, 270
Vietnam War, 24, 25, 269, 270
Vijayanagara Empire, 121
Villanovan culture, 50
Virgin Lands Campaign, 109
Vladimir Putin, 114
Volcano, 28
Von Kaufman, 106
Voyages of discovery, 244
V:Topic:Southeast Asian history, 275
V.V. Barthold, 115

Wade–Giles, 5
Wahhabism, 58
Wahhabist, 84
Wa (Japan), 201
Waka (poetry), 210
Wang Anshi, 160
Wang Mang, 144
Warfare, 41, 63
Warlord, 145
Warlord Era, 176
War of Attrition, 81
War of the Eight Princes, 147
War on Terror, 58, 84

Warring States period, 6, 125, 128, 132, 137–139
Wars and armed conflicts, 172, 174
Wars of the Diadochi, 96
Washukanni, 48
Watchtower, 141
Water Margin, 19
Wei River, 135
Weiyang Palace, 144
Wen Jiabao, 181
West Bank, 85
Western Asia, 35, 57, 58
Western Chalukya Empire, 120
Western Ganga dynasty, 120, 121
Western Han, 125
Westernization, 222
Western Jin Dynasty, 146
Western Regions, 143
Western Roman Empire, 65
Western Wei, 148
Western world, 129
Western Xia, 14, 126, 157, 158
Western Zhou, 125
West Java, 254
West Kalimantan, 265
West Malaysia, 245
Westview Press, 238
Wheat, 93
Wheel, 1, 41, 63
Wikipedia:Citation needed, 28, 83, 84, 96, 101, 133–135, 140
Wikipedia:Link rot, 52, 116
Wikt:lingua franca, 60
Wiley-Blackwell, 241
William M. Tsutsui, 238
William Tsutsui, 240
Winged sun, 61
Withdrawal of U.S. troops from Iraq, 85
Wokou, 169
Wolf, 28
Woodblock print, 160
Woodblock printing, 159
Woodcut, 36
World Heritage Site, 165
World Trade Organization, 181
World War I, 77, 176
World War II, 25, 57, 79, 177, 245, 247, 268, 269
World War II, 228
WP:NOTRS, 209
Writing system, 41
Writing systems, 27
Wuchang Uprising, 175
Wucheng culture, 45
Wu Ding, 31
Wuhan, 175

Wujing Zongyao, 156
Wu Sangui, 171
Wusun, 93
Wu Zetian, 13, 150, 152
W. W. Norton & Company, 240

Xenophobia, 167
Xia dynasty, 34, 125, 126, 132
Xian, 34, 131, 135, 139, 140, 144, 150, 153, 161, 174
Xianbei, 147, 148
Xianren Cave, 130
Xianyang, 139
Xianyu people, 95
Xiaochangliang, 34, 129
Xihoudu, 129
Xindian culture, 45
Xin dynasty, 125, 144
Xinglongwa culture, 2
Xinhai Revolution, 175
Xinjiang, 91, 95, 100, 104, 129, 172
Xinjiang Production and Construction Corps, 109
Xinye Village, 166
Xinzheng, 131
Xiongnu, 95, 99, 147
Xiongnu Empire, 143, 144
Xuanzang, 151
Xueyantuo, 99
Xue Zongzheng, 118

Yakub Beg, 107
Yamagata Aritomo, 223
Yamashita Cave Man, 199
Yamatai, 201
Yamato Province, 202
Yamhad, 48
Yam (route), 162
Yam (vegetable), 249
Yanan, 177
Yang Guifei, 13
Yangshao culture, 34, 131
Yangtze, 160
Yangtze civilization, 128
Yangtze River, 6, 128, 135, 143, 147
Yangzi River, 23, 131
Yasser Arafat, 82, 85
Yasukuni Shrine, 235
Yayoi, 196
Yayoi period, 198
Yazdânism, 60
Yellow River, 34, 126, 131, 135, 144
Yellow river civilization, 128
Yellow Turban Rebellion, 8, 145
Yemen, 66
Yemeni Civil War (2015–present), 85

Yemen Vilayet, 74
Yin and yang, 6
Ying Zheng, 138
Yining (city), 107
Yining City, 107
Yinxu, 134
Yom Kippur War, 58, 81
Yongle Emperor, 19, 166, 167, 264
Yongzheng Emperor, 23
Yoshida Doctrine, 232
Yoshinogari site, 201
Yoshino, Nara, 211
Yoshiwara, 218
Young Ottomans, 75
Young Turk Revolution, 75
Young Turks, 75
You (vessel), 135
Yuan dynasty, 126, 161, 165, 167
Yuanmou Man, 34, 129
Yuan poetry, 164
Yuan Shikai, 176
Yue Chinese, 257
Yueshi culture, 45
Yuezhi, 93
Yūkaku, 218
Yungang Grottoes, 147
Yunnan, 34, 249, 264
Yunyan Pagoda, 155
Yurt, 93

Zagros Mountains, 60
Zaibatsu, 224, 230
Zaju, 164
Zakāt, 70
Zen, 13, 210
Zhang Heng, 145
Zhang Qian, 143
Zhang Zeduan, 160
Zhang Zhung culture, 132
Zhejiang, 138
Zheng He, 19, 262, 264
Zhengtong Emperor, 168
Zhengzhou, 133, 141
Zhetysu, 105
Zhongshan (state), 95
Zhou Dynasty, 5, 34, 125, 128, 138, 256
Zhou dynasty (690–705), 126
Zhou Enlai, 178
Zhoukoudian, 28, 34
Zhu Rongji, 181
Zhu Wen, 153
Zhu Xi, 160
Zhu Yuanzhang, 18, 166
Zindan, 106
Zionism, 78, 79
Zionist, 79

Zizhi Tongjian, 160
Zoroaster, 4
Zoroastrian, 92
Zoroastrianism, 4, 60, 61, 66, 70, 96
Zuo Commentary, 138

www.ingramcontent.com/pod-product-compliance
Lightning Source LLC
Chambersburg PA
CBHW021142160426
43194CB00007B/662